A School in Arms

Uppingham and the Great War

Timothy Halstead

Helion & Company Limited

Helion & Company Limited
26 Willow Road
Solihull
West Midlands
B91 1UE
England
Tel. 0121 705 3393
Fax 0121 711 4075
Email: info@helion.co.uk
Website: www.helion.co.uk
Twitter: @helionbooks
Visit our blog http://blog.helion.co.uk/

Published by Helion & Company 2017
Designed and typeset by Mach 3 Solutions Ltd (www.mach3solutions.co.uk)
Cover designed by Paul Hewitt, Battlefield Design (www.battlefield-design.co.uk)
Printed by Short Run Press, Exeter, Devon

Text © Timothy Halstead 2017
Photographs © as individually credited

Front cover top photo: An OTC instruction class during the Great War; front cover bottom photo: The Uppingham OTC marching at its 1918 inspection; Rear cover photo: The East Block and School Memorial Hall. All photos from Uppingham School Archives

Every reasonable effort has been made to trace copyright holders and to obtain their permission for the use of copyright material. The author and publisher apologize for any errors or omissions in this work, and would be grateful if notified of any corrections that should be incorporated in future reprints or editions of this book.

ISBN 978-1-911512-64-6

British Library Cataloguing-in-Publication Data.
A catalogue record for this book is available from the British Library.

All rights reserved. No part of this publication may be reproduced, stored in a retrieval system, or transmitted, in any form, or by any means, electronic, mechanical, photocopying, recording or otherwise, without the express written consent of Helion & Company Limited.

For details of other military history titles published by Helion & Company Limited contact the above address, or visit our website: http://www.helion.co.uk.

We always welcome receiving book proposals from prospective authors.

Contents

List of Illustrations	iv
List of Tables	vi
List of Abbreviations	vii
Acknowledgements	ix
Introduction	xi
1 Public Schools and the Great War	21
2 A Brief History of Uppingham	35
3 The Threat of War	42
4 Spying on Germany	55
5 Taking Up Arms	68
6 Uppingham and the Home Front	98
7 Gallantry and Awards	110
8 Commanders in Arms	123
9 Teachers in Arms	135
10 Laying Down Arms	143
11 Taking Up Arms Again	154
Conclusion	161
Appendices	
I Record of Service for Old Uppinghamians	166
II Record of Service for the Assistant Schoolmasters of Uppingham School	242
III Account of the Dedication of the School War Memorial 16 October 1921	244
IV Order of Memorial Service 6 July 1919	254
Bibliography	273
Index	285

List of Illustrations

The Uppingham Bisley Shooting Team 1897 in old style Rifle Corps uniform. (Uppingham School Archives)	i
Edward Thring. (Uppingham School Archives)	i
The Uppingham Rifle Corps on parade 1898. (Uppingham School Archives)	ii
The officers of the Uppingham Rifle Corps 1901. (Uppingham School Archives)	ii
Edward Carus Selwyn Headmaster 1897-1907. (Uppingham School Archives)	iii
The Boer War Memorial utilised today as the School Theatre. (Uppingham School Archives)	iii
The Rifle Corps camp 1908. (Uppingham School Archives)	iv
C.R.W. Nevinson at Uppingham 1905. (Uppingham School Archives)	iv
Harry Ward McKenzie Headmaster 1908-1915. (Uppingham School Archives)	iv
Eric Dorman-Smith at Uppingham 1911. (Uppingham School Archives)	v
The OTC on parade, Leicester 1910. (Uppingham School Archives)	v
Brian Horrocks at Uppingham 1912. (Uppingham School Archives)	v
The Uppingham OTC officers 1913 C.H. Jones had been succeeded as C.O. by Major R.P. Shea. (Uppingham School Archives)	vi
OTC summer camp Mytchett, August 1914 which was attended by members of Uppingham OTC. (Uppingham School Archives)	vi
The Uppingham OTC at Mytchett August 1914 – Edward Brittain is third down on the right. (Uppingham School Archives)	vii
The Front Cover of Edward Brittain's Church Parade Order of Service at the 1914 OTC summer camp. (Uppingham School Archives)	vii
The Uppingham School Praeposters – Roland Leighton is in the centre of the middle row. (Uppingham School Archives)	viii
The newly promoted Lieutenant Colonel C.H. Jones. (centre front seated row) with the 5th Battalion of the Royal Leicestershire Regiment just after the outbreak of war in August 1914. (Uppingham School Archives)	viii
Harry Ward McKenzie with Mrs McKenzie and their son Harry, an OU, at Uppingham in 1915. (Uppingham School Archives)	ix
Battle of the Somme, the attack of the Ulster Division by J.P. Beadle – The officer leading the attack with arm raised is OU F.B. Thornely. (Belfast City Council)	ix

List of Illustrations v

General Sir Horace Smith-Dorrien inspects the Uppingham OTC in 1917 – Headmaster Owen is to the left of the picture. (Uppingham School Archives)	x
Reginald Herbert Owen Headmaster 1916 to 1934. (Uppingham School Archives)	x
R. Sterndale Bennett at the 1917 inspection of the Uppingham OTC. (Uppingham School Archives)	x
The Uppingham OTC marching at its 1918 inspection, Percy Chapman future captain of England is at the front. (Uppingham School Archives)	xi
The Uppingham Metal Workshop utilised to produce material for the war effort. (Uppingham School Archives)	xi
An OTC instruction class during the Great War. (Uppingham School Archives)	xi
The exterior of the Memorial Chapel dedicated in 1921. (Uppingham School Archives)	xii
General Sir Charles 'Tim' Harrington with R.H. Owen at the opening of the Memorial Hall in 1924. (Uppingham School Archives)	xii
Interior View of the Memorial Chapel. (Uppingham School Archives)	xii
The East Block and Memorial Hall immediately after opening in 1924. (Uppingham School Archives)	xiii
The East Block and School Memorial Hall today, Little exterior change has occurred since its opening. (Uppingham School Archives)	xiii
Godfrey Robinson prior to losing his sight in 1917. (RNIB)	xiv
Godfrey Robinson (right) attending the Braille centenary in his capacity as RNIB chairman. (RNIB)	xiv
Memorial plaque to John Colling-Wells, All Saints, Caddington, Bedfordshire with the more common rendition of *Dulce et decorum est pro patria mori*. (Peter Graham)	xiv
The Gleed Harvey Memorial Window, Gleed an OU is on the left. (*A Guide to the Stain Glass Windows in St Mary & St Nicolas Church*, 2nd ed., 2008). Photograph by Alastair Goodrum)	xv
Memorial plaque to Stephen Jalland in All Saints, Pavement, York with the more unusual version of 'It is a beautiful thing to die for one's country' – *Pulchrum est Pro Patria Mori*. (James Halstead)	xv
The section of the Gleed Harvey memorial window featuring John Gleed. (*A Guide to the Stain Glass Windows in St Mary & St Nicolas Church*, 2nd ed., 2008). Photograph by Alastair Goodrum)	xv
The Edwalton Alms Houses built in memory of OUs Lawrence and Oliver Hind. (James Halstead)	xvi
Lawrence A. Hind dedication plaque situated outside the Alms houses. (James Halstead)	xvi

List of Tables

1	Contribution of Public (HMC) Schools and Other Schools with an OTC Unit to the War Effort 4 August 1914 to March 1915	31
2	Analysis of Regular Army Officers Produced by Uppingham School 1903-1909	50
3	Analysis of pre Great War Certificate A Pass Rates	51
4	Analysis of OU Service by Rank in the Great War	74
5	Analysis of OU Service by Age in August 1914	75
6	Analysis of Uppingham OTC in the First World War	80
7	Analysis of Uppingham OTC Military Service in the First World War	80
8	Analysis of Past Uppingham OTC Cadets Commissioned in the Army to June 1915	82
9	Analysis of Deaths by Age	93
10	Analysis of Deaths by Rank	93
11	Analysis of Deaths by Year of War	93
12	1914-1919 Honours List. Summary of Military Honours	111
13	VCs awarded by School	114
14	Award of DSOs to OUs by Date of First Award and Type of Award	116
15	Comparison of Individual Medal Winners from Tonbridge, Uppingham and Winchester	120
16	Teachers who served in the Great War – Tonbridge, Uppingham and Winchester	140

List of Abbreviations

AEF	American Expeditionary Force
APD	Army Pay Department
BEF	British Expeditionary Force
CBE	Commander of the Most Excellent Order of the British Empire
CF	Chaplain to the Forces
CMG	Companion of the Order of St Michael and St George
CIGS	Chief of the Imperial General Staff
CO	Commanding Officer
CWGC	Commonwealth War Graves Commission
DAQMG	Deputy Assistant Quartermaster General
DSO	Distinguished Service Order
GCR	Great Central Railway
HMC	Headmasters' Conference
IEF	Indian Expeditionary Force
IWM	Imperial War Museum
IWT	Inland Water Transport
KCB	Knight Commander of the Order of the Bath
LHCMA	Liddell Hart Centre for Military Archives
LMS	London Midland and Scottish Railway
LNWR	London and North Western Railway
MBE	Member of the Most Excellent Order of the British Empire
MC	Military Cross
NID	Naval Intelligence Division
OBE	Officer of the Most Excellent Order of the British Empire
OCB	Officer Cadet Battalion
OTC	Officer Training Corps
OU	Old Uppinghamian
POW	Prisoner of War
RAF	Royal Air Force
RAMC	Royal Army Medical Corps
RAOC	Royal Army Ordnance Corps
RASC	Royal Army Service Corps
RFC	Royal Flying Corps
RMA	Royal Military Academy

RMC	Royal Military College
RNAS	Royal Naval Air Service
RMLI	Royal Marine Light Infantry
RND	Royal Naval Division
RNVR	Royal Naval Volunteer Reserve
SA	Somme Association
SASA	St Albans School Archives
SGSM	St Georges School Magazine
SR	Special Reserve
TF	Territorial Force
TNA	National Archives
USA	Uppingham School Archives
USM	Uppingham School Magazine
UVF	Ulster Volunteer Force
VAD	Volunteer Aid Detachment
VC	Victoria Cross

Acknowledgements

This book would not have been possible without the assistance of many and I would like to apologise to and thank anyone whose names I have overlooked in these acknowledgements. I am most grateful to everyone who has provided help to me while I was writing this book.

Although I already had a vague idea of writing a book about Uppingham and the Great War; the introduction by Dr Spencer Jones to Duncan Rogers at Helion was a crucial part in easing the way to making this possible. I would like to thank Duncan and Dr Michael Lo Cicero, my editor at Helion, for their support and assistance while I was writing this book. Dr Phylomena Badsey kindly read and commented on the second draft of this book. My son, James, proof read my early efforts and was of immense help in getting this book to a state where it could be submitted to the publishers.

A key source of material for this book was the Uppingham School archives. Jerry Rudman, the school's archivist, was a tremendous support to me in all my visits to the archives. On many occasions, my discussions with him led to him identifying material which was invaluable in developing the themes within this book. Paddy Storrie of St Georges School, Harpenden and Nigel Wood Smith of St Albans School also provided important assistance in locating important documents.

In addition to those named in the previous paragraph I have been provided with a great deal of support by those working at many other archives on top of those named above. I would like to thank Cliff Houseley of the Sherwood Foresters Regimental Museum, Richard Bourne of the Wanganui Collegiate School Museum, the staff of the Imperial war Museum archives and especially the late Rod Suddaby (OU), the staff of the London Metropolitan Archives, the staff of the Liddell Hart Centre for Military Archives, the staff of the Lincolnshire Archives, the staff of the Manchester Regiment Archives, the staff of the National Archives and Sue Bryant of the Royal Marines Historical Society.

The following have generously shared documents and other material with me while I was writing this book: Robert Aitken, David Ballantine, Professor Ian Baruma, Mark Bishop, John Callcut, Stephen Cooper, Stephen Edell, Mark Forsdike of the Friends of The Suffolk Regiment Website, Geoffrey Fox, Andrew Griffin, Martin Gossage, Richard Hill, Hans Houterman, Guy Lewin Smith, John Mott, Andrew Rice, Bruce Robinson, Hugh Robinson, Gwyn Thomas of the Suffolk Regiment Museum, Nick Thornely and Reverend John Woolmer. Fran Dignon provided invaluable post production assistance with some of the photographs taken for this book.

Many have provided invaluable support in helping me to check and gather information or acting as a sounding board for me. I would like to thank Professor John Bourne, Dr Jim Beach,

Dr Timothy Bowman, Brian Curragh, Jo Franklin of Uppingham School, Dr Paul Harris, Dr Simon House, Michael Latham, David Marks, Patrick Mulville of Uppingham School, Martin Purdy, Dr Trevor Robinson, Dr Michael Senior, Professor Peter Simkins, David Sneath and Alison Summerskill. Above all, my wife, Ann, has been a source of unstinting support and interest even when I have at times become overenthusiastic!

I am grateful to the following for granting me permission to use their copyrighted material: Uppingham School for permission to quote from its archives and School Magazine, St Georges School for permission to quote from its School Magazine, Mr Aymeric Jenkins for permission to quote from E H Jenkins, *A History of the French Navy* (London: Macdonald and Janes's, 1973), Lincolnshire Archives for permission to quote from *Letters from Christopher Wakefield Selwyn*, Ms Barbara Matthews for permission to quote from Bryan Matthews, *Eminent Uppinghamians* (Cranbrook: Neville & Harding 1987) and Ms Barbara Matthews and Whitehall Press for permission to quote from Bryan Matthews, *By God's Grace* (London: Whitehall Press, 1984). Uppingham School generously provided me with many of the pictures included in this book. The photographs of Godfrey Robinson are reproduced with the permission of the RNIB. The photographs of the Gleed and Harvey Memorial Window by Alastair Goodrum are reproduced with the permission of the Churchwardens of St Mary and St Nicolas Church, Spalding and are taken from 'A guide to the Stained Glass Windows in St Mary & St Nicolas Church, Spalding', 2008 (2nd ed 2015). The painting "The Attack of the Ulster Division, 1st July 1916" by James Prinsep Beadle is reproduced by the kind permission of Belfast City Council. The original painting currently resides in Belfast City Hall (2016). The picture of the memorial plaque to John Collings-Wells is reproduced with the permission of Peter Graham.

Despite my best efforts, I have been unable to contact all copyright holders. I would like to apologise to anybody whose permission has not been obtained and invite them to contact me so that the matter can be addressed.

I would like to make it clear that all errors and omissions in this book are my responsibility alone.

This book is dedicated to those associated with Uppingham School, known and unknown, who contributed to victory.

Introduction

For many the story of Uppingham School's involvement in the Great War is epitomised by Vera Brittain's *Testament of Youth*. The book is a personal account which, for many, demonstrates the tragedy of the war. It tells of the deaths in the war of her brother, Edward, her fiancé Roland Leighton and their close friend Victor Richardson all of whom had come to the school in 1909. The popular view of the book as a tale of personal loss, however, is only part of the story; it is also the story of her recovery from a personal tragedy. It is as much a mistake to treat Brittain's account as being about loss as it is to think of *Testament of Youth* as being a complete account of Uppingham's involvement in the Great War. Brittain's book was a personal memoir, not a history and there is no evidence that she was trying to suggest that she represented a wider set of views about the school's involvement in the Great War. The aim of this book is to provide an account of the school's involvement in the war and explain how it fitted into the Empire's war effort.

Structure

In explaining the school's involvement this book cannot be chronological and merely recount the deeds of various individuals. In doing that, it would fail to draw out a number of key themes about the school. To place the school and the war into context the book has been divided up into 11 chapters addressing different themes.

To understand Uppingham's role it is necessary to place it within the wider topic of public schools in the First World War. Chapter 1 looks at the growth of public schools in the Victorian era and in the years before the war. It touches on the reasons for this growth, the common factors in it and how different schools varied within this. Equally importantly, it attempts to define what a public school was in 1914; something significantly different to what we now understand by the term. Public schools in the years before the war were associated with the concept of manliness which has been used to explain their contribution to the war so it is important to explain what is meant by this.

As much as there are common factors in the development of all public schools each varies in its individual progress. For Uppingham, although founded in 1584, the key to its development was the appointment of Edward Thring as Headmaster in 1853. Chapter 2 provides an account of how Thring developed the school and its educational ethos and how this carried on after his death in 1887. In particular, it looks at what made Uppingham different including the importance of music within school life.

For the British Empire in the early years of the 20th century up to 1914 there was a rising concern about the threats to it especially from Germany. Chapter 3 considers how this mood reflected itself at the school and in wider society. During this period the Officer Training Corps (OTC) was introduced at nearly all public schools and this chapter provides some detail about its development. The chapter also discusses the development of the school during this period. In particular it discusses how falling numbers of pupils led to the departure in 1907 of Edward Carus Selwyn, Thring's successor as Headmaster. Chapter 4 provides, through the story of the involvement of two OUs in espionage, a demonstration of the tensions which were rising between Germany and Britain in the years before the Great War. Reference will be made to the qualities of an Uppingham education but this chapter will show how these did not always produce a satisfactory outcome.

When the country declared war on Germany in August 1914 the response of the school and its OUs was immediate as it was throughout Britain and Ireland. Like all parts of British society it would suffer terrible losses but despite this was committed to winning the war. Chapter 5 looks at Uppingham's contribution to the military effort offering comparisons with other schools and the wider country. Questions such as what branches of the army did OUs serve in will be asked. What skills did they bring to the armed forces? This book is not just about those old boys who died but it is important to reflect on those who died. Death did not come evenly to all families; some suffered totally disproportionately compared even to other families who had lost fathers and sons. Some of those who died bravely were not even at the front. For others death would be mundane and unglamorous. The attitude of OUs to the war will also be discussed; were they really jingoistic in their approach or was there something more measured about it?

Total war meant that the whole country was affected between 1914 and 1918 far more than it had been in previous conflicts. Uppingham was no different in this respect and Chapter 6 describes how it developed its response and made its own contribution to the war effort. The school responded in two ways, firstly by using the OTC to prepare boys for the duties of the junior officer and secondly by using its resources to support the wider war effort. OUs also found themselves used in activities other than fighting when it was considered they were better employed there and this chapter provides examples of this. Another aspect of the home front OUs were involved in was propaganda. Often this was because their exploits were used to demonstrate how the war against Germany was being won. Much of this propaganda recounted acts of gallantry which had led to medals being won.

These accounts only cover a very small proportion of the medals and honours won by OUs. At least 624 OUs were awarded medals or honours for their services during the war. Chapter 7 sets out the scale of the awards received and looks at some of the more notable cases including the VCs awarded and the DSO for Harold Howitt. Awards were not just given for gallantry and by analysing the DSOs awarded to OUs it demonstrates how awards were made for both gallantry and meretricious services. Examples of awards for OUs of different medals are used to demonstrate the different types of behaviour which were necessary for each type. A comparison of awards of medals to OUs with those made to the old boys of other schools is made which demonstrates the unique nature of each school's contribution to the war and the way in which it was recognised.

Another factor which demonstrated the nature of each school's contribution to the Great War was how they were represented within the higher ranks of the army. Uppingham was not a traditional supplier of officers to the army and as a result was not well represented at the higher levels of the army. However, a study in Chapter 8 of some of the OUs who held senior command demonstrates some of the problems the higher command faced as the army rapidly expanded. It also demonstrates that like any other large organisation had to deal with the tensions caused by internal politics. Most importantly it shows senior commanders to be far from the donkeys have they have been portrayed as by some.

Amidst all the discussion about the contribution of old boys to the war effort, that of the teachers and other members of staff are often forgotten. In many schools teachers made significant contributions to the war effort. In the case of Uppingham 26 members of staff were involved in the war. Not all were on active service but involved in other ways such as working with the OTC. Chapter 9 examines this and pays particular attention to the career of Lieutenant Colonel C H Jones who was Commanding Officer of the Uppingham School Rifle Corps and OTC. His role within the school has received a reasonably full account but Chapter 9 demonstrates the significant part he played in the formation of the national OTC which was a significant source of junior officers during the Great War.

The end of the war was seen by the School Magazine as a time to return to normality and look to the future.[1] This was a common view but the country wished to remember and give thanks as well. Remembrance took many different forms and a study of Uppingham and its OUs demonstrates how this could vary from simple thanksgiving to many gifts to benefit others. Many OUs were able to move on in their life but for others the effects of the war had a significant effect on them. For some it proved too much and for others it spurred them onto a positive response as Chapter 10 will demonstrate.

After just under 21 years war with Germany broke out again. Over 200 OUs who had fought in the Great War would once more be involved in the national effort. The contributions would vary from those in senior command who played a significant part in victory to those who were involved in the Home guard and onto those who used their expertise gained in a civilian capacity to provide advice to the government on the efficient prosecution of the war. The subject of the school's involvement in the Second World War merits a separate book but some discussion of what those who had served in the Great War contributed to the next world war is necessary. It demonstrates that experience gained between 1914 and 1918 did not guarantee success between 1939 and 1945.

The reasons for the revised roll of service for OUs in Appendix I have already been explained but the significant role of the teachers needs to be recorded as well. Therefore Appendix II provides a roll of service for all those teachers and staff connected with Uppingham. Appendix III reproduces the order of service when the memorial to those who served and died was dedicated in the chapel. Finally, Appendix IV provides the text of the sermon given by the Bishop of Southampton on that day.

Sources

The magnitude of the war made it a chaotic and confused affair and records about Uppingham's involvement are incomplete. J P Graham, old boy and master at the school, claimed to have gathered the names of over 2,500 old boys who had undertaken military service during the

---

1   *Uppingham School Magazine* (*USM*) July 1919 pp. 153-154.

war but the *Third List of Old Uppinghamians who served in H.M. Forces 1914-1919* which he compiled and was published in 1919 lists only 2,158 who served in the war.[2] The research and analysis carried out for this book has identified 2,343 old boys who we were in the armed forces in the war. Unfortunately, it has not been possible to locate Graham's list in the school or other archives and there is nothing to suggest where it might be.

By examining the *School Roll* and comparing it to the *Third List of Old Uppinghamians who served in H.M. Forces 1914-1919* it has been possible to identify names of old boys which had not been included in the 1919 list. Using other resources such as the internet it has been possible to add the extra names. The names were verified by matching them up with the information in the *School Roll*. As a result it was possible to add a further 192 names to the 1919 list while at the same time seven names who were in the *Third List of Old Uppinghamians* were removed where it was clear that the individual originally identified for the list had never been to Uppingham. In addition, the names of 14 OUs who had lost their lives during the war but are not on the memorial in the chapel were identified. Some, but not all, of these deaths have been recorded in the *School Roll* but in many cases the school was unaware they had died as a result of the war.

The lack of complete records is not unique to Uppingham; many schools have discovered over the years that their records are incomplete. Winchester is one of many schools who have added to the list of old boys who served since the sixth edition of the *Wykehamist War Service Roll* was published in October 1919. Even the CWGC database of those who died is not complete as it does not include all the names on the various war memorials throughout the country. The case of Howard Roderick Parkes who was at the school from 1892 to 1896 is a good example of how the school would not have been aware of the death of an OU as a result of the war. Parkes died on 20th May 1920 (the *School Roll* records him as having died in 1921) from TB contracted while on active service. Under the CWGC criteria as he had died as a result of the war before 31 August 1921 he was eligible to be included on its database. It was only as a result of an individual discovering Parkes's grave in Molesey Cemetery and researching his history that the CWGC added the name to its database in 2010.[3]

Uppingham's records are also somewhat depleted in respect of war service of those acting in a civilian capacity. Compared to the Second World War we know relatively little about the OUs who made a contribution as civilians during the Great War. The November 1916 edition of the School Magazine contained a somewhat indignant letter from Norman J. MacDonald (at Uppingham from 1908 to 1913) who complained that medical students were not being included in the list of those serving. He pointed out that medical students had been asked by Lord Kitchener to stay at home. In his view the work being carried out was more important than those listed as 'awaiting commission'.[4] The December 1916 edition published a response from J P Graham who explained the list was specifically of 'those Old Boys who are serving in *His Majesty's Forces* (Graham's italics)' which was drawn from official lists published in the newspapers. As the likes of MacDonald were not serving in this capacity they were not included. This did not mean many old boys were not doing 'excellent and patriotic work in other spheres' the

---

2   John P. Graham, *Forty Years of Uppingham* (London: Macmillan, 1932,) p. 138 and *Third List of Old Uppinghamians who served in H.M. Forces 1914-1919* (Oxford 1919).
3   New CWGC Commemoration <http://1914-1918.invisionzone.com/forums/index.php?showtopic=155966> Accessed 29th September 2015.
4   *USM*, November 1916, pp. 253-4.

lack of information from official lists made it too time consuming to gather this information.⁵ Even getting hold of information from official lists was problematic as a letter from a master, Reverend W J Constable, to Major Arthur Lee, 1890 to 1896, demonstrated; in it he pleaded for help in getting copies of the official lists as it was proving impossible to get reliable news of OUs.⁶

Obtaining information from official lists also meant that there was a bias towards the activities of those who were officers. The official lists reported on subjects such as men who had been given commissions, their subsequent promotions and changes in role. There were no official announcements about those who had enrolled in the ranks. One hundred years on it is even more difficult to gain information about OUs who served in the ranks. A large proportion of the records relating to the ranks were destroyed after the warehouse where they were kept was bombed during the Blitz. This means that there are severe limits on gaining any information on many of those who served in the ranks. The discrepancy between the figures cited in this work and the 2,500 plus figure Graham quoted could be explained by those who served in the ranks and were received by him too late to be included in any of the four editions of the *School Roll* he edited before he retired.

Some but not all OUs were diligent about sharing their news with the school and Graham. However, from conversations with the School Archivist and a past School Librarian it is clear that it has long been a problem getting OUs to share their latest news with the school. Even when information is provided there is always a risk that it will be provided in the way the OU wishes to be seen. For example, Bronson Albery, 1895 to 1899, is described in the *School Roll* as a barrister but is better known as a theatre impresario; between 1973 and 2005 what is now the Noel Coward Theatre was called the Albery Theatre in tribute to his management of it for many years. Lionel Beale, 1909 to 1914, was described as an electrical engineer which disguised the fact he had remained in the army and was engaged in secret work.

The way that Graham appears to have collected his information via the newspapers means that there was a high risk that he would miss news of OUs and on occasions include someone who shared the name of an OU. With the benefit of hindsight it is obvious from the information discovered that the *Third List of Old Uppinghamians* would benefit from a number of revisions to make it a more accurate document. This list has been revised and it is included in Appendix I. Constraints of time meant that it was not possible to follow up the cases where it was possible the man was an OU but considerably more research was required. It is not certain that all the 2,343 names on the revised list are all on Graham's list of 2,500 but it is likely that there is a high level of correlation between the two lists. Assuming that the total of those who served was not much more than 2,500 then it is possible to identify from the list I have produced roughly 94% of the old boys who undertook military service during the Great War. By understanding the problems with the information available it is possible to gain a fuller picture of Uppingham's contribution to the Great War. There will never be a complete set of information about the school in the Great War (much of it was never recorded) but there is enough to be able to draw out trends and patterns and tell a detailed story about its involvement in the war.

---

5   *USM*, December 1916, pp. 278-9.
6   Imperial War Museum: IWM 66/121/1; Papers of Lieutenant A. N. Colonel Lee. I am grateful to the late Roderick Suddaby for drawing to my attention to these and other papers of OUs held at the IWM.

During the early stages of research about Uppingham and the Great War in the archives at the Imperial War Museum it was most fortunate that the late Rod Suddaby was working there. Rod, an OU, was providing assistance to researchers at the enquiry desk and approached the author offering to help. He was able to provide a lengthy list of OU papers available with his detailed knowledge proving invaluable in pointing me towards the ones most relevant to the MA dissertation being worked on at the time. To the many historians who have used the IWM archives over the years this is no surprise as Rod was renowned for his ability to point people in the direction of the most relevant material for their research topic. As research for this book continued it has become obvious that the IWM holds a wider range of Uppingham related material than even Rod was aware of. This is not a criticism; if such a knowledgeable individual as Rod was unaware of this material it demonstrates the wide variety sources about Uppingham and the Great War.

Not only is material available from a wide variety of private collections but there is information in places as diverse such as the IWM, the RNIB, the National Army Museum, London Metropolitan Archives and the Lincolnshire Archives. The material includes taped interviews, diaries kept during the war, letters between those fighting on the front and privately published memoirs in honour of old boys killed during the war. Many of these accounts provide a personal view of the conduct of the war; written from the front line the views expressed are those arising from personal situations often without knowledge of the wider strategic situations. However, they do provide an insight into the conditions they found themselves in, their daily routine, reflections on those they fought with and views on the way the war was being fought.

There are a number of autobiographies and biographies relating to various old boys including E W Hornung, Brian Horrocks, Eric Dorman-Smith and C R W Nevinson. As well as accounts of their involvement in the war they often give us insight into Uppingham and the way it influenced them; often this influence was not as positive as some academic theories might suggest. It should be noted that many of these books were published because the subjects were either famous, controversial or there was a desire to explain something about the individuals or some combination of these three factors. As such they are not necessarily typical of the beliefs and attitudes of other OUs involved in the war. Nonetheless they can provide us with part of the often subtly different views about the war and how it was being conducted.

A book which attempts to place its subject within a wider context will not be complete without drawing on general histories of the war and public schools. The First World War was a hugely complex affair so inevitably a wide range of books have been drawn on. However, there are three books which have been particularly valuable while researching for this book. Adrian Gregory's *The Last Great War: British Society and the First World War* provides a valuable reminder that we must be careful not to assume our predecessors held the same views as we do. John de Symons Honey's *Tom Brown's Universe: The Development of the Victorian Public School* provides a useful and scholarly insight into the development of public schools in the nineteenth century. Finally, Christopher Moore-Bick's *Playing the Game* offers an insight into the lives, experiences and attitudes of the junior officer on the Western Front.

The Great War was a complex and chaotic war and it would be foolish to rely on any single source of information. By comparing and contrasting and understanding the shortcomings of single sources of information it is possible to gain an insight into the essential nature of Uppingham's involvement in the Great War. When examining these sources three key questions have been asked. What was the nature of Uppingham's role in the Great War? Were there particular aspects of an Uppingham education which were important in explaining the involvement of OUs and the school? How did the school's involvement fit into the wider war effort of the British Empire?

Uppingham and the War in Context

That the involvement of the school is more nuanced than the simplistic understanding of Brittain described above is illustrated by comparison with E W Hornung, creator of the *Raffles* books and an Old Uppinghamian, who had a different attitude to the war. Both Brittain and Hornung suffered personal tragedies in the war; Brittain with the loss of four individuals she was close to and Hornung with the death of his only child, Oscar. Their poetry in response to their loss demonstrates contrasting reactions. Brittain expressed her thoughts in *Perhaps* as ones where darkness and pain had overwhelmed her.[7] In contrast, Hornung's *The Boy's War: Consecration* spoke of his need to respond by taking action. His poem spoke of the example young men set with their sacrifice, inspiring their elders to follow in their footsteps: 'To be of England's flower that fell'[8]

Hornung is better known for his *Raffles* stories about a gentleman thief than he is for his personal views and values. Amongst these was an unwavering belief in the Empire. Bryan Matthews, author of the history of Uppingham, describes him as: 'a second Henry Newbolt in his stress on playing the game at School and later in the Empire, on manliness and on keeping a straight bat in life.'[9] These were values which are more closely associated with public school old boys at the start of the 20th century than Vera Brittain's expression of loss, darkness and pain. Today Brittain is seen as a pacifist but this does not reflect her views about the war while it was being fought. *Testament of Youth* was not published until 1933 and she did not become a pacifist until 1937; in 1915 she most admired the idealistic and patriotic poetry of Rupert Brooke.[10] Just from looking at Hornung and Brittain we can see that the approach of those connected with Uppingham is not quite what we might expect 100 years later. The losses experienced by Brittain, Hornung and others associated with the school were tragic but it is important to see the school's involvement as greater than these two individuals. At least 2,343 old boys served in the war and of these it is known 463 died. Nearly all of those old boys who were involved in the war were affected by it; the majority did not die and of those who survived most were neither maimed nor scarred. Most accounts and letters suggest the war was mainly a happy period of their life with small periods where it was described as hell. That did not mean that there were not extremely disagreeable experiences but in the main it was a happy time for them. 100 years on many believe the Great War to have been pointless and those who died did so in vain. There is a perception today of the war starting in a rather distasteful tide of jingoism and stupidity and ending as a most appalling tragedy. However, as Adrian Gregory has shown the majority of the British population feared an extremely militaristic German domination of Europe.[11] During

---

7   Vera Brittain, *Verses of a VAD 1918* (London: Imperial War Museum, 1995), pp. 20-21.
8   Peter Rowland, *Raffles and his Creator: The Life and Works of E.W. Hornung* (London: Nekta, 1999), pp. 220-221.
9   Bryan Matthews, *Eminent Uppinghamians* (Cranbrook: Neville & Harding 1987), p. 35.
10 Brittain, *Verses of a VAD*, p. x.
11 Adrian Gregory, *The Last Great War: British Society and the First World War* (Cambridge: Cambridge University Press, 2008), p. 2.

the war and for a considerable time afterwards most of the British people shared this view about Germany.[12] Many of the letters written by old boys reflect this view that Germany needed to be stopped. Hindsight must be put to one side and the involvement of the school needs to be understood as one where the vast majority of the old boys and staff held these views. Those who fought do not need to be pitied; volunteering to fight was, for them, their patriotic duty. The British Empire was under threat and it was their duty to defend it.

The fear of German domination made the national response between 1914 and 1918 an understandable one. The United Kingdom (which in 1914 included all of Ireland) became a nation in arms. It was a very British response to the war in that it was based on volunteerism. In France the idea of a nation in arms meant mass conscription but in Britain this was politically unacceptable.[13] Britain was unique amongst the major European powers in not having a conscripted army. Instead, Richard Haldane, Secretary of State for War, in the Liberal Government from 1905 to 1912 developed the idea of a small professional army backed by a larger base of volunteers who would be called upon in the event of war.[14] There is some debate about how successful this idea was in the years leading up to the war but when war broke out there was a flood of volunteers to serve in the army.

In 1914 the comparatively small British regular army was well prepared for war; its mobilisation and despatch to France was done efficiently and quickly but by the end of 1914 had been virtually wiped out when the Germans executed the Schlieffen plan and subsequent First Battle of Ypres. There was a need to rebuild the army but also to recruit one to fight the first total war the country had ever fought. It was total war because of the high intensity of the fighting, geographical range of the conflict, the extensive nature of the belligerents' war aims and the extent to which civil society was involved. Kitchener had recognised this in 1914 when he sought the cabinet's permission to recruit a large citizen army advising that it would take at least three years to train before it would be ready to win the war. To win the war it would also be necessary to direct all the nation's resources towards victory. Amongst other things industry would need to be directed towards producing the munitions the army needed to achieve victory and a vastly expanded army would need far more administrative support. Not only was it the first total war the country had been involved in but technological developments such as heavy artillery and machine guns made it the first industrial war Britain had been involved in. In response to its shortcomings during the Boer War from 1899 to 1902 the British Army had become far more professional in its approach; the training of its officers had become more technical and theoretical and the army had started to recruit from a wider base of potential candidates. When war came the army rapidly expanded, military technology developed at an increasingly rapid pace and there was a corresponding growth in the need for professional and technological skills. Amongst the skills and expertise needed were management skills to support the war effort, leadership skills for the front line and technical skills to develop increasingly sophisticated munitions. The army had to draw on civilians and citizen soldiers and their skills to meet its needs.

---

12   Gregory, *The Last Great War*, p. 5.
13   Ian Beckett, "The Nation in Arms, 1914-18," in Ian F.W. Beckett and Keith Simpson (Ed), *A Nation in Arms: A Social Study of the British Army in the First World War* (Manchester: Manchester University Press, 1985), p. 2.
14   Edward M Spiers, "The Regular Army in 1914," in Beckett and Simpson, *A Nation in Arms*, p. 38.

Eventually, the government was forced to introduce conscription to help it to direct the war effort more efficiently and effectively but this was no seismic change; it simply formalised the nation in arms approach which had already developed. Within this national effort, different sections of society varied in their contributions to the war; like every other school Uppingham's contribution was unique and this book attempts to describe it and explain its wider significance. It's important to move beyond a focus on the more prominent examples of Uppingham's involvement to get a broader understanding of the contribution it made to the war. One of the aims of this book is to highlight those who have not enjoyed so much prominence as Leighton and Brittain.

This does not mean we should see the school and its contribution through rose tinted spectacles; not every old boy had fond memories of the school. In general, those who fought were not unquestioning patriots, in their letters home while stating their belief in the cause they were fighting for they were more than ready to criticise the way the war was being conducted. Not all old boys were of the highest integrity and the behaviour of a few was deplorable. This should not be a surprise; society is made up of individuals with different qualities and failings. However, the vast majority of OUs like the vast majority of the country were committed to meeting the threat from Germany.

This book is not just about those died. It aims to explain why so many OUs were prepared to fight and how their efforts fitted into the wider one of the country. It is not the place of this book to pity the old boys who served. It is the place of the book to try and explain the contribution they made, the skills they contributed and why they nearly all believed in the cause they fought for.

1

Public Schools and the Great War

To understand Uppingham's role in the Great War it is necessary to provide a brief history of the development of public schools from the 1830s. It is important to understand the development of their ethos and why they became attractive to parents. Different schools varied in their approach but all schools shared some values. These values made public schoolboys attractive to the army as a source of officers. Part of the attractiveness of the boys to the army was the growth of cadet corps and their successor the Officer Training Corps (OTC). As a result of this, the public schools were an important source of officers for the army during the Great War.

Understanding of public schools in the Great War has been coloured by a number of different factors. British society was far more deferential in 1914 than it is now; the rise of social liberalism in the 1960's and economic liberalism in the 1970s led to a rejection of the idea of deference to one's social betters. This was reflected in sketches such as Monty Python's 'Upper Class Twit of the Year' which promoted the idea of the public school twit.[1] Disillusioned public school boys such as Edmund Blunden and Robert Graves who promoted the idea of the futility of war became more influential in the 1960s.[2] More recently, the brilliant comedy, *Blackadder Goes Forth* added to the idea of public school incompetence. In it we see the public schoolboy being sent up though two different characters, General Melchett played by the OU Stephen Fry, 1970 to 1972, and The Honourable George Colthurst St. Barleigh.[3] Melchett was portrayed as the archetypal public school twit whose callousness, stupidity and incompetence was typical of British Generals and led to senseless slaughter of British soldiers. George is a parody of the public school officer, being brave but in a profoundly stupid and patriotic way. He cannot wait to encounter Germans but has no idea there is a very high possibility he will die when he does so. Within public consciousness the works of Blunden and Graves alongside the comedy of *Blackadder* has become confused with historical accuracy. For example, Blunden did not write *Undertone of Wars* as a historian but as a poet.[4] Both Blunden and Graves supported Britain's role in the war and were proud of their part in the war even if they were disillusioned with some of

---

1 Monty Python's Flying Circus, 'Upper Class Twit of the Year' TX 4 BBC2 January 1970.
2 See Edmund Blunden, *Undertones of War* (Paperback edition, London: Penguin, 2010 [1928]) and Robert Graves, *Goodbye To All That* (London: Jonathan Cape, 1929).
3 TX BBC1 28 September 1989 to 2 November 1989.
4 Blunden, *Undertones*, pp. vii-viii.

the ways the war was fought.[5] The disillusionment of this small group of public schoolboys about the war is, therefore, more nuanced than it is often perceived to be. The individuals who gave rise to this idea of disillusionment were gifted writers and the prominence of their views is because of their literary qualities; not their historical authority. There are many less known memoirs about the war written by public school boys which are less jaundiced such as Guy Chapman's *A Passionate Prodigality*.[6] This less cynical outlook is typical of many other public schoolboys who did not write or publish memoirs. It is within this context that involvement of public schools within the Great War needs to be understood. It is necessary to move beyond the disillusioned minority and contemporary values to understand their involvement in the Great War.

The Development of Public Schools

The definition of a public school has provoked a great deal of academic debate and over the years has evolved. In 1914 even the most liberal definition of a public school would result in a far smaller group of schools than those included in today's definition. In 1861 when the Clarendon Commission was set up to investigate the leading public schools the definition was very precise: the schools investigated by the commission were Eton, Harrow, Westminster, Winchester, Charterhouse, Rugby, Shrewsbury, St Pauls and Merchant Taylors. This definition reflected that, up until 1870, it was believed that only these schools could claim the title of public school.[7] However, the Endowed Schools Act of 1879 which sprung from the Clarendon and Taunton Commissions made it possible for a wider range of older schools to adopt the public school model.[8] Although public schools have common features their individual characteristics vary in many ways. Therefore, any definition is somewhat clumsy but membership of the Headmasters' Conference (HMC) can be regarded as an acceptable way of defining a public school in 1914.

Uppingham was a founder member of the HMC in 1869 which was set up at a meeting at the school on 21st December 1869 which Thring, Uppingham's Headmaster at the time had called.[9] All the Headmasters who attended shared a concern about the effects on their schools of proposed government legislation.[10] The schools which met at Uppingham did not include the Clarendon schools but they all joined in the years immediately after its formation.[11] The speedy growth in HMC membership reflected the fact there was a growing body of schools which had many similarities in the way they operated. It was the appointment of Thomas Arnold as Headmaster at Rugby in 1828 which was to lead to the development of the model on which public schools would operate. Correlli Barnett attributes to Arnold the primary

---

5   Anthony Seldon and David Walsh, *Public Schools and The Great War: The Generation Lost* (Barnsley: Pen and Sword Military, 2013) p. 224.
6   Seldon and Walsh, *Public Schools and The Great War*, p. 224.
7   J. de Symons Honey, *Tom Brown's Universe: The Development of the Victorian Public School* (London: Millington, 1977), p. 238.
8   Honey, *Tom Brown's Universe*, p. 120.
9   Honey, *Tom Brown's Universe*, p. 247.
10 For a fuller explanation of Thring's involvement in the setting up of the HMC see Bryan Matthews, *By God's Grace* (London: Whitehall Press, 1984), pp. 99-100.
11 Seldon and Walsh, *Public Schools and The Great War*, p. 11.

responsibility for giving English education its 'concern with moral conduct and its distinctive mark of romanticism'.[12]

Arnold's ideas developed over the time he was headmaster and it is important to look at the end result rather than taking his thoughts in isolation. At the heart of his approach was the belief the headmaster should have a free hand in the way he ran the school on a day to day basis and imposed discipline. Arnold had no compunction about expelling unsuitable pupils. His belief was that a school should have a strong sense of identity and values. This was reinforced by his requirement that masters should only work for the school (and not hold a curacy at the same time) emphasising their pastoral role within the school. To recruit masters of the required ability he set up a system of houses for boarders. This enabled him to generate more revenue so he could pay attractive salaries for the most able teachers. One result of this was to bring masters and boys into closer contact and develop their pastoral relationship. Complementing this approach was the prefect system he set up where a select group of boys were not to enforce the system but to support Arnold in developing the right moral culture by being leaders and not dictators. Prefects in each house were given a great deal of discretion to run them as they saw fit.[13] This was part of Arnold's idea of the school as a Christian community. In the development of the school's curriculum he was more conservative. Classics remained at the heart of it but were used for the teaching of the moral values which he believed to be so important.[14]

One of the major factors in the growth in the number of public schools during the Victorian era was the growth of the railways as they provided a means of getting boys to and from schools with greater ease. As already discussed, the Endowed Schools Act gave schools the ability to adapt the new public school model, and provided parents with more choice of which school to send their sons to. Many schools chose this course of action as the demand for public school places increased, the demand came mainly came from the middle classes. In the second half of the nineteenth century, there had been a rapid growth of the middle classes at the expense of the land owning classes. The catalyst for this was the repeal of the Corn Law in 1846 was in the words of Arthur Balfour a decision by the country that it wished to be industrial and urban and not an agricultural and rural one.[15] The rise of public schools was a response to the requirements of middle class parents. They wished to cement their newly found prosperity by improving their social status. The ending of practices such as patronage, the purchasing of an army commission and the phasing in of competitive entrance by examination for bodies such as the Indian Civil Service were huge opportunities for public schools. Their ability to prepare pupils for these exams made it more attractive for parents to send their sons to them. It was not so much that they imparted 'a distinctive and valuable set of values' in the eyes of parents but that the educational services provided were a means to provide their sons with status.[16] It was important to the middle classes that their sons gain recognition by achieving the status of 'gentleman.' This could be achieved by passing entrance exams to bodies such as the army, the civil service and the

---

12 Corelli Barnett, *The Collapse of British Power* (Paperback edition, Gloucester: Alan Sutton, 1984), pp. 24-25.
13 Honey, *Tom Brown's Universe*, pp. 7-11.
14 Honey, *Tom Brown's Universe*, p. 10.
15 David Cannadine, *The Decline and Fall of the British Aristocracy* (Revised paperback edition, London: Papermac 1996), p. 450.
16 Honey, *Tom Brown's Universe*, pp. 151-152.

professions. It was the ability to help their sons achieve this which made public schools attractive to parents more than the set of values which the schools sought to represent.

To meet this increased demand from parents public schools varied from the model pioneered by Arnold and varied in the communities which they aimed to support as the needs of society changed. Epsom College was founded in 1855 to start the education of those who wanted to enter medicine or another profession. Between 1801 and 1841 the country's population had almost doubled and demand for medical care had outstripped the supply of doctors.[17] Even before the abolition of the purchase of army commissions in 1871 Cheltenham and Clifton were preparing boys for military careers. Many of the aristocracy sent their sons to Eton; Arnold preferred not to accept the children of the aristocracy and suggested to the Duchess of Sutherland that Eton was a far better school than Rugby for her son. His view was that it was better he was at school with others of a similar background than those who did not come from such an elevated background.[18] In the Great War the leadership of the army would be dominated by a relatively small group of schools who had a reputation for preparing boys for the army.

Despite these variances in approach by different schools there were common factors to many of them. In particular, Christian morality was seen to be more important than scientific knowledge in the education of boys.[19] The schools had many aspects in common; they had adopted the house system and chapel worship was at the centre of their lives but between 1890 and 1914 there would be a shift in the ethos of public schools. The romantic idea of Christian idealism merged together with a romantic idea of patriotism. A belief developed that the English principles of truth, liberty, equality and religion must be taken to the rest of the world. The public school response to the threat to this from countries such as France and Germany became idealised and the school playing field was seen as a preparation for the battles the Empire would be involved in.[20]

Christianity was not usurped but the concept of what it stood for changed from that set out by Arnold; even in 1914, of the 56 attending the annual meeting of the HMC, 30 headmasters were clergymen. However, the idea that being proficient at games was pleasing to God began to take hold and in the years leading up to the Great War the ideas of athleticism (the playing of games) and muscular Christianity developed within the public school system. The development of athleticism in public schools coincided with that within the universities and the clergy adopting games as an appropriate topic for sermons; one even suggested that poor performances by college teams were 'displeasing to God.' This evolution of values led to the rise of the playing of games at university. By the 1890's some Oxford colleges set about attracting games players by offering them scholarships solely based on their athletic ability. This meant that graduates joining public schools as teachers were more likely to be athletes. These men were attracted to public schools as the playing of games there gave them an opportunity to pursue their athletic interests.[21] The playing of organised games at public school during the second half of the nineteenth century also had a more practical purpose as it was an excellent way to occupy boys and

---

17 The History of Epsom College <http://www.epsomcollege.org.uk/a-unique-history> (accessed 7 October 2015).
18 Honey, *Tom Brown's Universe*, p. 16.
19 Honey, *Tom Brown's Universe*, p. 25.
20 Barnett, *The Collapse of British Power*, pp. 27-28.
21 Honey, *Tom Brown's Universe*, pp. 110-111.

keep them out of mischief.[22] Athleticism had its critics such as Ford of Repton and Lyttelton of Haileybury but it thrived in public schools because it had the support of the vast majority of boys, parents and masters.[23] The house system within the schools provided an effective mechanism for sporting competition to operate and thrive.

The playing of games at public schools was important but equally important was the way they were played; the playing of games was to reflect the chivalric way life which was to be lived. By 1914 this way was termed 'gentlemanliness' which 'stressed honour, bravery, loyalty, courtesy, generosity, mercy and self-sacrifice'. From this flowed a sense of responsibility towards team members and in the Great War manifested itself in a sense of paternalism in officers towards their men and their welfare.[24] This notion of chivalry and gentlemanliness and the connection between the playing field and the battlefield manifested itself in Newbolt's *Vitai Lampada* ("They Pass on The Torch of Life") which included these lines:

> The river of death has brimmed his banks,
> And England's far, and Honour a name,
> But the voice of a schoolboy rallies the ranks:
> 'Play up! play up! and play the game!'[25]

This heroic tradition, it is argued, was underpinned by the teaching of the classics which dominated the public school curriculum. For the 14- and 15-year-old boy at King's Canterbury the week's teaching included seven and a half hours a week of Latin with the possibility of a further five hours spent on Greek. In contrast, two hours a week was spent on English which included history and geography. Of the 114 schools in the HMC in 1914 92 had classicists as headmasters.[26] Arnold changed the way the classics were taught by switching the emphasis from Latin to Greek and using the ideas of the ancient Greeks to explain the problems of the Victorian world.[27] In the period from 1840 to 1870 the emphasis in the teaching of classics was on the ideals of Plato. From this stemmed the belief that physical prowess promoted moral behaviour. This underpinned an education where truth, courage and self-control were promoted; from this came the idea of serving the community and addressing the needs of others. This was the system which produced the muscular Christian and the ideal of manliness. This was to change, it is argued, with the rise of the games cult. One of the complaints the Clarendon Commission attempted to address was that schools gave no moral training; they proposed that this should be done by the playing of games. The emphasis in public schools changed to one where the emphasis was on producing leaders rather than men who would serve others.[28] It was a development that

---

22 Seldon and Walsh, *Public Schools and The Great War*, p. 18.
23 Honey, *Tom Brown's Universe*, p. 114.
24 Gary Sheffield, 'Officer – Man Relations: Morale and Discipline in the British Army 1902–22', (PhD thesis, London, 1994), p. 129.
25 John Lewis-Stempel, *Six Weeks: The Short and Gallant Life of the British Officer in the First World War* (Paperback edition, London: Orion, 2011), p. 22.
26 Seldon and Walsh, *Public Schools and The Great War*, p. 18.
27 Malcolm Tozer, '"To the Glory that was Greece": Classical Images in Public School Athleticism', in Tom Winnifrith and Cyril Barratt (eds) *Leisure in Art and Literature*, (London: Macmillan, 1992), p. 109.
28 Tozer, "To the Glory that was Greece", pp. 112-114.

would fit in well with the growth of athleticism at universities which the public schools would be keen to draw on. Those who led were to be gentleman displaying the qualities of chivalry; these qualities would be learnt on the public school playing fields. The emphasis in the teaching of the classics moved away from an emphasis on Plato to one where Homer dominated; the works of Homer concentrated on the deeds of heroes.[29] By 1914 it is claimed the classics taught focussed on heroes and stories of their deeds and reinforced the public school ethos.

This was an important development in public school life but it can be overstated and it is important to bear in mind a number of other factors. As has already been shown public schools varied in their character being set up for different purposes and to serve different groups. Memoirs which reflect on the influence on the classics in their approach to the Great War are not necessarily wholly representative. In the way that the disillusioned public school boys gained prominence because of their literary merit the same observation applies to those erudite ex-public schoolboys who wrote fondly of the influence of the classics on them. Not all boys would fully understand the classics as perfectly as they should have. Something Kipling satirised in his short story *Regulus* where school boys with a distinctly limited grasp of the classics got the wrong end of the stick in terms of what the right thing to do was. Not all schools had the same heavy emphasis on the classics. Some would continue to place a strong emphasis on the classics long into the twentieth century. Shrewsbury was in the 1950s still known for its emphasis on classical education while at Bedford it was not until 1976 that a boy was allowed to not sit his Latin O Level (the predecessor of the GCSE). Other schools moved away from an emphasis on the classics early on. By 1908 at Uppingham most boys were taught the bare minimum of Latin with the serious study of the classics reserved only for the most academically gifted. Oundle had developed by 1914 a reputation for its emphasis on science and engineering. It is difficult to see that the way the classics were taught was so influential on boys as is sometimes claimed.

Public Schools and the Army

Public schools are often blamed for the rise in the spirit of militarism within Britain but their response reflected wider concerns within Britain. There was, as E M Forster put it in *Howard's End* first published in 1910, a growing fear of Germany. Germany saw itself in a new way: 'Germany a commercial power, Germany a naval power, Germany with colonies here and a Forward Policy there.'[30] Although his book was a novel, Forster was touching on unease within British society which was stridently expressed in the press. In the years leading up to 1914 the British Empire was the largest one in history. It was an empire whose success was based on trade and commerce. Threats to the empire were a threat to the country's prosperity and security. Britain had a great deal to lose if Germany were to usurp its position of global domination.

This explains the patriotic response when the Boer War (1899 to 1902) broke out. A serious sense of crisis was felt by the country following the disaster of the 'Black Week' in December 1899. Stephen Badsey records that in response to a government appeal following these events, Erskine Childers along with thousands of others volunteered to serve in South Africa. It was part of a national response in which the public schools would make their own unique

---

29 Sheffield, 'Officer – Man Relations', p. 131.
30 E M Forster, *Howards End* (Paperback edition, London: Penguin, 1979) p. 42.

contribution. The Boer War also demonstrated that public school contribution to the war effort varied with a relatively small group of schools providing officers for the army in South Africa. Eton alone provided 11 percent of the officers who served in the Boer War and its old boys made up over 17 percent of the public school boys who served as officers in the war. In all, 62 percent of officers in the war had received a public school education.[31] The dominant position of public school boys developed as a result of the abolition of the purchase of commissions in 1871; prior to this the British officer corps had been dominated by the aristocracy and landed gentry.[32] These groups considered it their duty as the leisured class to defend the country in times of war. The attributes of chivalry, leadership and horsemanship were part of their way of life and something all members of this social group were brought up around.[33] The abolition of the purchase of commissions opened up the opportunity to be an officer to middle class public schoolboys; being an army officer remained an expensive business but the depression which afflicted agriculture in the late nineteenth century reduced the number of those from a landed background who could afford to be an officer. It was wealthy businessmen and industrialists who could financially support their public school educated sons as army officers and acquire for them the status of a gentleman. Furthermore, there had been significant technological developments in the way war was fought such as more sophisticated weapons and the development of the railways. Such developments led to the need for a professional officer corps and the introduction of entrance exams to Sandhurst and Woolwich; something public schools were well equipped to prepare their pupils for.[34]

The army moved away from a group who were assumed to be able to practice chivalry and leadership to one who would who would be educated in the public schools to practice these qualities. It was gradual and public schools attracted the sons of the landed classes as private tuition became ill equipped to meet their educational needs. It is significant that of the 41 percent of the officer corps who fought in the Boer War came from the 10 leading public schools; Eton alone, which attracted the sons of the aristocracy, provided 11 percent of the this officer corps.[35] The policy of the army until 1910 would be to recruit from its preferred background. The traditional sources of army officers had been 'families with military connections, the gentry and peerage and to some degree the professions and clergy'.[36] These were in general educated at a limited range of public schools. For example, in 1913 Wellington, Cheltenham, Clifton, Marlborough and Winchester provided nearly half the cadets at Woolwich.[37] However, by 1910

---

31 Christopher Moore-Bick, *Playing the Game The British Junior Infantry Officer on the Western Front 1914-18* (Solihull: Helion 2011) p. 21.
32 S. Badsey, 'Fire and the Sword: The British Army and The Arme Blanche Controversy 1871-1921' (Unpublished PhD thesis, Cambridge, 1981) p. 124.
33 Cannadine, *The Decline and Fall of the British Aristocracy*, p. 264.
34 Cannadine, *The Decline and Fall of the British Aristocracy*, pp. 274-275.
35 Edward M Spiers, 'The Regular Army' in Ian F W Beckett and Keith Simpson (ed). *A Nation in Arms: A Social History of the British Army in the First World War* (Manchester: Manchester University Press, 1985) p. 41.
36 Sheffield, Sheffield, 'Officer – Man Relations', p. 3.
37 S. Robbins, 'British Generalship in the First World War, 1914-1918' (Unpublished PhD thesis, London, 2001) pp. 48-49.

it was recognised by the army these sources of recruits were starting to dry up and there was a need to recruit officers from a wider range of public schools.[38]

As a solution to this shortfall public schools appealed to the army as a source of men because the playing of organised games was viewed as useful training. 'By teaching boys to take rapid decisions on the playing field, games prepared them to take similar decisions on the battlefield, boys learned to take risks and to disregard their personal safety.' An interest in sport was something public school boys shared with the working class soldiers they commanded.[39] This shared interest would be used by officers to package training as a form of sporting activity.[40] By drawing on a wider range of public schools the army believed it could obtain a supply of officers without disturbing the social status quo.[41]

The roots of the army's ability to efficiently recruit from a wider group of public schools stemmed from the response to the events of the 'Black Week' in December 1899. In January 1990, the government called for volunteers in response to this crisis and public schools were quick to respond. At its meeting In February 1900 the HMC agreed to the suggestion of Dr Edmund Warre, Headmaster of Eton, that public school boys over 15 should be enrolled for basic military training.[42] He followed this up with proposals for a voluntary scheme where public schools would become training and recruiting ground for army officers.[43] Since 1859 when the Volunteer Force had been set up in response to the threat of French invasion an increasing number of public schools set up Cadet Corps. The War Office supplied members of the corps with weapons for which they were required to pay a fee. In 1889 the first Public Schools Camp consisting of Bedford, Bradfield, Haileybury and Sherborne was held; after initially struggling to establish itself the camp continued to meet attended by an increasing number of schools at the start of public school summer holidays.[44] Although the number of Cadet Corps had been rapidly expanding the Boer War led to a further surge in the number set up.[45] The vast majority of these Corps had been established at public schools and Warre envisaged them as being the centre of his proposal. His original proposal was rejected by the government on the grounds of cost and a belief that the public would be hostile to compulsory military training in schools.[46] Within Britain there was longstanding opposition to conscription and it was not until 1916 that this opposition could be pushed aside. Warre continued to promote the idea of compulsory training in a lecture at the RUSI in June 1900 and at the annual HMC meeting in December but with no success.[47]

The scheme was revived in 1906 when a committee under Sir Edward Ward was set up to consider how to solve the problem of a shortage of officers which was a significant problem

---

38   Sheffield, 'Officer – Man Relations', pp. 97-98.
39   Sheffield, 'Officer – Man Relations', pp. 122-123.
40   Sheffield, 'Officer – Man Relations', p. 127.
41   Sheffield, 'Officer – Man Relations', pp. 97-98.
42   Ian Worthington, 'Antecedent Education and Officer Recruitment: An Analysis of the Public School-Army Nexus, 1849-1908' (Unpublished PhD., Lancaster, 1982), p. 242.
43   Worthington, *Antecedent Education and Officer Recruitment*, p. 243.
44   Captain Alan R. Haig-Brown, *The O.T.C. and The Great War* (London: Country Life, 1915), p. 1 and p. 10.
45   Haig-Brown, *The O.T.C. and The Great War*, p. 5
46   Worthington, 'Antecedent Education and Officer Recruitment', p. 244.
47   Worthington, 'Antecedent Education and Officer Recruitment', p. 245.

in the Boer War. Public schools were represented by Reverend David, Clifton's headmaster.[48] The committee identified that there was a shortfall of officers of 4,419 in the Regular Army while the Auxiliaries (Volunteers etc.) were short of 3,914. It looked at how Russia, Germany, France and Japan had addressed the problem of having a sufficiently strong reserve of officers in the event of war. In addition, it took evidence from 28 witnesses, seven of whom were school Corps Commanders including Captain C H Jones of the Uppingham Rifle Corps.[49] The views of Jones appear to have had a significant influence on the committee's proposals which will be discussed in Chapter 9. The Committee moved very quickly; it met for the first time in late October 1906 and by February 1907 it had produced a report after hearing evidence as well as holding a conference with the HMC to discuss its proposals. The committee's proposals were designed to streamline the system of Training Corps at both schools and universities. In order to ensure there were enough officers in the event of war it proposed that gentlemen could become officers by being attached to a unit for a period of a year after which they would retain a liability of service with a regular recall annually or biennially.[50] In return they would receive pay during their periods of attachment.[51] After completing their minimum period of service gentlemen would become officers in the Special Reserve. In a country where military service was not compulsory the committee recognised that a year's service would not be especially attractive to young men starting a career. It therefore proposed that earning a certificate of proficiency from the school corps (Certificate A) would entitle the holder to exemption from four months of the one year's service. Passing another certificate of proficiency in the University Corps (Certificate B) would provide a further exemption of four months. The University Corps had also started to develop from 1859 onwards as part of the volunteer movement. It was also proposed that similar exemptions would be offered to those joining the Territorial Force (now known as the Army Reserve) as officers.

These proposals provided incentives for young men to become officers and achieve the valued status of a gentleman. Equally important was the way the corps would be organised. All the 'University and School Corps' were to be organised into a single body, the OTC. They were to be placed under the direct control of a department of the War Office which would oversee the running and examination of the OTC.[52] The War Office would provide financial support for the OTC which would be based on the number of 'efficient' cadets.[53] Efficiency would be measured by the number of cadets over 15 who had met criteria which included a minimum level of attendance at parades and training camp and the unit passing an annual inspection.[54]

This was an improvement on the previous arrangements for the corps. Under the previous system the corps were attached to local Volunteer units who had discretion about what support

---

48 *Interim Report of the War Office Committee on the Provision of Officers (a) For Service with the Regular Army in War and (b) for the Auxiliary Forces (Hereinafter Ward Committee)*, Cd. 3204, (London: HMSO, 1907), p. 2.
49 *Interim Report of the War Office Committee on the Provision of Officers (a) For Service with the Regular Army in War and (b) for the Auxiliary Forces Minutes of Evidence (Hereinafter Ward Committee Evidence)*, Cd. 3205, (London: HMSO, 1907), pp. 3-4.
50 *Ward Committee*, p. 6.
51 *Ward Committee*, p. 15.
52 *Ward Committee*, p. 7.
53 *Ward Committee*, p. 10.
54 *Regulations for the Officers Training Corps* (London: HMSO, 1912), pp. 19-20 and p. 29.

and training the corps were provided with. Instead, under the War Office the training for all cadets was standardised. From 1908 the regulations were regularly revised to make sure they were in line with the army's approach to training which became more professional as part of its response to the Boer War. By 1912 the papers for the Certificate A examination at most schools were based on *Field Service Regulations, 1909* and *Infantry Training, 1911* which laid down how the British Army would fight in battle. The aim was that those who studied for them would have the basic skills to be a junior officer on being called up.

Richard Haldane, the Secretary of State for War responsible for the introduction of the OTC believed that the Japanese experience during the Russo-Japanese War had demonstrated it was possible to produce effective officers from the reserve even with a relatively short period of training. This, he claimed, had shown that 'short trained men could be put into the fighting line' so long as they were fed in one by one and not as units. The Japanese had found, he argued, they were able to use men who trained for six months and this was adequate when it was supplemented by further training during the campaign.[55] The Ward Committee said that Certificate A should train the cadet to a standard that made him suitable to be a second lieutenant in the Volunteers.[56] The training was to be practical with no military theory included.[57]

Early comments about the newly formed OTC were favourable. General Langlois, of the French Army, after a visit to observe British Army manoeuvres in August 1909, compared the OTC favourably with its French equivalent. He observed that in addition to being trained in drill movements and the handling of arms the training also included field work which was taken seriously and done well.[58] This was not merely good manners on the part of Langlois; he had a reputation for speaking bluntly about matters he considered unsatisfactory and had often criticised the French army. In his account he touched on the role of the OTC in addressing the shortage of officers for the regular army recounting the views of an unnamed officer; who remarked that those drawn from the 'upper and wealthier classes' had needed to 'give more time and attention to their work' during the Boer War. As a result, some of these officers had resigned rather than accept change. It also discouraged others from applying for a commission and as a result it became necessary to 'open the gates wider' to candidates from the middle and non-moneyed classes.[59]

Langlois may have been impressed by the OTC but in its early years it failed in its objective to provide officers for the Special Reserve. Haldane reported in March 1912 that of the nearly 18,000 who had left the OTC (Schools and University) only 283 had taken commissions in the Special Reserve with a further 500 having passed their Certificate A and Certificate B examinations.[60] Haldane conceded that as a piece of machinery for recruiting officers the OTC was working slowly. However, he maintained that it was a vast improvement on what had gone before during the Boer War where he implied lack of machinery led to a haphazard approach to recruiting extra officers required for the war. Most regular armies had sufficient officers for peacetime but war required many more officers. Mobilisation for war would be a 'ragged process'

---

55 P. Debs., 1908, Volume 185, 12 March, column 1862, Commons.
56 *Ward Committee*. p. 9.
57 *Ward Committee*. p. 7.
58 General H. Langlois, *The British Army in a European War* (London: Hugh Rees, 1910), p. 14.
59 Langlois, *The British Army in a European War*, p. 59.
60 Edward M Spiers, *Haldane: An Army Reformer* (Edinburgh: Edinburgh University Press, 1980), pp. 140-1.

but the existence of the OTC as a source of officers made this a great deal easier. He pointed out that while the figures for the Special Reserve were relatively small the OTC had not been in existence for long and that year on year the number of Special Reserve officers being provided by the OTC was increasing substantially; when war broke out in August 1914 the number of officers in the Special Reserve was 2,557 strong. Many of those who had been given a commission in the Special Reserves had received them in 1914. The official statistics record that only 81 had been granted in 1913.[61] Haldane maintained that he had never expected the OTC to be effective before 1914 and as a way of recruiting officers for the Special Reserve it had not failed.[62]

Haldane was working in extremely constrained financial circumstances as annual expenditure on the army was limited to £28 million.[63] The Liberal Government elected in 1906 had made this decision so it could fund social reforms. He needed to find a way to respond to emergencies while controlling costs and his solution was to have a small regular army into which bodies such as the OTC would feed if war broke out; an approach he described as 'a nation in arms'.[64] Haldane's achievement was not one that provided the best possible solution to the problem of a shortage of officers but one which given the political constraints used the available resources efficiently albeit not as effectively as they could be.

Although the OTC had many contingents from public schools it also had a large number of contingents who were not HMC members; a large number of these schools were grammar schools. However, in the period from August 1914 to March 1915 it was public schools who played the leading role in providing officers for the army. Table 1 summarises their contribution.

Table 1 Contribution of Public (HMC) Schools and Other Schools with an OTC Unit to the War Effort 4 August 1914 to March 1915[65]

	HMC Schools with OTC Unit	Other Schools with OTC Unit	Total	HMC Schools as a % of the Total
Number of Schools	97	69	166	58
Old Boys with a Commission on 4th August 1914	3,299	824	4,123	80
Old Boys granted a Commission 4th August 1914 to March 1915	9,668	1,934	11,602	83
Old Boys enlisted to other ranks 4th August 1914 to March 1915	4,511	4,513	9,024	50
Total Old Boys Serving	17,478	7,271	24,749	70

61 *Statistics of the Military Effort of the British Empire During the Great War* (London: HMSO, 1922), p. 234.
62 P. Debs., 1912 Volume 11, 13 May 1912, columns 984-6, Lords.
63 Spiers, *Haldane*, p. 73.
64 Spiers, *Haldane*, p. 191.
65 Based on analysis of Haig-Brown, *The O.T.C. and The Great War*, p. 97-106.

The table shows that HMC schools played the biggest part in the provision of officers to the army during this period, especially in terms of providing new officers to supplement the Regular Army. Conversely, the greatest percentage of old boys from OTC units of schools outside the OTC had gone into the ranks. Further analysis demonstrates that the army had 'opened the gates wider' to draw more extensively on HMC schools. The 10 leading schools in terms of contributing officers to the army (Charterhouse, Cheltenham, Clifton, Eton, Haileybury, Harrow, Marlborough, Rugby, Wellington College and Winchester) provided 38 percent of OTC cadets granted a commission between August 1914 and March 1915. Although this was similar to their contribution to the Boer War officer corps (41 percent) they provided half of the public school contribution from the OTC compared with 66 percent in the Boer War. This demonstrated that establishing the OTC had made it easier to recruit officers from a wider range of public schools. The existence of the OTC was useful to the army which was rapidly expanded by Kitchener after the war broke out. The battles of 1914 imposed a heavy toll on the British Expeditionary Force in France with 4,023 officer casualties (45% of the regular army officers) of which 1,230 had died and only 593 replacements had been sent.[66] With no structure for selecting the high number of officers required to replace casualties and to lead Kitchener's army the OTC was an attractive way of recruiting officers quickly. Its training programme was coordinated with that of the rest of the army so cadets would have some idea of what was required. The army's rapid, sudden and unplanned expansion meant there was no formal training structure in place for those recruited to the ranks. OTC cadets could be trained relatively quickly and be available to provide leadership for the new recruits.

The army clearly had a preference for public school boys to be officers as Table 1 demonstrates. This preference continued beyond the end of March 1915; in April 1915 the army's instructions about suitable men for commissions set out that the criteria included 'adequate military knowledge, a public school education and being under 27 years old except where there were 'exceptional circumstances'.[67] The approach of public school boys to sports with the spirit of team building and cooperation was clearly attractive to the army. In addition the schools were geared to producing gentlemen and to be an officer you needed to adhere to the concept of being 'a gentleman'. Playing the game in the right way was considered a key element of gentlemanliness which 'stressed honour, bravery, loyalty, courtesy, generosity, mercy and self-sacrifice'. From this flowed a sense of responsibility towards fellow team members which in war would be very important as one of the junior officer's key duties was care of his men.[68]

This belief in public school boys explains why it was the boys from HMC schools who were drawn on first to provide officers for the army in the early stages of the war. The British army's expansion can be demonstrated by the growth of the officer corps from 28,060 officers in August 1914 to 164,255 in November 1918.[69] The role of junior officers leading their men into action, often at the forefront of the advance meant that their mortality rates were far higher than the ranks. Second-Lieutenant Bertram Monk who was killed on 23 November 1914 was found close

---

66 Sheffield, 'Officer – Man Relations', p. 103.
67 Sheffield, 'Officer – Man Relations', p. 113.
68 Sheffield, 'Officer – Man Relations', p. 129.
69 *Statistics of the Military Effort*, p. 234.

to the enemy trenches with his right stretched out as though pointing the way to his men.[70] The mortality rate for the British army of the Great War was 12.3 percent but for schools such as Uppingham which provided many junior officers the mortality rate was often over 20 percent. 37,452 officers died during the war which meant that the public schools could no longer fill all the gaps and the army had to be more flexible about recruitment as the war went on.[71] Lastly, it meant that public schools such as Uppingham which had not traditionally been drawn on to provide army officers would begin to be drawn on more heavily as the war went on.

Recruitment from public schools went beyond membership of the OTC, which reinforces the idea that the army placed a premium on a public school education. At Uppingham 46 percent of those who served were 27 or older when war broke out and came from a variety of backgrounds, not just the army. To have been a member of the OTC which was not established until 1908 a boy could have been no older than 24 when war came in 1914. These figures show that while the OTC was an important source of officers the army, faced with a rapid expansion, was flexible about who it recruited. It needed men quickly and would consider anyone with what it considered to be the right background. The figures for those OUs 27 or older when war came demonstrated that those with public school backgrounds were attractive to the army. After February 1916 the recruitment of officers was formalised with the establishment of Officer Training Units from which men could only progress to a commission if they passed the course.[72] However, the qualities of leadership men were taught reflected those that the army found attractive in public school boys. Officers were expected to display resolution, self-confidence and self-sacrifice if they were to be leaders of men.[73] One qualification to join an Officer Training Unit was to have been a cadet in the OTC. This meant it was likely that public school boys would be officers, if they wished but the pool of possible candidates had been widened by recruiting from the ranks as well. All, those with or without a public school background would be trained to think like officers; it was no longer assumed that they had these skills.[74]

Necessity meant it was essential from the start of the war to draw from a wider group of public schools than in the past and as officer casualties mounted. At the higher levels of leadership in the army, the schools which had traditionally been the main source of officers for the army continued to dominate. Simon Robbins has carried out analysis of what he described as the BEF's managers; these were either high ranking officers or men on the staff who were involved in the planning and management of the war on the Western Front. The top three schools in Robbins's table were Eton (93 officers), Wellington (44) and Harrow (38): between them they provided 175 officers which was 25 percent of the group. The army did not draw exclusively from long established schools; the top 10 schools which accounted over 50 percent of the 'war managers' included Wellington, Cheltenham, Clifton, Haileybury and Marlborough which had all been established in the Victorian period.[75] Westminster which was a Clarendon school and

70 Paddy Storrie, *"Here I am; Send me" The War Dead of St George's School 1914-1918* (Harpenden: St Georges School, 2004), p. 10.
71 *Statistics of the Military Effort*, p. 237.
72 *Statistics of the Military Effort*, p. 237.
73 Sheffield, 'Officer – Man Relations', p. 344.
74 Sheffield, 'Officer – Man Relations', p. 142.
75 Sheffield, 'Officer – Man Relations', pp. 510-511.

founded in 1560 only provided three 'war managers' despite its elite status. The less established Uppingham provided seven.

Seeing the public school contribution to the Great War in terms of brave but stupid individuals is not helpful to understanding the contribution of public schools to the Great War. The creation of the OTC provided a source of officers for the army from public schools. Their ethos developed men whom the army considered suitable for leadership. However, in the years before the war it mainly recruited from a small group of schools it favoured. Public schools were far from homogeneous in their nature. While there were common characteristics in many of them they varied in their emphasis. For example, Epsom had a focus on producing boys to enter the medical profession while Clifton and Cheltenham were focussed on preparing their boys to serve in the army. Uppingham in its own way varied from the stereotype as the next chapter discusses.

2

A Brief History of Uppingham

It was under Edward Thring that Uppingham developed its unique approach to education. The school was founded in 1584 by Archdeacon Robert Johnson alongside nearby Oakham School with the purpose of providing free education to boys with poor parents. The statutes of both schools clearly stated that the schools were for those local boys whose parents could not afford fees.[1] Johnson also attached to each school at a later date hospitals or alms houses providing accommodation for poor men. In the statutes governing the school and in his will Johnson set up a number of exhibitions so pupils could go to Oxford or Cambridge. Preference was to be given to pupils from impoverished backgrounds.[2] In the early part of the eighteenth century the school started to take fee –paying pupils some of whom boarded in the hospital.[3] This made the school attractive to better-off parents who were often not local but saw it as an opportunity to obtain a place at university for their sons. As a result, a gradual erosion of the school's original charitable purposes took place over the years, and by 1820 it had virtually ceased to be a school for local children.[4]

Edward Thring was appointed in 1853 to succeed Henry Holden as Headmaster who had accepted the headmastership of Durham. Since being appointed Holden had made a number of changes to the school which greatly improved its reputation but these would be overshadowed by the work of Thring who became known as the school's 'Second Founder'. For Uppingham his significance was that he converted it from: 'a small but high quality grammar school which only a few academics had heard of into a well-known public school.' He made the school 'part of the history of education'.[5]

Outside the school, Thring developed a reputation in Britain and America as an original thinker and author on education. Thring's influence on the educational system remains to this day but is barely acknowledged. His role in developing public schools gets scant attention when compared to the influence attributed to Thomas Arnold of Rugby. Arnold died in 1841 12 years before Thring became Headmaster at Uppingham and although this was his only appointment

---

1 Matthews, *By God's Grace*, p. ix.
2 Matthews, *By God's Grace*, p. 13.
3 Nigel Richardson, *Thring of Uppingham* (Buckingham: University of Buckingham Press, 2014), p. 25.
4 Don Farr, *None That Go Return* (Solihull: Helion, 2010), pp. 39-40.
5 Matthews, *By God's Grace*, pp. 73-74.

as a Headmaster Thring would have a significant influence on the way the wave of new public and private schools would develop.

In 1907, 20 years after Thring's death, St Georges School opened in Harpenden, Hertfordshire. It was established by Reverend Cecil Grant as "a co-educational public School Trust", he had moved from Keswick where he had been Headmaster but had become frustrated with interference by the local authority.[6] Thring's ideas remained highly influential in 1907 as the second page of the prospectus directly quoted his views expressed in *Education and School* as to the purpose of education:

> True education is nothing less than bringing everything that men have learnt, from God or from experience, to bear first upon the moral or spiritual being by means of a well-governed society and healthy discipline, so that it should love and hate aright; and through this, secondly, making the body and intellect perfect, as instruments necessary for carrying on the work of progress; training the character, the intellect, the body, each through the means adapted to each. This is the object of education; and all the work of discipline and self-government, of exercising the intellect, of exercising the body, go on at once, and in a good system mutually support each other in their appointed places. But all this requires time.
>
> It follows then that no falseness in the government, no falseness in the working plan, in or out of school can make boys true. Whatever is professed must be done.
>
> If a school professes to teach, then every boy must have his share of teaching. There must be no knowledge scramble, or the untruth will make itself felt.
>
> If a school professes to train, then every boy must be really known, his wants supplied, his character consulted, or the untruth will make itself felt.
>
> If a school professes to board boys then every boy must find proper food and proper lodging and no meanness, or the untruth will make itself felt.[7]

The appointment of Thring was a decision many of the governors at Uppingham would regret as he would give them no respite with his dynamism and ideas for the development of the school until he died in October 1887. One of Thring's successors, Lord Wolfenden (Headmaster from 1934 to 1944), speaking in 1953, summarised the fundamentals of Thring's educational philosophy under four headings.

Firstly, all boys must receive equal and full attention and not lack for any support that they needed. Classes were to be small enough for each boy to get the personal attention he deserved. From this the second principle flowed which was that ordinary and brilliant boys should have an equal amount of time spent on them in the classroom. This was in contrast to Arnold's approach where he wished only to have boys of ability within his school. It was a matter of pride to Thring that the best should be brought out of the less able boys as well as the most academically gifted pupils. A feature of the school, even after Thring, was that more intelligent boys were sent to other schools such as Rugby while the less intelligent brother was sent to Uppingham because it was recognised that the school would bring the best out of him. From this idea of equality of attention Wolfenden identified the third fundamental element as being that boys who were

---

6   St George's School, School History <http://www.stgeorges.herts.sch.uk/About-Us/School-History> (accessed 21 October 2015).
7   St Georges School Archives: 1907 Prospectus.

not intellectually gifted should have opportunities to succeed in other occupations. In Thring's time this idea was entirely novel. The public school syllabus was based on teaching the classics and mathematics which many boys struggled with. Thring introduced subjects such as modern languages, history, sciences, art, music and carpentry. The result was that boys of lesser ability developed a greatly improved self-confidence. The fourth element of Thring's philosophy was that a school must be underpinned by efficient organisation and adequate buildings and equipment; what Thring called the machinery of the school. He was critical of Arnold for failing to set up this machinery which could enable a school to operate effectively in the face of less able Headmasters and teachers.[8]

These four aspects underpinned Thring's fundamental aim which was to prepare boys to serve their fellow men. As part of his plan to achieve this he significantly increased the amount of games played and sport became increasingly important in the school's life.[9] He saw PE as playing an important part in preparing boys to serve their fellow men. Fitness and physical ability were important basics but the training was designed to promote the ideas of truth, courage and self-control; from this would follow the exercise of Christian ideals of recognising the needs of others and serving the community.[10] It reflected his belief that religion should be practiced and not preached.[11]

Games, however, were only to be part of a boy's moral development in Thring's approach; in much of the rest of the public school movement games were to become more prominent and become important in developing leadership. Matthews argues that Thring was aware of the danger that a love of games could get out of control. He wanted the boys to enjoy games but he did not wish too much importance to be placed on them.[12] To the end of his life, he resisted pressure to replace Uppingham football with Rugby Union football which he disliked because it involved too much brute force. To do so he said was: 'the old, old story of rising by goodness, and when risen and admitted to be great, imitating the vices of the great.'[13]

Thring's idea that boys should be prepared to serve others is reflected in the choice of profession by his old boys; from 1853 to 1870 of the professions the church was most frequently chosen.[14] The decline after 1870 in old boys going into the church is not surprising even though Thring remained strongly committed to the idea until he died in 1887. Other public schools had already experienced a decline in old boys who were being ordained, at Rugby the figure declined from nearly 40% in the 1830s to 5% in the 1880s.[15] The reasons for this decline appear to be complex but amongst them may have been an increasing secularisation of society and the rise of the middle class. Many of Uppingham's parents were from a commercial and business background and wished their sons to follow a similar career. D W Carmalt Jones who was at the

---

8   Matthews, *By God's Grace*, pp. 81-82.
9   Matthews, *By God's Grace*, p. 228 and Farr, *None That Go Return*, p. 41.
10 Tozer, "To the Glory that was Greece" p. 114.
11 Malcolm Tozer, 'Manliness: The Evolution of a Victorian Ideal' (Unpublished PhD thesis: Leicester 1978), p. 137.
12 Matthews, *By God's Grace*, p. 230.
13 Matthews, *By God's Grace*, p. 232.
14 Tozer, "To the Glory that was Greece", p. 127 footnote 17.
15 Patrick A Dunae, *Gentlemen Emigrants: From the British Public Schools to the Canadian Frontier* (Manchester: Manchester University Press, 1981), p. 49.

school from 1888 to 1893 and before that in the Lower School recalls that many fathers were either in the City or involved in the Liverpool shipping industry.[16]

Thring's other significant innovation was the introduction of music to the school's curriculum. No other public school had done so and England was not a country celebrated internationally for its music.[17] Since 1855 he had appointed music masters but in 1865 he appointed Paul David as music master with the aim of making music central to school life. When Thring died the school had seven full time music staff and 108 boys, approximately a third of the school, were learning an instrument.[18] The importance of music in the school is reinforced by C R W Nevinson's description of David as 'almost headmaster' and such was the esteem music was held, he would remain at Uppingham until 1908 which included the 20 years Thring's successor, Selwyn, was Headmaster and from whom he would enjoy an equal amount of support.[19] He would only retire after Selwyn had left and been succeeded by McKenzie who was equally supportive of music. One of the many innovations which David initiated was the introduction of a school orchestra in 1890.[20] It was an important development which stood in contrast to many other public schools where music was not considered to be manly and even in the eyes of a few of their masters to be decadent.[21] Under David's successor, Robert Sterndale Bennett, music at the school would continue to be known for its excellence and its quality improved even further.[22] Support for music at Uppingham is demonstrated by the way it appears to have been attractive to the parents of boys who were gifted at music, long after the death of Thring. Ernest Moeran, the composer, was at the school from 1908 to 1912. His brother, William, had been sent to Marlborough but the family had sufficient funds to send their children where they wished so it seems Uppingham was selected as the most suitable place for Ernest. He had already displayed musical ability at his prep school so the decision to send him to Uppingham would have been logical.[23] Many more boys were sent to Uppingham because of the quality of its musical education: Edward Brittain, brother of Vera, was a talented musician and as the son of a paper mill owner it is no surprise he was sent to Uppingham which was popular with industrialists.[24] Selwyn's support for David is important to bear in mind when criticisms are made of his period in office and in particular the cult of games which developed during his time from 1888 to 1908.

Selwyn has been much criticised for the changes he made when he became Headmaster but nearly all Headmasters wish to place their own stamp when they go to a new school so it should come as no surprise that Selwyn, who might have felt he was in the shadow of such a prominent figure as Thring, wished to make a mark. He also faced different circumstances to when Thring had become Headmaster. By the late Victorian period the number of public schools had

---

16 D W Carmalt Jones, *A Physician in Spite of Himself* (London: Royal Society of Medicine Press, 2009), p. 36.
17 Tozer, 'Manliness', pp. 190-191.
18 Richardson, *Thring of Uppingham*, p. 65.
19 C.R.W. Nevinson, *Paint and Prejudice* (New York: Harcourt, Brace and Company, 1938), p. 11 and Matthews, *By God's Grace*, p. 220.
20 Farr, *None That Go Return*, p. 42.
21 Honey, *Tom Brown's Universe*, p. 223.
22 Ian Maxwell, 'The Importance of Ernest John: Challenging the Misconceptions about the Life and Works of E.J. Moeran' (Unpublished PhD: Durham, 2014,) p. 77.
23 Maxwell, 'The Importance of Ernest John', pp. 76-77.
24 Farr, *None That Go Return*, pp. 31-34.

greatly increased and there was more competition for boys.[25] Carmalt Jones says that Thring predicted that the school could not continue to be run along his lines and there was a belief that no one else could have run it in the way he did. There was, he said, a wish that amongst parents Uppingham should more closely conform to the way most other public schools were run.[26] A view reflected in Selwyn's obituary in the School Magazine which stated that there was a real fear that the school was so unique under Thring and would not survive his death.[27] A move to being a more orthodox public school is understandable in these circumstances.

There were many areas where Thring had not conformed to the general public school model. It has been argued that Selwyn remained loyal to Thring's educational philosophy but with increasing competition from other schools, expanding the size and making adjustments to the nature of the school was understandable in order to meet expectations about what great public schools should do. There was a change in the approach to games which led to the dominance of and awarding of special privileges to the top games players at the school; a development which chimed with the development of the cult of games in other public schools. Amongst the changes to games were the introduction of compulsory rugby, colours for the first, second and third teams and a system of promoting and relegating boys from different games.[28] As already discussed, Thring disliked rugby and the school played Uppingham football which was a mix of rugby and soccer. From Carmalt Jones's point of view the introduction of rugby was welcome to many who wished to play football elsewhere and were now able to do so under the same rules.[29] Amongst other changes Selwyn made shortly after his arrival at the school was the introduction in 1889 of a rifle corps after advising the Trustees 'that other Great Schools have a Rifle Corps'. This needs to be understood in the context of the continuing and long standing tensions between Britain and France. After the Crimean War these tensions had risen again as the two countries' colonial ambitions clashed. In the 1880s concern about the French threat had led to the abandonment of work on the Channel Tunnel and led to the growth of the Volunteer movement with more public schools corps being established as described in the previous chapter. The introduction of a Rifle corps was something Thring had long resisted and there was some hesitation amongst the Trustees before they agreed to this innovation.[30] The typical Victorian public school headmaster was an autocratic individual who fiercely protected his right to develop and run the school as he saw fit. Thring had clashed with the Trustees on many occasions over his plans to develop the school; the relationship between Selwyn and the Trustees would also often be strained and he would regularly be challenged over his decisions and recommendations.[31]

One strain between Thring and the Trustees over a considerable time was the pressure they had applied on him to increase the size of the school beyond 330 boys as they were anxious to earn more revenue; he had resisted it on the grounds it would cause overcrowding and that the school would be too big for the Headmaster to be able to know all the boys adequately. Selwyn

---

25 Tozer, 'Manliness: The Evolution of a Victorian Ideal', unpublished PhD thesis (Leicester 1978) p. 410.
26 Carmalt Jones, *A Physician in Spite of Himself*, p. 29.
27 USM, February, 1919 p. 9.
28 Matthews, *By God's Grace*, p. 233.
29 Carmalt Jones, *A Physician in Spite of Himself*, p. 29.
30 Matthews, *By God's Grace*, p. 120.
31 Matthews, *By God's Grace*, p. 120.

almost immediately after coming to the school had accepted the plan of the trustees to expand the size of the school and during his time this increased by 100 boys but this sort of agreement between him and the trustees was not guaranteed.[32]

The 'machinery' which Thring introduced would continue to work well in many areas of the school's life; despite the rise of the cult of games. His successors would continue reforms to the curriculum with further moves towards emphasising the teaching of the moderns and away from the teaching of the classics.[33] In some areas these were not always a resounding success. Carmalt Jones describes French as a farce because as a subject it did not count enough for boys to care; both masters who taught French, when he was at the school, found it almost impossible to control their classes.[34] Selwyn, despite his strong personality, was not immune to parental pressure. The introduction of the Army Classes and Engineering Classes which did not involve the teaching classics and concentrated on the moderns were introduced as a result of the demands of parents rather than Selwyn's belief in their educational merit.[35]

Selwyn has been criticised for the changes to the school after he became Headmaster but much of Thring's approach continued. A point made by Nevinson, an Official War Artist, who was at the school from September 1903 to April 1907.[36] His father had wanted him to go to Shrewsbury, his old school, and then onto Balliol, planning a classical education for him. However, Nevinson was more interested in mechanics at the time and while his journalist father was abroad in South Africa his mother agreed to send him to Uppingham which he described as a great public school with the traditions of Thring and more modern than any other at that time. In his words: "Science was not regarded as "stinks," and music and painting were not looked upon as crimes." Nevinson was no friend of Uppingham and claimed to have learnt nothing there, although he did start to develop an interest in art, so in the context of this his words are surprisingly positive.[37]

The commitment to giving every boy a chance no matter what his ability was continued and can be seen by examining the school prize lists. The prize lists for 1913 show awards ranging from the more traditional subjects such the classics and mathematics to modern subjects including Modern History, English literature, German and science. There were six prizes for music together with prizes for practical subjects such as pencil sketching, metalwork and carpentry. This was an indication that Thring's ideal of giving an equal opportunity to do well continued.[38] By the time boys got to the sixth form classics were not compulsory except for the Oxbridge exams where it was still required; there were only 19 of a total of 83 in the Upper VI and therefore considered to be Oxbridge material. An examination of the *School Roll* shows a diversity of occupations for boys after they had left the school. Three of the most prominent were the army, business and law. In the case of these first two occupations the classics were certainly not required. Here the focus was on technical and professional skills. Latin had been

---

32 Matthews, *By God's Grace*, p. 121.
33 Matthews, *By God's Grace*, p. 82.
34 Carmalt Jones, *A Physician in Spite of Himself*, pp. 31-32.
35 USM, February 1919, p. 11.
36 *School Roll*, p. 224.
37 David Boyd Hancock, *A Crisis of Brilliance* (Paperback edition London: Old Street Publishing 2010), p. 43.
38 Uppingham School Archives, Uppingham School Prize Lists Easter 1907 to Christmas 1913.

made optional for Woolwich and Sandhurst exams and had declined in importance as there were other subjects where it was considered easier to gain marks.[39] The army needed officers who could deal with increasingly complex technology and tactical developments. Despite what Selwyn and others may have felt the classics were no longer considered to be an essential part of an army education. Likewise, there was an increasingly utilitarian approach which valued technical skills. As noted above, Uppingham boys were often the sons of northern industrialists who placed a premium on the ability of their sons to master technical processes. Thring had set out an educational philosophy which promoted independence, inquisitiveness and self-confidence in boys and this was attractive to parents. Despite the rising importance of games the prize list demonstrates that Thring's ideals still had an important place in the school's philosophy.

It was not only the technical and professional skills that Uppingham instilled in its boys. The rise of public schools had partly been the result of their ability to give boys the opportunity to be gentlemen. This desire of parents for their sons to be gentlemen had become a particular obsession in late Victorian and Edwardian times. Since the 1880s there had been a decline in the wealth, power and influence of the landed classes and a rise in the wealth, power and influence of industrialists and other members of urban society. British society did not have formal and rigid boundaries and industrialists started to replace the old landed classes in positions of political and social influence. An example of this was Joseph Shuttleworth who had set up the engineering company Clayton and Shuttleworth with his brother-in-law; he purchased the Old Warden estate in Bedfordshire and became a prominent local gentleman while applying his technical skills to making agriculture more efficient. The acquisition of property was not the sole condition to be a gentleman. Social skills were important as well and his appreciation or practice of music was valuable in this respect. An Uppingham music education was not just for the musically gifted. It was also attractive to those parents who wished their sons to make their way in polite society as gentlemen.

The Uppingham Thring had created had focussed on bringing the best out of every boy and it was very much his personal creation. It was his drive which had created such a unique institution in the face of opposition from various parties such as the Trustees and even on occasions his own staff. This was in the face of a growth in a public school culture where the cult of games was becoming increasingly dominant. His own idea of public schooling had diverged away from what many parents apparently wanted. Selwyn would have found it difficult to continue Thring's approach even if he had wanted to. Despite the changes made by Selwyn, many of Thring's ideas continued to be prominent in the school's culture. There were still opportunities for boys of all abilities to thrive and music continued to play a high profile part in the life of the school. Thring's approach which promoted independence, inquisitiveness and self-confidence in boys continued to be a central part of the school's approach. In the early years of the 20th century Selwyn discovered to his cost that this was far more important to parents than the cult of games he developed.

---

39 USM, February 1919, p. 11.

3

The Threat of War

The early years of the 20th century before the Great War broke out have often been presented as a period of rising militarism within Europe. Countries throughout Europe strengthened their armed forces and senior military figures became increasingly influential within governments. Within public schools it has been suggested there was an increasing spirit of militarism. The growth of the cadet corps and the OTC has often been used as a central tenet in arguing that there was a case of rising militarism within public schools in the early 20th century. The development of public school militarism reflected growing concern about Germany. That concern only went so far: as is demonstrated by the difficulties that a relatively small army had in recruiting officers before 1914. It was only with the outbreak of the war that there was a rush to take up arms. At Uppingham developments between 1900 and 1914 show that militarism was not as prevalent as some have claimed. Close analysis of the *School Roll* suggests that the tie between the school and old boy is not as strong as has been suggested.

The Boer War

The early days of the Boer War which broke out in October 1899 caused a great deal of concern in Britain. By December the British Empire had suffered three defeats within the space of a week. An army which was used to fighting colonial wars against ill-equipped natives had come up against a far more effective opponent and had its shortcomings badly exposed. The defeats by what were two small countries (Transvaal and the Orange Free State) led to a closing of ranks in the country and a determination that the British Empire's position as a world power be protected.[1] The government decided to send vast amounts of reinforcements and to recruit civilian volunteers as part of this response. Stephen Badsey records that following the disaster of the 'Black Week' Erskine Childers along with thousands of others had volunteered to serve in South Africa.[2] The Headmaster Selwyn's response was prompt and in February 1900 he made it compulsory for every boy to pass a shooting test. He ruled that no boy would be allowed to participate in inter-house competition and would be ineligible for a school prize until he had

---

1 Thomas Pakenham, *The Boer War* (Paperback edition, London: Abacus 1993), pp. 247-248.
2 Badsey, 'Fire and the Sword', p. 124.

passed the test. It is part of the post 1896 rise of the military spirit at the school described by Tozer.[3]

It is important to see that Uppingham was not acting alone even if this increased militarism received a mixed response, within the school community.[4] As discussed in Chapter 1 there was a rise in volunteerism in the country across the second half of the 19th century as concerns about the threat of French invasion rose. There was public concern about the situation and Selwyn would have been keen to be seen to be doing his bit. Selwyn's response was echoed by the public school movement when later, in February 1900, the HMC agreed that boys over 15 should be enrolled for basic military training.[5] As previously noted, this was at the initiative of Dr Warre, Headmaster of Eton, who followed this up with a proposed voluntary scheme where public schools would become an officer training and recruiting ground for the army.[6] Selwyn was not acting in isolation and his proposal for a shooting test was designed to make pupils ready for service. Good accuracy was vitally important to operating in the new circumstances of the South African War and in its call for volunteers the government laid down a number of requirements including that any man volunteering should be a first class shot.[7]

The school history records that 222 old boys served in the war nine of whom lost their lives. As with the Great War the school's involvement is understated; there are at least 10 old boys who served but are not recorded on the *School Roll*. A reliance on *The Times* as in the Great War could not be depended on for complete information. Some of those missed had served in Canadian units as volunteers and their involvement was not reported. The compilation of the list would also have been reliant on the vigilance of the master compiling it. The scale of the school's involvement is considerably smaller than the Great War as this was a smaller war but there are themes which would be repeated between 1914 and 1918. There were a large number of volunteers many of whom served in units such as the Imperial Yeomanry and the City Imperial Volunteers. Included within this group were so-called gentlemen emigrants who had gone to work in the Dominions; mainly in Canada. Hugo Beaumont Burnaby who was at the school from 1887 to 1891 emigrated to Canada in 1893 and worked in ranching but as soon as war broke out returned to Britain and enrolled with the Wiltshire Yeomanry.[8] Many OUs served in the ranks as Uppingham was not one of the top 10 army public schools so were not relied on so heavily for officers. Clifton which was among these top 10 had 347 old boys serve in South Africa, nearly all of whom were officers.[9]

The losses Uppingham suffered in South Africa were small in number and in the overall percentage of those who served when compared to those of the Great War. In South Africa nine died which was four percent of the 232 known to have served; in the Great War at least

---

3   Tozer, 'Manliness', p. 403 and Farr, *None That Go Return*, p. 43.
4   Tozer, 'Manliness', p. 408.
5   Worthington, 'Antecedent Education and Officer Recruitment', p. 242.
6   Worthington, 'Antecedent Education and Officer Recruitment', 243.
7   Ian Beckett, *Britain's Part-Time Soldiers: The Amateur Military Tradition 1558-1945* (Revised paperback edition Barnsley: Pen and Sword Military, 2011) p. 202.
8   Roll of Honour, Buckinghamshire <http://www.roll-of-honour.com/Buckinghamshire/Wendover.html> (accessed 29 October 2015) and DNW The Brian Kiernan Collection <http://www.dnw.co.uk/auction-archive/special-collections/lot.php?specialcollection_id=53&specialcollectionpart_id=21&lot_id=74147> (accessed 29 October 2015).
9   Derek Winterbottom, *Henry Newbolt and The Spirit of Clifton* (Bristol: Redcliffe, 1986), p. 53.

2,344 are known to have served of whom 463 (20 percent) died. Similarly when compared to the leading army public schools Uppingham's losses were smaller in absolute and percentage terms; Eton lost 129 old boys during the war, Wellington lost 65, Clifton 43 (twelve percent of the 347 who served) and Charterhouse 27 (Seven and a half percent of the 360 who served).[10]

The numbers who died may have been comparatively small but the school nonetheless wished to remember those who, in the words of Selwyn, 'went forth and returned not again.'[11] The chivalric values of public schools espoused honour, bravery, loyalty, and self-sacrifice and it was therefore natural Uppingham wished to honour them and an understandable reaction given public concern about the threat to the Empire especially at the time of the 'Black Week.' On the day peace was signed Selwyn launched an appeal for a combined gymnasium and concert hall to replace the highly inadequate facilities which already existed. The appeal was necessary because the Trustees had agreed only to fund the building of a new water supply for the school at a cost of £17,000 and did not have the resources to fund other development schemes. Selwyn chose to present the appeal as not only being a memorial for those who had died but also as a celebration of Paul David, the music master, who was close to retirement and whose work had given music a far higher prominence than other schools. When compared to other schools it was as much a thanks for those who had given their lives as the celebration of a cultural activity central to the school's life. Selwyn was drawing on national sentiment to raise funds to boost both the athletic and musical aspects of the school.[12] In the words of the School Magazine David's name stood for 'an inspiring force in music' and many OUs would be glad to see his name connected with a Concert Hall to replace the overcrowded School Room, while a new gymnasium was needed as 'the new developments of military exercise' rendered it imperative.[13] When compared to the memorials at other public schools there was more than militarism at the heart of it. Other schools used appeals to boost their facilities; both Eton and Harrow built memorial halls but there does not appear to have been the same diverse approach as at Uppingham.[14] In other schools there was a more romantic approach; Tonbridge chose to place a window in its chapel the theme of which was knightly chivalry.[15] Clifton, under the influence of Henry Newbolt, selected a Gothic pedestal with a figure of St George.[16] While Charterhouse placed a bronze of the angel of victory holding a dying hero in its memorial cloisters.[17] When compared to other schools it suggests that the concept of romantic patriotism combined with knightly chivalry had not taken quite such a grip at Uppingham. The motto above the entrance 'Caesorum Comitum Memores' (Mindful of our fallen Comrades) was balanced by the motto above the orchestral platform 'Res severa est verum gaudium' meaning 'true pleasure is a serious business.'

The importance of music within the school was reflected when the June 1905 School Magazine provided extensive coverage of the first concert in the hall. It said 'this truly magnificent hall

---

10 Peter Donaldson, 'The Commemoration of the South African War (1899-1902) in British Public Schools' *History & Memory*, 25: 2. p. 34, p. 52 and p. 60 and Winterbottom, *Henry Newbolt*, pp. 53-55.
11 USM, April 1905, p. 45.
12 Matthews, *By God's Grace*, pp. 124-126.
13 USM, November 1904, p. 4.
14 Donaldson, 'The Commemoration of the South African War', pp. 40-41.
15 Donaldson, 'The Commemoration of the South African War', p. 47.
16 Winterbottom, *Henry Newbolt*, p. 55.
17 Donaldson, 'The Commemoration of the South African War', p. 46.

proved as good for its sound as it is to look at.'[18] The concert featured Josef Joachim the most eminent violinist in Europe who performed Beethoven's violin concerto and declared the concert hall open. The hall itself was a copy of the interior of the Leipzig Gawandhaus (Concert Hall).[19] The Memorial Hall was a development which reflected the importance of both music and games to the school but also reflected national concern about threats to the empire. The £5,000 required came in relatively quickly; by December 1903 the School Magazine was listing 660 subscribers who had contributed £2,432.[20] To the contemporary mind an interest in both military matters and music are viewed as being incongruous but in the early twentieth century this was not so. R Sterndale Bennett, David's successor, commanded the OTC during the Great War and in 1920 remarked in a lecture that he had spent a good part of his life 'teaching boys the art of music and the art of soldiering'.[21] There was no barrier between music and the military, both being integrated into school life which reflected a concern about the threats to the Empire mirroring the social and political concerns of the period.

A Temporary Decline

If the opening of the hall appeared to be the culmination of Selwyn's leadership of the school with its celebration of athleticism and music he was shortly to discover this was not enough. In October 1906 he was forced out by the Governors and told to leave by the end of 1907.[22] Like many headmasters of his time he was an autocrat who expected to be given a free hand to run the school as he wished. Sir Harold Howitt and later Chairman of the Trustees who was at the school from 1901 to 1904 described him as 'a terrifying character held in great awe.'[23] Selwyn took his belief in having a free hand to extremes and refused to account for his actions to the Governors.[24] He might have been able to co-exist with the governors if other problems had not led to a decline in school numbers.

In September 1903 the number of boys had reached the maximum of 450 but then started to fall so that by September 1906 numbers had fallen below 380.[25] One significant factor was the number of boys who left within two years of joining the school which suggests parents considered Uppingham was not right for their sons. In 1903 eight percent left in their first year and 14 percent in their second. In 1905 the figures were seven percent and nine percent. This can be compared with the figures for 1930 which were nil and two percent.[26] It must be remembered that even during Thring's time boys might stay for only two years or less. Sir Sidney Burrard was only at the school from 1873 to 1874 and then left to go to Wellington; mainly because the

---

18 USM, June 1905, p. 94.
19 Matthews, *By God's Grace*, pp. 125-126.
20 Matthews, *By God's Grace*, p. 124 and *USM* December 1903, pp. 286-289.
21 Uppingham School Archives (USA), Notes on Uppingham School OTC, From the files of R Sterndale-Bennett (1910-1921).
22 Matthews, *By God's Grace*, pp. 128-129.
23 USA, Harold Howitt Reminiscences, p. 6.
24 Matthews, *By God's Grace*, p. 128.
25 Matthews, *By God's Grace*, p. 128.
26 Matthews, *By God's Grace*, p. 131.

journey from his home to school was considerably shorter.[27] However, it appears that there was an increase in shorter stays and it is likely that Uppingham's reputation was damaged making it less likely that parents would send their boys there. The cult of games which had been introduced by Selwyn had seen the development of the worship of the 'games blood', the top athletes who enjoyed privileges by virtue of their status and who were at the heart of his fall. Nevinson, in typically vivid language described the bullying and sexual abuse which took place:

> It is now the fashion to exclude the "hearties" from accusations of sexual interest or sadism or masochism; but in my day it was they, the athletes and above all the cricketers, who were allowed these traditional privileges. Boys were bullied, coerced and tortured for their diversion, and many a lad was started on strange things through no fault nor inclination of his own.[28]

This vivid language demonstrates Nevinson was not in the habit of pulling his punches and this would have made him the target of bullying himself and this probably influenced his recollections.[29] His autobiography is more known for its drama than its reliability but there are other less vivid accounts which provide support for bullying at Uppingham.[30] Canon Charles Raven, who was at the school from 1898 until 1904, expressed hatred for his time at the school, admitting that he did not fit in. In a school where games came first a boy who was interested in nature, cerebral and capable of sarcasm was, he concedes, unlikely to fit.[31] Similarly Professor William King who was at the school from 1904 to 1908 believed he had not fitted into the school because he was neither a gifted games player nor good at Latin.[32] Nevinson, Raven and King all enjoyed success in different fields so it can be argued the school did not harm them but it is certainly indicative of the games cult at the school. A view reinforced by Howitt who was good at games recalled that he enjoyed his time at Uppingham.[33] Matthews speaks of the fashion at the time for 'bloods' to have attractive favourites, usually younger boys. He cites Howitt as recalling that when he arrived at the school in 1901 several in his house were expelled during a period of 'low morality'. In 1903 Selwyn made sex and morality the subject of a closed session of chapel.[34] Even after the Great War, Uppingham appears to have suffered from a reputation for 'immorality.' Alec Waugh suggested his father send his brother Evelyn to Uppingham even though it had a reputation for being immoral.[35] It appears homosexuality, then a crime, had become a significant problem, although in most cases an over-emotional interest by senior boys in younger ones stopped at that.

---

27 *Nature* obituary Sir Sidney Gerald Burrard Bart., K.C.S.I., F.R.S. <http://www.nature.com/nature/journal/v151/n3832/abs/151414a0.html> (accessed 2 November 2015).
28 Nevinson, *Paint and Prejudice*, p. 12.
29 Nevinson, *Paint and Prejudice*, p. 16.
30 Boyd Haycock, *A Crisis of Brilliance*, pp. 323-324.
31 Charles E Raven, *A Wanderer's Way* (London: Martin Hopkinson, 1929) pp. 11-12.
32 The Royal Society Biographical Memories William Bernard Robinson King. 1889-1963 <http://rsbm.royalsocietypublishing.org/content/roybiogmem/9/171> (accessed 2 November 2015).
33 USA, Howitt Reminiscences, p. 6.
34 Matthews, *By God's Grace*, p. 130.
35 Peter Parker, *The Old Lie* (Paperback edition London: Hambledon Continuum, 1987), p. 112.

The decline in numbers in the 1900s is not surprising if Nevinson's account is broadly accurate: social and sexual norms would have prevented any hint of homosexual practices at the school becoming public. Other factors could explain this decline, for example, between 1900 and 1914 national income hardly rose while prices continued to increase.[36] Economic hardship may be one reason but after Selwyn's departure school numbers increased again so it is difficult not to attribute much of the fall to parental dissatisfaction.

As has already been argued parents did not send their children to public schools because of their ethos, but because they were giving them something they wanted for their sons: the education necessary for attaining the status of gentleman. Selwyn was removed because a significant number of parents and prospective parents were concerned about the games cult getting out of control which resulted in low moral standards. Although the playing of games and the values of romantic patriotism were important they were not sufficient in themselves to meet the requirements of parents. The public school system was one where boys were given substantial responsibility for the running of houses and other activities such as sports. Selwyn appears to have taken a *laissez faire* attitude to this and not intervened when things were going wrong. He believed that discipline was not about keeping rules but something more ethical.[37] Those who enjoyed privileges do not appear to have exercised the responsibilities which went with them. Support for Selwyn was not unconditional despite innovations such as the building of the gym and the introduction of a shooting test to equip boys for military service was not unconditional. The welfare of their sons was more important to parents than sporting and military developments.

A Rising Concern

The Boer War prompted a rising concern within the country about the Empire. The Kaiser's support for the Afrikaans in the Boer War prompted further concern about the threat from Germany both from a military and economic point of view. These concerns were reflected in the contents of the School Magazine. As with most other School Magazines its basic content covered school events such as sport, the OTC and other content together with a liberal smattering of poetry. In addition there were articles which reflected various concerns about the welfare of the nation. The School Magazine of March 1906 reported on a debate in the Union Society about Free Trade; a topic which had divided the Conservative party much as the EU did nearly 100 years later.[38] Military matters were covered on a number of different occasions. In April 1904 a letter from the Navy League was published which explained its role to promote the importance of British naval supremacy to protect the Empire arguing that the navy had been underfunded by both parties and drew on the Boer War as an example of the cost of being unprepared, citing the support it enjoyed in many public schools pupils while inviting OUs to join.[39] In November 1904 the magazine reported on a debate at the school Union Society on a motion which proposed: 'That this house considers the introduction of Compulsory Military Service into England a necessity.'

---

36   Sir R. Ensor, *The Oxford History of England 1870-1914* (Oxford: Clarendon, 1936), pp. 500-502.
37   *USM*, February 1919, p. 11.
38   *USM*, March 1906, p. 1.
39   *USM*, April 1904, pp. 50-54.

The proposer's main concern was the need to defend the country against invasion from Europe. The arguments for a volunteer system were that a compulsory system would produce too large an army and, as the Boer War showed, in times of threat there would be a voluntary patriotic response with 'Englishmen' prepared to lay down their lives to defend the Empire. The motion was lost by 22 votes to 13.[40] It was an indication that, at Uppingham, the view was that it was the patriotic duty for men to respond when a threat to the Empire came but that compulsory service was too militaristic.

This was a reflection of the wider public view rather than being exclusive to Uppingham and other public schools. Even if a boy was good at games it did not mean he would be sympathetic to the games ethos and the school. Gordon Wills, who was at the school from May 1906 to July 1910, 'disliked it intensely'.[41] Wills was in the Shooting VIII in 1908, 1909 (when he was Captain) and 1910 a status which would have placed him in a favoured position but despite this he did not think well of the school. He served in the war but his motivations to do so are unlikely to stem from values acquired at Uppingham.[42] Likewise Professor King was in the Shooting VIII but did not think of Uppingham in glowing terms.[43]

Visitors to the school in Selwyn's final years, however, had a military nature; the magazine of July 1905 reported the speaker was Rear-Admiral W F S Mann of the National Service who also presented the League's medal to the school for its implementation of compulsory shooting tests. In the words of the *Grantham Journal* whose report of the day was reproduced in the School Magazine the value of the training was: 'too obvious to need more than the merest mention'.[44] It was not usual for the *Grantham Journal* to pass comment on developments at the school; usually it merely reported on the addresses at Speech Day. It is indicative of a national mood after the Boer War that the country needed to be prepared for further threats although compulsory military service was not considered to be part of this. However, after Selwyn's departure the heady tone of debate about national issues appeared to die away. The chief guests at speech days, if there was one at all, were more likely to be of an educational background; in 1910 the invited guest was the Master of Trinity College.[45]

Under Selwyn's successor, The Reverend H W McKenzie, there was a move away from the more stridently militaristic tone and the cult of games was brought under control by ending special privileges for athletes.[46] His style was understated as can be seen in his reports to the governors. In 1911 he recorded that there was 'nothing very startling to record' and in 1913 'nothing very noticeable.'[47] This understated style perhaps made the words he used during the 1914 speech stick so much in the memory of Vera Brittain when she recalled them in *Testament of Youth*. In a wide ranging speech he offered the advice of Count Nogi. 'Be a man – useful to

---

40 *USM*, November 1904, pp. 257-261.
41 J. Wills, *World War 1 experiences of my grandfather, Gordon Wills* <http://www.oceanharmony.ca/Alfred%20Gordon%20Wills.html> Chapter 1 (accessed 1 September 2012).
42 *School Roll*, p. 241.
43 The Royal Society Biographical Memories William Bernard Robinson King. 1889-1963 <http://rsbm.royalsocietypublishing.org/content/roybiogmem/9/171> (accessed 2 November 2015).
44 *USM* July 1905 pp. 129-133.
45 *Grantham Journal*, 16 July 1910, p. 2.
46 Tozer, 'Manliness', pp. 452-453.
47 Matthews, *By God's Grace*, p. 135.

your country; whoever cannot be that is better dead.'⁴⁸ On 11 July 1914, when he spoke, the crisis following the Archduke Ferdinand's assassination had not yet come out into the open. The Austro-Hungarian government was still discussing its response and would not issue an ultimatum until 23 July. McKenzie's words were not designed to address a current crisis but were more a reflection of possible threats to the country.

McKenzie also made changes to the school which included the building of a music school, the installation of a new organ and the introduction of a new curriculum which shifted its focus significantly away from the classics. The new curriculum was introduced in 1908 and made the moderns a distinct part of the curriculum; although Latin remained compulsory, as many universities and professions still required it, it was nevertheless now possible to go through Uppingham concentrating on subjects such as modern languages, history or the sciences. With a reduced emphasis on the classics for most boys the opportunity for them to have been indoctrinated by deeds of military heroism was even less likely. That is, if they had even been capable of being indoctrinated by the classics in the first place. Above all the changes that he made also restored the moral tone of the school and the number of boys returned to the threshold of 431 required by the governors.⁴⁹

The Uppingham OTC

McKenzie modified the approach at Uppingham but did not make radical changes'; he continued to support the Rifle Corps and its successor the OTC although it would have been difficult for him to have withdrawn support even if he had wanted to. The HMC of which Uppingham was a founder member played a leading part in the OTC's creation; the commander of Uppingham Rifle Corps, Captain C H Jones, having played a role in the creation of a detailed plan for the OTC. The OTC had come into existence in McKenzie's third term in October 1908 and in the years that followed it quickly expanded. The Junior Division for schools expanded from 85 contingents on formation to 166 by the end of 1914.⁵⁰ Nearby Oakham School only established an OTC unit in 1911; the Headmaster saying the interesting training provided as part of being an officer made it useful. He added, the school was also increasing the amount of Army class work within it.⁵¹ The expansion of the OTC and Army class work within many public and grammar schools was part of a response to the rising threat which would accelerate in the years before 1914. In the light of these rising concerns McKenzie's support for the OTC should not come as a surprise. It fitted in with the ethos of public schools but as the developments at Oakham showed there was a demand from parents for schools to have an OTC.

After its formation in 1889 the Rifle Corps had enrolled 106 members by the end of its first term – about a third of the school. It would remain a relatively leisurely organisation until the appointment of Jones in 1898 as the commanding officer and the master in charge of the Army class. Tozer describes Jones as a bad teacher, a poor housemaster but 'an outstanding

---

48   USM, July 1914, p. 167.
49   Matthews, *By God's Grace*, pp. 135-137.
50   Based on analysis of Haig-Brown, *The O.T.C. and The Great War*, pp. 97-106.
51   *Grantham Journal*, 5 August 1911, p. 2.

corps commander'.[52] He had a reputation for producing interesting training schemes at a time when school corps often had a reputation for dull training.[53] Under his command the corps was expanded and from 1899 participated in the Public Schools Camp at Aldershot.[54] Jones was the epitome of the part-time soldier and would serve as a Volunteers officer in the Boer War and with the Territorial Force in the First World War.[55]

While it is believed that team games and the existence of the OTC made public school boys attractive to the army, evidence from Uppingham suggests that in reality there was a conflict between the OTC and games. Membership of the OTC remained voluntary in the years leading up to the war, and[56] The best sportsmen often declined to join the OTC because they were too busy training. George Horridge, at Uppingham from 1908 to 1912, stated he did not join the OTC because he was too busy participating in games. He joined the Territorials in 1913 and, in 1914, agreed to fight overseas.[57]

As discussed in Chapter 1, one of the aims of establishing the OTC was to address the shortage of officers in the regular army. The traditional sources of officers were drying up so it was necessary to widen the field of potential candidates. Uppingham was a potential new source of officers. Table 2 suggests that the Ward Committee's innovation was successful so far as Uppingham was concerned. In the years that followed the formation of the OTC the number of boys from the school who became regular officers increased.

Table 2 Analysis of Regular Army Officers Produced by Uppingham School 1903-1909[58]

Academic Year of Entry	Served in the Regular Army	Total Number of Entrants	% becoming Regular Army Officers
1903-1904	1	113	0.08
1904-1905	3	95	3.16
1905-1906	4	115	3.48
1906-1907	5	110	4.55
1907-1908	12	134	8.96
1908-1909	13	112	11.61
1909-1910	10	119	8.40

The entrants of 1903 have been selected as the first year of the table because it is the last one in which boys could have entered the school and not served in the OTC; 1909 has been selected as the final year because it is the last possible one a boy would have entered and left before the war broke out. After the war broke out the demands of the army vastly increased and this makes analysis more difficult.

52 M. Tozer, 'Physical Education at Thring's Uppingham' (MEd diss., University of Leicester 1974), p. 228.
53 *Grantham Journal*, 5 August 1911, p. 2.
54 Tozer, 'Physical Education at Thring's Uppingham', p. 229.
55 See Chapter 9 for a fuller account of Jones and the development of the OTC.
56 Matthews, *By God's Grace*, p. 246.
57 IWM, Taped Interview with G. Horridge, 7498 Produced 1984 Downloaded 16th September 2012.
58 Based on analysis of the *School Roll*.

These figures suggest that the introduction of the OTC led to an increase in the number of entrants into Woolwich and Sandhurst and that the Ward Committee's scheme to widen the recruiting base for officers had worked. The numbers of boys becoming regular officers had multiplied by a factor of 10 and the percentage of entrants achieving this status had multiplied by a factor of eight. An indication that while it was making an increased contribution to army the fact that no more than 11.6% of entrants became regular officers means that it was not an 'army' public school in the way that the likes of Eton, Wellington and Clifton were. One of the Ward Committee's suggestions had been that there should be incentives for OTC members who wished to gain a commission. After the introduction of the OTC in 1908 its regulations had offered, to those with Certificate A, 200 marks in the entrance examinations for Woolwich and Sandhurst and this partly explains the increased entry.[59] The existence of the Army class would have been helpful to those boys who hoped to gain a commission. In its desire to broaden the recruiting base for its officers from its traditional sources which included the landed families and military families the army looked to more middle class schools like Uppingham for more recruits. There was also a need, as was discussed in Chapter 1, for the army to become more professional and the focus of Uppingham on bringing the best out of every boy would make it a good source of potential recruits.

The other main aim of establishing the OTC had been to increase the supply of officers for the Special Reserves and the Territorial Force. The introduction of the Certificate A examination was meant to make it easier for boys to achieve this and not spend too much time preparing for it. As Table 3 shows there was not a spectacular pass rate in the Uppingham OTC before the Great War.

Table 3 Analysis of pre-Great War Certificate A Pass Rates[60]

Number of Cadets enrolled	499
Passed Certificate A	68
% Pass Rate	13.6

On the face of it a pass rate of 13.6% cannot be described as spectacular and in other areas of school life would have been viewed with disappointment. There were, however, good reasons for the disappointing pass rate. The syllabus for Certificate A was demanding, required coaching outside normal school activities and passing was not guaranteed. In addition, to be eligible a cadet had to be deemed to be efficient the conditions for which were substantial.[61] He also must have completed the musketry training and been passed physically fit. Within a busy school life these requirements were not necessarily easy to achieve. Alan Haig-Brown, who wrote an account of the OTC and the Great War and was commanding officer of the Lancing OTC, commented that those involved in the OTC at schools had 'been watched with a jealous eye to see that they did not encroach an inch upon the claims of work or the necessities of games.'[62]

---

59 Regulations for the OTC 1912, 22 and The National Archives (TNA): WO 92/9034: Regulations for Officers Training Corp 1908 & Royal Warrant.
60 Analysis based on USA, Junior Division Officers Training Corps Uppingham School Contingent.
61 Regulations for the OTC 1912, 19-20.
62 Haig-Brown, *The O.T.C. and The Great War*, p. 62.

Life for boys at all public schools was busy with the competing demands of academic work, games and the OTC and at Uppingham there were also the demands of music; part of a deliberate attempt to stop them getting into mischief.[63] Edward Brittain, brother of Vera, was not a gifted sportsman but was a talented musician and part of the Uppingham School Orchestra which is likely to have kept him busy with lessons and practice and therefore limited the opportunities he had to study for Certificate A.[64] It was only prodigies such as Roland Leighton who were able to participate in a wide range of school activities and excel in all of them who succeeded in passing Certificate A alongside their other commitments. Leighton was academically gifted; at his last speech day he won all of the top seven prizes while his literary gifts made him a good choice as editor of the School Magazine in his last year. He also found time to pass the OTC Certificate A and gain a high rank within it but he was the exception which proved the rule.

Bearing in mind the demands on boys' time it is better to judge the success of the Uppingham OTC by the level of participation rather than Certificate A success. It is notable that although membership was voluntary, as the First World War approached, membership of the OTC increased. In 1908 membership had been 200, in March 1912 the School Magazine reported there were 281 members (63% of the school) and by June 1914 it had a full complement of 350.[65] It's difficult to know how much parental pressure there was on their sons to enrol but given OTC membership was voluntary it indicates a response by pupils to threats to the Empire. Incidents such as the Agadir crisis of 1911 where German behaviour was seen as a threat to British interests and in particular its naval power led to a general concern within the country about a possible future conflict. Joining the OTC was one way in which a response could be made to an unstable international attitude and affirmed the boys support for the Empire.

Militarism and the School

Looking at the *School Roll* might lead one to the conclusion that a large number of old boys were involved in the army; supporting the idea that militarism was rife. The figures in Table 2 for those going into the regular army suggest otherwise so some explanation is needed of why this perception has arisen. It is dangerous to assume that the *School Roll* is a complete record of the activities of old boys while they were at school and after they left it. The information recorded was very much dependent on what information old boys chose to share about themselves with the school. In the records for entrants during the 1900s there are many individuals which provide no information at all about their post school life. In many cases the information provided related to service in the Great War. This would have been gleaned by the compiler (imperfectly as already discussed) from announcements in *The Times*. Including this information gave a natural bias towards the idea that many old boys made a career in the army. Many old boys developed careers in the professions and business and would have been considerably more difficult to gather information about unless they chose to share it. Nevinson had no reason to keep in touch with the school after he left. It is no surprise that the list of the old boys who

---

63 Seldon and Walsh, *Public Schools and The Great War*, p. 18.
64 Farr, *None That Go Return*, pp. 46-49.
65 Matthews, *By God's Grace*, p. 245. USM, March 1912, p. 5, USM, October 1913, p. 277, and USM, June 1914, p. 103.

served does not include him even though he served in the RAMC before he was declared unfit. It would not necessarily be dislike of the school which led to old boys not keeping in touch. Many would simply not get round to it if they were leading a busy life. Burnaby, who had returned from Canada to serve in the Boer War, was killed at Delville Wood in September 1916 and was at the school from 1887 to 1891. His private papers show that after he left he went to British Columbia where he was ranching. When he returned and volunteered to serve in the Boer War he initially served as a Trooper and ending it as a Captain. After the war he set up a Game Farm near Wendover volunteering in 1914 to serve again.[66] The *School Roll* merely details his military career making no reference to other activities.[67] Burnaby like many of his generation shared the patriotic values espoused by Uppingham and other schools and he had to make a great deal of effort to gain a command in the Great War.[68] Despite sharing the values of the school he appears to have made no real effort to keep in touch. Rather than suggesting an increasingly militaristic approach by its incomplete nature the *School Roll* suggests an apathy on the part of OUs which implies that the bond between school and OU is not as it is sometimes to be perceived to be in the notion of the old school tie.

The dangers of overstating the influence of Uppingham can be seen in the examples of Brian Horrocks and Eric Dorman-Smith who were friends for much of their lives and entered the school in September 1909 and also left at the same time to attend Sandhurst in December 1912. They both served in the Great War and became senior army officers in the Second World War.[69] Even before they went to Uppingham an army career was planned for them and after leaving they harboured no great nostalgia for the school. After leaving, Dorman-Smith never returned to the school.[70]

It is dangerous to attribute to Uppingham too much responsibility for the attitudes of the boys who it educated. Many boys never received much exposure to the deeds of military heroes in the classics so it is difficult to see that many influenced by this. As the final years of Selwyn's spell as Headmaster showed an emphasis on games the espousal of romantic patriotism was not enough for parents to keep their boys at the school. What they also expected was discipline and high moral standards within the school. The rise of the games 'blood' and the development by some of over emotional relationships with younger boys was obviously a concern to many including Selwyn. However, his failure to intervene because he believed it was the senior boys who should have responsibility for many aspects of the school allowed the situation to get out of control. The playing of games may have been attractive to the army but there was often a conflict between them and the OTC. While the number of boys becoming officers in the regular army increased Uppingham did not become a school whose boys predominantly joined the army when they left. While voluntary membership of the OTC rose in the years before the Great War the passing of Certificate A was not at the level desired by the army. The concern which led to the increased OTC membership was one that was shared by much of the country.

---

66   Liddell Hart Centre for Military Archives, Burnaby Papers, GB 0099 KCLMA Burnaby H B.
67   *School Roll*, p. 125.
68   See Chapter 5.
69   *School Roll*, p. 262-263.
70   B. Horrocks, *Escape To Action* (New York 1961) p. 13 and L. Greacen, *Chink A Biography* (London 1989) p. 3, pp. 13-14.

Many old boys who served appeared to have had an ambivalent attitude towards Uppingham and its values. Only Charles Raven of those discussed in this chapter became a pacifist; both he and Vera Brittain joined the Peace Pledge Union in the 1930's. Wills and King who were both in the Shooting VIII were indifferent or worse to Uppingham yet both served as officers in the Great War and received the MC and OBE respectively for their work. Likewise those who became officers in the regular army would not necessarily have a strong affection for the school. Horrocks and Dorman-Smith both became senior officers in the British army but showed no great affection for the school. It was probably the training they received in the Army class and the OTC, both passed Certificate A, which gave them the foundations to become the sort of professional the army required.

The response of those at Uppingham before the war to the threat of Germany very much reflected the concerns of the whole country. It was not necessarily the case that a keen commitment to games within the school automatically bred young men keen to serve their country. There are a number of examples of old boys who had a distinctly ambivalent view about the games ethos but still went on to give distinguished service. Their response to the war reflected the qualities of independence, inquisitiveness and self-confidence which the school aimed to produce in boys. In the years before the war like many of the British people they became concerned about Germany's threat. A view reflected in the Government and armed forces who were taking steps to address it. Two OUs would be involved in one of the more dramatic examples of this exercising the qualities of independence, inquisitiveness and self-confidence in an unfortunate way.

4

Spying on Germany

The concerns of the British population about Germany were shared by the government and its armed forces. Both army and navy (there was no separate air force service until 1918) were, in the years before the war, increasingly considering the nature of the German threat and how to respond. The response was not that of a 'nation in arms' with no conscription and no scheme to expand the army although the navy had grown in size in response to the expansion of Germany's. Plans for mobilisation were being prepared by the British and both sides were engaging in espionage in an effort to understand the military and naval capabilities of their opponents. The increasing level of espionage added to the tension developing between the two countries. An incident at Borkum in 1910 involving two OUs is an interesting and dramatic illustration of this tension. Borkum can also be used to demonstrate that the qualities of independence, inquisitiveness and self-confidence the school aimed to produce in its boys could also be counter-productive.

British Naval Supremacy and the Threat from Germany

Since the Franco-Prussian War of 1870-71 and especially after 1890 there had been a move by the military authorities of the major European powers towards preparing for the possibility of war; such as mobilisation schemes and the moves to be made in initial stages of any war.[1] International tensions had led to the development of two alliances, the Triple Entente and the Triple Alliance, within Europe. The Triple Entente was between Russia, Britain and France and the Triple Alliance consisted of Germany, Austro-Hungary and Italy. After the Prussian victory of 1871 a new German Empire had emerged and when Kaiser Wilhelm II came to the throne in 1888 Bismarck's cautious foreign policy had been replaced by a more assertive one. The result was that Germany became diplomatically isolated and found itself with potential enemies on its eastern and western borders. Britain remained aloof from continental European politics until 1904 when it had made the Entente Cordiale with France. The reasons for this in the words of E H Jenkins were that:

---

1   Donald F Bittner, 'Royal Marine Spy 1910-1913 Captain Bernard Frederic Trench Royal Marines Light Infantry', in *Royal Marines Spies of World War One Era* (Royal Marines Historical Society, Portsmouth, 1993). p. 1.

The United Kingdom had hitherto maintained a policy of 'splendid isolation' to avoid entangling alliances. But Kaiser Wilhelm II had flamboyantly proclaimed his country's big naval programme which, since Germany had no colonial need for a large navy, could only mean an intention to seize colonies from Britain or France; and Britain had also realised from the enmity shown to her during the Boer War (1899-1902) that isolation could be dangerous.[2]

By 1907 Britain had signed an Entente with another old rival, Russia. The key to this diplomatic action by the British Government is that in the years before the Great War the country was a naval power and had a relatively small army when compared to the other European powers.[3] France and Russia were concerned about the threat from Germany's army and these agreements, while not binding Britain to a military commitment, offered a diplomatic commitment to challenging Germany. The effect was to remove old antagonisms between the countries and provide Britain, France and Russia with more security against Germany. In contrast to its small army Britain had the largest navy in the world; the viability of its empire depended on a strong navy to defend the trade routes which linked the empire. British naval superiority was a key part of maintaining the Empire so the expansion of the German Navy was viewed with considerable alarm.

The British had good reason to be concerned as the German naval threat was reinforced by an atmosphere of animosity towards Britain within Germany. Lieutenant Colonel Frederic Trench, military attaché in Berlin from 1906 to 1910, regularly reported on this animosity and how it was, in his opinion, leading Germans to see England (as the Germans referred to Britain) as a global rival and enemy. Not only did most German army officers share this view but the general population was being prepared for the idea of war by bodies such as the Navy League.[4] On the 20 December 1907 Lieutenant Colonel Trench reported on the German Navy League; he described it being set up as a pressure group to argue the case for a high level of expenditure to develop a navy which could challenge British naval supremacy. It was, he wrote, 'the most powerful organised body in the state outside the army and navy' and a key part of the effort to mobilise Germany for war. With just under a million members its influence was substantial and Trench believed that in a time of tension before war broke out it would play a vital role in rapidly mobilising public German public opinion behind war increasing the risk of a sudden attack.[5] The growth of German naval and military strength alongside an increasingly hostile public mood gave Britain good reason to be concerned that there was a substantial threat to its naval supremacy.

Matching the animosity of the German public, British public opinion had developed into a mutual animosity towards Germany. One of the factors underpinning this was a concern about the threat of German invasion partly fuelled by the genre of invasion literature from authors such as William Le Queux. It was a genre that in 1903 produced what is often considered to be the first modern spy novel *The Riddle of the Sands* by Erskine Childers. The novel, which was immediately popular, told a story of Germany making preparations to invade Britain

2   E H Jenkins, *A History of the French Navy* (London: Macdonald and Janes's, 1973), p. 308.
3   Matthew S Seligmann, *Military Intelligence from Germany* (Stroud: Army Records Society, 2014) p. 2.
4   Seligmann, *Military Intelligence from Germany*, p. 10.
5   Seligmann, *Military Intelligence from Germany*, pp. 61-2.

from the Frisian Islands on its North Sea coast. In 1897 Childers had made the first of six voyages through the islands in his yacht and this had alerted him to the possibility of invasion. Childers was somewhat put out by its success as he had intended it to be a way to alert the British Government to the threat of a German invasion and not primarily as a piece of fiction.[6] However, Childers was well connected and the novel struck a chord with the government and the Admiralty who stepped up their efforts to counter the threat.[7]

The development of the German threat presented two problems which needed to be addressed to successfully counter any invasion. Traditionally, Britain's naval rivals, running from the time of the threat of the Armada and through the Napoleonic Wars and the Battle of Trafalgar until the end of the nineteenth century, were considered to be France and Spain. To deal with this threat the navy's main bases had been at Plymouth, Portsmouth and Chatham. The German threat came from the Baltic and the North Sea so the navy's existing bases were in the wrong place to be able to respond.[8] This was addressed in two ways; in 1904 a decision was made to develop northern naval bases which would eventually be established at Invergordon, Rosyth and Scapa Flow in the Orkneys. Complementing this was an increasing level of co-operation with the French Navy culminating in a formal agreement in 1912 which enabled the Royal Navy to concentrate more of its resources in the North Sea in return for a French focus on the Mediterranean.

In addition to having its bases in the wrong place to effectively address the expansion of the German Navy the Royal Navy had an urgent need for intelligence about the nature of the threat. It was not just details about the ships in the fleet which were required; every aspect of Germany's naval strength needed to be understood. This also included information about German bases and coastal defences. In the event of war this would all be needed if the navy decided that it wanted to make a pre-emptive strike on German naval berths.[9] The navy's curiosity about these facilities was increased by an increasing tendency for the Germans to cloak their military activities in secrecy. On 24 June 1909 Lieutenant Colonel Trench had commented that the Germans were making it increasingly difficult for overseas observers to attend military exercises.[10] It was through their involvement with naval intelligence that two OUs, Captain Cyrus ("Roy") Hunter Regnart and Captain Bernard Frederic Trench, both serving with the RMLI, became involved in significant and high profile work to assess German naval developments.

Regnart and Trench

Bernard Trench and Roy Regnart had a number of things in common. Not only were they OUs serving in the RMLI but they had long careers in military intelligence and were gifted linguists. It is not likely that they knew each other at the school as their time there only overlapped by two terms and they were in different houses, the Hall and West Deyne. At Uppingham the houses are spread throughout the town which made interaction between boys in different houses

---

6   Alan Judd, *The Quest for Mansfield Cumming and the Founding of the Secret Service* (London: Harper Collins, 1999, pp. 33-4.
7   Judd, *The Quest for Mansfield Cumming*, p. 35.
8   Bittner, 'Royal Marine Spy', p. 12.
9   Bittner, 'Royal Marine Spy', pp. 17-18.
10 Bittner, 'Royal Marine Spy', pp. 93-97.

more problematic unless they were in the same classes, which is highly unlikely as they were in different years. Regnart came to the school in September 1892 and left in August 1895 while Trench had arrived in January 1895 and left in December 1898.[11] It was unusual for OUs to be serving in a section of the navy as the navy did not draw on public schools in the same way that the army did. For those wishing to serve as officers in the navy they would go to Osborne at the age of 13 and stay there until they were 15 when they went on to Dartmouth where they would start sea training at the age of seventeen. Trench had been commissioned into the RMLI in January 1899 having gone straight to the Royal Naval College in January 1899; Regnart had gained his commission in the RMLI in September 1897. It was not a coincidence that two officers from the RMLI should be involved in intelligence work. As Donald F Bittner has pointed out there were limited opportunities for officers of the RMLI. Although it was the navy's light infantry there was no formal structure to make it properly prepared to support the navy onshore in its operations. Thus the career progression for an officer serving in the RMLI's normal activities was somewhat curtailed. If an officer chose to pursue another option such as intelligence work then his opportunities were greatly improved.[12]

It is not clear whether they came to know each other because they both went to the school but both were typical of Uppingham having fathers from middle class backgrounds. Trench's father was an engineer while Regnart listed his father as an upholsterer.[13] This played on the humble origins of his father who had come to London from Jersey in the 1850s and joined Maples, the furnishers of Tottenham Court Road; he had been promoted through the company until, in 1903, he became President. Roy's oldest brother would also become President of Maples in 1926 on his father's retirement.[14] This family business connection was useful to Roy Regnart in his subsequent career in the intelligence services.

Regnart joined the Naval Intelligence Division in 1904 and although he would become better known for his work with the Secret Intelligence Service (subsequently MI6) Matthew Seligmann states that the more important part of his work was with Consuls and Intelligence Officers after 1911.[15] This work was probably more varied than that of the military attaché who worked at embassies and reported on what they learnt from their official contacts and through analysis of matters such as press comment and public opinion. The work of the Consuls would be to collect from open (i.e. not secret) sources such as shore agents and captains of Merchant Navy ships on the movements of German ships and analyse it to identify potential threats.[16] This information gathering system was to prove a great success in tracking the movement of German warships and gaining a better understanding of wider German naval war plans.[17] Regnart was also a gifted linguist; amongst the languages he was fluent in were Russian, Danish and

---

11 *School Roll*, p. 153 and p. 167.
12 Bittner, 'Royal Marine Spy', pp. 15-16.
13 Bittner, 'Royal Marine Spy', p. 48 and p. 50.
14 M V Seran Charles Clare Regnart <http://www.seran1926.com/charles-c-regnart.html> (Accessed 11 December 2015).
15 Matthew S Seligmann, *The Royal Navy and the German Threat, 1901-1914: Admiralty Plans to Protect British Trade in a War Against Germany* (OUP: Oxford, 2012), p. 121.
16 Seligmann, *The Royal Navy and the German Threat*, p. 114.
17 Seligmann, *The Royal Navy and the German Threat*, pp. 123-5.

German.[18] It made him well suited to the espionage work carried out by the secret service he was to become increasingly involved with in the years leading up to the war. He was a complex character who Mansfield Cumming, the first head of MI6, at times would find very difficult to work with.[19] Within the intelligence community he was not popular because of his behaviour which, at times, was obstinate, arrogant and resentful. Cumming usually backed him in the face of criticism from the intelligence community because he was conscientious, frank, dedicated and perceptive. Cumming in his diary recognised the value of Regnart's understanding of the, at times, dubious motives of those who spied for Britain and the need to handle them with care.[20]

Like Regnart, Trench was a talented linguist being fluent in German, French and Danish.[21] It might seem curious that it was an advantage for an agent to be fluent in Danish but for espionage work this did offer considerable benefits. Copenhagen was in a good position to receive reports on German naval activity especially those from the Baltic and North Sea ports. Activity in North Sea ports and the threat of an invasion being launched from them was of particular concern to the navy. It was also believed that Danes were well suited to employment as secret service agents.[22] An ability to speak Danish fluently was thus an essential factor in conducting espionage operations from Denmark.[23] His father was Lewis Trench who was in charge of the Engineering Department of the London and North Western Railway.[24] It is not clear when Trench started his intelligence work but the intention for him to do this must have been in place by January 1907 when he qualified as a German interpreter having studied in Germany the previous year. In the years up to 1910 he paid a number of visits to Germany.[25] During his visits his uncle, Lieutenant Colonel Trench, mentioned above was military attaché reporting on military developments.[26] It is not recorded whether he saw his uncle during his visits, it's entirely possible that he did and this had an influence on his decision to work in intelligence. On one of his visits in 1908 he visited Kiel, the headquarters of the German Baltic Fleet, with Lieutenant Vivian Brandon to collect information on the port's naval facilities. In 1907 work started to widen the canal so that the fleet including its Dreadnoughts could enter the North Sea without having to sail through the Danish Straits from the Baltic. This was important because it was far easier for the Royal Navy to prevent the German Baltic fleet from entering the North Sea as the Straits are comparatively narrow. The ability to enter the North Sea directly made the German navy far more of a threat to Britain. Gathering information on Kiel became much more important as a better understanding of its capabilities and its defences was required. The work Trench and Brandon did had been considered to be useful by the Admiralty and Trench

18 Bittner, 'Royal Marine Spy', p. 50 and Keith Jeffery, *MI6: The History of the Secret Intelligence Service 1909-1949* (Paperback edition, London: Bloomsbury, 2011), p. 24.
19 Judd, *The Quest for Mansfield Cumming*, p. 124.
20 Judd, *The Quest for Mansfield Cumming*, p. 163.
21 Bittner, 'Royal Marine Spy', p. 16.
22 Jeffery, *MI6*, p. 23.
23 Danish is one of the most complex languages to learn and become fluent in as someone who is not raised in the country. At this time it was very rare indeed for anyone to learn the language, French & German being the usual languages. I am grateful to Dr Phylomena Badsey for pointing this out to me.
24 Espionage in Germany, *New Zealand Herald*, Volume XL VIII, Issue 14596 <http://paperspast.natlib.govt.nz/cgi-bin/paperspast?a=d&d=NZH19110204.2.148.10> (Accessed 14 December 2015).
25 Bittner, 'Royal Marine Spy', p. 16 and p. 49.
26 Bittner, 'Royal Marine Spy', p. 53.

had an official commendation placed on his service records which noted he had produced a useful report on Kiel's coastal defences. This sort of information gathering exercise was the type of activity that the Directorate of Naval Intelligence considered to be one of its main activities.[27] When a similar exercise was proposed to gather information about Borkum in the Frisian Islands Trench was an obvious choice to undertake the task.

Spying on Borkum

Lieutenant Colonel Trench's successor as military attaché in Berlin, Lieutenant Colonel Russell, reported on 7 December 1910 on the development of German North Sea Coast defences; he observed that the island of Borkum was closed to civilians.[28] Borkum had been placed under military control as it attracted an increasing interest from the Admiralty in its defences for a number of reasons. The closure was probably the result of the events of August 1910 which Trench and Regnart were involved in. Borkum was at the centre of the coastline in which *The Riddle of the Sands* was set; it was not, however, a case of naval judgement being distorted by popular fiction. The island (see map) lay at the mouth of the estuary of the River Ems and in 1908 the Admiralty was aware that coastal defence batteries had been built. The role of the defences was to provide protection to Emden, a town on the river where it was believed there were plans to build a torpedo boat base.[29] In addition, Emden was at one end of the Ems-Jade canal. The other end of the canal came out at Wilhelmshaven which with Kiel was one of Germany's two main naval bases. The existence of the canal provided both a threat and an opportunity for Britain. The canal, if widened, provided Germany a means to move some of its naval fleet from Wilhelmshaven to Emden and give another way for it to get into the North Sea. From the point of view of the Royal Navy the canal could provide an opportunity to make a pre-emptive attack on the German fleet at Wilhelmshaven. It was a threat the Germans were very much aware of and the lessons of the second battle of Copenhagen of 1807 were very much in their minds. At this battle the British had made a pre-emptive assault on the Dano-Norwegian fleet and confiscated much of it to prevent it falling under the control of France and its allies. The Germans wanted to prevent a pre-emptive strike and building defences at Borkum was an important part of this. The British appreciated this, and the construction of defences on the island was bound to make them curious.

Roy Regnart approached Trench to carry out a visit to the Frisian Islands to gather information on their defences. Trench agreed and obtained agreement to take Brandon, who had been in Kiel in 1908, with him.[30] In a memoir he wrote, now in the Royal Marines Museum, Trench was clear the trip had not been at his own initiative. Regnart had told him that the Director of Naval intelligence had agreed that an officer could be a sent on a tour of German North Sea defences and had asked him whether he was willing to do it. Trench had been provided by Regnart a list of questions about the defences on which he should gather as much information as possible.[31] On 6th August 1910 Trench and Brandon set out on their tour with Borkum being

27 Judd, *The Quest for Mansfield Cumming*, p. 177.
28 Seligmann, *Military Intelligence from Germany*, pp. 119-20.
29 Bittner, 'Royal Marine Spy', p. 20.
30 Judd, *The Quest for Mansfield Cumming*, p. 177.
31 Bittner, 'Royal Marine Spy', pp. 55-6.

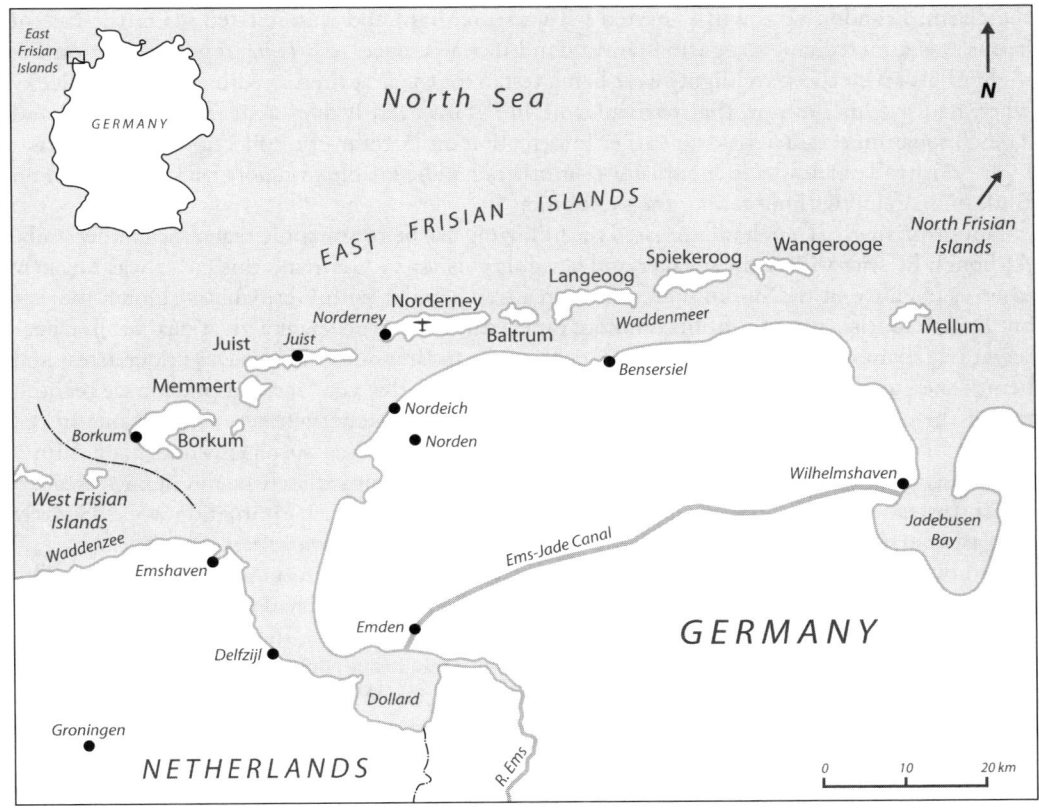

East Frisian Islands.

of most interest to them. As a result of his work at Kiel, the NID had decided Trench was a good officer to undertake the Borkum mission. Unfortunately the qualities of independence, inquisitiveness and self-confidence which he had displayed on that occasion degenerated into incompetence and carelessness which would lead to his and Brandon's arrest. Their original plan had been to enter Germany from Holland where they were going to leave all incriminating paperwork. However, when they learnt that military exercises were to take place on Borkum they had decided to go straight to Germany and not take the precaution of leaving the paperwork outside the country.[32] This cutting of corners would have disastrous consequences. Their tour of Germany had started in Kiel before including Brunsbittel, Bremen, Sylt, Fohr, Amrun, Heligoland and Nordeney.[33] On their arrival in Borkum Trench was successful in getting into the restricted area and gathering intelligence. The next night (22 August), Brandon entered the restricted area with a camera and flash, which he used and it was spotted by a sentry who raised

32 Bittner, 'Royal Marine Spy', p. 21.
33 *The Times*, 21 December 1910, p. 8.

the alarm; Brandon was swiftly located with a searchlight and was arrested.[34] On the face of it this was a mixture of staggering naivety and incompetence. *The Times* reported that on the night of his arrest the searchlights were being tested for the first time so perhaps he was unlucky when he used his flash on that particular night.[35] However, it does appear that both he and Trench took unnecessary risks to gather information on Borkum the collection of which was a high priority. Trench was to learn later that others had been able to report back to London on Borkum in detail without taking the same risks.[36]

Not surprisingly, Trench was arrested the following day before he could reach the Netherlands. Although he was a German speaker and a regular visitor to Germany this cover was unlikely to be as effective in the Borkum area. The area was popular with German and Dutch tourists but British tourists were far from common; especially, those who spent a great deal of time near secret installations.[37] Rather curiously, Trench spoke to Brandon while he was under arrest and being taken to Emden for interrogation.[38] It is no surprise that the Germans must have realised that if there was one British spy in the area it was highly likely there was another one in the vicinity. Trench's conversation with Brandon would have excited suspicions and made him a prime suspect. If he had chosen to leave for the Netherlands immediately he might have escaped arrest. Instead Trench had taken an unnecessary risk which made a bad situation worse. Shortly after their arrest Trench and Brandon were moved to Leipzig to await their trial.[39]

Although, the press had reported on the circumstances of their arrest in general the tone of its reports was low key. The two officers' solicitor, Sir William Bull MP, had used his influence with the press to ensure nothing that would inflame public opinion was said. The Foreign Office, as was the usual practice, denied any knowledge about Trench and Brandon and told Berlin on 5 September that any of their movements were unauthorised. While official involvement may at this stage have been officially deniable the Germans were quickly gathering evidence that the men had been on a spying mission. Much of this was possible because of their incompetent and careless approach. Having carried out activities in a way which attracted attention they made it easy for the Germans to gather this evidence. On the face of it, their behaviour was amateur and naïve and the exercise of a little common sense might have made their position easier. Brandon had not helped his case by agreeing to allow the examining magistrate to gain access letters which had been sent to him for collection from Delfzyl in the Netherlands. Unfortunately, one of these letters clearly indicated that Brandon was gathering intelligence. Within a month the Germans also had substantial evidence of Trench's involvement in espionage. After meeting Brandon under arrest Trench had realised that the Germans were likely to search the hotel in Emden where they had been staying; therefore, before attempting to escape to the Netherlands he had attempted to hide the documents in his possession. Unfortunately, he had not been very imaginative in the places he had chosen to hide them. On 23 September proprietor of the hotel where they had been staying had found documents behind the bolster of the bed Trench had been sleeping in. The proprietor called the police, who presumably had already made enquiries

---

34 Judd, *The Quest for Mansfield Cumming*, p. 179.
35 *The Times*, 26 August 1910, p. 3.
36 Bittner, 'Royal Marine Spy', p. 36.
37 Bittner, 'Royal Marine Spy', p. 22.
38 Judd, *The Quest for Mansfield Cumming*, p. 179.
39 *The Times*, 22 December 1910, p. 8.

at the hotel and more documents were found hidden in equally unimaginative places in the room including between two mattresses.[40] In 1914 Trench and Brandon would blame Regnart for their actions telling Cumming he had sprung the need to observe the military exercises at the last moment and had made them take short cuts to respond to this need. Unbeknown to Cumming, Regnart had arranged to meet them in the Netherlands and they had thought in the week since their arrest he would have had the time to remove the incriminating mail in Delfzyl before the Germans got to it so had given permission to have access to them.[41] If accusations of a cavalier and incompetent approach can be made against Trench and Brandon they can also be made against Trench's fellow OU, Regnart, for his failure to remove incriminating material.

Thanks to this slapdash approach by the time the trial of Trench and Brandon opened in Leipzig on 21 December before the Supreme Court the prosecution had a large number of documents to support the charge of espionage. Indeed, the trial mainly revolved around the documentary evidence discovered; the defence would produce no witnesses and the prosecution very few. The key points in securing a conviction were proving the information had been communicated to the British, that it was in the interests of national defence for the information gathered to be secret and finally knowing that the communication of the information was a threat to national security. The prosecution was unable to prove that the information had been transmitted but was able to demonstrate a connection to the British intelligence services. Amongst the letters found at Delfzl was one from 'Reggie' which it was argued must be from someone in British Intelligence as it expressed concern about the arrest at Borkum and made funds available for a second tour.[42] 'Reggie' was Regnart which makes it more surprising he had not arranged to remove documents.[43] Despite this relatively unsophisticated cover name the Germans do not appear to have worked it was Regnart and he was able to carry out espionage work in Europe in the years before the war. However, within London there were understandable fears that the Germans would work out who 'Reggie' was.[44]

The list of documents found included a list of questions the officers were asked to obtain information on. An indication of the sort of information to be collected could be seen in the detailed and intricate information which had been recorded. At Borkum information recorded included the diameters of the gun and there were detailed observations on the Kiel Canal. At Sylt the information collected covered the measurements of a pier, the depth of water and the rails laid on the shore. The only use of this information the prosecution argued was for the planning of landing operations. Therefore, it was claimed, the information collected was a threat to national security. The naval background of the men made them expert enough to understand exactly the significance of what they were collecting and that the information was secret. The defence argued that just because the government wanted to keep something secret this did not make it secret in law pointing out that with the exception of Borkum there had been no trespass into restricted areas.[45]

---

40 Bittner, 'Royal Marine Spy', pp. 22-5.
41 Judd, *The Quest for Mansfield Cumming*, p. 261.
42 *The Times*, 21 December 1910, p. 10.
43 Bittner, 'Royal Marine Spy', p. 55.
44 Jeffery, *MI6: The History of the Secret Intelligence Service*, p. 25.
45 *The Times*, 22 December 1910 p. 9 and 23 December 1910, p. 8.

The court disagreed on 22 December and ruled that the men had tried to transmit secret and essential information about German security by carrying out a general study of coastal defences. The weight of evidence Trench and Brandon had left behind them in their hasty approach to the mission counted against them. However, the court also ruled there was no proof that the information had been delivered to other parties. This final finding was politically convenient to the Germans. If this had been proved the court would have had to impose a sentence of penal servitude. As it was Trench and Brandon were sentenced to four years' detention in a military fortress which was a considerably more comfortable punishment.[46] Both men were quickly sent to their place of captivity. In the case of Trench this was the Fortress of Glatz in Silesia (now in Poland).[47]

In an atmosphere of increasing tension the Germans had been keen to mount a trial which appeared to be lenient and fair. The propaganda opportunities outweighed other considerations. Although the military had been keen to have much of the trail held in secret the prosecution was keen that as much as possible of it should be held in public. In an era when the British press regularly accused the Germans of spying, the prosecution wished to demonstrate it was the British who were just as guilty of espionage. On 7 September British authorities arrested a German officer, Lieutenant Helm, at Portsmouth for carrying out the same activity as Trench and Brandon. He had been treated leniently and allowed to return to Germany, possibly as an encouragement to the Germans to treat the two British officers in a similar manner.[48] Both sides regularly engaged in spying against each other and there is plenty of evidence of German espionage in Britain. Gustav Steinhauer who supervised German espionage in Britain before the war had had a total of 40 agents under his control at different times.[49] Being found guilty was not a matter of disgrace for Trench and Brandon; it was conceded that they were doing their duty.[50] They had done nothing that was un-gentlemanly and un-officer like as they were doing their patriotic duty. It was not only in Britain that it was considered necessary for an officer to be a gentleman.[51] The punishment imposed reflected that their behaviour was considered to be gentlemanly; detention in penal servitude would have involved hard labour but detention in a fortress, while depriving them of their freedom, meant they were free to spend their time as they wished. It would even be possible for them to visit the town adjacent to whatever fortress they were held in.

The case was extensively reported not only in the British Press but also in newspapers in other parts of the Empire such as the *Advertiser* in Adelaide and the *New Zealand Herald*. From time to time after his imprisonment reports about Trench would appear in the papers. On 19 January 1912 the *West Australian* reported on Trench's letters to his relatives in which he had denied he had attempted to hang himself and criticising a French officer, Captain Lux, for escaping when it was understood that a condition of lenient treatment was not attempting to escape.[52] Trench explained his apparent suicide attempt as, after Lux's escape, conditions become a lot more

---

46 *The Times*, 23 December 1910, p. 8.
47 *The Times*, 20 May 1913, p. 8.
48 Judd, *The Quest for Mansfield Cumming*, pp. 179-81.
49 Nicholas Hiley, 'Spying for the Kaiser', *History Today*, 38: 6 (1988), p. 37.
50 Bittner, 'Royal Marine Spy', p. 55.
51 Judd, *The Quest for Mansfield Cumming*, p. 180.
52 *Western Australian*, 19 January 1912, p. 7.

restrictive so he decided to escape himself. He had therefore decided to tunnel through the wall of his cell but the exit point was high up so he had hung himself high in the cell on looped putties. He had nearly been discovered by the Germans who on entering his cells had seen the hanging putties and concluded he was trying to commit suicide.[53] An attempt at suicide seems unlikely as he spent the last 20 years of his life confined to a wheelchair because of arthritis and it seems unlikely that he was the type of man to have attempted suicide. His obituary spoke of his courage in spite of the pain he suffered and suggested he was a man who could cope with adversity.[54]

Any hope of an early release in 1911 on the occasion of George V's coronation was thwarted by a nationalistic German press which campaigned against his release. In particular, they argued that Trench and Brandon should be detained until the information they had gathered was out of date. The *Hamburger Nachrichten* argued that care should be taken to ensure they did not communicate with the Admiralty. It was a well-placed concern as, in 1912, *The Times* reported that Trench had been able to send two letters to unknown persons.[55] Trench and Brandon were pardoned in May 1913 on the occasion of the visit of King George V and Queen Mary to Berlin for the wedding of the Kaiser's daughter.[56] Also released from Glatz with Trench was Bertrand Stewart who had been caught spying on German naval facilities in August 1911 just after the Agadir crisis, a time of great international tension.[57]

Trench and Stewart arrived back in England to a noisy reception from Stewart's family and friends. In the pandemonium of the welcome from Stewart's party Trench was able to slip away telling *The Times* he intended to report immediately to the Admiralty.[58] He quickly returned to duty at the Plymouth Division and would continue to serve in intelligence. He kept his own counsel about his time in Germany. In August 1913 the School Magazine reported its disappointment that he was under orders not to comment on his detention in Germany.[59] Trench was not always restricted from providing reports to the School Magazine; the October 1914 edition contained a report from him on the sinking of the *Kaiser Wilhelm* in August 1914. After serving on the *HMS Highflyer* he served with the Admiralty War Staff Intelligence Division for the rest of the war.[60] In both World Wars he gained a reputation for being an excellent interrogator of German prisoners. This was a marked contrast to his botched tour of Germany in 1910.

Regnart and the Secret Intelligence Service

The Secret Intelligence Service with which Roy Regnart would eventually work for had been established as the Secret Service Bureau in October 1909. The German threat and a concern about German spying with the help of the press and 'invasion scare' literature had developed

---

53   Bittner, 'Royal Marine Spy', p. 35.
54   The Alpine Journal <http://www.alpinejournal.org.uk/Contents/Contents_1968_files/AJ%201968%20129-142%20In%20Memoriam.pdf> (accessed 17 December 2015).
55   Bittner, 'Royal Marine Spy', pp. 33-34.
56   *The Times*, 20 May 1913, p. 8.
57   Judd, *The Quest for Mansfield Cumming*, pp. 222-224.
58   *The Times*, 20 May 1913, p. 8.
59   USM, August 1913, p. 210.
60   The Alpine Journal <http://www.alpinejournal.org.uk/Contents/Contents_1968_files/AJ%201968%20129-142%20In%20Memoriam.pdf> (accessed 17 December 2015).

into a public spy fever. 'Invasion scare' literature was a prolific genre; apart from *The Riddle in the Sands* there had been a series of other books with titles such as *Spies of the Kaiser* designed to play on public fears. In 1909, unlike Germany and France, Britain did not have a secret service and neither was it able to assess espionage being carried out within Britain or effectively collect intelligence about foreign powers. Although the Admiralty and War Office collected intelligence they were placed in a difficult position by having to work directly with agents; without intermediaries it was difficult to deny British involvement if their spies were caught. A sub-committee of the Committee of Imperial Defence proposed that a Secret Service Bureau be established to monitor espionage within the country. It would also act as the front for the Admiralty and the War Office and their spies and recruit agents overseas to gather information from foreign countries.[61] Mansfield Cumming was appointed to the new bureau and given responsibility for foreign work.

Regnart's secret service career was held back by the Borkum incident. Cumming first proposed that Regnart be appointed the overseas agent (for the whole of Europe) based in Copenhagen. Afterwards, however, there were concerns about the way Regnart had handled the incident. The way he had exercised the qualities of independence, inquisitiveness and self-confidence was understandably questioned. A number of concerns were raised about his suitability as an overseas agent including whether his identity would become known and, in the end, fears about his involvement in the Borkum incident meant the position was not filled and Regnart stayed in Naval Intelligence.[62] Regnart appears to have been somewhat of a loose cannon; at the same time as he sent Trench and Brandon out on their mission to Borkum he had proposed sending an agent called Wren to photograph the shipyards at Pola. This was something that Cumming objected to on the grounds that Wren was bound to be arrested but Regnart had persisted with the plan expressing indifference as to whether the agent was caught as he was of little use.[63] He was unpopular with many of those he worked on a day to day basis because of his maverick behaviour. George McDonough of the War Office complained that Regnart's involvement with foreign agents was contrary to the Foreign Office's wish that there should be no direct link between naval and military intelligence and agents in the field. If he had had his way Regnart would have been dismissed.[64]

Cummings was aware of Regnart's shortcomings but he understood that within the intelligence services one worked with a variety of unusual characters. In the years between 1910 and 1913 Regnart made regular visits overseas, including to Brussels, often meeting agents. The position of overseas agent remained unfilled until 1913 when Cumming once again proposed that Regnart be appointed but this time be based in Brussels. There were objections from the Director of Naval Intelligence, Thomas Jackson, that Regnart was not suitable. Cumming persisted by arguing that Regnart was suitable for the position and received support from the Director of Military Operations, Henry Wilson. Wilson, an arch intriguer himself, pointed out that it was impossible to get the perfect man for the job but believed Regnart was committed to his work, a good linguist and well-practised in secret service ways. In the end it was agreed that

---

61 Jeffery, *MI6: The History of the Secret Intelligence Service*, pp. 4-7.
62 Jeffery, *MI6: The History of the Secret Intelligence Service*, p. 25.
63 Judd, *The Quest for Mansfield Cumming*, p. 190.
64 Judd, *The Quest for Mansfield Cumming*, p. 202.

Regnart would be appointed once he retired from the RMLI.⁶⁵ This was entirely understandable if the Bureau was to provide some separation between military intelligence and its spies.

Regnart's role was to run a network around Belgium's eastern frontier and the area around Maastricht in the Netherlands which was located on a southerly spur of Dutch territory where Belgium was on the east and south sides of it with Germany to the East. In the event of a German attack on Belgium it was expected its armies would pass through this part of the Netherlands. The role of the networks was to provide warning of an attack and to provide a foundation for intelligence reporting if war broke out.⁶⁶ As cover for his activities, Regnart was able to use his family connections with Maples to set up a furniture shop in Brussels from which he could recruit agents.⁶⁷ When war broke out in August 1914 all the networks, including Regnart's, failed to predict the time and precise direction of the German attack on France.⁶⁸ On the outbreak of war he was recalled to the RMLI and spent the war as commanding office at Loch Ewe naval base. It is not clear what his role was there but he did cease to be a problem for Mansfield Cumming and the intelligence services. It is worthy of note that throughout the war Trench remained in the intelligence service but Regnart did not. It is fair to say that it was not inconvenient for the troublesome Regnart to be given a posting outside the intelligence service. In July 1921 he committed suicide by shooting himself in the head after he had been discharged from the Auxiliaries in Ireland.⁶⁹

A Different World

Trench and Regnart's involvement in the fight against Germany before the Great War is representative of how much changed after war broke out. Before the war, Britain's power rested in its navy and not its army. Military tensions with Germany mainly arose from the expansion of the German navy and the ensuing suspicion with which both sides viewed each other. Given this suspicion, it was inevitable that the two empires would wish to spy on each other and why Regnart and Trench were so involved in working against Germany. Their involvement was a mixed story; both of them appeared to be guilty of naivety bordering on incompetence at times. On the other hand, they both made their mark in other areas of their work. Regnart made a great contribution to the gathering of information about the German naval capability from open sources while Trench became very effective at interrogating German prisoners in both wars. In the end the complexities of Regnart's personality would bring his intelligence career to an end. The outbreak of the war would see a significant change with the emergence of a 'nation in arms' and the development of a citizen army. Uppingham, as a public school, would make a significant contribution in providing officers to lead this citizen army. However, it was not just the young men who had been in the OTC who would serve. They were joined by a wide range of OUs who provided a wide range of skills valuable in the prosecution of the war.

---

65 Jeffery, *MI6: The History of the Secret Intelligence Service*, pp. 27-28.
66 Jeffery, *MI6: The History of the Secret Intelligence Service*, p. 33.
67 Judd, *The Quest for Mansfield Cumming*, p. 251.
68 Jeffery, *MI6: The History of the Secret Intelligence Service*, p. 34.
69 Major Cyrus Hunter Regnart, RMLI <http://theauxiliaries.com/men-alphabetical/men-r/regnart/regnart.html> (accessed 14 December 2015).

5

Taking Up Arms

August 1914 saw a dramatic and sudden increase of involvement in meeting the German threat to one which involved many. Britain became a 'nation in arms' and many in the country volunteered to serve and the outbreak of the war led to the size of the army increasing several times over. The concerns about Germany that were felt by many led to a response by many OUs when war broke out. The school's philosophy stressed a strong sense of duty, leadership skills and taking responsibility and OUs, in general, believed it was their duty to respond to this threat. The motivation to volunteer varied in its precise nature with some keen to serve but many others doing so out of a sense of duty. Their letters home demonstrated this sense and their commitment to protecting the British Empire. The school's educational ethos produced men who displayed independence, inquisitiveness and self-confidence. The rapid expansion of the army meant the army had to spread its net wider to find suitable men to become officers. In the transition from a small professional army to a mass citizen army a far more sophisticated organisation developed and a wider range of skills were required to make it work effectively. Uppingham became a significant source for the new skills required. The vast majority of OUs who served were officers and provided leadership both in military actions and in the welfare of their men. As junior officers many OUs found themselves more vulnerable to death than others. The men from Uppingham who served accepted the deprivations of war and while happy to criticise aspects of its prosecution almost none of them expressed disillusionment.

A Nation Divided

When Vera Brittain attended the Uppingham Speech Day in July 1914; there was no perception that the assassination of Franz Ferdinand several weeks before would lead to war. She later remembered it as an idyllic day and the end of a care free life.[1] The response to the outbreak of the war has often been portrayed as one of patriotic enthusiasm within a united country and, while it is true that many in Britain were worried about the threat from Germany but there were also serious internal tensions with the early years of the 20th century seeing widespread industrial unrest and continued problems in Ireland.

---

1   Vera Brittain, *Testament of Youth* (Paperback edition London: Virago, 2004) pp. 72-73.

The Curragh Incident of March 1914 was the centrepiece of the problems in Ireland with the incident seeing a serious standoff between the Liberal Government and elements of the army. The crisis had its immediate roots in 1912 when the government introduced a Home Rule Bill; the primary aim of which was to create an autonomous Irish Parliament. There was considerable opposition to Home Rule, especially within Ulster and the wider Unionist community and there were threats of active resistance if it was implemented. Matters came to a head in March 1914 when orders were issued for the army to protect arms supplies which militant opposition to home rule, the Ulster Volunteer Force (UVF), might try to seize. Rather than coerce Ulster into accepting Home Rule 60 officers based at the Curragh, the army's main base in Ireland, threatened to resign.[2] The government backed down in the face of this claiming there had been a misunderstanding but the damage to the relations between the government and army was immense; leading to serious divisions within the senior ranks of the army and was one of the reasons for the Army's troubled relationship with the Liberal Party throughout the war.[3]

At Uppingham the concerns about the threat to Ulster were articulated in a letter which appeared in the March 1914 edition of its magazine. An unnamed OU expressed his concerns about the threat to Ulster which would follow the granting of home rule. Fundamentally, he explained, the Protestant north was opposed to being ruled by a parliament in Dublin dominated by Catholics. As a result a provisional government had been set up to take power if home rule came into effect. A military wing, the Ulster Volunteer Force (UVF), had been set up to protect the north and boasted over 100,000 members.[4] The writer was a member of the UVF but we do not know who he was. However, at the same time as the letter appeared Lieutenant Joseph Lister Cheyne, 1901 to 1906, who was with the 16th Lancers based in Ireland was one of the officers taking matters into his own hands and resigning. Cheyne was involved in the subsequent discussions by acting as a go-between when he passed a message from the Prime Minister, Asquith to Brigadier-General Hubert Gough one of the leading dissenters within the army. Cheyne's father wrote to his son following a conversation with Asquith's wife in which Gough was asked to accept the withdrawal of a government guarantee that the army would not be forced to take military action against those opposed to Home Rule. Gough refused to do so and in the end Asquith publicly withdrew the guarantee anyway.[5] The army was not united in the matter and there were many officers who believed it should keep out of politics; Major-General Sir Charles Ferguson took this view and played a key role in limiting the numbers of officers involved in the stand-off.[6] Although, a serious confrontation had been ended it left the army badly divided. Cheyne's and the anonymous OU's involvement are demonstrations of the strength of feeling within the country. The political crisis over Home Rule continued over the summer of 1914 so that, while news of the Austrian ultimatum to Serbia was reported to a cabinet meeting discussing Home Rule on 24th July the cabinet hardly discussed the matter. Within two weeks Britain was at war with Germany and the British Army and country rapidly

2   Ian F W Beckett (ed.), *The Army and the Curragh Incident* (London: Army Records Society, 1986) p. 1.
3   Robert Blake (ed.), *The Private Papers of Douglas Haig 1914-1919* (London: Eyre and Spotiswoode, 1952) p. 26.
4   *USM* March, 1914, pp. 10-12.
5   Beckett (ed.), *The Army and the Curragh Incident*, pp. 357 and 363.
6   Beckett (ed.), *The Army and the Curragh Incident*, pp. 1-2.

reunited. It was yet another testament to Kaiser Wilhelm's remarkable ability to bring harmony where there was discord.⁷

A Sense of Duty

War may not have been on anyone's mind at the school speech day on 11 July 1914 but for many connected with Uppingham there was no doubt that a personal response was required. Amongst those OUs who were quick to enlist in response to Lord Kitchener's call for volunteers were Vera Brittain's future fiancé Roland Leighton, brother Edward Brittain and their friend Victor Richardson. Her book *Testament of Youth* is often thought of solely as an account of loss however it is not just an account of the personal tragedy she suffered but also one of her recovery.⁸ Similarly, Uppingham's response must not be seen in isolation as one inspired by public school ethos but as a wider one by the whole of the country. The commitment of the wider British public to the war is demonstrated by the large numbers who quickly volunteered for military service Trevor Wilson believes that even if the men who volunteered had known the nature of the war which lay ahead they would still have done so.⁹ When Germany invaded Belgium in August 1914 as part of its attack on France many believed that there was no alternative to war. To do nothing would lead to German domination of Europe and the vast majority in Britain believed that would be a disaster. It was a belief that, even after the heavy cost of war, many still believed to be the case in 1918 and would do so for the rest of their lives.¹⁰ Many in Britain in 1914 held a liberal and Christian perspective that war was wrong but believed that values embodied in this perspective must be defended against the German threat to them. Today, the British response to the German invasion of Poland in 1939 is seen as a response to the evils of Nazism in 1939. The horrors of the concentration camps and the German occupation of Europe make this easier to understand from a modern perspective but in 1914 the British also thought of Germany as a serious threat to their way of life.¹¹

Therefore, the response of Uppingham and its old boys to war needs not be seen as that of a small exclusive elite who were out of touch with the rest of the country but as reflective of the mood of the rest of the country which believed there was a threat to the nation and its empire. To some modern students of the topic this response can be seen as overly militaristic. However, when seen in wider context of the times Uppingham's response in 1914 was not militaristic and merely reflects the concerns of many within the country.

The public response to the outbreak of the war is often understood as being one as one of excitement epitomised by cheering crowds in front of Buckingham Palace on 4 August 1914. In reality, the evidence is there was an overwhelmingly enthusiastic response to war is not as strong as the accounts we are familiar with suggest.¹² London was crowded on 4 August but this was because it was a bank holiday. Contemporary accounts suggest crowds were more interested

---

7   Beckett (ed.), *The Army and the Curragh Incident*, p. 29.
8   Brittain, *Testament of Youth*, p. 608.
9   J. Grigg, 'Nobility and War: The Unselfish Commitment?', *Encounter* 74 (1990), pp. 21-27.
10 A. Gregory, *The Last Great War: British Society and the First World War* Cambridge: Cambridge University Press, 2008) p. 2.
11 Gregory, *The Last Great War*, p. 5.
12 Gregory, *The Last Great War*, p. 11.

in enjoying the bank holiday although groups of people did gather to discuss the situation and others scanned the newspaper posters for the latest news.[13] It's important to remember that crowds would have gathered in public places to get news when there was no television or radio.[14]

It is in this light that the response of OUs to the outbreak of war of 1914 needs to be seen. *Testament of Youth* and *Letters from a Lost Generation* give us an insight into the attitudes of three boys who had just left school towards the outbreak of war but there are many other sources which also give us an insight into the attitude of old boys. It was not just young men who went off to war in 1914. Arthur Lee had been at Uppingham between 1890 and July 1896 and was 37 at the outbreak of war. As a partner in a firm of solicitors, had a great deal to lose from the war and took a far from jingoistic point of view. He believed it would damage his career and lead to a loss of income. As a father with a 16-month-old son and a wife expecting another child very soon he knew it would also create problems for their education. It is no surprise that he had mixed feelings about the war but knew once Germany became involved in the crisis in the summer of 1914 'that a European War was a certainty'. He said in his memoirs that his 'feelings were none too pleasant' but neither his wife nor she had any doubts about: 'whether or not I should serve in the War – we hardly discussed the point: it was understood.'[15]

Dudley Carmalt Jones was 40 when war broke out and was, like Lee, a member of the Territorial Force. In August 1914 he was Dean of Westminster Medical School and attached to the Territorials as a medical officer. He enlisted with the Territorials before the war because he believed war between Germany and Britain was inevitable. For him the way that war came was entirely unexpected; he had anticipated a surprise German invasion. This was the view of many in the country and was behind the spying by Trench on Borkum. However, if war came, he realised that the small size of the British Army meant there would be a great deal of improvisation. He preferred to have some sort of pre-defined role when war came. For this reason he had enlisted with the Territorials to be part of the second line needed in the event of war.[16]

Younger OUs shared this sense of duty as well and this is reflected in a letter of 31st August 1914 to J E B Gray, a pupil from September 1909 to April 1914. Gray joined the school in the same term as Edward Brittain and Roland Leighton but left a term earlier than them. The letter from a fellow OU, the signature is indecipherable, urges him to enlist quickly because his country needs him. The letter states the collective view of many of his contemporaries: 'This is not only my opinion but that of all the OUs I have met who are doing something.'[17] Not all OUs had the same reasons for volunteering. Philip Howe, who was at the school between 1905 and 1909, saw an opportunity for adventure by volunteering. He was bored of living at home and enlisting was a way of escaping from this. When he received a letter from the War Office, one of 2,000 sent to recent members of the OTC, encouraging him to apply for a commission he was quick to follow this up.[18] Howe's account was given 50 years after the event for *The First Day on*

13 Gregory, *The Last Great War*, pp. 13-15.
14 Catriona Pennell, 'Responses to the Outbreak of War: The Myth of the "Spirit of 1914"', University of Wolverhampton First World War Study Group 26 April 2014.
15 IWM: IWM 66/121/1; Lee Papers.
16 Carmalt Jones, *A Physician in Spite of Himself*, pp. ix and 95.
17 IWM Con Shelf: Papers of Captain J. E. B. Gray.
18 Martin Middlebrook, *The First Day on the Somme* (Paperback edition, London: Classic Penguin, 2001), p. 17.

the Somme so he may have presented his motivation in a different manner to what he felt at the time but it does suggest that the opportunity for adventure was a reason for enlisting.

Some Uppinghamians sought to enlist in the belief that the war would not last long and wanted to fight in the war. One such man was Frank Bodenham Thornely, 1910 to 1914, who was 18 in August 1914 just after war came and had planned to stay at the school until July 1915. Having already played for the cricket 1st XI he hoped to be captain in 1915. The arrival of war led him to the decision that he wanted to serve so he wrote to Major Kington Phillip Blair Oliphant, who was married to an aunt and second in command of the 11th Royal Irish Rifles, for advice. Blair Oliphant advised him to apply to his battalion as he would be able to help him get a commission. Having passed his Certificate A examinations while serving with the OTC Thornely was attractive officer material for the army as he had successfully completed all the training available to him at school and regiments would have been keen to have him. In the chaotic conditions of the early part of the war in order to speedily enlist and become an officer it was very helpful to have connections. So Thornely, who had no connections with Ulster enlisted with a regiment that would form part of its 36th Division. It was a choice of regiment which would have interesting consequences (See Chapter 10).[19]

For Roland Leighton, who came to the school the term after Howe left, it was a matter of a sense of duty which motivated him to volunteer which was supported by his parents, while Edward Brittain's desire to serve in the army was opposed by his father.[20] When war broke out Brittain was 18 years and eight months old which was four months short of the minimum age for enlisting. He could only do so unless he obtained his father's permission. This was angrily denied by his father who took a great deal of persuading by his family to provide the written consent required. Farr ascribes Brittain's determination in the face of this opposition to the sense of patriotism and duty installed by Uppingham but this seems to ignore the wider public mood.[21] In the period from 4 August to 12 September 1914 nearly 479,000 men had volunteered and by the end of the year the total number of volunteers had risen to 2,466,719 men. Of this volunteers from a public school background probably made up no more than 40,000 of the total. OUs tended to have a middle class background and while it is suggested the middle class were more in favour of going to war there were no strong class division on this subject within the country.[22] Although the views held by OUs may have been a slightly more exaggerated than those from other backgrounds there was a sense of duty shared by many within the country. The army which was recruited in 1914 and 1915 was the second largest volunteer army in history.[23]

This did not mean everyone wanted to serve and some OUs chose not to volunteer. Some made this decision because they had other responsibilities which they felt prevented them from doing so; such as those in holy orders. Men such as Alfred Hale, at the school from 1889 to 1893, believed themselves to be unsuitable for military service. Hale was a composer who appears to have had the means to survive without the need to perform other work. He was a deeply impractical bachelor; Fussell says that he was unfit for physical work and found even the telephone to

19 Discussion with Nick Thornely, 24th February 2016.
20 Farr, *None That Go Return*, p. 59.
21 Farr, *None That Go Return*, pp. 65-66.
22 Gregory, *The Last Great War*, p. 25.
23 Gregory, *The Last Great War*, p. 73.

be a challenge.²⁴ Hale believed that Britain should fight if war broke out in Europe. On several days he had been at Liss and Petersfield stations waiting for the evening papers to arrive with the latest news. Like others, he was inspired by the events of August and September 1914 to play his part. After meeting an elderly doctor at his club who had told him he had just heard his son had been killed in action Hale had returned home and enrolled as a Special Constable. He believed himself to be unsuitable for military life. To him the idea of conscription was unpatriotic. When conscription was introduced in 1916 Hale who was not quite 41, at which point he could not be conscripted (he was 40) was called up.²⁵ Military service as a batman in the RFC and RAF would prove to be a deeply unhappy experience for him. Like Hale, C R W Nevinson considered he was unfit for military service and doubted he would pass the medical. Through his father, a war correspondent, he was able to join the Red Cross as an ambulance driver, eventually joining the Royal Army Medical Corps (RAMC) in 1915 from which he was invalided out in the same year. He believed he had no patriotism but felt he needed to do something and described his war service as being in the war but not of it.²⁶ Something he would demonstrate from 1917 when he became an official war artist and producing work which did not always meet with official favour.²⁷ Some OUs simply did not believe they should fight in the war; Hope Bagenal, 1902 to 1905, held Quaker beliefs but volunteered to serve in the RAMC. Old boys such as Nevinson and Bagenal, were not influenced by the values of public school ethos, were ambivalent about fighting but still felt a need to be of service.

It cannot be assumed that there is a universal rule that public opinion, parental influence or educational background were decisive factors in deciding whether or not to serve. The example of the Shove brothers is a useful example of this point. Gerald was at Uppingham from 1902 to 1906 and Ralph from 1903 to 1908 yet both had entirely different careers and attitudes. Ralph became a barrister and later a County Court Judge and served in the Royal Field Artillery during the war. After graduating Gerald was a Cambridge academic, a member of the Apostles and a pacifist.²⁸ As a conscientious objector he worked on a poultry farm during the war. Even when individuals came from the same background it was not necessarily the final determinant of attitudes towards war. The vast majority shared a common concern about Germany but their precise motives for serving varied. Nearly all of those who had reservations about military action found a way of serving such as by driving ambulances.

Uppingham and the Citizen Army

In the years before the First World War the government had pursued the 'nation in arms' approach championed by Haldane to provide a second line of part-time officers which would be fed into the army once war broke out. The development of the OTC formed part of this scheme and, as discussed in Chapter 3, the introduction of the OTC had seen an increase in the number of boys joining the regular army (see Table 2). Between 1903 and 1910 the numbers

---

24 Paul Fussell (ed.), *The Ordeal of Alfred M Hale*, (London: Leo Cooper, 1975), p. 2.
25 Fussell (ed.), *Hale*, pp. 28-31.
26 Nevinson, *Paint and Prejudice*, pp. 94-105.
27 See Chapter 6 for a discussion on Nevinson's time as a war artist.
28 *School Roll* p. 219, p225 Obituary G.F. Shove *The Times*, 8 August 1947, Obituary R.S. Shove *The Times*, 3 February 1966.

of boys taking up a regular commission each year had increased from one to ten. This was a substantial increase from one percent of the intake to eight percent of those joining the school but the numbers still remained a low percentage of the overall student body. Most boys were not sent to Uppingham with a view to taking up a military career; an analysis of the available data of the professions of those who served in the war shows that 26 percent of OUs had a career in business. The second most popular occupation was the army which attracted 19 percent of those who served with law in third place on 11 percent. The figures for the professions of OUs are not complete because, as previously explained, they were not always good at keeping in touch with the school. However, there is information for 65 percent of those who served which is statistically significant and we can draw reasonable conclusions from this information. Because it was easier to collect information via *The Times* on the army careers of old boys it is likely the percentage of OUs joining the army is overstated and that of those in business is understated. Many fathers were involved in business and many of their sons would have followed them into these occupations.

Christopher Moore-Bick suggests that junior officers were part of a 'citizen army 'and were volunteers and not predominantly Regular Army.[29] By 'citizen army' he meant an army that consisted mainly of civilians with very few regular soldiers. Analysis of the records for OUs shows that many of them were part of this 'citizen army.

Table 4 Analysis of OU Service by Rank in the Great War

Rank	Number	% of Total
Major & Above	400	17.1
Junior Officers	1,689	72.2
Ranks	114	4.9
Other	140	6.0
Total	2,343	100.0

This is demonstrated when Uppingham is compared with the figures for Winchester drawn from the *Wykehamist War Service Roll 1914-1919*. Winchester was one of the top 10 contributors of officers to the army before the war.[30] When compared with Uppingham there is a higher proportion of senior officers (26 percent compared with 17 percent for Uppingham) and a lower proportion of junior officers (66 percent vs 72 percent). The senior ranks were populated by a far greater proportion of officers from the regular army. The status of Winchester as an 'army' school is demonstrated in the analysis by Simon Robbins of the sample of 700 officers who were part of the senior officers and staff officers who ran the war effort on the Western Front. The vast majority of these men had a background in the regular army.[31] To this group Winchester contributed 33 men compared with seven from Uppingham; that is nearly five times as many.[32]

---

29   Moore-Bick, C., *Playing the Game* (Solihull: Helion 2011), p. 12.
30   See Chapter 2.
31   Robbins, *British Generalship in the First World War*, pp. 27-28.
32   Robbins, *British Generalship in the First World War*, p. 510.

Uppingham was not part of the elite who made up the army leadership and its old boys who fought came from a predominantly civilian background.

This did not mean that OUs had no interest in the army. Analysis shows that up to 505 served with a Territorial unit or were members of the Special Reserve; that is 22 percent of those known to have served. Not all of these men were part-time soldiers before the war and some enlisted with the Territorials or Special Reserve after the war broke out. They include men such as Gordon Wills, who was 22, and on holiday in South Africa when the war broke out; he immediately volunteered to serve with the South African Army and in 1915 he managed to engineer a recall to Britain to serve in the Cambridgeshire Regiment (a territorial unit) which was commanded by the father of his brother-in-law.[33] Roland Leighton used membership of a territorial battalion in the Norfolk Regiment as a route to his commission with the Norfolk Regiment after his original application was turned down on account of his poor eyesight.[34] Despite this a substantial number of OUs were pre-war part-time soldiers. A large number of OUs demonstrated a commitment to serve if war came through part time involvement with the army but retained a civilian status and approach to life pre-war.

A War for all ages

For many the war is seen as one in which young men were predominantly involved. The figures in Table 5 demonstrate that the picture is far more nuanced than this.

Table 5 Analysis of OU Service by Age in August 1914

Age in August 1914	Number	% of Total
Under 20	609	25.99
20 to 29	942	40.21
30 to 39	529	22.58
40 and over	263	11.22
Total	2,343	100.00

A significant portion of OUs (33.80 percent) were 30 or older when war broke out and many of these men were just as keen to sign up quickly as the likes of Howe, Leighton, Brittain and Richardson were. Kitchener's call for volunteers aged between 19 and 30 in August 1914 did not deter men such as Charles Mott, Hugh Graham Peachey and Hugo Beaumont Burnaby. Mott was 44 years old in August 1914; like Arthur Lee he was a solicitor with children but unlike Lee he was not in the Territorial Force. Nonetheless, he was determined to volunteer but initially was told he was too old. This did not put him off and he used a friend in the War Office to get a commission in the Army Service Corps. In many ways he was physically unsuited to the army and needed to learn to ride and shoot before he joined his unit. This was accomplished with some difficulty and during the war he would serve in Gallipoli and the Middle East where

---

33 World War 1 experiences of my grandfather, Gordon Wills <http://www.oceanharmony.ca/Alfred%20Gordon%20Wills.html#Chapter 2> (accessed 5 February 2016).
34 Farr, *None That Go Return*, pp. 61-62.

one of his main responsibilities would be the supply of food for the soldiers and the horses.[35] Peachey was a stockbroker who had served with the 10th Imperial Yeomanry in the Boer War, like Mott he was 44, but a bachelor.[36] When war came, he also gained a commission in the Army Service Corps. By October 1914 he was at Aldershot writing to his family describing the demanding training programme he was undergoing. It is clear from his letters that the army was not giving volunteers aged over 30 an easy time. Something he questioned when he remarked that a man who had served in the Boer War for 18 months with 1,200 men under him was not guaranteed to be an officer.[37] Peachey spent most of the war in France with a responsibility for supplying men and horses.[38] Burnaby was 40 years old, and married with young children on the outbreak of war and had immediately volunteered but was informed by the War office he was not required. Having served as an officer in the Boer War and won a DSO, on the face of it, he had more to offer to the army than Mott or Peachey. Unlike Mott and Peachey he had made a formal approach to the War Office and been rejected. Like Mott he was not deterred taking charge of the guard at the Chiltern Water Works and, later in 1914, gained his commission as Captain in the Durham Light Infantry after applying directly to the HQ of the 21st Division in Aylesbury. In 1915 he was promoted to Lieutenant-Colonel of the 11th Battalion The Queens which had been raised by the Mayor of Lambeth.[39] Many older OUs appear to have gained a commission by using their contacts to get round the official War Office recruitment policy.

The examples of Mott and Peachey demonstrate an improvised approach to recruitment in 1914 and the early stages of the war. As Carnforth Jones had realised, a country which was militarily unprepared for a significant commitment would need to improvise in recruiting an army and its officers speedily. In the period from August to December 1914 Kitchener devolved the recruitment of officers to Battalion COs. Men who had connections within the army and were known quantities would have been attractive as it needed quick solutions to meet the immediate military threat. By January 1915 Peachey was writing in a letter to his father that he could no longer help anyone to get a commission in the army. There was a 2,000 strong waiting list and commanding officers no longer had the power to nominate men.[40] Despite this older OUs continued to get commissions. Wilfred Parr, 1888 to 1891, was 41 when war broke out but was appointed to a commission in April 1915; before the war he had been working in the family coal merchant business.[41] He volunteered in September 1914 and entered the army as a private. Promotion through the ranks followed rapidly and he was made a Lance Corporal on 15 December 1914, promoted to Corporal on 15 January 2015 and eventually appointed a Sergeant on 30 January 1915. This rapid promotion is likely to have bought him to the attention of the army who, as a result, awarded him a commission. The experience of Burnaby shows that the War Office in 1914 was not keen on men of 40 or older. Parr got round this problem by lying

---

35 John Mott (2015), 'OUs in WW1'. E-mail (7 January 2015).
36 TNA: WO 339/10422: Major Hugh Graham Peachey. Royal Army Service Corps and *Uppingham School Roll*, p. 109.
37 London Metropolitan Archives (LMA): F/PEY 261, 262, 263 & 264: *Peachey Papers*.
38 LMA: F/PEY: Letters to Family 1914 to 1919.
39 Liddell Hart Centre for Military Archives (LHCMA): Papers of Burnaby, Lt Col Hugo Beaumont
40 LMA: F/PEY271: Letter to Father 14 January 1915.
41 Roll of Honour and Biographies Officers of the Gloucestershire Regiment Who Died in the Great War <http://www.remembering.org.uk/glosregtofficers/glos_regt_offrs_biographies_P.htm> (accessed 8 February 2016).

about his age; on his discharge form (when he left the ranks to become an Officer) he gives his age as 34 years and 11 months when he was actually 40.[42] It was not just under age boys who were prepared to lie about their age in their eagerness to serve their country. Parr's commission had not come about as a result of string pulling or personal connections but because he had potential to lead men. The army either was unaware of his real age or turned a blind eye because it was considered he was extremely well qualified for a commission.

Despite this not all old boys volunteered immediately and it is not always clear why they delayed but within the country many men felt there were good reasons why they should not volunteer such as physical (as in the case of Hale) family and business considerations.[43] The reasons for delaying enlistment varied. Harry Becker, 1907 to 1908, had been a Second Lieutenant in the Territorial Force but resigned to go and work in the USA. By July 1915 he had returned to England and enrolled and was posted to the Army Service Corps as a Private. In May 1917 he was granted a commission. It is not clear why there was a delay but by 1917 the high rate of junior officer casualties meant there was an urgent need for replacements. His previous service in the TF and membership of the OTC made him an obvious choice to be an officer.[44]

Others appear to have made a commitment to some sort war service but as the war progressed volunteered for active service. Edward Bindloss, at the school in 1887, spent the early part of the war working in the York Remount Depot but in May 1915 had gone a stage further and taken a commission in the Royal Field Artillery. He was 41 in May 1915 but it appears his ability to ride and his previous service at York made a difference.[45] Others appear to have avoided seeking a commission until the alternative was conscription. Humphrey Baker, a barrister, 1896 to 1900, and 32 when war broke out was deemed to have enlisted in June 1916 after conscription was introduced but was not posted until October 1917 whereupon he was awarded a commission in the Labour Corps.[46]

Apart from those who volunteered other OUs who found themselves in the army included the 'dugouts'. These men were the officers and men who had retired but remained on the reserve list. When war came they found themselves rapidly recalled to service. Uppingham 'dugouts' included Brigadier-General Charles Henry Alexander, 1868 to 1872, who had been retired for five years when war broke out. He was recalled to the Army in October 1914 and given the task of forming the artillery section of the 21st Division. The 21st Division was part of the New Army which had emerged from Kitchener's recruitment drive. He went out to France in September 1915 with the division but was removed on 6 October 1915 after the division's poor performance at Loos. From 1915 until 1917 he commanded a Royal Field Artillery training brigade at Luton.[47] Alexander's experience was a familiar story for many 'dugouts' who were

---

42 TNA: WO 339/13666: Captain Wilfred Wharton Parr The Gloucestershire Regiment and *Uppingham School Roll*, p. 129.
43 Gregory, *The Last Great War*, pp. 92-93.
44 TNA: WO 339/108894: 2/Lieutenant Harry Thomas Alfred Becker The Suffolk Regiment.
45 TNA: WO 339/1270: Lieutenant Edward Hugh Bindloss Royal Field Artillery.
46 TNA: WO 339/124614: Lieutenant Humphrey George Ambrose Baker Labour Corps.
47 World War One Luton <http://www.worldwar1luton.com/individual/brigadier-general-charles-henry-alexander> (accessed 8 February 2016) and Profiles of Western Front generals <http://www.birmingham.ac.uk/research/activity/warstudies/research/projects/lionsdonkeys/a.aspx> (accessed 8 February 2016).

deemed to be ineffective commanders on the front line. The circumstances surrounding his alleged ineffectiveness are discussed in Chapter 8.

Alexander had mainly served in India during his military service and had not fought in the Boer War although 73 OUs had fought in it as officers. Although the war had ultimately been won it had been a chastening experience for the British and in its aftermath reforms were implemented to make the army more professional. At least 232 OUs had fought in the Boer War and of these 149 fought in the Great War. Not all of the 76 men with no regular army background were welcomed back into army; Burnaby had to be extremely persistent to get a commission in 1914 in the face of disinterest from the War Office.

With the exception of Becker, who was 22 at the start of the war all the men discussed in this section were outside the army's preferred age range for recruiting officers in 1914. By the end of 1914 the regular army had suffered 4,082 officer casualties in France and Belgium; of these 1,230 were fatal.[48] Not only did these officers need to be replaced but officers needed to be found to lead the Territorial Force and the New Army established by Kitchener. So in April 1915 the army had laid down new criteria for selecting officers. Suitable candidates for commissions included those with a public school education and who were under 27 years old except where there were 'exceptional circumstances'.[49] At the outbreak of the war 1,264 of the OUs who served were 26 or younger. That is 54 percent of the total known to have served fell into the age qualification laid down by the army. By April 1915 the percentage of OUs over 26 would have been a little higher but we can conclude from this that at least 1,079 were 27 or older in April 1915. A small number of these men were never officers, such as Hale who was conscripted, but by analysing the data it can be concluded that in the region of 960 officers who were in the army's view fell outside this criteria.

Of these 180 (nineteen percent of the 960) were serving or had previously served in the armed forces. Despite the army's age criteria 780 OUs who were outside it were awarded commissions. Not all of them gained commissions before April 1915; men such as Parr and Bindloss were given them from April 1915 onwards. Although there was some string pulling along the way this on its own does not explain why there were so many. It suggests that many OUs had skills which the army valued as it expanded rapidly after 1914 and then had to replace lost men. Men such as Parr who by his rapid promotion to sergeant had displayed leadership qualities and Bindloss whose horsemanship was considered to be useful to the Royal Field Artillery had skills which fell into the category of 'exceptional circumstances' which allowed the recruitment of men of 27 or older.

The examples of a few more OUs demonstrate the reasons for which 'exceptional circumstances' might apply. They can be applied to H G Ivatt 1901 to 1904 and would later become the Chief Mechanical Engineer of the LMS. He left school to start an apprenticeship at Crewe with the LNWR and during the war served on the staff of the Director of Transport in France. That this was important to the army is demonstrated by his civilian background being recorded on his army file.[50] It is an obvious case of a man's talents being applied to the army's requirements for a good logistical system to provide the supplies of food and munitions it needed to

---

48 Sheffield, 'Officer – Man Relations', p. 103.
49 Sheffield, 'Officer – Man Relations', p. 113.
50 TNA: WO 339/24071: Major Henry George Ivatt Royal Army Service Corps.

successfully prosecute the war.[51] The army was prepared to draw on those with no previous army experience where their skills could be applied to tasks which were undertaken in the civilian world. The Directorate of Inland Water Transport (IWT) recruited a number of individuals from the LNWR on this basis.[52] George Tryon who went to the school in January 1901 and left in August 1905 did not have a specialist role and was killed in action on 7th November 1918 having volunteered in 1914. Tryon had been a member of the Uppingham Rifle Corps and the Cambridge University Rifle Volunteers and after graduation had eventually become a Housemaster at Oundle School where he served in the OTC.[53] Although he had not served in the OTC at school or university, his involvement as a teacher and an ex-public school boy made him attractive army officer material.

The vast majority of OU enlistment for military service took place in the first 20 months of the war. By February 1916, just after conscription was introduced, 72 percent (1,694) of 2,343 OUs who served in the war were known to have enlisted; demonstrating a strong and immediate response by OUs to the declaration of war.[54] From analysing the records of those who served 217 of them can be identified as having left the school after February 1916. The increase from February 1916 to the total who served was 649 so in 1916 there were 432 individuals eligible to serve who enlisted after that date. Only 114 OUs served in the ranks so it can be concluded that of those who enlisted after February 1916 the majority of them served as officers.[55] The figures demonstrate a strong and immediate response to the call to sign up to the civilian army by a group of men whose age covered a range from 18 to 69.

The OTC

Of those OUs who served just over half of them (1,264) were aged 26 or under when war broke out. The vast majority of them were eligible to have served in the OTC and as Table 6 shows 904 of them had received their early training in the OTC. There are a few conclusions which can be drawn from number and proportion of boys who were in the OTC. Of those under 26

---

51 Grace's Guide Henry George Ivatt <http://www.gracesguide.co.uk/Henry_George_Ivatt> downloaded 9th September 2012 and *School Roll* p207. A more famous example of a railwayman's involvement in the war is Sam Fay of the GCR who was Director of Movements at the War Office from 1917.
52 Christopher Phillips, Logistics and the BEF: The development of Waterborne Transport on the Western Front, 1914-1916 *British Journal of Military History*, 2: 2 pp. 42-58, p. 57.
53 Roll of Honour – Lincolnshire – Market Rasen, De Aston School <http://www.roll-of-honour.com/Lincolnshire/MarketRasenDeAstonSchool.html> downloaded (7 September, 2012), *School Roll* p. 207 and *The London Gazette* 7 December 1909 p. 9331.
54 *USM*, March 1916, p. 7 The total figure derives from a detailed analysis of the *Third List of Old Uppinghamians*.
55 See the letter to the School Magazine (December 1916 pp. 278-279.) which explains how the information about military service is gathered, the problems caused by a lack of access to official information and why the coverage of non-military involvement is very difficult. It can be surmised that of the 432 some were already serving but information about their service had not reached Uppingham. See the previous comments about the apathy of OUs in providing information. Some OUs wished to serve such as Boris Karloff who was at Uppingham as William Henry Pratt from September 1903 to April 1907 and volunteered in 1914 but was rejected because of a heart condition. See the *School Roll* p. 225 and Matthews, *Eminent Uppinghamians* p. 48.

who served 72 percent actually participated in the OTC; leaving another 360 who chose not to but still served in the war. Some of these would have been the sportsmen, such as George Horridge, who preferred to spend their time training for sports as opposed to training for future military service. It demonstrates that when OTC membership was genuinely voluntary a significant amount chose not to enrol. The pressures to join the OTC were not overwhelming at Uppingham unlike some other schools. In some of them it was obligatory to join the OTC while in others there was considerably more pressure to enrol even if this was on a voluntary basis. Lancing, which also had a contingent where membership was voluntary, claimed to the first public school where every eligible boy was a member of the OTC.[56] For this to have happened there must have been considerable pressure within the school to do so. Uppingham appears to have reflected the national mood which opposed conscription but was strongly in favour of responding to threats to the nation when they came.

Table 6 Analysis of Uppingham OTC in the First World War[57]

Category	Number	Percentage Split
Served or Awaiting Commission	788	87.2
Rejected	28	3.1
Under Eligible Age	41	4.5
No Known Military Service	47	5.2
Total	904	100.0

As Table 7 shows Uppingham OTC served its purpose in producing young men who were suitable to be officers.

Table 7 Analysis of Uppingham OTC Military Service in the First World War[58]

Category	Number	Percentage Split
Commission in Army, RAF or Navy	664	84.3
Ranks	35	4.4
Awaiting Commission	89	11.3
Total	788	100.0

From this it can be seen that those holding or awaiting commissions made up nearly 96 percent of all those from the Uppingham OTC who served during the war. It was an even more impressive figure than the 89 percent of OUs who served as officers during the war. Even when those from the OTC who did not serve but are included the figures demonstrates that

---

56 Lancing College War Memorial <http://www.hambo.org/lancing/view_man.php?id=132> (accessed 19 February 2016).
57 USA: Sterndale-Bennett Papers.
58 USA: Sterndale-Bennett Papers.

Edward Thring.
(Uppingham School Archives)

The Uppingham Bisley Shooting Team 1897 in old style Rifle Corps uniform.
(Uppingham School Archives)

The Uppingham Rifle Corps on parade 1898. (Uppingham School Archives)

The officers of the Uppingham Rifle Corps 1901. (Uppingham School Archives)

The Boer War Memorial utilised today as the School Theatre. (Uppingham School Archives)

Edward Carus Selwyn Headmaster 1897-1907. (Uppingham School Archives)

The Rifle Corps camp 1908. (Uppingham School Archives)

C.R.W. Nevinson at Uppingham 1905.
(Uppingham School Archives)

Harry Ward McKenzie Headmaster 1908-1915.
(Uppingham School Archives)

Eric Dorman-Smith at Uppingham 1911. (Uppingham School Archives)

Brian Horrocks at Uppingham 1912. (Uppingham School Archives)

The OTC on parade, Leicester 1910. (Uppingham School Archives)

The Uppingham OTC officers 1913 C.H. Jones had been succeeded as C.O. by Major R.P. Shea. (Uppingham School Archives)

OTC summer camp Mytchett, August 1914 which was attended by members of Uppingham OTC. (Uppingham School Archives)

The Front Cover of Edward Brittain's Church Parade Order of Service at the 1914 OTC summer camp. (Uppingham School Archives)

Keep this Book for the Evening Service.

Evening Service in Recreation Tent, 8.15 p.m.

Officers' Training Corps

(Junior Division),

2nd August, 1914.

1914.
E. W. Langham, Printer, Farnham.

The Uppingham OTC at Mytchett August 1914 – Edward Brittain is third down on the right. (Uppingham School Archives)

The Uppingham School Praeposters – Roland Leighton is in the centre of the middle row.
(Uppingham School Archives)

The newly promoted Lieutenant Colonel C.H. Jones. (centre front seated row) with the 5th Battalion of the Royal Leicestershire Regiment just after the outbreak of war in August 1914.
(Uppingham School Archives)

Harry Ward McKenzie with Mrs McKenzie and their son Harry, an OU, at Uppingham in 1915. (Uppingham School Archives)

Battle of the Somme, the attack of the Ulster Division by J.P. Beadle – The officer leading the attack with arm raised is OU F.B. Thornely. (Belfast City Council)

General Sir Horace Smith-Dorrien inspects the Uppingham OTC in 1917 – Headmaster Owen is to the left of the picture.
(Uppingham School Archives)

R. Sterndale Bennett at the 1917 inspection of the Uppingham OTC.
(Uppingham School Archives)

Reginald Herbert Owen Headmaster 1916 to 1934.
(Uppingham School Archives)

The Uppingham OTC marching at its 1918 inspection, Percy Chapman future captain of England is at the front. (Uppingham School Archives)

An OTC instruction class during the Great War. (Uppingham School Archives)

The Uppingham Metal Workshop utilised to produce material for the war effort. (Uppingham School Archives)

The exterior of the Memorial Chapel dedicated in 1921. (Uppingham School Archives)

Interior View of the Memorial Chapel. (Uppingham School Archives)

General Sir Charles 'Tim' Harrington with R.H. Owen at the opening of the Memorial Hall in 1924. (Uppingham School Archives)

The East Block and Memorial Hall immediately after opening in 1924. (Uppingham School Archives)

The East Block and School Memorial Hall today, Little exterior change has occurred since its opening. (Uppingham School Archives)

Godfrey Robinson prior to losing his sight in 1917. (RNIB)

Memorial plaque to John Colling-Wells, All Saints, Caddington, Bedfordshire with the more common rendition of *Dulce et decorum est pro patria mori*. (Peter Graham)

Godfrey Robinson (right) attending the Braille centenary in his capacity as RNIB chairman. (RNIB)

The Gleed Harvey Memorial Window, Gleed an OU is on the left. (*A Guide to the Stain Glass Windows in St Mary & St Nicolas Church*, 2nd ed., 2008). Photograph by Alastair Goodrum)

The section of the Gleed Harvey memorial window featuring John Gleed. (*A Guide to the Stain Glass Windows in St Mary & St Nicolas Church*, 2nd ed., 2008). Photograph by Alastair Goodrum)

Memorial plaque to Stephen Jalland in All Saints, Pavement, York with the more unusual version of 'It is a beautiful thing to die for one's country' – *Pulchrum est Pro Patria Mori*. (James Halstead)

The Edwalton Alms Houses built in memory of OUs Lawrence and Oliver Hind. (James Halstead)

Lawrence A. Hind dedication plaque situated outside the Alms houses. (James Halstead)

Uppingham's OTC was an effective source of recruits for the armed forces and that a high percentage of its output became officers.

Not all school OTC units were as successful as Uppingham in producing officers for the war. Wellington School in Somerset was distinctly less successful. In the period up to the end of March 1915 41 percent of its OTC cadets had gained a commission.[59] In the same period 79 percent cadets from Uppingham, nearly twice as many, had been awarded a commission. Figures for the whole war are not available for Wellington, Somerset but by looking at the overall split for the war we can see that the school was not as rich a source of officers as Uppingham. In the case of Wellington, Somerset only 40 percent of its old boys were awarded commissions. Compared with the 89 percent equivalent for Uppingham it demonstrates that Wellington's OTC was not as successful in producing officers. The background of OUs was one where their parents were often from professional and business backgrounds with army and business classes. In contrast, the boys of Wellington, Somerset often came from an agricultural background; the emphasis in its curriculum was on agricultural science and handicrafts.[60] Those from an agricultural background were more likely to be needed on the home front and rates of volunteering were lower in the agricultural community.[61] Many of those who did not volunteer would have been conscripted into the ranks as the war continued.

In the early stages of the war when the army was expanding rapidly there was an urgent need to recruit officers to lead Kitchener's New Army. This citizen army had no military experience; Britain's policy of building a small professional army and having no national service meant the New Army consisted of untrained men. This was in contrast to Germany and France who, as a result of having national service, had large numbers of men who had served in the army, received military training, and could be called up from the reserves in the event of war. In contrast, the New Army would have to be trained from scratch. Officers were needed to train this army of raw recruits. The men who served in the OTC were attractive to the army because they had received some training. The training provided had integrated with the army's training scheme by basing the scheme on documents such as the *Field Service Regulations, 1909* and *Infantry Training, 1911*.[62] Their understanding of what was required of them made OTC cadets an obvious source of officers. The former OTC cadet's training meant that they were more likely to pass their officer exams. Peachey, 42 at the start of the war, in a letter from Aldershot in October 1914 spoke of the demanding training and exams for a commission. He remarked that not one man over 30 had passed yet but 'schoolboys and Sandhurst cadets have it at their fingertips' when it came to passing the necessary exams.[63] The opportunity to accelerate the training of men to be officers was very attractive to the army. As the figures for commissions of former OTC cadets in Table 8 show the army placed a premium on these men.

---

59   Based on analysis of Haig-Brown, *The O.T.C. and The Great War*, pp. 97-106.
60   Honey, *Tom Brown's Universe*, p. 68.
61   Gregory, *The Last Great War*, p. 81.
62   *Regulations for the Officers Training Corps*, (London: HMSO, 1912), pp. 41-47.
63   LMA: F/PEY261: Letter to Steph October 1914.

For Uppingham up to June 1915; over 80% of past OTC members eligible members were serving in some capacity. Of those not serving some were applying for a commission while others were 'debarred physically from serving' and others were under age.[64]

Table 8 Analysis of Past Uppingham OTC Cadets Commissioned in the Army to June 1915[65]

Total OTC cadets commissioned	286
Serving in Special Reserve (SR)	31
Serving in Territorial Force (TF)	59
Total Prior Service SR & TF	90
% with SR or TF Service	31.5

It is likely that several those recorded as TF or SR enlisted after war broke out but it also indicates that OTC membership was attractive to these bodies in urgent need of officers as the army rapidly expanded in a somewhat haphazard manner in 1914 and early 1915.

The importance of OTC membership to the army is demonstrated by it being specifically mentioned in the announcements of commissions for a number of old boys. The most extreme example of this was when the commission of Herbert Edward Boucher, 1910 to 1915, was announced as being given on 1 March 1915 although he did not leave school until April 1915.[66] Arthur Egerton Claude Daniel who left the school in December 1914 was granted his commission on 2 February 1915.[67] Edmund Risley Hearn left the school in July 1914 and was awarded a commission on 21 October 1914.[68] James Herbert Morrish who, like Hearn, joined the school in September 1910 and left in July 1914 was commissioned on 23 September 1915.[69] In many cases the army, desperate for officers, accelerated former cadets into service.

From March 1916 the army stopped offering commissions via direct entry and introduced the Officer Cadet Battalion (OCB) system for officer selection and training. The OCB accepted men from both the ranks and the OTC as potential officers with all successful applicants required to undergo four and a half months of training. Cadets from the Uppingham OTC continued to gain favour in the OCB scheme. After March 1916 216 boys left the school and went on to serve in the armed forces; given that levels of OTC membership at the school increased after August 1914 the vast majority of these boys would have been OTC cadets. As Table 7 shows only 35 OTC cadets served in the ranks during the war and it is clear that from the point view of the army Uppingham OTC cadets remained attractive officer material. This was despite R Sterndale Bennett expressing reservations about some of the men who gained commissions. On Alan Stanley Hett's application, 1912 to 1916, he remarked Hett had no marked ability as a

---

64 USA: Officers Training Corps Record of Commissions gained by Uppingham School Contingent to June 1915.
65 Based on USA, Officers Training Corps Record of Commissions gained by Uppingham School Contingent to June 1915.
66 *The London Gazette*, 2 April 1915, p. 3257.
67 *The London Gazette*, 2 February 1915, p. 1024.
68 *The London Gazette*, 20 October 1914, p. 8404.
69 *The London Gazette*, 22 September 1915, p. 9400.

leader.[70] Hett was not the only OU he expressed reservations about; he described Cyril Reginald Bascombe, 1913 to 1916, as having 'no distinct capacity in any direction.'[71] The OCB system had the advantage that with a more formal training scheme it was easier to weed out those not up to the job so a risk could be taken with those who had poor references.[72] Both Hett and Bascombe received commissions in the RFC. Sterndale Bennett was also prepared to praise; of Walter William Gordon Beatson, 1912 to 1915, he said he was 'a conscientious officer with some power of command.'[73] Ironically, both Bascombe and Beatson would be killed in training with the RFC before they went to the front.

As Uppingham was not one of the traditional suppliers of officers to the army it is clear that the OTC cadets produced by Uppingham had qualities which were attractive to the army. There was probably an element of it being considered one of the better public schools by the army but there would have been other factors. Inspection reports by the War Office about the school's OTC were consistently good and the skills which came from OTC training together with those produced by the school's curriculum, much of it practical, made the school's OTC attractive officer material. Despite Sterndale Bennett's reservations about some of the cadets under his command the army appears to have regarded the Uppingham's OTC cadets with great favour.

The OCB was set up to manage the recruitment and training of officers when the casualties in the early part of the war led to a shortage from the army's traditional sources. The Uppingham OTC remained an important source of officers but it was in the early part of the war that its contribution was the most crucial. The army was able to process through cadets to commissions as a result of the training they had received. This was acknowledged when in April 1919 the School Magazine reported the War Office had written to express its appreciation of the 'great work' carried out. In particular it said:

> In the early months of the war the number of vacancies filled in the commissioned ranks of the Army by ex-cadets of the Officers Training Corps fully justified the formation of the Corps in 1908 and afforded an able testimony of the standard of training and powers of leadership which had been inculcated.[74]

That nearly all Uppingham OTC cadets gained or awaiting commissions by the end of the war is testament that in the case of the school this was no general platitude.

Skills and Expertise

A study of the role of the school's OTC cadets only provides a partial understanding of the school's contribution to the military effort. Only 34 percent of those who served had been members of the school OTC's contingent. The cadets from the OTC were one group of old boys who provided skills which were attractive to the army. However, it is necessary to examine

---

70   TNA: WO 339/60216: Lieutenant Alan Stanley Hett Royal Flying Corps.
71   TNA: WO 339/115814: 2/Lieutenant Cecil Reginald Bascombe Royal Flying Corps.
72   C. Moore-Bick, *Playing the Game* (Solihull: Helion 2011), p. 73.
73   TNA: WO 339/58484: 2/Lieutenant Walter William Gordon Beatson Royal Flying Corps Special Reserve.
74   *USM*, April 1919, p. 94.

the pattern of service for all OUs to gain a better understanding of the school's contribution to the military effort in the Great War. This is a mixture of men with specific skills having them applied to specific military activities and the civilian experience of OUs proving valuable in a more general sense. The contribution of each public school varied and this is demonstrated by a comparison of the military involvement of the school with that of Winchester; one of the traditional sources of army officers.

At both schools approximately half of those old boys who served spent a period in the infantry. This is no surprise as the infantry formed a significant part of the strength of the army. On 1 December 1918 the infantry made up 43 percent of the British army with infantry officers forming 41 percent of the army's total number of officers.[75] In the war, many officers served in more than part of the army (e.g. the infantry and the artillery) but deeper analysis of the figures shows that OUs were more likely to stay in the infantry than the old boys of Winchester. Uppingham provided more men who remained in the infantry as a result of it not being a traditional source for the army. Its OTC syllabus was based on the infantry training manuals as was that of its predecessor the Rifle Corps which had been attached to the Leicestershire (infantry) Regiment. With no real professional army background it was an obvious place to post those with no professional military experience. In the case of Winchester as an 'army school' it would have provided officers for a wide range of arms of the army; for example, Wykehamists made up a significant proportion of the Woolwich intake in 1913 which trained cadets destined for the more specialist artillery and engineers.[76]

Winchester's more professional army background is demonstrated by examining the contribution of staff officers by each school. Staff officers were at the heart of the professional army; they were the men who planned and provided the means to execute military campaigns. These officers performed activities such as preparing the detailed orders for a battle and arranging the necessary logistics. Although men from outside the regular army did serve as staff officers, Ivatt served on the staff of the Director of Transport in France, it was a role naturally suited to the professional soldier.[77] The status of Winchester when compared to Uppingham can be seen in the number of staff each school provided. The number of men from each school is almost the same but by examining their respective war service rolls it can be seen that Winchester provided 120 men who spent at least part of the war as staff officers compared to 10 from Uppingham. There were probably more staff officers from each school but these figures demonstrate that Uppingham's contribution was that of citizens lending their skills to a volunteer army.

Despite not being an 'army school' like Winchester there were areas where Uppingham's traditional strengths more than matched Winchester. One area was the air arm where there was a rapid expansion in its size. Initially the army and navy had their own air wings; the army having the Royal Flying Corps (RFC) and the navy the Royal Naval Service (RNAS). In April 1918 the two services were merged to form the RAF when it was decided a more integrated approach was required. Although the air forces remained relatively small compared to the army there was a huge increase in their size. From August 1914 to the end of March 1918, there was

---

75 *Statistics of the Military Effort*, p. 79.
76 Sheffield, 'Officer – Man Relations', pp. 48-49.
77 Grace's Guide to British Industrial History, Henry George Ivatt <http://www.gracesguide.co.uk/Henry_George_Ivatt> (accessed 22 February 2016).

over a 100 fold increase as the RFC grew from 1,200 men to 144,078 men.[78] Until September 1918 all pilots had to be officers and the first source for pilots was the public schools. A training memorandum in 1917 identified school boys as being the best source because of their esprit de corps.[79] Proportionally the contribution of Uppingham was greater than Winchester's; Seven percent of the OUs who served would spend at least some of their services in an air force while the equivalent figure for Winchester was four percent. Winchester's stronger connections to the army meant that its old boys were more likely to have found commissions in the army. The memorandum expresses a reluctance to recruit too many officers from the leading public schools (Uppingham did not fall into this category in the mind of the army). It was therefore easier for the air force to recruit from Uppingham; its OTC had a good reputation and, as discussed, the army was prepared to set aside the concerns of Sterndale Bennett. Uppingham also had a reputation for the strength of its science and this would have made its old boys more likely to have the necessary mechanical skills. The Commander of the Cambridge OTC reported that Bascombe was able to ride motorbikes, drive cars, understood their mechanisms and was able to carry out ordinary running repairs.[80] An ability of the pilot to check his machine and ammunition belts before a mission was an important skill. In an age when the mechanics of planes were simple this would have been a good recommendation. Men such as Hett applied for a commission with the RFC probably knowing from their own research that that there was an urgent need for pilots and an Uppingham background was well regarded by the RFC.

The strength of its scientific education meant that Uppingham was able to make the same level of contribution as Winchester to providing men to the artillery and provide a greater proportion to the engineers. This was despite Winchester's strong tradition of providing officers for the artillery and engineers (see Chapter 1). Like the air force during the war there was a dramatic increase of the sizes of the Royal Engineers and the three branches of the artillery (the Royal Horse Artillery, the Royal Field Artillery and the Royal Garrison Artillery) because of the protracted nature of the Great War as a four year long siege operation. In the case of the Engineers it had expanded from 24,035 men (1,565 officers and 22,470 other ranks) in August 1914 to 357,389 men (16,493 officers and 343,471 men) in November 1918.[81] At the same time the artillery had grown from 86,041 men (3,331 officers and 82,710 other ranks) in 1914 to 529,068 men (21,091 officers and 529,068 other ranks) in 1918.[82]

With this level of growth it was impossible for a small group of schools to provide all the officers required for expansion and the army had to spread its net wider. The role of engineers was crucial during the Great War with a wide range of responsibilities which included infrastructure, communications, equipment maintenance and building fortifications; not to mention tunnelling. This was a huge range of responsibilities in a war fought on an industrial scale and where technology played a vital role. Uppingham with its good reputation for science was an obvious source and proportionately more OUs (five percent) spent at least part of the war with the artillery than Wykehamists (three percent). Men joined the Royal Engineers with an engineering and manufacturing business background. Major Charles Gamble Bishop, 1892 to

---

78 *Statistics of the Military Effort*, p. 227.
79 TNA: AIR/1/120/15/14/80: Officer Cadets for Officers Cadet Technical Corps.
80 TNA: WO 339/115814: 2/Lieutenant Cecil Reginald Bascombe Royal Flying Corps.
81 *Statistics of the Military Effort*, p. 212.
82 *Statistics of the Military Effort*, pp. 209-211.

1897, worked in the family glass works business in St Helens before joining the Royal Engineers when the war broke out.[83] Both his business and technical skills were attractive to an army which required them as it became increasingly complex as an organisation requiring strong management skills and the technology employed became more advanced requiring an aptitude for technological matters. One area where relevant experience became particularly important was the transport system. Men with the skills and background to carry out the maintenance and running of railways and other means of transport were very attractive to the army. Frederic Eugene Campion, 1907 to 1911, spent from 1912 to 1916 working as an engineer on British railways. By 1916 it was recognised that British arrangements for transport were inadequate. Sir Eric Geddes was sent out to France in 1916 to investigate the management of transport in France producing a highly critical report and was sent out to France again to implement the required changes. As a result, the British took over lines used to transport their troops and by the end of the war had control of 1,800 miles of standard and light railways. In addition, another 800 miles of railway was been built. Geddes was a railway man and understood the manpower requirements to achieve the necessary improvements.[84] Campion's skills were required to assist in the development and maintenance of the railways as the war effort increased and more lines were laid. After the war, when he returned to civilian life the skills in bridge design and permanent way maintenance he had developed during the war were employed while working for the Southern Railway.[85] Other OUs whose skills were used during the war to support the military effort included Dudley William Sanford, 1905 to 1909, who graduated from Cambridge with a BA (Honours) in Mechanical Science Tripos. He had been employed by the Midland Railway at Derby before the war and In September 1914 enlisted with the engineers whose responsibilities included the maintenance of transport.[86]

Like the engineers the artillery played a significant part in winning the war; from early in the war it was recognised that artillery superiority was decisive.[87] To be an artillery officer also required a high level of scientific skill; in particular it required mathematical ability. A competence in maths was essential to calculate the gun setting required to successfully hit targets as well as calculating where the enemy artillery was. By August 1918 at the Battle of Amiens these capabilities had been so successfully developed that British artillery was able to successfully neutralise its German opposition by destroying large parts of it in the early stages of the battle. These techniques had been gradually developed to deal with the new situation where enemy guns could not be seen because they were often further back behind the front lines and hidden behind slopes. The RFC, which had been formed out of the Royal Engineers, by the early part of the war in 1914, was already working closely with the artillery to identify enemy targets. Donald Swain Lewis, 1900 to 1902, played a key part in the early developments in this

83   Information provided by Mark Bishop.
84   Christian Wolmar, *Engines of War How Wars Were Won & Lost on the Railways* (Atlantic Books London 2010), pp. 181-184.
85   Proceedings of the Institute of Civil Engineers Obituary Frederic Eugene Campion 1893-1967, <http://www.icevirtuallibrary.com/doi/abs/10.1680/iicep. 1967.32691>, (accessed 23 February 2016).
86   Derby Engineers, etc. Sanford, Dudley William <http://www.steamindex.com/people/derby.htm> (accessed 23 February 2016).
87   Shelford Bidwell and Dominick Graham, *Fire-Power: The British Army Weapons and Theories of War 1904-1945*, (Paperback edition, Barnsley: Pen and Sword, 2004), p. 94.

field. Along with Captain B T James he developed a grid square reference system for giving the artillery the location of targets. Through the use of two way radio it became possible to direct any barrage on to a target. Over time this system developed in sophistication so that it became possible to bring down fire on any target without a sighting shot thus taking the enemy by surprise and not allowing them to move targets ahead of barrages. It was this system which played an important part in the victory at Amiens. The work of Lewis was important in the early development of this capability.

Away from the battle front OUs also made significant contributions. William King, later a Professor of Geology at Cambridge, played an important part in identifying water supplies for troops on the Western Front. His work involved overseeing the drilling of bore holes and interpreting the results. Although war tends to be seen in terms of fighting victory cannot be won without effective logistics. One of the army's requirements on the front was an adequate supply of water. The existing water supply infrastructure was not adequate enough to keep a large number of men supplied either in its capacity to supply or the physical location of water supplies. King was responsible for supervising many of the 414 bore holes drilled by the army. The soldiering and leadership skills gained in the OTC were important but the war could not have been won without other technical and administrative skills. King was also able to employ his technical skills for more overtly military purposes. The static trench warfare made the digging of mines underneath the other side's lines with a view to blowing them up and destroying the enemy's positions a practical proposition. King's knowledge of water tables made him proficient at optimising the depth of the mine and identifying the lowest possible depth which would avoid flooding. His geological skills were also put to use in proving that the Germans were using Dutch canals to transport material including concrete aggregates for military purposes to Belgium. The Germans used concrete extensively for defensive structures and as a result of King's work the British government was able to apply pressure on the Dutch government to close this supply route.[88]

Like Campion, King was able to apply his war experience in peace, publishing a number of papers based on his experience from 1919 onwards.[89] Another OU who used his war time experience to produce an academic paper based on wartime experience was Carnforth Jones. By the time war came he was a bacteriologist but he had also spent time before that working in neurology at Queens Square. Initially, his work was in bacteriology but in 1917 he was moved to use his experience of neurology running a shell shock centre. Before the war he had already published 14 papers on vaccine therapy but after the war he published two papers in *Brain* and the *Quarterly Journal of Medicine* on shell shock.[90] He described his work in the shell shock centre as the most useful clinical work he did but he believed those in charge did not share this view because he often held back men from returning to the front because he believed they would not be effective soldiers.[91] Judged in one of his obituaries to be a diffident man these strongly

---

88   F W Shotton, 'William Bernard Robinson King 1889-1963', *Biographical Memories of Fellows of the Royal Society*, 9 (Nov. 1963) pp. 171-182.
89   Archives Hub The Papers of William Bernard Robinson King <http://archiveshub.ac.uk/data/gb590-wbrk> (accessed 29 February 2016).
90   Obituary D W Carmalt Jones, D.M., F.R.C.P. F.R.A.C.P. *British Medical Journal* (March 16 1957), pp. 649-650 and Alastair Compston, 'From the Archives', *Brain*, 2013: 136, pp. 1681-1686.
91   Carmalt Jones, *A Physician in Spite of Himself*, p. 104.

held views about sending troops back are on the face of it are surprising but Uppingham's philosophy stressed a strong sense of duty, leadership skills and taking responsibility.[92] These were the qualities he showed in sticking by his judgements in the face of apparent official disapproval. Like Carnforth Jones William Douglas Harmer, at the school from 1888 to 1892, served in the RAMC during the war. As part of the professionalisation of the British Army after the Boer War the RAMC had gained a central role in it. There had been many improvements such as standards of sanitation minimising deaths from disease which had been the main problem for an army at war. Similarly the RAMC's capacity to develop effective treatment for the wounds and other medical conditions caused by modern warfare was significant. Harmer like Carnforth Jones made a significant contribution to medical practice during the war by his study of throat wounds.[93]

Carnforth Jones and Harmer were respectively 40 and 41 when the war broke out and analysis, as Table 5 shows Uppingham's involvement was not overwhelmingly dominated by youth. Eleven percent were aged over 40 and used their skills in vital non-combat roles. Mott and Peachey used their skills in their RASC working with horses; Mott in his eagerness to serve learnt how to ride. Others over 40 used their professional skills in other ways to support a national war effort. William Glynes Bruty, at the school from 1881 to 1887, was 44 and a lawyer when war broke out and in January 1915 received a commission as a Second Lieutenant in a Special Supply Company. He spent the war serving at home and in March 1917 was appointed an Assistant Provost Marshal. In this role he was in charge of the military police at Eastern Command Headquarters; it was a good fit for his legal background.[94] George Algernon Fothergill, 1882 to 1887, was 46 when the war started; he is better known as an artist but had trained as a doctor. By 1918 the army was starting to suffer from manpower shortages and there was a need to replace men serving at home who were now needed at the front. Fothergill was commissioned into the RAMC at the age of 50 in October 1918 and served in hospitals at home in the late stages of the war.

There are many other examples of OUs using their specific skills and experience to support the war effort. The school's educational philosophy stressed a strong sense of duty, leadership skills and taking responsibility also produced men whose approach was useful to the army. Harold Howitt was a Partner in a firm of Chartered Accountants when war came but too old to have served in the OTC. By the end of the war he held the staff responsibility of Brigade Major. He recalls that his business skills were judged to be of great value. He quotes a Major Rose who wrote of him: 'In place of long staff training he brought business powers. He was indulgent of everything save fear, laziness and inefficiency.'[95]

OUs contributed to the war a large number of skills needed by the military as it became an increasingly complex and technological organisation. As sections such as the engineers developed, OUs provided skills previously unused by the British in war. Their training as well as their

---

92 Obituary D W Carmalt Jones, M.A., D.M. Oxfd, F.R.C.P. F.R.A.C.P. *The Lancet* (March 16 1957), pp. 59-60.
93 Plarr's Lives of the Fellows Online Harmer, William Douglas (1873-1962) <http://livesonline.rcseng.ac.uk/biogs/E005034b.htm> (accessed 29 February 2016).
94 Law Society, *Record of Service of Solicitors and Articled Clerks with His Majesty's Forces 1914-1919* (London: Law Society, 1920), p. 72.
95 USA, Reminisces of Harold Gibson Howitt p. 52.

independence of mind was valuable as the army sought officers to lead it. Skills were not only applied to specific technical requirements but also to more traditional military functions.

Writing Home

The examples described above of Fothergill, Mott and Bruty together with all the other OUs in general suggests that they were patriotic men who left their peace time occupations to serve their country in resisting what they believed to be a serious threat. This is not to say that they were unquestioning in their service and their opinions on the war's prosecution. Their letters often reflected this but also covered other interests such as the questionable delights of trench life and requests for items to ease the discomfort of them and their men.

Frank Thornely's letters were usually a mixture of descriptions about army life in France and requests for supplies. On 5 December 1915 he described his billets, the bathing arrangements, the training the weather (inevitably) and the supply of plum puddings along with a request for further supplies to be sent after Christmas.[96] At the end of the war on 22 November 1918 talk of training had been replaced by a description of the classes, for the men planned for the men to relieve the boredom. As ever, there were requests for supplies; in this case for fresh clothes as he felt what he had was not suitable for peace time soldiering.[97] The description of the routine and requests for supplies were a way of escaping from the realities of the war. James Thursby Roberts, 1910 to 1915, also described trench life and kept in a sense of reality by writing about his passion for horse racing.[98] This was the nature of many letters from OUs to home and higher matters were only touched on from time to time. In their letters there is little to suggest they were influenced by the classics and their focus on heroes and their deeds. Even among those gifted at the classics (and bound for Oxbridge) there is little evidence in their letters they were influenced by them.

Roland Leighton, Edward Brittain and Victor Richardson had planned to go to Oxbridge after they left Uppingham in July 1914. Leighton at the July 1914 speech day had won a number of prizes given for the classics. He was a prodigy and very gifted at the classics but within his wartime letters and those of his two friends there is no real evidence that they were influenced by the classics in general or the more heroic scripts it is alleged they would have been taught.[99] There are the love letters between Vera Brittain and Roland Leighton; the letters of Leighton, Edward Brittain and Richardson cover topics such as the conditions in the trenches and their billets, the loss of friends, relationships with their commanding officers and reminisce of their time at Uppingham. If they were imbued with a militaristic spirit acquired at Uppingham it is extremely well disguised. There is little talk of the Germans in terms of a hatred for them but inevitably mention of attacks by them. When there is talk of poetry between Vera and Roland it is the romantic patriotism of Rupert Brooke and not that of disillusioned public schoolboys.

---

96   Somme Association (SA): Frank Thornely Letters: Letter to Mother 5 December 1915.
97   SA: Thornely Letters: Letter to Mother 22 November 1915.
98   Private Collection, James Thursby Roberts Letters.
99   See Bishop, A., and Bostridge M., (eds.) *Letters from a Lost Generation: First World War Letters of Vera Brittain and Four Friends: Roland Leighton, Edward Brittain, Victor Richardson, Geoffrey Thurlow*, (Paperback edition, London: Abacus, 1998).

The mood in Britain at the start of the war was that to do nothing would lead to German domination of Europe and that would be a disaster. It was not an obsession but a strong belief that was articulated in letters from serving OUs from time to time. Victor Richardson in a letter to Edward on 18 May 1916 spoke of the Allies being God's means to protect Christian values.[100] This reflected a belief that Germany was an evil force which needed to be defeated to preserve a civilised way of life. It was a view that was shared by many OUs; Christopher Wakefield Selwyn, the son of McKenzie's predecessor Edward Selwyn who had been at the school from 1905 to 1907 and was killed in action in May 1915, reflected this point of view in his letters. On 17 March 1915 he wrote of German behaviour towards the woman on whose farm he was billeted. She had since the start of the war had billeted on her Germans, French, Belgians, Indians, Canadians and English. She had spoken of the gentleness of the Indians contrasting it with the brutality of the Germans who had arrived with wounded men and demanded at gunpoint coffee for them. Selwyn spoke of her bravery describing how at the same time she had been hiding a wounded French soldier in the loft knowing that if caught she would have been shot. He was in no doubt about German brutality saying: 'The deeds these brutes committed in the villages are unspeakable and unwritable, and I fear these outrages by German troops are not the exception but the rule.'[101] He was in no doubt Germany must be defeated; it was the only reason Britain was fighting and in his view Germany must be 'humiliated' and, at worst, cease to be a great power. Otherwise, he believed a future generation would find itself fighting Germany again. Yet, he did not believe he hated the Germans; to him the British were God's instruments in dealing with this problem and as God could not hate he did not believe hate did not enter into his fighting the Germans. Like Richardson he strongly believed that he was fighting to protect Christian values.[102] It was part of the chivalric ideal that 'civilisation' must be protected.[103]

Many OUs shared this belief; Hugh Peachey spoke of Germany being a nation without honour who were lying to conquer the whole world. Reflecting the belief that he was fighting for Christian values he quoted from the bible saying it did not profit to gain the whole world if you lost your soul. The Germans, he believed, would be ostracised by the world for a whole generation.[104] It is mistaken to think that Peachey and others were unquestioning about the way the war was being conducted. The school's educational ethos was designed to produce boys with independence, inquisitiveness and self-confidence who, as a result, were equipped to take leadership roles. OUs were prepared to challenge and disagree where they thought something was wrong. Peachey strongly and contemptuously dismissed the armchair critics at home remarking that they should go to the front line before passing judgement.[105] Nor did 'one nation' mean everything was harmonious within the army; a regular complaint from Peachey was about the attitude of regular army officers towards temporary officers. As the war went on he became more

---

100 Bishop and Bostridge (eds.) *Letters from a Lost Generation*, pp. 256-258.
101 Lincolnshire Archive: Letters from Christopher Wakefield Selwyn, p. 24.
102 Lincolnshire Archive: Letters from Christopher Wakefield Selwyn, p. 36.
103 Alisa Miller, Modern War and Aesthetic Mobilisation: Looking at Europe in 1914, *British Journal of Military History*, 2: 2 pp. 12-41 p. 40.
104 LMA: F/PEY283: Letter to Father 23 September 1915.
105 LMA: F/PEY321: Letter to Father 10 January 1917.

and more trenchant in his view that it was the temporary officers who did all the hard work while regular army offers, and staff officers in particular, took all the credit.[106]

The strength of his exasperation demonstrates Peachey considered how important it was to win the war. As a stockbroker he had extensive experience of running a business and seeing things being done, in what he considered was the wrong way, would have been frustrating. The complaints about regular army officers came in the later stages of the war but between 1914 and 1918 his letters are full of observations about what he thought was being done wrong. Another of his frustrations was the way training was conducted. When remarking about how younger men had an advantage in passing officer exams he had remarked on the shortcomings of this. In particular, he found it ridiculous that a man who had served in the Boer War and had 1,800 men under him should struggle to pass exams. Perceptively, in August 1916, he touched one of the major problems the army had during the Battle of the Somme; speaking of new recruits and conscripts having no training and stating it was a disaster to use these men in an attack.[107]

Selwyn, who was 17 years younger than Peachey, was equally critical, at times. Before the war he had spent nearly seven years mainly working as a locomotive engineer before a brief spell as a lay missionary in Canada.[108] He had gained a commission as a temporary officer for the duration of the war but with a background in solving problems it is not surprising that he criticised the way the war was being conducted. On 1 April 1915 he commented that the German lines were so thinly held that were it not for a shortage of ammunition for the guns they could be breached. The demands of the Gallipoli campaign meant that it would be a few months before the situation would be rectified. It was an overoptimistic point of view; the British army was far from ready and it would not be until 1918 that this was the case but there was some truth in his views when he said: 'How galling it is to feel that we are waging war out here with one hand tied behind our back!'[109]

In Gallipoli Reginald Arthur Savory, 1908 to 1910, a regular officer in the Indian Army was even more critical about the performance of the army. Of the attack on Gully Ravine on 4 June 1915 he was bitterly critical of an assault undertaken without the commanding ground being taken. It seemed to him that one of the main tactics learned in frontier warfare had been ignored and dismissed as useless by the high command.[110] War was to be taken seriously and like Peachey he became exasperated with the way it was regarded in Britain. In a letter to his mother he was contemptuous about a story in the *Daily Graphic* which cast the Sikhs as using knives as their main weapons against snipers. The story may have been graphic in its description but it was complete rubbish.[111] For Savory it was disrespectful towards his men. War was a serious matter and death was always near as Savory himself knew.

---

106 LMA: F/PEY321: Letter to Father 10 January 1917, LMA: F/PEY344: Letter to Sybil 3 January 1918, LMA: F/PEY345: Letter to Sybil 2 February 1918 and F/PEY346: Letter to Father 20 February 1918.
107 LMA: F/PEY307: Letter to Father 15 August 1916.
108 Rutland Remembers Christopher Wakefield Selwyn <http://www.rutlandremembers.org/fallen/692/selwyn-second-lieutenant-christopher-wakefield> (Accessed 4 March 2016).
109 Lincolnshire Archive: Letters from Christopher Wakefield Selwyn, p. 31.
110 Peter Stanley, *Die in Battle Do Not Despair: The Indians on Gallipoli, 1915* (Solihull: Helion, 2015), p. 137.
111 Stanley, *Die in Battle Do Not Despair*, p. 258.

OUs were only too aware of the danger of death and those on the front line would be cautious about how they addressed this risk in their letters home. John Sinclair Martin, 1910 to 1914, worried about how much he should tell his parents about the war. In a letter dated 13 April 1915 he sought advice about whether it was better to shield them from the realities or to tell them everything.[112] By his last letter home on 7 May 1915 he appeared to have decided to be completely open. Writing just before taking part in the Battle of Aubers Ridge he described the wire work he had been undertaking in preparation for the battle before turning to the brutal reality of the forthcoming battle:

> It is altogether a desperate business, but everyone is very calm about it. Inwardly we are all dreading it, outwardly we joke about it. In many ways I feel indifferent about what happens to me, at other times I do not. It is often a frightening thought. However I have a sort of feeling I shall get through it somehow, and it will be a great thing to have taken part in it. If I do not get through it will be equally great. The only thing I am really afraid of is that I shall get the Company messed up. Commanding a Company in a thing like this is a bit thick but there is no one else to do it. I only pray I shall do it all right. If we succeed in breaking through it will be worth everything.
>
> I know this letter will be bound to make you worry but I thought it better to write now that I know it is coming. I put it off as long as possible. I also know it would be no good minimising the dangers, as you know them as well as I do from the last one. We can only pray that I shall get through it all right and get home again. If I do not, it cannot be helped. It will be a great thing to have taken part in it and I shall try not to disgrace the family.[113]

Two days later Martin was killed in action aged 19. His letter reflected the strong sense of duty of many public school boys. The needs of the nation were greater than those of the individual and the emphasis was on commitment, endurance and sacrifice.[114]

Death

Of those who served 463 (20 percent of the 2,343 who served) lost their lives during the war. Tables 9, 10 and 11 provide some analysis of the nature of these deaths. The figures in them are stark and require further interpretation and explanation. Those who were aged between 20 and 29 suffered disproportionately compared with other groups. Some of the reasons are obvious; of those under 20 at the start of the war many would not have served for the whole of the conflict and in the case of the 284 who were 16 or under in 1914 would have served for two years or less. To put it crudely, the under twenties enjoyed a statistically lower chance of being killed. Almost all of those in the groups who were aged between 20 and 39 would have been eligible to serve for the whole war. Those who were 40 or older included those who retired part of the way through the war as well as others who served away from the front line. Bruty, who was 44 when war came, spent the entire war at home and Peachey, who was also 44 and ended the war as a Major, spent from 1915 in France but was never on the front line and although he had a few

---

112 USA:, J S Martin to Majorie 13 April 1915.
113 USA: Letter from J S Martin to Family 7 May 1915.
114 Moore-Bick, *Playing the Game* (Solihull: Helion 2011) p. 240.

close encounters with shells and air raids did not lead a particularly dangerous existence. It was those who were junior officers who were in the most vulnerable position. They were the officers who led their men in combat, flew planes and as such were often on 'the sharp end' of fighting. Seventy-nine percent of those who fell into the 20 to 29 group were junior officers; of those 40 and over only 35 percent were junior officers making their lives considerably safer.

The vast majority of OUs who went to war were junior officers and part of the citizen army. They were volunteers and many of them had no background in the army and were less likely to hold positions away from the front line. The planning and execution of the war was more likely to be carried out by professional army officers. Of those in the over 40 category many more held higher rank and had served in the regular army before the war.

Table 9 Analysis of Deaths by Age

Age at the Start of the War	Number Dead	% of Total Dead	Total Served as a %
Under 20	42	9.07	25.99
20 to 29	265	57.24	40.21
30 to 39	117	25.27	22.58
40 and over	39	8.42	11.22
Total	463	100.00	100.00
Total dead as a % of those who served			19.76

Table 10 Analysis of Deaths by Rank

Rank	Number Dead	% of Total Dead	Total Served as a %
Major & Above	49	10.58	17.07
Junior Officers	377	81.43	72.09
Ranks	31	6.70	4.87
Other	6	1.30	5.98
Total	463	100.00	100.00

Table 11 Analysis of Deaths by Year of War

Year	Number Dead	% of Total Dead
1914	30	6.48
1915	94	20.30
1916	123	26.57
1917	119	25.70
1918 to 1921	97	20.95
Total	463	100.00

The timing of the deaths of OUs reflected the fact that Uppingham was not a traditional army school. For the traditional army schools the majority of deaths came earlier in the war than Uppingham. Eton suffered 19 percent of its deaths by the end of 1914 and by the end of February

1916 it had already suffered about half of its losses.[115] Haileybury, another school the army drew heavily on, had suffered 34 percent of its losses by the end of 1915. In contrast Uppingham, not a traditional provider of officers, had suffered nearly 27 percent of its losses by the end of 1915. At Uppingham the point at which over half its losses had been suffered was on 5 October 1916, seven months after Eton. Uppingham and Eton had similar levels of losses during the war (both losing about 20 percent of the old boys who served). The losses for Uppingham were skewed towards the second half of the war because many of the OUs had started enlisting in August 1914. OUs, as we have seen, were quick to enlist but many of them were part of the citizen New Army formed by Kitchener which did not become significantly involved in fighting until 1916. In contrast, the regular army suffered catastrophic losses in 1914 combatting the initial German assault. The Battle of the Somme between 1 July 1916 and 18 November 1916 was the first significant action of the New Army and it was while leading this army that the heaviest losses of OUs took place. Haig had been worried about the lack of training for and the inexperience of the New Armies and had tried to postpone the start of the battle. However, the French under dreadful pressure at Verdun were insistent on 1 July 1916 as the start date and that the assault should take place with less French soldiers than previously planned.[116] The demands of the Franco-British relationship made heavy losses inevitable. Between the start and end of the battle 85 OUs died which was just over 18 percent of the total OU deaths. While not all these deaths took place on the Somme many of them did and the losses were heavy. From the end of the Somme to the end of the year only another four OUs died. The 85 who died during the period of the Somme was 69 percent of OU deaths for the whole of 1916. In 1917 when the Battles of Arras and Third Ypres (popularly known as Passchendaele) were fought the losses were almost as high as those of 1916. By this time little was left of the Regular Army of 1914 and it was Britain's citizen army which was bearing the brunt of the losses. A further 80 OUs lost their lives in 1918 before the armistice on 11th November 1918.

That OUs were officers in a citizen army, is demonstrated when we examine the records for the 112 boys who entered the school in the academic year 1908 to 1909. This was the year that suffered most heavily with 31 (28 percent of the entrants and 30 percent of those who fought) of these boys losing their lives. Of the boys who entered the school that year 103 (92 percent) undertook some sort of military service. Ninety-eight (95 percent) were officers of which 94 (91 percent were junior officers but only 13 (12 percent) were regular army officers. Only two of those who died were regular army officers; both of these men were killed in late 1914 as the British Army fought to halt the German advance in Belgium and Northern France. The majority of the others who died were killed in 1916 (nine) and 1917 (13). The men who served from the year 1908 to 1909 are in many ways representative of the predominantly citizen army officers Uppingham provided.

The two OUs who had the unfortunate distinction of dying on 5 October 1916 and being the median point of OU deaths were Hugh Pollock Bunce and Francis Bedford Marsh. Both had been at the school between 1910 and 1914 and had left in July 1914 at the same time as Leighton, Brittain and Richardson. The manner of their deaths demonstrates the diverse ways that OUs lost their lives; not all deaths were as a result of action on the front line. Whereas

---

115 Gregory, *The Last Great War*, p. 124.
116 Brian Bond, *From Liddell Hart to Joan Littlewood: Studies in British Military History* (Solihull: Helion, 2015), p. 226.

Marsh died of wounds he suffered fighting on the Somme Bunce was killed in an accident. Yet as much as Marsh's death was a valiant death Bunce's was just as gallant. Richardson in a letter to Vera Brittain on 31 October 1916 described how Bunce had fallen on a bomb which was about to go off during practice to protect his men from the explosion. At Uppingham, Bunce had not been athletically gifted and had been the victim of teasing about this perceived shortcoming.[117] Despite not falling into the games playing category his actions reflected the qualities of honour, bravery, loyalty, courtesy, generosity, mercy and self-sacrifice; these were the qualities expected of a gentleman and officer. It reflected the school's philosophy which stressed a strong sense of duty, leadership skills and responsibility.

Not all of the deaths were in any way brave or heroic. Edward Molyneux Cohan was the first OU to lose his life on 5 August 1914. An officer in the Territorials he was at the annual training camp on Salisbury Plain when war was declared. As he returned to the station his horse took fright at a passing motor tractor and bolted catching its foot in a rabbit hole. It fell on Cohan who suffered a fractured skull and died in hospital a few days later. His brother Harry Molyneux Cohan is also on the Uppingham memorial and died of heart failure on 6 August 1919 while on active service in Sri Lanka.[118] Richard Godolphin Hume Chaloner was shot dead by a sentry on 3 April 1917.[119] Other men such as Basil Terah Hooley, who was awarded an MC for gallantry in leading a tank company, were victims of the flu pandemic which broke out in 1918.[120] A relatively peaceful death did not mean that a man had had a quiet war. Men killed at the front were vulnerable even when they were not fighting. Roland Leighton lost his life when he was shot by a sniper while repairing wire. Philip Aubrey Hill, 1888 to 1891, was killed by a sniper at Arras just after his regiment had been withdrawn from the front line. His servant was killed by a shell as he went to his aid.[121] Deaths often came about as a result of the strength of the relationship between the officers and the men. Alfred Percy Brewis, joined and left the school at the same time as Leighton and Brittain and like them had been planning to go to Oxford. He left his dugout during shelling to check none of his men had been injured and was killed by a shell.[122]

Officers, Paternalism and Welfare

The nature of the death of Brewis is representative of the attitude of officers and the bond they often formed with their men. To be an officer and a gentleman laid stress on the qualities of honour, bravery, loyalty, courtesy, generosity, mercy and self-sacrifice.[123] These were qualities which inspired loyalty and self-sacrifice in their men. In the attack at Gallipoli on Gully Ravine, Savory passed out after being hit in the head by a bayonet. The Turks mistakenly believed he

---

117 Bishop and Bostridge (eds.) *Letters from a Lost Generation*, p. 285.
118 Merseyside Roll of Honour Edward Molyneux Cohan <http://www.merseysiderollofhonour.co.uk/get2.php?cwgc=374842> (accessed 9 March 2016).
119 The North-East at War <http://www.thenortheastatwar.co.uk/in_your_town/redcar/parochial-church-uses-10k-grant-to-remember-war-heroes> (accessed 9 March 2016).
120 Derbyshire War Memorials Basil Terah Hooley <http://derbyshirewarmemorials.wikispaces.com/BASIL+T.+HOOLEY.+M.C.> (accessed 9 March 2016).
121 Richard Hill (2016) 'Philip Aubrey Hill', Letter (8 February 2016).
122 North East war Memorials Project Brewis T/Capt A P 1917 <http://www.newmp.org.uk/article.php?categoryid=99&articleid=1421&displayorder=19> (accessed 9 March 2016).
123 Sheffield, 'Officer – Man Relations' p. 129.

was dead (his family were initially notified he was dead) but he was eventually able to stagger back to his own lines where one of the men from his battalion, the 14th Sikhs, who was a wrestler picked him up and carried him under fire to a dressing station.[124] Savory was vigorous in sticking up for the rights of his men; this included complaining about the poor postal arrangements for his men.[125] He kept in touch with Ude Singh, the soldier who had rescued him for the rest of his life as well as other men who had served under him. After Singh died he continued to keep in touch with his son. When Savory died in 1980 on the same day his wife sent Singh's son a telegram with the news.[126] The interests of the Sikhs remained of great interest to him to the end of his life. In 1976 he supported a campaign to exempt Sikhs from wearing motor cycle helmets saying that they were not required to wear headgear in war and it would be 'ignoble' to force them to wear helmets in peace time.[127]

Thornely also maintained relations with men who served under him. For the rest of his life he kept in touch with Sergeant Calvert who had served with him on the Somme.[128] His letters regularly requested items he could give to his men such as cigarettes.[129] It was a duty of care exercised by many OU officers. Howe in the hours before the attack on the Somme realised that his men's rum ration was missing and went in search of it. His success in tracking down the missing supplies made him very popular with his men![130] Men often kept in touch with the widows of officers in the years after the war. Burnaby's papers include a letter from his batman, Clinch, who wrote to Burnaby's widow describing a visit to his grave and speaking of him as a father figure.[131] Men would often express their gratitude directly to the officer's family for supplies sent out. A former servant of Lee, Private J Truman, wrote to Lee's wife to thank her for a parcel.[132] It's impossible to provide to carry out a scientific assessment of the relationship between OU officers and their men but these examples do suggest a strong paternalistic one. This paternalistic relationship was based on chivalric qualities required of officers of officers in their care for their men such as that of self-sacrifice. Even when men reciprocated it was not an equal relationship and there was always distance between officers and their men. Selwyn spoke of his isolated position as an officer describing being in charge of 80 men billeted at a barn two miles away from a village saying it was 'a curiously lonely position for an officer; he has nobody to talk to as an equal; and everybody treats him as a lord of creation!'[133]

The OU officer was in a position where he was apart from his men. As strong as the mutual bonds of solidarity were it was the obligation of the officer to care for his men. Some of it would have better in this role than others but nearly all would have seen themselves as bound to live up to the standards of honour, bravery, loyalty, courtesy, generosity, mercy and self-sacrifice. Thus it

124 Great War London R A Savory: death reports exaggerated https://greatwarlondon.wordpress.com/tag/reginald-savory/ (accessed 9 March 2016).
125 Stanley, *Die in Battle Do Not Despair*, p. 186.
126 Stanley, *Die in Battle Do Not Despair*, p. 298.
127 Hansard Motor-Cycle Crash-Helmets (Religious Exemption Bill) <http://hansard.millbanksystems.com/lords/1976/oct/04/motor-cycle-crash-helmets-religious> (accessed 9 March 2016).
128 Discussion with Nick Thornely, 24th February 2016.
129 Somme Association, Frank Thornely Letters, Letter to Mother 5 December 1915.
130 Middlebrook, *The First Day on the Somme*, p. 114.
131 LHCMA: Burnaby Papers.
132 IWM: Lee Papers.
133 Lincolnshire Archive: Letters from Christopher Wakefield Selwyn, p. 12.

was not an equal position between the officer and his men even when strong bonds were formed between them. At the heart of the relationship was the idea that it was a gentlemen's duty to care for those under him.

Conclusion

In the years before the war the vast majority of OUs who fought led a civilian life. No more than one fifth of OUs served in the Territorials or Special Reserve but even then they were still, basically civilians. Many but not all OUs had experience of serving in the OTC or its predecessor, the Rifle Corps, but this was not a group of men who actively sought war. Many were concerned about the threat of Germany and some like Carmalt Jones and Lee joined the Territorials because of this. The majority however had no significant military experience outside the school before the war started. When war came they believed it was their duty to serve their country and empire against the threat to it. For most of them there was not a militaristic desire to go to war but a strong belief that Germany must be stood up to. For them it was the right thing to seek a commission; in the early months of the war there was a backlog while applications were processed but they still volunteered. This was a reflection of the school's philosophy which stressed a strong sense of duty, leadership skills and taking responsibility. Thring's educational philosophy promoted independence, inquisitiveness and self-confidence in boys; this was attractive to parents for whom a career in the army was not first choice but they were also the skills required for leadership in the armed forces. The rapid expansion of the army meant that there was a greatly increased need for officers. The expansion also meant that there was an increased demand for a variety of different skills needed for a modern army. These included legal skills in the management of discipline, medical skills in the treatment of men, technical skills to run the railways and business skills in areas such as logistics. The Army could no longer rely on the schools it had predominantly relied on to supply its officers. The training provided by the OTC provided the basic skills to rapidly give commissions to many young OUs but the wider age range of OUs who volunteered suggests there were many more that had a background attractive to the army. In particular, their paternalism was an important factor. As many in the country took up arms to fight Germany so too did many OUs. Britain became a 'nation in arms' between 1914 and 1918 with all parts of the country involved; at the same time Uppingham turned into a school in arms. The nature of being a nation in arms was that all parts of the British people became involved in the war. It was not just on the front line but also on the home front that Uppingham went to war.

6

Uppingham and the Home Front

The last chapter analysed the nature of the school's military contribution in the war. The Great War was the first time however that Britain had been engaged in total war and this required the country's resources to be dedicated to the war effort. It was no longer a question of the army and navy being sent overseas to fight: the implications of war on an industrial scale were that the whole country needed to be involved. Production needed to be geared towards producing munitions and the skills of the population employed to the best effect. Involving the whole country meant sacrifice by everyone and this required the government to make the case for fighting the war and showing it would be won. The role of the school and its OUs on the home front has received relatively little attention. This is partly because there is relatively little material available but it is possible to gain idea of this involvement and better understand it from the limited sources available. In the early days of the war the emphasis was on the military side and there was little comprehension that to be a school in arms also required a substantial effort on the home front. As the war progressed this changed and the school and OUs were used in a more effective way. The school was slower than others in taking these developments forward but it is not surprising when the Government was so poorly prepared for total war.

At one level Britain's entry into the war in 1914 was a well-run and efficient exercise. In the years leading up to 1914 the 'War Book' had been prepared by the Government. This laid down the administrative arrangements which covered the actions to be taken by each government department in the event of an emergency. It was a highly detailed document with a chapter for each department detailing the actions it needed to take as well as indicating related actions being taken by other departments.[1] The most obvious demonstration of the success of the 'War Book' is the way the railways were taken over so that the regular army could be rapidly mobilised and sent to France. Military Planners had developed a plan for the troops to be sent to Southampton to be embarked. The detailed timetable allowed for troop trains to arrive at the port every 12 minutes for 16 hours each day. By 31 August 1914 670 trains had carried nearly 120,000 soldiers to the port. This was not something the Germans had been expecting.[2] The 'War Book' was an administrative triumph which helped to stop the Germans from rapidly

---

1 David French, *British Economic and Strategic Planning 1905-1915* (London: George, Allen and Unwin, 1982) p. 82.
2 Wolmar, *Engines of War*, p. 155.

knocking the French out of the war but as David French has pointed out an administrative plan was not enough. The highly detailed plan in the 'War Book' ended a few days into the war. Beyond that it made no attempt to put in place plans for how the civilian and armed forces war effort worked in tandem. More seriously it made no effort to address the strategic question as to how industry and manpower should be mobilised in the prosecution of the war. The British government as well other combatants in the war had believed that the war would be a short one.[3] It was believed that the 120,000 strong expeditionary force would be sufficient to assist the French and Russians to speedily win the war. The substantial part of increased military expenditure had gone into the navy to deal with any German threat to the Empire. The government's view was that Britain's main contribution would be to the war at sea which would include a blockade of Germany. Britain would support the war through its economic strength and providing financial and logistical support to its allies. To successfully do this it would not be necessary to raise a large army. When Lord Kitchener was appointed Secretary of State of War in August 1914 he rapidly disabused the cabinet of this belief. He argued that the war would last at least three years and he set about gaining parliament's approval to expand the army. On 6 August 1914 he gained parliamentary approval to expand the army by 500,000 men. Later that day set out his plans to the cabinet. The war could not be won solely at sea, he said, and therefore Britain must prepare to raise an army of millions which would be needed for some time.[4]

The consequences of this radical change to the cabinet's approach were far reaching. As was discussed in the last chapter the response of OUs from a wide range of ages was to enlist almost immediately. In the absence of conscription which was believed to be politically impractical there was no constraint on who could serve and who could not. Conscription is often thought of as being about compelling men to serve in the armed forces but is more concerned with the Government having the power to direct men towards where they would have the most beneficial effect on the war effort. The effect of the raising of the new armies was to deprive industry, commerce and agriculture of the resources they needed to maintain the economic strength necessary to support its allies. The new armies also required a whole range of goods and services such as munitions which Britain's domestic economy was not set up to supply.[5]

For Uppingham the dislocating effects were immediate; the October 1914 edition of the School Magazine reported that four teachers together with the OTC instructor had already departed on service. One of those who departed was of R P Shea, the CO of the OTC, to join the Leicesters on the outbreak of war. Another teacher was expected to receive his commission shortly.[6] The Bursar, Captain Constantine Bland, also departed on war service.[7] All of those men already held commissions in the Territorials and were an immediate source of men as reinforcements were urgently needed. Territorials were not obliged to serve overseas but by August 1915 in excess of 70 Territorial battalions had volunteered to serve overseas. By the end of December 1914 23 Territorial battalions had been sent to the Western Front while another

3   French, *British Economic and Strategic Planning*, pp. 82-83.
4   Peter Simkins, *Kitchener's Army: The Raising of the New Armies, 1914-1916* (Barnsley: Pen and Sword, 2007), p. 39.
5   French, *British Economic and Strategic Planning*, p. 127.
6   *USM*, October 1914, p. 203.
7   USA: Minutes of the Trustees 21 October 1914.

four had relieved army units overseas who were urgently needed at the front.⁸ The postings of teachers were reported in a matter of fact way with little comment. The magazine, however, reflected the national view that the war was about standing up for Belgium. In November 1914 it reported that Belgian refugees had arrived at Uppingham, one of whom provided a long account of his experiences after leaving Liège on 6th August until departure for Britain on 22nd September speaking gratefully of the reception received. Other changes would take place in time but initially they were solely of a military nature. The November 2014 School Magazine also reported the OTC was now meeting three times a week in response to the declaration of the war.⁹ Although the War Office had withdrawn the support of officers and instructors after war broke out the Army Council continued to direct the nature of the training it wished OTC units to carry out. The OTC had been designed to provide an integrated approach to training and this continued and was supplemented; over the Christmas holiday of 1914 several OTC cadets from the school spent Christmas with mobilised units. The March 1915 magazine reported a reorganisation of OTC meetings to twice a week with an entire afternoon made available for 'Field work' to provide a more efficient use of time. Its activities were mainly concerned with the development of training and concentrated on the lessons of trench warfare and equipping officers with the skills to instruct soldiers. Several members had also spent Christmas with mobilised units.¹⁰ Those involved with the OTC took their obligations seriously. R Sterndale Bennett, the Director of Music assumed command on the departure of Shea. His papers in the school archives include regular applications by him to attend training courses. He took his duties very seriously and the courses he attended indicate that the Army Council and War Office continued to co-ordinate the training of the OTC so it produced candidates for a commission.

The willingness of the Trustees to release teachers to serve in the war rapidly diminished as it became obvious the war would not be a short one. In March 1915 the Trustees agreed financial terms for Frank Street, Housemaster of Fircroft, until he received a commission but in June 1915 a decision was made not to allow any more masters to be released to serve.¹¹ The consequences for the school of the loss so many teachers were severe. In December 1915 McKenzie had retired as Headmaster on doctor's advice. The pressures on him as a result of the war having added to the health problems he already had. The replacements for teachers who had departed for war were not of a high quality and this led to disciplinary problems.¹² The pressures of war caused many headmasters a great deal of suffering and stress. Sanderson at Oundle never recovered from the effects of the war and died in 1922 while he was still in office. Grant at St Georges, Harpenden, keenly felt the losses at the school and was forced to take an extended break in Switzerland because of the strain the war had placed on his health.¹³ McKenzie was replaced by Reginald Herbert Owen who was only 28 when he was appointed.

The appointment of Owen was controversial; many asked why so young a man was not serving. He had been passed unfit to serve at the front because of a history of pneumonia and

8 Simkins, *Kitchener's Army*, pp. 45-46.
9 *USM*, November 1914, p. 243, pp. 258-262.
10 *USM*, March 1915, pp. 55-56.
11 USA: Minutes of the Trustees 3 March 1915 and 8 June 1915.
12 Matthews, *By God's Grace* p. 140.
13 Storrie, P., *"Here I am; Send me": The War Dead of St George's School 1914-1918* (Harpenden: St Georges School, 2004), p. 55.

had decided he would be more useful as Headmaster than as a training officer. Matthews says that there is no record of his illness on his service file but it must be remembered that many officer files from the War Office are known not to be complete. Some files can offer a great deal of interesting detail and others next to nothing. Owen chose not to speak about his illness and was labelled by many as a shirker with so many OUs serving at the front. His unpopularity appears to have been a feature of his headmastership and 65 years later OUs still spoke of him in highly critical terms. It was not only the OUs who considered him to be a shirker. He also attracted the contempt of members of staff including Jones, the former OTC commander, who was serving in France and the boys many of whom were expecting to serve on the front line with all its inherent dangers. Owen's reluctance to speak about his efforts to be passed fit were typical of the attitude of the time of 'keeping a stiff upper lip.' However, his single minded approach and his lack fear of unpopularity meant that combined with this strong sense of privacy meant that he made it easy for others to label him a shirker. The lack of official documents about his war service has meant that to this day his motives and reputation are questioned. Early on he asserted his authority by dismissing three athletic 'bloods' as Praeposters for misdemeanours.[14] Under Owen there would be no danger of the games cult prevalent under Selwyn returning to the school. Jessell, his biographer, argues his commitment to the war effort was shown when, before he had even arrived in December 1915, he agreed to release those masters who wished to serve with a place on the staff guaranteed at the end of the war.[15] Jessel is highly sympathetic towards Owen but there is plenty of evidence to suggest Owen was reluctant to release staff for war service. At the Trustees meeting of 1 March 1916 it was confirmed that no more teachers would be released to the armed forces. This was in the interests of efficiency and discipline and it was noted this was in accordance with the views of the Board of Education and the War Office. There is no evidence that Owen argued against this decision.[16] On 12 June 1917 he reported that J A Lumsden, Housemaster of Fircroft, had been called up but this was being appealed against with Owen's support.[17]

The war had also created restlessness within in the school with the boys' minds focussed on forthcoming military service.[18] Owen accelerated the process of moving the school from one where its war effort focussed on the OTC to one which embraced a wider range of activities essential for the war effort and made it a 'school in arms.' McKenzie had already initiated this by arranging that in future the school's carpentry school would be dedicated to the production of splints for the war effort.[19] Owen developed this approach in June 1916 when the Trustees agreed to purchase a more powerful engine for the Metal Workshop; this was required to support production for the war effort. At the same time he made his first offer to local farmers of boys to provide labour during term time afternoons.[20] Between 1916 and 1918 several farmers accepted this offer of as much labour as they required; up to 70 boys at a time were engaged in

---

14 Matthews, *By God's Grace*, pp. 140-145.
15 Penelope Jessel, *Owen of Uppingham* (London: A R Mowbray 1965) pp. 20-22.
16 USA: Minutes of the Trustees 1 March 1916.
17 USA: Minutes of the Trustees 12 June 1917.
18 Jessel, *Owen of Uppingham*, pp. 20-22.
19 USA: Minutes of the Trustees 26 October 1915.
20 'Farmers Offered School Students' Assistance', *Grantham Journal*, 3 June 1916, p. 2 and 'Labour for the Land. Uppingham School to the Rescue, *Grantham Journal*, 17 February 1917, p. 2.

this work. School Harvest Camps were held in 1917, when 50 boys were employed, and 1918, when the number involved rose to 150, all remuneration being given to War Funds. From the second half of 1916 all work undertaken in the Metal Workshop was war-related making items such as plunger bolts while splints, bed tables and lockers for hospitals were made in the woodwork shop.[21] During the war production included 7,500 shell bases and over 2,600 dies and punches for .303 cartridge cases.[22]

That Uppingham initially was disproportionately committed to the military effort can be seen by a comparison. Oundle School, under the leadership of Sanderson, developed a strong reputation through a strong emphasis on science and engineering in the school's curriculum. From January 1915 the school's workshops had been recognised by the Munitions Board and following the summer of 1915 there was a rapid expansion in the range of machinery in Oundle's workshops. The significance can be seen in its wartime production figures of 13,376 torpedo components, 32,008 tools for Woolwich Arsenal, 1,393 horseshoes for the Munitions Board and a large number of bed screens for local hospitals.[23] Uppingham was 18 months behind Oundle in making a serious effort to support the war effort and never made the same level of investment. Its strength was in preparing its boys for positions of leadership and business but it was not a specialist school in the way that Oundle was. Belatedly, it came to understand that the war effort was not just a military one. Something the government was equally slow in realising.

As the war progressed there was a change of emphasis in the way the School Magazine reported Uppingham's contributions especially in comparison with other public schools. It was a slow process but by 1917 an increasing emphasis was being placed on the support for the local farmers as well as events such as the Harvest Camp held during the summer holidays. It has been suggested that the school was becoming tired of the war and the magazine increasingly reported on sporting activity. Although the magazine became shorter as the war went on, because of paper rationing, there does not appear to have been increased coverage of sport. Contributions from OUs who were fighting continued; some were more enthusiastic than others but in general they were not especially militaristic in tone. Brief summaries of the activity of OUs appeared including an ever increasing list of those who had died. Eventually, the list became so long and paper rationing tighter that it became necessary to only publish the names of those who had died since the last edition. When compared with other schools Uppingham did not attempt to over romanticise the loss of its old boys. No obituaries were published in the magazine during the war. In contrast, many other schools published fulsome obituaries of old boys who had been killed. At St Georges the first death of an old boy, Bertram Monk, led to a tribute from Grant in the March 1915 School Magazine together with a reprinting of the letters his father had received from his fellow officers.[24] The death of Geoffrey Frangcon-Davies was reported in the July 1915 edition with the same reprinting of letters and other tributes including a poem by Grant built around theme of Christian sacrifice. Frangcon-Davies having done his best for the school reflected in the lines: "God bless the dear old school" he wrote "and if I chance to

---

21 Uppingham School Archives.
22 USM, April 1919, p. 94.
23 Richard John Palmer, 'The life of F W Sanderson (1857-1922)' with special reference to his work and influence at Oundle School (1892-1922) (Hull, 1981) pp. 220-225.
24 *St Georges School Magazine* (SGSM), March 1915, pp. 3-4 and 24-25.

fall, /A Georgian will have done his best, as Georgians will know."²⁵ Compared to Uppingham St Georges was a small school and it could be argued had more room in its magazine for such tributes but many larger and older schools published similar tributes in their magazines.

It appears at Uppingham there was a policy decision not to provide detailed news of OUs in the war in the way other schools did. Just after Roland Leighton died Edward Brittain wrote to Vera saying Victor Richardson thought it would be a good idea not to include anything about him in the School Magazine.²⁶ Given that there were no tributes to any old boy killed in the magazine this was probably a tactful way of ensuring that Vera was not upset by there not being one. This was a change from the Boer War when news of OUs and C H Jones was far more jingoistic in tone and the reporting of the death of OUs far more romanticised. By the time of the Great War an attitude of keeping a stiff upper lip prevailed. That is not to say the school did not care. Teachers remained, as they do today, interested in and took pride in the progress of their former pupils. A master, W J Constable, wrote to Lee on 2nd January 1916 congratulating him on his promotion to Major and also appealing for help in obtaining a copy of the Army Lists as the school was finding it impossible to get reliable news of OUs. He noted 'More than 100 O.U.s have fallen in this war – and some of the very best.'²⁷ Constable's attitude was not one which glorified war and more one of thanks and regret at the sacrifice.

The school's losses may not have been commented on in the School Magazine they were recognised in the school's daily life. Every day after evening prayers the Housemaster would read out the names of the old boys who had been killed. Eric Mott, 1916 to 1920, remembered that every day at 11 a.m. the school bell tolled and was followed by a two minute silence.²⁸ Marie Leighton, in a highly emotional book she wrote after her son's death, claimed that the bell tolled each day once for each old boy who had died.²⁹ It seems unlikely that there were two separate occasions the bells were rung but the sense of loss within the school could be overwhelming. Mott recounts that his class Master's son, Spencer Mansell-Carey, had been killed in February 1916. Every day when the bell tolled the teacher would cover his head in his hands and weep.³⁰

In addition to the disciplinary problems previously mentioned other changes affected school life. John P Graham, the OU and a teacher at the school for over 40 years, wrote of the gradual change to the school and its life. Food rationing and other necessary economies made for a more austere life. Travelling to other schools for matches became a thing of the past; although the School Magazine shows these were substituted for with matches against armed forces teams. This together with the increased emphasis on the OTC and other war work pushed games into the background. The OTC became virtually compulsory under Owen although, in theory it remained voluntary, a great deal of pressure was applied on boys to join.³¹ Adrian Bell wrote of OTC parades being held three days a week and Field Days with Rugby and Oundle becoming virtual hand to hand combat, rather than a military training exercise, against the boys from the

25 SGSM, July 1915, pp. 57-59.
26 Bishop and Bostridge (eds) *Letters from a Lost Generation*, p. 208.
27 Lee Papers, IWM.
28 Mott (2015), 'OUs in WW1'. E-mail (7 January 2015).
29 Marie Leighton, *Boy of My Heart* (London: Hodder and Stoughton, 1916) p. 249.
30 Mott (2015), 'OUs in WW1'. E-mail (7 January 2015).
31 Adrian Bell, *My Own Master* (London: Country Book Club, 1962) p. 72.

other schools.³² It's possible this is an exaggeration on Bell's part but it does demonstrate the problems of discipline faced within the school.

The military conflict was felt more directly within the school as well. Air raids by Zeppelins on Midland towns meant that the restrictions of a blackout came into effect.³³ It is possibly an apocryphal story but it is said that during one Zeppelin raid a housemaster began his evening prayers with "Darken our lightness, we beseech Thee"! Of life at Uppingham and the difficulties caused by the war there is little mention in the School Magazine during the war and in the years which followed. It was not the way of the school either to glorify the dead or make reference to the difficulties which war brought to school life. The school's philosophy stressed a strong sense of duty, leadership skills and taking responsibility. In the light of this it is perhaps not surprising that the School Magazine did not linger on the hardships of war.

This is reflected in the attitude of many OUs to conscription. In 1904 a debate at the school had voted against conscription. Throughout 1915 the effects of Britain's failure to prepare for the economic consequences of war were becoming increasingly apparent. The supply of munitions had become a political issue in May 1915 when the shortage of shells at the Battle of Neuve Chappelle became public knowledge. Kitchener who was responsible for munitions came under attack from newspapers such as *The Times* and the *Daily Mail*. One problem had been munitions workers volunteering for military service with their loss to the industry having a detrimental effect on shell production. The Munitions Act of August 1915 started to deal with the shell shortage problem by only allowing munitions workers to enlist with the permission of their employers. The Act was part of a series of reforms leading up to conscription and was a consequence of the government's piecemeal approach to the economic mobilisation. A voluntary system had led not only to problems with munition production; during the summer of 1915 it was becoming increasingly obvious that there was a finite limit to the number of men available if industry was to operate efficiently.³⁴ In Parliament in May 1915 Sir Ivor Herbert had called for a system to be set so that the supply of men could be regulated. He proposed a census of the country's male population to establish the skills of each male.³⁵ In July 1915 the National Registration Act was passed into law which set up the census proposed but was presented as a measure to understand manpower resources in the country rather than as a tool to enable conscription. The Derby scheme which commenced in October 1915 was the final attempt by the Government to make volunteering work. All men on the National Register were asked to sign up or attest that they would serve if summoned. Many men failed to attest; of bachelors who would be first to be called up nearly half had failed to do so. Conscription was now unavoidable and in January 1916 the Military Service Act came into effect.³⁶

Although inevitable the end of the British tradition of volunteering for military service was met with disapproval from OUs. Edward Brittain believed that volunteering led to a superior morale to that in other armies. Conscription he believed would destroy that.³⁷ Other OUs found

---

32 Bell, *My Own Master*, p. 71.
33 John P Graham, *Forty Years of Uppingham Memories and Sketches* (London: Macmillan, 1932) pp. 132-136.
34 Simkins, *Kitchener's Army*, pp. 126-128.
35 Simkins, *Kitchener's Army*, p. 143.
36 Simkins, *Kitchener's Army*, pp. 15-157.
37 Bishop and Bostridge (eds) *Letters from a Lost Generation*, p. 115.

the idea of conscription to be offensive. Norman MacDonald, 1908 to 1913 wrote to express disappointment that his work as a medical student in Cambridge was not properly recognised. Many Cambridge medical students, he wrote, were working at the First Eastern General Hospital having been asked to stay at home by Lord Kitchener. In this role they wore an officer's uniform 'without rank and without pay.' In his view, conscription was an insult to his sense of duty:

> It may surprise you to learn that I am in the Navy. A large number of Medical Students have joined the Senior service, because they are annoyed (disgusted would be a better word) at receiving conscription papers, after work at the direction of the War Office – work for which they benefit only slightly, and for which they receive no pay and no recognition. How many will return to the Army when qualified? Not many; I, for one, will not.[38]

He had also complained that the school did not recognise the efforts of those who were not in the armed forces. However, as previously noted, the school was reliant on announcements in *The Times* to keep up to date on news of OUs and their involvement in the war. It was mainly dependent on OUs writing in with their news or reports about eminent OUs in the national press. Thus in July 1916 it quoted a report from the *Daily Graphic* that Ernest Newton, 1870 to 1872, who was President of RIBA had been appointed an adviser to the Ministry of Munitions.[39]

This information was not recorded in the *School Roll* and in general it is noticeable that far less information is available about the home front activity of OUs. It is possible to gain a hint of what service was rendered by OUs through their contributions to the School Magazine. Professional skills were often used to support the war effort. Thomas Eccles, 1879 to 1884, an architect, provided an account of his role in the building of a 260 bed mobile hospital. This had been funded by 'merchants' from Liverpool and Eccles had been appointed as architect. In his account he provides a detailed account of the process of erecting the hospital and the involvement of other OUs.[40] A significant proportion of the information about OU service outside the armed forces relates to their work with the Red Cross. This is not surprising as news about these men is likely to have been provided by other OUs they met while serving at the front. As with military service it was the way of OUs to play down their role. Eccles is modest about his own role and describes it as a 'privilege' and his entry in the *School Roll* for the war simply states 'Served with Brit. Red Cross in France 1915-18.'

As with military service OUs such as Eccles were keen to use their professional and business skills in the best way possible. Archibald Henderson, 1902 to 1905, who was a Glasgow shipowner, spent the war at the Admiralty. He was 26 when the war started and in theory would have been liable for conscription from 1916 onwards. The information about why he was not conscripted into the armed forces is sketchy but it is likely that his skills and expertise were better employed away from the front. One OU found himself withdrawn from the front because of his expertise. Lionel Brook Holliday, 1894 to 1898, served with the West Riding Regiment until 1915 when he was recalled. The family firm, Read Holliday and Sons, originally a dye manufacturer had moved into the production of picric acid during the Boer War. Picric acid was used in

38 *USM*, November 1916, pp. 253-254.
39 *USM*, July 1916, p. 125.
40 *USM*, December 1915, pp. 278-282.

the manufacture of explosives and when the Great War started the firm moved away from its core business of dye manufacturing back to the production of explosives. Germany had dominated European chemical industry in the years before the war and the British chemical industry was relatively undeveloped. The growing concern about munitions production in 1915 made the recall of Holliday inevitable. In a relatively undeveloped industry he was one of the few men in Britain with knowledge of the production of picric acid. He was placed in charge of a government plant producing picric acid which by the end of 1915 was producing 100 tonnes a week.[41]

Others with a business background found themselves serving on the home front when, no longer able to serve on the front line, their expertise was employed elsewhere. Oliver Lyle, 1905 to 1907, of the family which owned sugar company Tate and Lyle was badly wounded at Loos on 25 September 1915 while serving as a Captain with the 11th Highland Light Infantry. The regiment's Chronicle noted that he was one of the few officers to survive action.[42] As a result of his wounds he was released from military service to work in the Inventions Department of the Ministry of Munitions. In 1954 he was knighted for his services in promoting fuel efficiency but he also developed a reputation as a highly competent works engineer. The technical skills he had already developed in the family business made him a valuable addition to a Ministry which urgently needed to improve and increase the production of weapons and ammunition.

The early part of the war had seen men in their forties being pressed into service at the start of the war. George Grant Daglish, 1881 to 1883, was a member of the RNVR before the war. In August 1914 he was 48 and served with the RND at Antwerp in September and October 1914. This was an action which had delayed the Germans and weakened their advance in Northern France. After that he served at Gallipoli where he was wounded and in September 1915 he was transferred to work at the Camel Laird shipyard. As the government started to understand the implications of total war and there was an increasing need to use its resources efficiently it made sense for a man who was nearly 50 to be employed elsewhere. As an engineer by training working in a shipyard was a good use of his skills. Camel Laird in Birkenhead were involved in ship building for both the Royal and Merchant Navies as well as converting vessels for war service and repairing over 500 ships.[43] Without this vital work Britain would have found it difficult to maintain the supplies of food and other material for the war effort. As a result, the country found itself in a considerably better position than Germany whose failure to adequately feed its population would be a contributory factor to its collapse at the end of the war.

Other OUs who did not perform military service carried out important roles in the Government. Sir Charles Walker, 1885 to 1891, had been at the Admiralty since 1895. In 1902 he was appointed Private Secretary to Sir John ('Jackie') Fisher who had been made Second Naval Lord.[44] Fisher who as First Sea Lord modernised the navy as the threat from Germany grew was responsible in 1902 implemented reforms to officer training. Sir Charles was involved with this and Fisher's reforms of navy personnel management the following year. Included

---

41   Grace's Guide to British Industrial History L. B. Holliday and Co <http://www.gracesguide.co.uk/L._B._Holliday_and_Co> (accessed 21 March 2016).
42   DNW Orders, Decorations and Medals <http://www.dnw.co.uk/auction-archive/catalogue-archive/lot.php?auction_id=249&lot_id=84076> (accessed 25 March 2016).
43   Grace's Guide Camel Laird and Co <http://www.gracesguide.co.uk/Cammell,_Laird_and_Co> (accessed 25 March 2016).
44   Sir Charles Walker, *Thirty-Six Years at the Admiralty* (London: Lincoln Williams, 1933) p. 36.

within this was the modernisation of the mobilisation plans in the event of war. A system was devised so that the location of officers in the reserves was known as well as officers abroad. As with the army the technical aspects of mobilisation went well and in one case it was possible to get a senior naval officer, Sir Rosslyn Wemyss, out of Germany hours before its frontier was closed. By the end of the war Wemyss was First Sea Lord.[45] However, the navy was not ready for all aspects of a world war. The support role of the Admiralty expanded rapidly and there was a lack of staff to meet all the demands placed on it. There was little thought given to future requirements and as a result, Sir Charles said, Merchant Navy Captains who had offered their services but been declined had to be extricated from the army later. For much of the war Sir Charles would oversee the department which dealt with staff and enquiries about casualties.[46]

A little is known about Sir Charles because his memoirs were published in 1933. Of other senior civil servants little is known beyond the ministries they served in. This is a reflection on the way that, as with the army, senior civil servants were drawn from a small group of public schools of which Uppingham was not one. Likewise, little is known about individual OUs who remained in civilian life. Anecdotally, apart from the examples above, there is evidence that many did make a contribution through organisations such as the volunteer battalions. This was the Great War equivalent of the Home Guard in the Second World War. Started informally, they took upon themselves activities such as guard duty. As noted in Chapter 5 Burnaby, before he received his commission, took charge of mounting a guard at the Chiltern Water Works.[47] It was felt in Britain that it was the duty of the army to fight the enemy overseas while voluntary militias would be responsible for home defence. Many OUs believed that even if they were not able to serve in the armed forces then they should serve in some way. A view reflected within the school through OTC parades, production of components needed for the war effort and the provision of support to agriculture.

Total war required a high level of commitment from all parts of society but the war also saw the development of propaganda to reinforce the worthiness of the country's cause. From the start of the war the underlying aim of Government propaganda was to give a positive message about the country's participation in it. In the context of the German atrocity stories which appeared in the press this may be a little difficult to understand. However, there is no doubt that the Germans did carry out atrocities especially in Belgium early in the war. Given the British population's belief that the country had gone to war in aid of Belgium it is not surprising that a hatred for Germany developed within it from early in the war. Adrian Gregory has pointed out that for newspapers while being hostile to the Germans was good for their circulation being fair was not. German attacks such as that on the *Lusitania* inflamed public opinion. An atmosphere developed within the general public where the enemy was believed to be so uncivilised and in many cases of the press reporting of atrocities the benefit of doubt was not given to it. This was an approach driven by public opinion whereas the government wished to promote something more positive. As the war went on this exemplified itself as a desire to assure the public that victory would come and that the war was a cause which justified the public's participation and sacrifice.[48]

45 Walker, *Thirty-Six Years at the Admiralty*, pp. 44, 127.
46 Walker, *Thirty-Six Years at the Admiralty*, pp. 93-94.
47 LHCMA: Papers of Burnaby, Lt Col Hugo Beaumont.
48 Gregory, *The Last Great War*, pp. 67-69.

One way of demonstrating that Britain would be on the winning side was to encourage the publication of stories about air aces. These were often brief summaries of the pilot's success which accompanied an artist's impression of them in action. William Sanday, 1897 to 1898, appeared in a book depicting acts of heroism by pilots which was published in the second half of the war. The picture was one of him bringing down an enemy aircraft in flames together with the information provided that he had been awarded the DSO for his courage and gallantry.[49] The message was clear; it would be difficult to defeat the Germans but with Britain's brave fighting forces this could be achieved. Propaganda was designed to show that even in the most adverse circumstances it was possible to get the better of the enemy. John Alan Lyde Caunter, 1905 to 1908, was the author of a book designed to make this point. In *13 Days*, published in 1918, he gave an account of his escape in 1917 from the POW camp at Schwarmstedt. Much of the book is a detailed account of his escape from the camp and journey to the Dutch frontier. The introduction, however, gives a clear summary of why the war needed to be fought and why it was being won. Germany was a nation of bullies but if stood up to they would back off.[50] He provides an account of how badly the Germans had behaved towards him after his capture; other OUs such as Horrocks and Johnston also gave similar accounts. British Prisoners of War by standing up to the Germans and regularly escaping were playing their part in tying Germans down and taking men away from activities such as agriculture. He wrote of how the Germans were tired of war and the deprivations they suffered from including a substantial decline in the supply of food. Meat was unobtainable, bread and vegetables such as swedes, black peas and turnips formed a substantial part of the diet. The shops were devoid of goods to sell and the children wore wooden shoes. It was a country close to collapse and he assured his readers and conditions in Britain were considerably better.[51]

The message given out via Caunter was that Britain was winning and that the Germans needed to be stood up to. Another strand to British propaganda was that the country's way of life was worth fighting for. This was something the official war artist scheme was designed to demonstrate. Overseen by Charles Masterman, a friend of Nevinson's father, the war artists would not only produce propaganda but also produce a historical record of the war. Masterman avoided directing what the artists should draw an attitude which had a more subtle intention. This was that it demonstrated a freedom of expression in contrast to Prussian *Kultur*. British artists would play a part in demonstrating the ideals of Britain which the country was fighting to protect. Nevinson was accepted in June 1917 and was soon in France at work. Unusually, he was too keen to toe the official line and his first drawings were disappointing. Soon he returned to his typical forthright approach demonstrating the defence of freedom in a way officials had not intended. At his first exhibition of his war art in the Spring of 1918 his painting *Paths of Glory* demonstrated that, to those involved in censorship at the War Office, there were limits on what could be painted.[52] The picture is of two dead British soldiers in wasteland and was censored by the OU, Arthur Lee, who was the BEF staff officer responsible for censorship. Nevinson

---

49   Cranston Fine Arts, <http://www.directart.co.uk/mall/more.php?ProdID=11653> (accessed 24 March 2016).
50   Captain J A L Caunter, *13 Days: The Chronicle of an Escape from a German Prison* (London: G Bell and Sons, 1918), pp. ix-x.
51   Caunter, *13 Days*, pp. x-xv.
52   Hancock, *A Crisis of Brilliance*, pp. 269-273.

ignored the ban and exhibited it anyway covering the dead bodies with a piece of brown paper which had 'censored' written on it.[53] He was rebuked for this flagrant defiance of censorship but succeeded in making the point that British values were worth fighting for. It also had the equally agreeable effect of generating a great deal of publicity for his exhibition.

Nevinson had demonstrated the sort of initiative Uppingham's educational ethos created but not quite in the way that it was intended. Like much of the rest of the country Uppingham's war effort at home was directed towards military aspects. It was only as the war progressed that it was realised life at home could not continue in the way it had before the war. If the war was to be won then the school would have to support the war in every way it could. No longer would carpentry be dedicated to the making of tables and chairs; it would be directed towards producing splints. Metalwork would be dedicated to supporting munitions production and boys would help out on farms. OUs would find that their skills were not necessarily best used on the front line but details remain light on OUs and their role on the home front. Of those who fought their efforts in some cases were used to demonstrate the justice of the British cause and that it was one which would prevail. Propaganda also concentrated on gallantry and service and the awards received by OUs demonstrate how the nation recognised this.

---

53   Imperial War Museum, Paths of Glory, <http://www.iwm.org.uk/collecticns/item/object/20211> (accessed 24 March 2016).

7

Gallantry and Awards

Medals are not awarded solely for bravery or duty but as a formal recognition of service to others. An analysis of the awards of the Distinguished Service Order (DSO) and Military Cross (MC) to OUs illustrates this. These medals were not just awarded for specific acts of gallantry but also for duties and operations carried out well. An examination of the awards of medals and honours to OUs shows that, like any system for recognising achievements, the British system was flawed. It demonstrates that during the war OUs made valuable contributions to the war effort not only through their gallantry but in the way they applied their technical and professional skills in the service of the country. The system which existed in 1914 for recognising gallantry and excellent service was not equipped to recognise gallantry and excellent service in a total war. The scale and ferocity of the war was such that by December 1914 the MC had to be created because so many DSOs had already been awarded.[1] Without this change the status of the DSO would have been devalued. This was not the last innovation; the problems of recognising different types of service when Britain became 'a nation in arms' required a far more sophisticated approach than the pre-war one. In June 1917 King George V introduced the Order of the British Empire with five different classes as a way of recognising the efforts of non-combatants.[2] In this way it was possible to get a little closer to a position where there was fairness about the way medals were awarded. Despite this, there was always an element of arbitrariness in the way medals and honours were awarded and a comparison of the awards made to Uppingham and other schools demonstrates this. This chapter will also show that the dividing line between being awarded different types of medals was often blurred. It also discusses how the exploits of medal winners were used for propaganda purposes to demonstrate the risks and sacrifice individuals were prepared to make to win the war.

Table 12 summarises, the information held by the school about the OUs who were honoured for their work in the Great War. It is unlikely to be a complete account of every single OU who was recognised with an award or honour, although it covers the vast majority of awards. From other information available it is possible to identify at least 624 OUs with military service who received a British award (many of whom received more than one award). That is nearly

---

1   Moore-Bick, *Playing the Game*, pp. 218-219.
2   Richard Holmes, *Tommy: The British Soldier on the Western Front 1914-1918* (Paperback edition, London: Harper Perennial, 2005) p. 583.

27 percent of the 2,343 known to have served. There were also old boys who did not serve in the armed forces and were given honours for their work in the war. Together, the military and civilian awards demonstrate the recognition of the efforts of OUs was substantial.

As so many OUs received some sort of recognition it is not possible to provide an individual account of each case. By analysing some of the awards made by category and looking at some of the individual awards it is possible to gain a better understanding of why OUs were honoured. At least 87 percent of the awards in Table 12 were for those serving in the military but there were also OUs who received honours for their war work outside the military. Sir Charles Walker whose service in the Admiralty throughout the war was discussed in the last chapter was made a KCB for his work. The school's educational ethos aimed to produce boys with independence, inquisitiveness and self-confidence; the high level of awards suggests that in many cases as a result of this ethos Uppingham produced men who provided high quality leadership in the war and were rewarded for this.

Table 12 1914-1919 Honours List. Summary of Military Honours[3]

Award	Number
Victoria Cross	4
KCB	1
KCMG	1
CB	11
CMG	19
KBE	1
CBE	7
OBE	30
DSO with bar	9
DSO	79
DSC	2
DFC	6
MC with two bars	2
MC with bar	18
MC	226
AFC	4
DCM	2
MM	2
Albert Medal in Gold	1
Albert Medal in Silver	1
Mentions in Dispatches	561
Foreign Orders and Decorations	59

3   Figures provided by Jerry Rudman, Uppingham School Archivist.

The Victoria Cross

Mike Garrs has written an account of the five OUs who have won the VC, with four out of these five being awarded during the First World War.[4] Therefore this section briefly summarises the circumstances which led to each award and draws out some wider points. The OUs who were awarded the VC during the Great war were Lieutenant-Colonel John Stanhope Collings-Wells, 1895 to 1900, Captain Arthur Moore Lascelles 1895 to 1898, Captain George Allan Maling 1903 to 1907 and Captain Harold Broadbent Maufe 1912 to 1915. Collings-Wells was awarded a posthumous VC for his action on 25 March 1918 during the Spring offensive. The offensive was launched on 21 March 1918 and was designed to knock Britain and France out of the war before sufficient American forces had arrived on the Western Front. Having signed the Treaty of Brest-Litovsk with Russia, Germany had been able to move a significant amount of its forces to the west to mount the offensive. It was a final and desperate effort by the Germans to win the war. The initial phases of the assault were of high intensity and the British were forced to withdraw. On 25 March Collings-Wells took the decision to lead volunteers in a final rear-guard action while the rest of his battalion got away. Two days later he was ordered to mount a successful counter-attack and led his men, despite being wounded in both arms. Reluctantly dragged away to be treated for his wounds by his sergeant he was killed when a shell hit the bunker he had been taken to. The letters in his tribute spoke of his qualities of leadership in the actions between 25 and 27 March.[5] The school's philosophy stressed a strong sense of duty, leadership skills and taking responsibility and Collings-Wells put this into effect in the actions for which he was posthumously awarded a VC.

Putting this philosophy into effect was a strong feature in the actions of all the OUs who won VCs. Lascelles's VC had been awarded for his part at Masnieres during the Battle of Cambrai in meeting a German counter-attack on 3 December 1917. Like Collings-Wells although severely wounded he led the 12 remaining men of his company of the Durham Light Infantry against heavy machine gun fire without any artillery support and drove 60 Germans back. Later in the day he was captured but managed to escape. His dedication to duty and leadership was such that after he had recovered he returned to active service from his desk job, even though his right arm was beyond repair. He was killed in action on 7 November 2018, four days before the end of the war.[6]

Maling was the first OU to be awarded the VC and unlike Lascelles and Collings-Wells, who served in the infantry, was in the RAMC. Like these men his bravery carrying out his medical duties between 25 September 1915 and 26 September 1915 during the Battle of Loos was almost reckless. A large number of British soldiers had been cut off in a ruined house by a ferocious artillery barrage. The screams of the wounded could be heard from the British lines but their comrades were unable to provide support because of the ferocity of the barrage. Exercising the qualities of independence and self-confidence, Maling picked up his medical bag and ran through the barrage miraculously arriving at the house in one piece. He treated the wounded

---

4   Mike Garrs, *Valiant Hearts: The Story of Uppingham School VC's* (Nettleham: Private published, 2010).
5   The Bedfordshire Regiment in the Great War John Stanhope Collings-Wells V.C., D.S.O. <http://www.bedfordregiment.org.uk/4thbn/collingswellsvc.html> (accessed 7 September 2016).
6   Victoria Cross Durham Light Infantry Arthur Moore Lascelles <http://www.lightinfantry.me.uk/vcamlasclles.htm> (accessed 7 September 2016).

as the barrage continued and on two occasions he was blown from his feet by shells which had exploded nearby. On the second occasion, Maling's orderly was wounded and his medical equipment scattered which he promptly set about recovering. In over 24 hours, until the barrage ended, he treated over 300 wounded.[7] The School Magazine reported on the first award of a VC to an OU in a typically understated manner reprinting the official announcement and devoting one sentence to a comment: 'But it is gratifying to know that while many receive the decoration for destroying life, our first V.C. was won by a man who freely risked his own life to save others.'[8] Other schools tended to make more of such achievements. The school was committed to the war but was under-stated in the way it reported on the deeds of its old boys much like it was in reporting on the demise of old boys.

Like Maling, Maufe won his VC for his actions under a heavy artillery fire without which a considerable number of lives would have been lost. As with the others he exercised his initiative without regard for his personal safety. During the Battle of Arras in June 1917 Maufe had realised that a forward observation point's communications, which was vital for effectively directing artillery fire, had been cut off. He repaired the telephone line under heavy artillery fire at one point surprising the officers in the forward position, who considered themselves cut off, by arriving and requesting some more insulation tape to complete the repairs. After returning to the command point he lay down to rest but was woken up by a large explosion. Discovering that boxes by his battery's dump were on fire he dragged them away and put them in a water-filled shell hole. He then set about helping to out a fire in the dump of the adjacent battery before gas shells exploded. When another part of the dump exploded burying several men he went to extricate them and assisted the wounded while they waited to be taken to the dressing station. Maufe's actions like those of Lascelles and Maling attracted the attention of the propaganda unit, MI 7 (b) 1. The unit specialised in producing articles about fighting in France which were provided to newspapers throughout the world. The article about Maufe presents an image of him as a decisive man who remained calm under the most trying of circumstances. It explained he had taken it upon himself to repair the line and displayed considerable bravery and initiative in dealing with the fire. Not only had he saved a considerable amount of ammunition from exploding, his actions had prevented the loss of several lives.[9] As discussed, in the last chapter this was in accordance of the theme that victory was worth fighting for and highlighting these acts of bravery.

In the case of all the VCs won it seems that their actions reflected the school's philosophy stressed a strong sense of duty, leadership skills and taking responsibility. However, they were not supermen, of the four of them, only Maufe appears to have been truly outstanding in all aspects of his life at the school. He was a School Praeposter, Captain of Games, a member of the Rugby XV and after the war read engineering at Cambridge.[10] Despite this all of the VC winners rose to the occasion and displayed considerable qualities when the situation demanded it. The aspect which seems to tie them together is the qualities which Uppingham aimed to

---

7   George Allen Maling VC by Arthur Lockyear <http://www.tunsilk.co.uk/page303.html> (accessed 30 March 2016).
8   *USM*, November 1915, p. 258.
9   Europeana 1914-1918, Thomas Harold Broadbent Maufe ["Tales of the V.C."] <http://www.europeana1914-1918.eu/en/contributions/5380#prettyPhoto> (accessed 30 March 2016).
10 Garrs, *Valiant Hearts*, p. 45.

produce in boys. In themselves, their actions were insignificant but they demonstrated the commitment of OUs to winning the war.

In an age of education league tables it is wise not to draw too much from assessing a school solely on the basis of the academic achievement of their alumni. Schools themselves were unwilling to involve themselves in press attempts to draw such comparisons of how many VCs each school had won. Of the VCs won by public school old boys Seldon and Walsh point out that they were awarded to the alumni of 92 different schools.[11] The bravery which earned a VC was not the monopoly of a small group of schools. However, it is worth noting that in Table 13 which shows the 10 public schools which won the most VCs only Dulwich and Uppingham were not from the group of 10 public schools which traditionally had provided the army with most of its officers. Of the schools listed Uppingham had the lowest number of boys serving. It suggests that Uppingham with a large number of its old boys serving on the front line produced men who were capable of extraordinary levels of bravery in leadership. While it was not the sole reason for the VCs awarded it is likely the school's philosophy stressed a strong sense of duty, leadership skills and taking responsibility had some effect on the actions of the men who won them.

Table 13 VCs awarded by School[12]

School	VCs Awarded	Number Who Served
Eton	13	5,656
Harrow	8	2,917
Cheltenham	6	3,540
Haileybury	6	2,825
Wellington	5	3,500
Clifton	5	3,063
Dulwich	5	3,036
Rugby	4	3,244
Uppingham	4	2,343
Winchester	4	2,418

Gallantry and Service

Valour and bravery are important aspects of military service but there are different levels at which it is exercised. The behaviour for which a VC was awarded was almost reckless but there were other acts which were brave but not quite as selfless. There were at least two other OUs whose names were put forward for a VC but were instead awarded the DSO which was considered to be the award for the second level of gallantry behind the VC. The citations for a DSO suggest a high level of bravery which did not display an almost reckless disregard for one's own safety. Harold Howitt was awarded a DSO for his 'conspicuous gallantry and devotion to duty

---

11 Seldon and Walsh, *Public Schools and The Great War*, p. 244.
12 Based on Seldon and Walsh, *Public Schools and The Great War*, pp. 244, 259-260 and author's Uppingham database.

in action' in the Spring Offensive of 1918. From his own account, he recounts how he was taken prisoner but escaped soon afterwards. After getting back to the British lines he took part in an eight day long rear-guard action in which he recalled getting no sleep. During this time as a Brigade Major his role was to patrol the line encouraging the troops to hold their position. The citation describes how he 'displayed complete fearlessness in moving about in the open, under heavy fire, in order to clear up obscure situations.' Howitt recorded that his name had been put forward for a VC but this had been 'squeezed out' somewhere in the higher levels.[13] The citation for his medal bears similarities with other DSOs awarded. There is no doubt that he displayed 'conspicuous gallantry' in the actions for which he received his medal but it can be argued what he did was at the extreme of what was expected of him. He was an officer and had duty to lead his men in action and this is what he was doing when under heavy fire by his actions he had rallied men to carry on fighting. Maufe was under no obligation to go out and repair telephone lines under heavy artillery fire. He was under no obligation to take tremendous personal risks to tackle the fires in the ammunition dumps. He chose to take risks way beyond what was expected of him. This is not to say that Howitt did not reflect the school's philosophy of a strong sense of duty, leadership skills and taking responsibility. There were other factors which affected the level of the award given; an award was dependent on how the man's commanding officer wrote his recommendation. There was a real skill to this and some COs were better than others at doing this while others were, by their nature, more grudging in their praise.[14] This may have come into play when the recommendation for Howitt's VC was rejected and a DSO substituted.

This could also have been the case for Harold Inglis, 1900 to 1904, who was also recommended for a VC as a result of his actions at the Battle of the Somme. His citation reveals a high level of bravery;

> For conspicuous gallantry in action. He led his company with great dash in the attack. When checked forward he went forward with a sergeant and private and captured nine of the enemy, at the same time gaining another 80 yards of trench.[15]

Like Howitt the citation suggests he was doing something that was part of his job. His task was to capture objectives and this was what was behind the attack in which enemy trench was captured. The way in which he led his men as an officer and inspired them, is what was recognised by his award. In a citation for a VC the opening sentence begins with 'for most conspicuous bravery' as opposed to 'conspicuous gallantry' at the beginning of a DSO citation for a particular action. Gallantry suggests courageous behaviour to achieve an end while bravery suggests an action regardless of the risks. There are very blurred boundaries between the two and in different circumstances Howitt and Inglis might have been awarded a VC. The awards of DSOs were also used as part of the government's propaganda campaign. John Buchan was inspired to use the account of Howitt's escape for his *Mr Standfast* spy story series in a newspaper;[16] Buchan was involved in propaganda activities throughout the war and this fitted

---

13 USA, Reminisces of Harold Gibson Howitt, pp. 45-47.
14 Holmes, *Tommy*, p. 585.
15 *The V.C. and D.S.O. Book Distinguished Service Order 1916 – 1923* (London; Naval and Military Press, 2009), p. 19.
16 USA, Reminisces of Harold Gibson Howitt, pp. 45-46.

into the theme of giving accounts of men who had displayed great bravery as their contribution to winning the war.

The DSO, like many other medals, could be awarded for different reasons. It could be awarded for a specific act of gallantry and it could also be awarded for distinguished service. Normally awarded to those who were a Major or higher rank, officers of a rank lower than this (such as Inglis) were awarded it when the act of gallantry was considerably higher than what was normally expected of them. To preserve the integrity of the medal the circumstances for which it was awarded were tightened up to address the concern that the DSO and other medals were not diluted by a high volume of awards. The aim was to ensure that it demonstrated an exceptional effort towards winning the war. For this reason much of the war there were limits on how many could be awarded in a month. Until May 1918 there was a monthly limit for each theatre of war on the number of DSOs and MCs which could be awarded (after 1 January 1917, for France this was 200 DSOs and 500 MCs).[17] One example of a tightening of the qualifications was the removal of staff officers after 1916 from the list of those eligible.[18] The OU, Louis Vaughan, was awarded a DSO in 1915 while serving on the staff. After January 1917 the criteria were changed so that officers were only awarded the DSO for gallantry or distinguished service in the field after being in contact with the enemy. In future those who had previously qualified for it because of their distinguished service away from the front line were recommended for honours such as the OBE. An analysis of medals awarded during the war demonstrates that the DSO was not easily won. The war saw 9,761 officers being awarded the DSO (including bars to the DSO – each bar representing the award of a further DSO to an officer).[19] This may appear to be a high figure but by the end of the war the army had an establishment of 164,255 officers; this figure which does not take into account those officers who died or retired during the war so the total number of officers who served was higher.[20] From this we can surmise that less than six percent of officers were awarded the DSO. In all, 229,434 honours were conferred for services in the field during the war and DSOs formed four percent of them.[21] The medal was, therefore, won by a relatively small group of officers and represented distinguished service and gallantry.

Table 14 Award of DSOs to OUs by Date of First Award and Type of Award

Year of Award	Distinguished Service	Gallantry	Total
1914	0	2	2
1915	10	0	10
1916	12	6	18
1917	18	7	25
1918	9	10	19
1919	10	4	14
Total	59	29	88

17 *Statistics of the Military Effort*, p. 558.
18 Holmes, *Tommy*, p. 587.
19 *Statistics of the Military Effort*, p. 554.
20 *Statistics of the Military Effort*, p. 234.
21 *Statistics of the Military Effort*, p. 534.

Fifty-seven percent of the DSOs awarded to OUs were won in the second half of the war; this should not be a surprise because the majority of awards came from 1916 onwards. Similarly the majority of the awards were for 'distinguished service in the field' so it is no surprise that 67 percent of the first DSOs won by OUs fell into this category. Early in the war it was more likely that the nature of the distinguished service would be specified in announcements but as the war went on the volume of awards made it impractical to summarise the nature of it. D S Lewis who played an important role in the development of the grid square system for artillery spotting (see Chapter 5) was one OU whose distinguished service was explained in the announcement of his DSO. It demonstrates that distinguished service in the early years of the war was often more than good staff work and also hints at what it was awarded for later in the war when no citations were provided. The *Gazette* of 1 January 1915 announced Lewis had received it for 'valuable information repeatedly furnished to the Royal Artillery with regards to the position of the enemy's guns.'[22] The information he had provided had been valuable in silencing the German artillery. The citation, for obvious reasons, did not provide details of the technical innovations behind it. Lewis, without revealing technical details, provided a brief account to the School Magazine of what had he had been doing while playing down the considerable risks he had been taking:

> I'm having a great time now: they're at last beginning to use my wireless machine properly, and the last two days I've been observing artillery fire. It is simply topping, seeing the lyddite bursts getting closer and closer as one signals back the observations, and finally one sees one go plump into a gunpit and you know there's an end of a gun and its crew. It is exciting too as they blaze away merrily with anti-aircraft guns and rifles and one jigs about like a snipe to put them off. I had shells bursting all around last night after I'd ranged the guns on three different batteries. One hit my top plane and a bullet went through my propeller, but no damage to me. Today I'm putting on a new wing and propeller, hence this letter.[23]

The school's educational ethos aimed to produce boys with independence, inquisitiveness and self-confidence and the citation and letter demonstrate that Lewis had exercised these qualities in developing the grid square system. Although wireless was in its infancy Lewis's inquisitiveness had led to his recognition of its potential in eliminating enemy artillery positions. It is clear from his letter that it had had the self-confidence to persuade others of the value of it in counter-battery work. The school's philosophy stressed a strong sense of duty, leadership skills and taking responsibility. A key part of this was team work and his description of the elimination of the batteries demonstrates of this. He took pride in being part of a team; the information he provided was being used by British artillery to great effect. The qualities of the team player were something the British army looked for in its officer.

What Lewis demonstrates is that a DSO award which did not involve gallantry was often for excellent work, often at considerable risk. Lewis had understood an effective use of new technology and had shown a high level of commitment in its application and working as part

---

22 *The V.C. and D.S.O. Distinguished Service Order 1886-1915: Distinguished Service Order. 6th September 1886 to the 31st December 1915* (London, Naval and Military Press, 2009), p. 346.
23 *USM*, November 1914, p. 283.

118 A School in Arms

of a team to make it work. Other citations for OUs awarded DSOs for gallantry suggest a high level of teamwork as well as outstanding leadership skill in modern parlance it might be called 'going the extra mile'. The first OU to be awarded a DSO was Charles Liveing, 1886 to 1889, for gallantry at the Battle of Le Cateau on 26 August 1914. This was a rear-guard action designed to slow down the German advance and was significant in that it bought time for the British to slow the German advance and for the BEF to escape without heavy losses. Under heavy fire, Liveing was ordered to abandon his battery as the German artillery fire was too fierce to enable the horse teams to move up and withdraw the guns. The crew refused to abandon their guns and manhandled all six guns to a position where they could be limbered up and withdrawn.[24] For his 'bravery and devotion' in this action he was awarded the DSO but is clear that the successful withdrawal was a fine piece of team work, which he led.[25] The awards of DSOs for gallantry to OUs would continue to be the result of excellent leadership. Captain J E B Gray (see Chapter 5), who had been urged to enlist in 1914 by his friends, was awarded the DSO for his gallantry and 'skilful leadership' on the night of 4 and 5 November 1918, just a week before the armistice. In the face of fierce machine gun fire he led his company from the front over a bridge crossing the River Scheldt and succeeded in establishing a machine gun section on the opposite side before the bridge collapsed. The qualities of initiative, independence and self-confidence which the school aimed to produce in its boys were at the heart of the qualities that underpinned the actions which led to the award of his DSO.

That 246 OUs won the MC is a reflection of the large number of them who were junior officers; the medal could only be awarded to officers of the rank of Captain below and warrant officers. In all, 39 percent of the OUs who were honoured for their role in the war were awarded an MC. Like the DSO it could be awarded for gallantry and continued good service over a defined period.[26] The recommendation for the MC awarded to Sydney Humbert, 1898 to 1901, provides evidence for what constituted continued good service:

> Has commanded W18 Airline Section since the latter came to France in July 1915. During the whole time he has done excellent work, often under very trying circumstances, and by his energy and devotion has set a praiseworthy example to his Section – Previously bought to notice.'[27]

The announcement of the award which appeared in *The London Gazette* of 4 June 1917 simply lists his name so the recommendation helps to provide a better understanding of continued good service meant. In the recommendation four main factors are involved; the carrying out of excellent work in difficult circumstances together with a display of energy and devotion which set an excellent example. It is also clear that the quality of Humbert's work had already been noticed

---

24 Andrew Rawson, *British Expeditionary Force – The 1914 Campaign* (Barnsley: Pen and Sword, 2014), p. 47.
25 *The V.C. and D.S.O. Distinguished Service Order 1886-1915: Distinguished Service Order. 6Th September 1886 To The 31st December 1915* (London, Naval and Military Press, 2009), p. 342.
26 Scott Addington, *For Conspicuous Gallantry ... Winners of the Military Cross and Bar during the Great War Volume 1 – Two Bars and Three Bars* (Leicester: Matador, 2006), p. ix.
27 Australian War Memorial Honour and Awards Sydney Francis Morten Humbert <https://www.awm.gov.au/people/rolls/R1607217/> (accessed 15 April 2016).

and that this was a powerful support on top of the work by him which was being recognised. The school's philosophy stressed a strong sense of duty, leadership skills and taking responsibility; it is noticeable that these qualities shine through in this recommendation. Humbert had carried out his role in a way which was beyond what was expected for a man of his rank. The initiation of the MC enabled this to be recognised without diluting the value of medals such as the DSO. In the same way acts of gallantry could be recognised that might not normally qualify for a DSO. Frank Jameson, 1907 to 1912, won an MC with two bars; as with the DSO a bar to the MC could only be awarded for an act of gallantry. Jameson also won a DSO; one of only 21 officers to win a DSO and an MC and a comparison of the citation for the DSO and for one of the bars to his MC offers a useful understanding of the differences underpinning the award of each medal.

The first bar to his MC was gazetted on 15 March 1918 and awarded:

> For conspicuous gallantry and devotion to duty. He, together with another officer, was ordered to reconnoitre the front line and report upon communications. On returning, the officer was wounded in the foot and unable to walk. 2nd Lt. Jameson thereupon carried this officer on his back for half a mile through a heavy barrage, which the enemy put down in preparation for a counterattack. Throughout this period he displayed great courage and cheerfulness, and eventually brought his companion to an aid post. This officer has constantly shown coolness and a fine determination throughout the operations.[28]

Just over six months later on 15 October 1918 his DSO was gazetted:

> For conspicuous gallantry and devotion to duty, when in command of the brigade signal section during an enemy attack. Under heavy shell he superintended the placing under cover of the equipment and personnel. He then went out with his linesmen to repair communications with both front-line battalions. All day long he kept going round his various lines under heavy fire, and it was entirely due to his courage and energy that communication was maintained for certain periods.[29]

Scott Addington suggests that the difference between a DSO and an MC award was that the former medal was awarded for superintending an effort rather than a specific action.[30] There is more to it than this and it lies in the way leadership is displayed. In the DSO citations for Howitt, Irwin, Gray and Jameson an action is described where they are not only overseeing the action but also displaying leadership through the part they play in it. Gray was the first across the bridge across the Scheldt as part of a team. In MC awards there is more of a theme of leadership by example and use of initiative. Jameson used his initiative in picking up the wounded officer and set an example by his courage and cheerfulness. In an MC award the key factor was leadership by individual example whereas for a DSO the key factor was that the leadership was also exercised through leadership of and participation in the action. The qualities of leadership developed at Uppingham were recognised in particular through the award of DSOs and MCs.

---

28 Addington, *For Conspicuous Gallantry*, p. 123.
29 *The V.C. and D.S.O. Book Distinguished Service Order 1916 – 1923*, p. 129.
30 Addington, *For Conspicuous Gallantry*, p. 123.

Not Quite Fair

There does appear to have been discrepancies in the way medals were awarded. Some officers expressed embarrassment at their award of a DSO for distinguished service and it does appear that some commanders were more willing than others to make recommendations for honours.[31] Although some of these officers who felt they were undeserving were engaging in the British habit of underplaying their achievements. However, a comparison of medals awarded to the old boys of Tonbridge, Uppingham and Winchester does suggest there were some inconsistencies. As Table 15 shows the number of old boys from each school who served is broadly similar. There is, however, a discrepancy in the number of medals awarded when Winchester is compared with Uppingham and Tonbridge. Winchester, as already noted, was one of the leading sources for army officers before the war. Uppingham and Tonbridge were similar in many ways. Both while significant public schools were not part of the group of elite public schools made up of the likes of Eton, Harrow and Winchester. They drew their boys from less aristocratic backgrounds than Eton, Harrow and Winchester; in 1914 the backgrounds the fathers of boys at both schools were similar with many being engaged in commerce and the law.[32] Neither was known as an army school either and their contributions to the upper reaches of the British army were relatively small. In Uppingham's case Louis Vaughan was the most significant figure and Tonbridge's Major-General Robert Lecky was the most prominent old boy to serve in the Great War. The vast majority of those who served from these schools were junior officers whereas Winchester provided a far greater proportion of officers who were Major or a higher rank; 26 percent of its old boys fit this criteria compared with 17 percent for Uppingham. For Winchester, 66 percent of its old boys were junior officers compared with a figure of 72 percent for Uppingham. If you were from Winchester you were considerably more likely to be a senior officer which demonstrates its stronger connections with the army.

Table 15 Comparison of Individual Medal Winners from Tonbridge, Uppingham and Winchester

School	Served	VC	DSO	MC
Tonbridge	2,225	1	85	241
Uppingham	2,341	4	88	246
Winchester	2,418	4	188	303

It is no surprise to see that the number of medals won by old boys from Tonbridge and Uppingham are almost the same given the similarities of the social backgrounds of their old boys. The figures for Winchester when compared to the other two other schools show that Wykehamists were far more successful in winning medals. The number of DSOs won by them is more than Uppingham and Tonbridge combined. This could be explained by there being more Wykehamists in the senior ranks of the British army. However, this does not explain why double the number was awarded to them than OUs; 613 Wykehamists fell into the category of senior officer compared with 399 OUs. So Winchester only provided 50 percent more senior

---

31   Holmes, *Tommy* p. 587.
32   I am grateful to David Walsh Archivist at Tonbridge for providing information about this.

officers than Uppingham but its old boys won twice as many DSOs. There may be other factors but the figures strongly suggest a bias towards Winchester. When the comparative figures for the award of the MC are examined it becomes clearer that there is an element of who you knew and not what you did behind the award of medals. As Winchester provided 1,531 junior officers compared with 1,689 OUs it might be expected that the number of OUs whom won MCs might be broadly similar to the number won by Wykehamists. This is not the case as Winchester's old boys won 57 (23 percent) more than Uppingham's. It could be that this is a statistical fluke but the similarity of the figures for Tonbridge and Uppingham point to specific factors underpinning the discrepancy. The central factor in the discrepancy was that Winchester was an army school; as has been demonstrated in the years before the war it provided a significant number of officers to the army. The officers from the pre-war army dominated its management and higher levels of command during the Great War. At the start of the war more Wykehamists had substantial experience of army leadership than OUs. They already had the skills and expertise which when applied in a conspicuous manner would have made them more likely to receive medals and honours. There is, however, more to the discrepancy in awards than Wykehamists being better equipped and qualified to win medals. Those in senior and management positions within the army or were influential in the making of these decisions about the awards of medals or honours. It is inevitable that there was a bias amongst these decision makers towards favouring those they were connected with or aware of. This would not necessarily a conscious decision; those in command would have favoured Wykehamists over OUs because they knew them better. Having a better understanding of someone would have influenced their decision in being able to make better judgements about their merit. In the case of those they did not know so well they would have trod more cautiously and not given them the benefit of doubt. Some OUs suspected this and believed that there was a bias in favour of officers from the regular army over those from the temporary officers and men who had volunteered or been conscripted for the duration of the war. By January 1918, Peachey was becoming increasingly disillusioned with the way honours were awarded; commenting that while the honours list might be longer it contained the same names and in his view, staff officers had 'collared the lot.'[33] A month later he complained that the temporary officer was not treated fairly and their efforts were not recognised by the regular officer.[34] The resentment he expressed was symptomatic of what he described as bad feeling between regular officers and temporary gentlemen.[35] After nearly three and a half years on active service it is not surprising that these sorts of tensions had developed. Peachey was a successful and experienced businessman in his own right (42 when war broke out) and a sense of frustration at being undervalued is understandable. Since enlisting in 1914 he had risen to the rank of Major and his efforts had been recognised when he had been mentioned in despatches on 15 June 1916.[36] This was probably the result of him coming to the attention of Major-General Ivor Maxe who had sent him a note after a visit commending him for his work with the 180th Divisional Train.[37] Peachey's views and the comparison between medals won

---

33   LMA: F/PEY344: Letter to Sybil 3 January 1918.
34   LMA: F/PEY345: Letter to Sybil 2 February 1918.
35   LMA: F/PEY345: Letter to Father 20 February 1918.
36   *The London Gazette*, p. 59543.
37   LMA: F/PEY344: Letter to Sybil 21 December 1915.

by Wykehamists and OUs offers support for the view that Uppingham's contribution was not recognised enough.

The medals won by OUs demonstrated that their qualities of independence, inquisitiveness and self-confidence were recognised and they were not just awarded them for acts of bravery and gallantry. They were recognition of a wider contribution to the war effort which propaganda often used to demonstrate commitment to winning the war. Especially, in the case of DSOs the awards reflected exceptional leadership skills which were not just exercised through acts of gallantry. Over two thirds of DSOs to OUs were for distinguished service and not a specific act of gallantry. Many MCs were awarded for good work which reflects the practical skills many had developed and were able to employ in positions of leadership. The recognition of men such as Peachey was often the result of the management skills they had acquired in business and the professions over many years. Despite the substantial recognition of OU achievement there was a bias with in the army towards those with a regular army background. The evidence points towards the achievements, skills and expertise of OUs not being recognised as much as they should have been.

8

Commanders in Arms

In popular opinion, the British commanders of the Great War are often seen as blinkered, privileged, incompetent old men who are detached from the plight of the men on the front line. Something captured by General Melchett in *Blackadder Goes Forth* who lives a life of great comfort in a chateau and apparently cares more about his pet pigeon than the lives of his soldiers. This is a myth which distorts rather than explains the role of senior commanders in the Great War. With the pre-war regular Army almost completely wiped out by the end of 1914 and severely limited as an efficient fighting organisation the story of the British army is one where an army of civilians was created from scratch. The problems of creating an effective mass army in a country that had traditionally shunned conscription were immense. Throughout the war there were immense problems for the high command such as training new recruits and developing and using new technology. A study of the OUs who held higher commands offers some interesting case studies on the problems of command in the Great War and provides a more nuanced picture of British high command during the war. In exercising their command they all exhibited a strong sense of duty, leadership skills and taking responsibility. This chapter discusses how OUs contributed to the urgent need for retired officers to command this army, the younger men who replaced them and provides four case studies to illustrate the wider problems of command.

At its highest levels of command the army was dominated by the old boys of the 10 traditional 'army public schools. Schools such as Uppingham made a relatively small contribution at this level. A study of the commanders of the BEF in France on 11 November 1918 demonstrates how it was dominated by just a few schools. On the day the war ended Haig, commander of the BEF, met with his five army commanders, their chiefs of staff and the Cavalry Corps Commander. Of the six commanders, Haig and the five army commanders, three had gone to Eton, two to Clifton and one to Harrow. All these schools were in the top 10 public schools that provided the officers who led and managed the BEF. In the wider group 10 out of 13 (77 percent) of the commanders had been educated at one of the 10 leading 'army' schools. One of the three educated at a school outside this group was the OU Louis Vaughan. He together with Couper, Lake and Wilkinson provide the case studies which demonstrate some of the problems of command in the Great War.

As was discussed in Chapter 5 a number of retired OU army officers returned to service in 1914 to respond to the emergency; such was their maturity that they earned the nickname 'dugouts'. Often maligned they were a victim of circumstances. Charles Alexander, one of the 'dugouts', was removed from his command during the Battle of Loos and returned to Britain to command an artillery training brigade. He may appear to fit the stereotype of the elderly and incompetent high command but there are mitigating factors in his defence. Aged 59 with no recent experience of modern warfare at the Battle of Loos, he did his best but was overwhelmed by the circumstances and lack of resources. The army after August 1914 rapidly expanded in response to Kitchener's call to arms and in the process forced to improvise. It was not just 'dugouts' who were called upon to fill the gaps in leadership; former OTC cadets with only basic training were seen as a good source of officers. Men in their forties such as Peachey were enlisted as the army drew on its connections to find men with appropriate skills. It was an improvised approach which over time would become more formal but improvisation was necessary to cope with the rapid expansion. It also meant experienced men were urgently needed to fight and lead in the war. Experienced officers such as Alexander were 'dug out' to set up units, take positions of command and advise the new army created by Kitchener. Alexander was probably no different to many others in Britain in August 1914 in considering it his duty to respond to the German invasion of Belgium. Although he had spent his army career in the artillery after five years of retirement he would not have been up to date with the latest army thinking about its deployment but as a reservist it was decided he could fill a role there were relatively few candidates for. Alexander was blamed for the chaotic performance of his division and removed even before the battle was over but the performance of most of the artillery at Loos was totally inadequate. The use of gas by the British for the first time at Loos was a sign of weakness. The British did not have the artillery guns and munitions to provide support for the offensive and to compensate for this shortage improvised by using gas.[1] Blown towards the German lines the wind conditions were unfavourable and it was ineffective in its aim of neutralising the Germans. Had it been delivered by artillery shell it might have been more effective but there was a shortage of artillery. Considering Alexander's lack of recent experience and his age, he was 59 by the time of Loos; it would appear there were unrealistic expectations about what retired officers such as him could provide without the proper resources. He was redeployed in artillery training units for the rest of the war; it suggests that although he was blamed for some of the artillery shortcomings at Loos the army remained keen to use his skills and expertise which had no doubt been got up to date as a result of his experience in France. It also suggests that the army recognised that dugouts' had not always been deployed in the most effective way.[2] In the early stages of the war all the allies removed commanders who had proved to be ineffective. In 1914 after the Battle of the Marne Joffre sacked 50 senior commanders who had demonstrated an insufficient grasp of the way modern wars needed to be fought.[3] The French Generals who were sacked were part of an army which was 910,000 strong in peacetime and was able, thanks to its national service laws, to mobilise 1,865,000 men in August 1914.[4] In contrast, the British regular army was

1 Philpott, *Attrition*, p. 156.
2 World War One Luton <http://www.worldwar1luton.com/individual/brigadier-general-charles-henry-alexander> (accessed 8 February 2016)) and Profiles of Western Front generals <http://www.birmingham.ac.uk/research/activity/warstudies/research/projects/lionsdonkeys/a.aspx> (accessed 8 February 2016).
3 Philpott, *Attrition*, pp. 39-40.
4 Philpott, *Attrition*, p. 26.

247,432 strong in August 1914.⁵ The BEF which went to France in 1914 initially consisted of four divisions (approximately 72,000 men). It was from this very small establishment that the British army was expanded and it was inevitable that retired officers had to be recalled to assist in this expansion. The 'dugouts' were even more out of touch than the 50 commanders sacked by Joffre. Alexander's ineffectiveness was not solely the result of his age and lack of grasp of what was required; a lack of experienced men within the new army and a chronic shortage of suitable equipment and munitions made failure at Loos inevitable. After Loos Repington, *The Times* war correspondent, with the behind the scenes encouragement of Sir John French, the then BEF commander, provoked public outrage with his reports about a shell shortage. It took some time to develop supplies of munitions and suitable equipment to fight modern warfare. Even when the equipment was developed it would take time for officers and men to understand the most effective way to deploy it.

Other OUs also found themselves recalled to take senior commands at the start of the war. Bridges Lewis, 1869 to 1872, was 57 in August 1914 and retired from the army in 1910. In the Boer War he had been awarded a DSO 'in recognition of services during the operations in South Africa.'⁶ He was recalled to command the 56th Brigade in the 19th Western Division when it was established in September 1914. Like many of the new army units its early days were, to put it mildly, confused. Apart from the problems of a lack of equipment and experienced men it suffered from a lack of accommodation. In such a desperate situation the experience of men such as Bridges was urgently needed to bring some organisation to the running of the brigade. He served in this position until December 1915; by this time younger officers were starting to come through with more appropriate expertise and skills and he could stand aside. Uppingham's philosophy stressed a strong sense of duty, leadership skills and taking responsibility and this was something reflected in the 'dugouts' such as Alexander and Lewis who returned to the army when the war came.

The 'dugouts' could only be phased out as the younger men developed the experience and leadership skills, one example of these younger men was Wilfred Evans, 1893 to 1897. Evans had gained operational experience in the Boer War by the end of which he was a Lieutenant. In the early period of the Great War he built up these skills and experience as well as displaying the abilities required for senior command. Starting the Great War as a captain he was despatched to France in September 1914. During fierce fighting a few weeks later he found himself in command of a battalion as other more senior officers were killed or wounded. For his service during the early part of the war he was awarded the DSO. After that he spent the period from August 1915 to July 1916 on the staff of Plumer's Second Army. Promotion followed again and in July 1916 he became a Brevet (temporary) Lieutenant-Colonel of one of the service battalions established as Kitchener expanded the army. While commanding the battalion he won a bar to his DSO in an attack on an objective which resulted in the capture of many guns and prisoners. The citation spoke of his 'dash and initiative', his 'great coolness' and setting a 'fine personal example' which had saved a critical situation.⁷ In the period from 1914 to 1917 he had proved himself as a front line leader but had also gained important experience as a staff officer. Staff work gave him insight into the planning and management of operations. His appointment as

5   *Statistics of the Military Effort*, p. 30.
6   *Distinguished Service Order 1886-1915*, p. 163.
7   *Distinguished Service Order 1886-1915*, pp. 370-371.

a Temporary Brigadier-General drew on the experience he had developed of modern warfare and made it possible for younger men like him to take on senior command. These qualities of leadership and initiative were something an Uppingham education aimed to produce. These were demonstrated during his spell commanding 182 Brigade of 61st (2nd South Midland) Division which he led during Cambrai in November 1917, bearing the brunt of the German Spring Offensive in March and April 1918 and after rebuilding the brigade in the 100 days offensive during October 1918.[8] Like many other officers holding temporary ranks he returned to his substantive rank of Major in 1919 when his unit was disbanded.

The first case study demonstrates that the Uppingham philosophy of developing men with a strong sense of duty, leadership skills and taking responsibility also produced OUs who were prepared to take calculated risks even if it meant endangering their career. For Major-General Percy Wilkinson, 1879 to 1882, it involved becoming involved in organisational politics. Before the war, he had spent a substantial part of his career serving throughout the empire; in 1915 was appointed to command the 50th (Northumberland) Division.[9] When the division moved to France it fought at Second Ypres in 1915 and on the Somme in 1916. By April 1917 it was a battle hardened and experienced division and preparing for action in the Battle of Arras. The 50th Division formed part of the Third Army under the command of General Edmund Allenby. After an encouraging start to the battle Field-Marshal Douglas Haig, Commander of the BEF, perceived that something was going wrong. It appears that the inexperienced Allenby had lost control of the battle.[10] Haig's suspicions were confirmed when he visited three divisional headquarters including Wilkinson's on 13 April. He discovered that the orders they were receiving differed from those BEF HQ had issued.[11] Later that day Wilkinson was wounded but this did not stop him from meeting with the other two divisional commanders Haig had visited together with the Chief of Staff of VI Corps, Lord Loch on 15 April. The result of the meeting was an expression of dissatisfaction with the way Allenby was handling the battle which was passed to Haig. As Gary Sheffield remarks, this was potentially damaging to the careers of Wilkinson and his fellow divisional commanders. However, on this occasion this did not prove to be case and on the same day Haig ordered a pause in operations to regroup the day after Allenby had ordered further operations.

It is extremely unusual for the British *Official History* to record such dissent, its account attempts to gloss over the event but despite that it provides some indication of the ferocity of the disagreement. It claimed that despite the commanders offering a strong opinion about Allenby's orders it was not in the form of an 'expostulation'. That they did not offer any reasoning about their reservations appears to be unusual in that the commanders expressed them by means of passing a 'resolution.' It seems unlikely that a strong opinion would have been passed to Allenby without some reasoning to support the resolution; the *Official History* suggests the resolution

---

8 Museum of the Manchester Regiment The Men Behind the Medals Wilfred Keith Evans <http://www.themenbehindthemedals.org.uk/index.asp?page=full&mwsquery=(%7BPerson%20identity%7D=%7BEvans,%20WK%7D)> (accessed 22 April 2016).
9 Robbins, British Generalship, p. 503.
10 Gary Sheffield, *The Chief: Douglas Haig and the British Army* (London: Aurum, 2011), p. 217.
11 Gary Sheffield and John Bourne, *Douglas Haig: War Diaries and Letters, 1914-1918* (Paperback edition, London: Phoenix, 2006), p. 282.

was passed to Allenby who agreed with it.[12] Other accounts suggest Allenby knew nothing of it until he received orders to halt operations. The discrepancy lies in the nature of the *Official History* whose purpose was to present an agreed interpretation of events. James Edmonds who oversaw its production engaged in a great deal of correspondence with different participants as he sought to arrive at an agreed point of view on all the events recorded; this was a lengthy process and the volume covering these events was not published until 1940. Allenby had died in 1936 and the purpose of recording events in this way was probably to allow him to escape from the event with some honour and protect his reputation. Despite what the *Official History* says the incident appears to have been a brutal exercise in internal politics. Haig does not mention the incident in his diaries but it seems to be an extraordinary coincidence that the three division commanders he had met a few days before should protest directly to him. Haig and Allenby had great difficulty in communicating with each other which led to tensions in their relationship. There must be a suspicion that Haig, if not directly, offered support indirectly to Wilkinson and his fellow commanders. This suspicion is reinforced as, despite their insubordination, the three divisional commanders remained in post with Allenby's authority seriously damaged.[13] The development of the BEF and its approach to warfare owed as much to reasoned debate as it did to the imposition of approaches through the manoeuvrings of internal politics. Wilkinson showed independence in expressing his views about Allenby's approach but it appears before doing so he had judged that there was a low risk of him suffering adverse consequences as a result of his actions. Early in June Allenby was replaced as GOC of the Third Army and sent to the Middle East where he restored his reputation. Wilkinson continued to command the 50th Division until February 1918 when he was appointed Inspector of Musketry.

A senior commander could develop an excellent reputation but this status was often tenuous and one incident could lead to their removal. Victor Couper, 1870 to 1876, was 55 when war was declared; he commanded 14th Division from October 1914 to March 1918. Such longevity in one role was unusual, especially as the BEF went through a period of substantial growth and development. During this period, many senior commanders, especially older ones such as Alexander, were found not to be up to the job and were removed from their positions. Couper, however, had led the division in while it fought at Second Ypres in 1915, on the Somme in 1916 and at Arras and Third Ypres (also known as Passchendaele) in 1917. He appears to have been considered to be an influential leader within the army; in January 1917 he was member of a group of influential commanders and promising junior officers who visited the French army at Verdun.[14] On 22 March 1918, however, he was removed from his command after his division had collapsed in the face of the German assault on the first day of the Spring Offensive. The suddenness of the collapse justifies his removal but there are mitigating factors which suggest that he was a scapegoat when the British army suffered one of its worst days of the war. He was the first British Commander to be sacked for the handling of his unit during the battle. Before the battle, the commander of the 36th Ulster Division had complained that the 14th

---

12   Captain Cyril Falls, *History of the Great War Based on Official Documents. France and Belgium 1917 Volume I: The German Retreat to the Hindenburg Line and the Battles of Arras* (London: Macmillan, 1940), p. 378.
13   Sheffield, *The Chief*, pp. 217-218.
14   Peter Simkins, *From Somme to Victory: The British Army's Experience on the Western Front 1916-1918* (Barnsley: Praetorian, 2014), p. 48.

was not deploying in depth and was placing too many men on the front line. Despite this few adjustments were made by Couper and on the 21st the 14th's front line positions were overrun enabling the Germans to break into the British lines. It should be noted that the 36th Division's performance was not much better in holding up against the German offensive. Couper's successor, Greenly, did little better, cracked up under the strain and was removed from command only a few days later.[15]

The accusation made against the BEF and Haig about its failures in March 1918 is that it was unprepared for the German offensive. While there were many problems which badly hampered preparations for the expected offensive the BEF command appreciated their implications and this was reflected in the way it deployed its forces. In January 1918, the BEF had 78,500 fewer men than it did in January 1917;[16] the cabinet preferred to conserve manpower and wait for the Americans to arrive in force. The manpower shortage was made worse by an agreement by the British to take over 28 miles of the line from the French.[17] If that did not create enough problems in itself the government also decided that a reorganisation of the divisions was required to improve the proportion of their firepower. Whatever the merits of this, the reorganisation was only completed on 4 March 1918, just over two weeks before the German offensive commenced. The immediate effect was to disrupt the BEF's fighting effectiveness while it adapted to the changes and there was little time to provide men with rest and training before the German offensive.[18] Given this shortage of resources Haig made a decision to deploy manpower where he could least afford to lose ground. To the north of the River Scarpe the Channel ports were only 50 miles from the frontline. If the Germans broke through there, the British line of escape would be under threat and the British control of the Channel broken. The centre and left was kept strong at the expense of the Fifth Army on the right in the south of which Couper's 14th division was part of. The reserves were held in the north and it was decided the Fifth Army would be allowed to withdraw gradually with the purpose of delaying and exhausting the enemy. The Germans would have to advance 40 miles in the south before any serious danger to the British position arose.[19] Gough, commander of the Fifth Army estimated that his 14 divisions were outnumbered by 40 German divisions.[20] 14th Division was posted at the southern end of the British lines in trenches recently vacated by the French. It had only recently arrived from Ypres, was tired and had had little time for rest and training as it prepared its new defensive positions. It was required to defend just over 17 miles of the lines with two other divisions. Normally, just under half of this line would have been afforded extra protection from the River Oise but in the early part of 1918 very little rain had fallen. Marshes and channels had dried

---

15   Martin Middlebrook, *The Kaiser's Battle* (Paperback edition, London: Classic Penguin, 2000), pp. 327-328.
16   John Terraine, *Douglas Haig: The Educated Soldier* (Paperback edition, London: Phoenix, 2005), p. 392
17   Terraine, *Douglas Haig: The Educated Soldier*, p. 390.
18   Brigadier-General Sir James E Edmonds, *History of the Great War Based on Official Documents By Direction of the Historical Section of the Committee of Imperial Defence. Military Operations: France and Belgium, 1918, The German March Offensive and its Preliminaries* (London: HMSO, 1995), p. 61.
19   Chris Baker, *The Battle for Flanders German Defeat on the Lys, 1918* (Barnsley: Pen and Sword, 2011), p. 14.
20   Lieutenant Colonel Charles à Court Repington, *The First World War, 1914-1918: Personal Experiences of Lieut.-Col. C. À Court Repington Vol. 2* (Boston and New York: Houghton Mifflin, 1920), p. 268.

up which made the river far more easily fordable than normal.[21] The position of Couper and his 14th Division was highly perilous and when it was faced with the full brunt of the German offensive it is not surprising that it gave way on 21 March. It did not fight well but had had little time for rest and training since it had arrived in its new positions. Couper's division failed badly on 21 March but within the wider strategic situation it is little surprise it did. The war diary of his Corps commander is charitable about Couper and notes that he was in need of sleep and rest and unfit to manage the situation so had been replaced by Greenly.[22] The deployment of his forces by Haig worked; although the Germans made substantial progress in the south but further north with reserves available Byng's Third Army successfully held back the German advance. When a situation goes sour it is easy for an organisation to look for a scapegoat; Couper was the first commander chosen to fill this role in March 1918. Couper was the first of a number of commanders, including Gough at the insistence of the war cabinet, who were removed from command.

Couper fell from influential commander to failed commander in a relatively short period of time and in the heat of the war there was no time to reflect more fully on his performance. Percy Lake who would also be made a scapegoat was at least exonerated of any blame in the inquiry which followed his removal. Lake, 1867 to 1873, is one of three army OUs who are included in Matthews's *Eminent Uppinghamians*. His parents came from Canada and after leaving the school he was given a commission in the East Lancashire Regiment.[23] His experience from 1887 was that of a staff officer and in that capacity developed an excellent reputation for the quality of his work. Most noticeably in Canada, where he was Chief of Staff for the Militia from 1904 to 1908 followed by a further two years as Inspector-General and Chief Military Advisor to the Dominion Government. He increased its efficiency by extending the training period and encouraging the development of cadet corps as feeder units. This work was important in equipping the Canadian forces so that they could expand and make a valuable contribution during the Great War. In 1912 he became Chief of General Staff in India where he played an important part in improving the efficiency of the Indian Army and equipping it for the Great War. His qualities of leadership and initiative show in the way he had carried out his roles in Canada and India. In India, as a member of a commission reviewing the required level of military forces he had disagreed with the proposed level of forces to be maintained. With Sir Robert Scallon he submitted a minority report arguing for a stronger Indian Army.[24] Subsequently, his work as Chief of General Staff played an important part in the Indian preparation for war in August 1914. It was in a position to mobilise with specialist equipment in place.[25] When war was declared by Turkey in November 1914, the Indian Army was sent to Mesopotamia (modern day Iraq) to protect the supply of oil to the British navy. By December 1914, with the taking of Basra this aim had been achieved but the ease of this victory led to more ambitious and unrealistic plans being developed. The commander of the Indian Expeditionary Force (IEF), Sir John

---

21 W Shaw Sparrow, *The Fifth Army in March 1918* (London: John Lane, 1921), p. xx.
22 Middlebrook, *The Kaiser's Battle*, p. 327.
23 Matthews, B., *Eminent Uppinghamians* (Cranbrook: Neville & Harding, 1987) p. 8.
24 *The Times*, Lieutenant-General Sir Percy Lake, 20 November 1940.
25 Rob Johnson, '"I Shall Die Arms in Hand, Wearing the Warriors' Clothes": Mobilisation and Initial Operations of the Indian Army in France and Flanders', *British Journal of Military History*, 2: 2 pp. 107-119.

Nixon, ordered further advances and by September 1915 the IEF had reached Kut-al-Almara. Despite severe logistical problems Nixon ordered General Townshend to advance up the Tigris to Baghdad. Twenty-five miles short of Baghdad Townshend decided he could not reach the city and hold it and ordered a retreat back to Kut. The Turks anticipating this were able to cut his army off and by December 1915 Townshend and his soldiers were under siege in town. Nixon was relieved of his command in December 1915, officially because of ill health, and Lake replaced him. In the period between January and April 1916 four attempts were made to relieve all of which failed. On 29 April 1916 Townshend and his 13,000 men surrendered. Coming after so soon after the withdrawal from Gallipoli this was regarded as a humiliating defeat and in August 1916 Lake was replaced by Sir Frederick Maude.

Lake was unfortunate on a number of accounts. When he was appointed the conduct of the campaign was controlled from India but early in 1916 control was passed to the War Office in London. Sir William Robertson, the CIGS, had different ideas about the sort of commander he wanted. In a letter dated 10 February 1916 he expressed concern about Mesopotamia and stated a young active commander was needed.[26] Lake, who was 60 by the time he took command, did not fit the category of young. His health was not as good as it could have been and combined with his age led to a less energetic approach than might have been expected of a younger man.[27] Robertson believed that Lake had not shown enough energy replacing him with Maude whom he believed would display these qualities.[28] Forced to agree to a parliamentary enquiry into the surrender at Kut it suited Robertson to recall Lake to give evidence. Although he wanted a more energetic commander, Robertson believed that the events in Mesopotamia were not Lake's fault.[29] Lake was in a difficult position and earlier had requested more logistical support and men. When Townshend had advanced he had enjoyed the support of six steamers and eight tugs. By the time Maude started his advance to retake Kut in December 1916 he had the support of 446 tugs and steam launches, 774 barges and 414 motorboats not to mention considerably more men.[30] Maude appreciated this and believed that Lake had done everything humanly possible to save Townshend.[31] The Mesopotamia Commission which was set up by parliament blamed Nixon for the defeat at Kut and attached no blame to Lake. It was, however, in effect the end of Lake's military career. No new command was found for him and he spent the rest of the war in the Ministry of Munitions retiring in 1919. After taking up the position of commander of the IEF he soon found himself under a new commander who had different ideas about what was needed from a commander. With the fall of Kut it was politically expedient for the government to the time honoured approach of looking for a scapegoat; his recall was an obvious and visible thing for the government to do. By the time he was publicly exonerated no command opportunities were available for an elderly general and he became a victim of circumstance however unfair this appears to be.

26 Liddell Hart Archives, Papers of Field Marshal Sir William Robertson, 8/10/1, 10 February 1916 Letter to General AJ Murray.
27 *The Times*, Lake.
28 LHCMA, Robertson Papers, 8/1/40, 11 July 1916 Letter to General B Duff.
29 LHCMA, Robertson Papers, 8/4/13, 9 August 1918 Letter addressed to 'Your Royal Highness'.
30 David Stevenson, *1914-18: The History of the First World War* (Paperback edition London: Penguin, 2005), p. 122.
31 Andrew Syk (ed), *The Military Papers of Lieutenant-General Frederick Stanley Maude 1914-1917* (Stroud: Army Records Society, 2012), p. 151.

Mesopotamia although strategically important to the extent that the navy's oil supplies needed to be protected was always a sideshow. Victory required the defeat of Germany on the Western Front and it is there that Louis Vaughan came to prominence. His role in the defeat of Germany was the most significant of all the OU commanders. Vaughan is not included in *Eminent Uppinghamians;* apart from Lake the other two army OUs included are Brian Horrocks and Clive Liddell. His exclusion is understandable because the three OUs included all rose to the rank of General and Vaughan never reached this rank. Despite his lack of high rank/office his career demonstrates how the army and its commanders came to grips with the concepts of modern warfare. He made a significant contribution to winning the war on the Western Front but, partly owing to his modest nature, this has not been discussed in detail. By nature he was the antithesis of the Great War general portrayed in popular culture. When discussing Vaughan many have repeated Sir Philip Gibbs description of him as 'that charming man, with his professional manner, sweetness of speech, gentleness of voice and gesture, like an Oxford don analysing the war correspondence of Xenophon.'[32] Xenophon was an ancient Greek historian, soldier and mercenary whose books included *Hellenica* about the later stages of the Peloponnesian wars. Vaughan's character stands in contrast to public perceptions of the Generals of the Great War as boorish, uncaring and incompetent.

Vaughan's background was typical of many Uppinghamians. He came from a middle class background; his father was an engineer. Like many others who went to the school his other brothers were sent to different schools; his youngest brother, Percy, was sent to Rugby and became a barrister.[33] His parents, it appears, were more interested in picking the right school for their sons' abilities than blind loyalty to a particular one. After leaving Uppingham in 1892 he went to Sandhurst and after being gazetted transferred to the Indian Army in 1896. A commission in the Indian Army was especially attractive to those of limited means. Living in India was a good deal cheaper and it was possible to live without an independent income. As a result there was a great deal of competition to gain a commission in the Indian Army.[34] The dominance of schools such as Eton among the officer corps before the war is partly explained by their old boys coming from backgrounds with independent means required to be able to afford to be an officer in the British army. The background of OUs was from the professions and business and they were far less likely to have independent means. Vaughan served in India in various regimental roles until 1907 when he entered the Staff College at Camberley. This was the body which trained future commanding and staff officers. After graduating from Camberley he served in a number of staff roles. When war broke out he was 39 and held the rank of Major.[35] Unlike the elderly Alexander, who was 58 when war came, Vaughan had not reached the senior ranks of the British Army in 1914 but his promotion after that was relatively speedy. By April 1916 he had attained the rank of Brigadier-General having been Chief of Staff (G.S.O.1) for the Second Division at the Battles of Festubert and Loos. Neither of these battles was a success for the British but as already noted the BEF was severely constrained by limited resources. As a G.S.O.1 his responsibilities included training, intelligence, planning operations and directing the division in battle as it was fought. Unlike Alexander, it appears he was not blamed for the

32   Philip Gibbs, *Now It Can Be Told* (London: Harper, 1920), p. 486.
33   *Memorials of Rugbeians who fell in the Great War Volume V* (Rugby: Privately published, 1919), p. 266.
34   I am grateful to Professor John Bourne for this information.
35   *The Times*, Lieutenant-General Louis Ridley Vaughan, 8 December 1942.

poor performance at Loos. He was promoted because it was believed he had potential while Alexander's performance at Loos and, despite all the handicaps he faced, deemed to be not good enough and it was judged to be better employed elsewhere. In May 1917 Vaughan was promoted again to Major-General and appointed to be Chief of Staff of the Third Army. This was coincided with Byng's promotion to commander to replace Allenby following the latter's inadequate performance at Arras, which Wilkinson had protested about. Paul Harris argues that Vaughan's promotion was the result of the meritocratic system which operated for the staff officers system. A sign of his relatively rapid promotion was that he was one of the younger army Chiefs of Staff. He had a reputation for leading staff teams by setting exacting standards. This was partly achieved by the training he conducted which included an exercise for the prompt issuing of operational orders.[36]

The role of an army's staff is little understood; it was to put in place the required framework (orders, logistics etc.) so a commander's battle plans could be put into action. Staff Officers in the Great War are often portrayed as being out of touch sitting in their chateaus living a languid existence and oblivious to the predicament of the men on the front line. This is far from the case; they worked long hours, frequently visited the front line and often found themselves under fire. The chateaus they worked in were a long way behind the front line but for very good reason; in 1914 some British commanders and staff had lost their lives when their headquarters came under fire from German artillery. Sensibly, the decision had been taken to move these headquarters further back to avoid severe disruption to a key part of the army's operations. Where headquarters were in chateaus they were far from luxurious. In other cases headquarters were not based in chateaus; Vaughan's Third Army headquarters were based in a far from luxurious railway carriage.

Far from being out of touch Vaughan demonstrated at Cambrai in November 1917 his grasp of how modern warfare needed to be conducted. Kitchener had predicted in 1914 that it would take three years to get Britain's citizen army into a position where it would be able to win the war. This was a substantial achievement as it had involved the recruitment and training of a mass army together with the equipping it. Ever since 1916 the army had made immense progress from one of predominantly raw soldiers to an experienced fighting unit. Technology had developed substantially but equally importantly so had the army's understanding of how to use it effectively. No longer would gas be used, as it had been at Loos, in an indiscriminate way in the vain hope that it was a panacea to other equipment shortages. In late 1917 and 1918 it was used in artillery shells aimed at specific targets where it was judged it could be used effectively. There was an understanding of how to use different arms to gain an advantage quickly. Equally importantly, during 1918 the army also developed the ability to understand when an attack was running out of steam and that it was time to switch the focus of the attack to another part of the line. Cambrai is best known as the first tank battle but more importantly it was when the British first applied the tactics which were to lead to victory in 1918. Vaughan as Chief of Staff for the Third Army was responsible for the planning and implementation of this approach. Tanks were used to bridge the huge German defensive ditches by carrying and releasing bundles of fagots into them thus easing the advance of the infantry. The improved technology of the artillery

---

36 Paul Harris, *The Men who Planned the War: A Study of the Staff of the British Army on the Western Front, 1914-1918* (Farnham: Ashgate, 2015), p. 163.

meant that no sighting shots were required. It was possible to it move artillery into place at night without the Germans being aware and its first shots to be on target taking the Germans by surprise. Using a much improved ability to locate German artillery and the reconnaissance information from the RFC it was possible to neutralise enemy batteries. The new approach meant that preliminary barrages over several days were no longer needed; the barrage would be short enough to surprise and neutralise the enemy while the infantry advanced behind it. As a result, the British were able to seize positions before the enemy had a chance to respond. The brevity of this explanation cannot give justice to the huge amount of work and thought given to the planning of Cambrai. The German counter offensive meant that the battle did not result in British victory but it proved the effectiveness of the army's tactics. Vaughan described this more effective use of resources as cutting 'our coat according to our cloth.'[37]

In 1918 after its successful part in blocking the German Spring Offensive in March, the Third Army played one of the leading roles in the final victory over Germany.[38] In the 100 days offensive from August until the Armistice in November the Third Army advanced 60 miles, captured 67,000 prisoners and in the region of 800 guns. Casualties, however, were substantial; in the region of 100,000 although the Germans suffered equivalent if not greater casualties.[39] The difference between the British and the Germans was that the latter were worn down to the point where they were forced to seek an armistice. The British tactics which included a regular switching of the point of attack meant that that the German line was pushed back and their reserves used up. As Jonathan Boff puts it, the Germans were unable to keep up with the pace of British operations.[40] The Great War was one of attrition where the side which used up its resources first would lose. The Allies were able to deploy their resources in a more effective way and wore the German war machine out. It was not enough to have more resources; resources needed to be employed in an effective manner and used in a way where the Germans were always playing catch-up. They were combined to give the maximum effect in their use and to gain the maximum element of surprise. It was the role of the commander to set the plan and vision as to how this was to be achieved, the role of the Chief of Staff was to plan the details of the operation so that the maximum surprise could be achieved and resources used most effectively. Vaughan achieved surprise at Cambrai by developing plans to use tanks to breach the defensive ditches. He developed techniques such as the RFC flying at night before the assault to enable the tanks and artillery to be moved up without the enemy hearing. To achieve surprise required the use of initiative, strong leadership skills and taking responsibility for the details of the plan. Vaughan displayed leadership in his creation of battle plans but also in the way he delivered them. Gibb speaks of him explaining his plans and strategy in a charming and gentle-mannered way.[41] This was hardly the stereotypical blustering and callous general. Leadership did not need to be loud and aggressive in its style. Vaughan understood the need to only exploit success only so far as the

---

37 Gibbs, *Now It Can Be Told*, p. 486.
38 Philpott, *Attrition*, p. 330.
39 Jonathan Boff, *Winning and Losing on the Western Front: The British Third Army and the Defeat of Germany in 1918* (Cambridge: Cambridge University Press, 2012), pp. 36-37. By the end of the war German administration had broken down to the extent that it could no longer collect accurate information about its losses.
40 Boff, *Winning and Losing on the Western Front*, p. 38.
41 Gibbs, *Now It Can Be Told*, p. 53.

initial surprise justified.⁴² Cambrai failed because the British tried to go beyond this after Haig insisted that costly attacks should be continued although afterwards he accepted responsibility for it.⁴³ The 100 days offensive which commenced in August 1916 was not a textbook success. Victories in war rarely are but Boff argues the British made better decisions than the Germans and followed them through. In the 100 days the British ability to improvise and deal with the different military problems which arose was far superior to that of the Germans.⁴⁴ That Vaughan and other senior commanders had created an environment where this was possible demonstrated a high quality of leadership. Vaughan played an important part, as Third Army Chief of Staff in winning the victory which finally came in November 1918.

These four case studies of high ranking OUs demonstrate the problems of high command throughout the war. In the early days they demonstrate the huge amount of improvisation in the early days of the war as a mass British army was built from scratch. This involved putting square pegs into round holes and men such as Alexander did their best even if they were judged not to be long term solutions. Others who lost their commands such as Couper were the victims of politics and the need to have scapegoats when things went wrong. Lake became the victim of circumstances when he found himself in a position where he acquired a new commander who had different ideas about the sort of leader he wanted; his successor would have far more resources to complete the job Lake had been unable to finish. Others such as Wilkinson became involved in the politics which are so typical of large organisations and contributed to the removal of an underperforming commander. In Vaughan that we see how the British army learned many lessons, developed technology and the way it was used ultimately becoming a war winning machine. It is in him that we see the shallowness of seeing all generals as being one dimensional such as the fictional Melchett. In all these four OUs we see the qualities of a strong sense of duty, leadership skills, taking responsibility and independence of thought. These were qualities that were instilled in them by their teachers. The teachers who went to war would display these same qualities.

---

42 Gibbs, *Now It Can Be Told*, p. 490.
43 Peter Simkins, 'Haig and the Army Commanders', in Brian Bond and Nigel Cave (eds) *Haig: A Reappraisal 70 Years On*, (Barnsley: Leo Cooper, 1999), p. 92.
44 Boff, *Winning and Losing on the Western Front*, pp. 248-250.

9

Teachers in Arms

> It was pointed out to me last year that though every Public School was keeping a Record of Service of its "Old Boys" little was heard of the Schoolmasters who have supplied the O.T.C. with Officers and Instructors' and who have also supplied the fighting forces with excellent time in our national history.[1]

Little has been written of the teachers and staff from Uppingham who served in the Great War and their service was not included with the list of OUs who served. The School Magazine of April 1919 listed 12 masters who had served overseas during the war but this was an incomplete account of their contribution to the war effort.[2] It was only when the Record *of War Service 1914-1918 Officers Training Corps (Junior Division) Public School Officers and Other Members of the Staffs* was published later in 1919 that a full account was provided. The contribution of the masters and other staff reflect the involvement and commitment of the whole of the school community to the war effort. At the heart of this there is one teacher who made a particularly significant contribution; Charles Herbert Jones, as previously discussed, was the teacher responsible for the development of the school's OTC into a leading unit but he also made a significant contribution to the development of the OTC throughout the country. Before discussing the involvement of all of the school's teachers in the war it is necessary to discuss the role of Jones.

Born in 1865 Jones was 49, the oldest of all the school's teachers who served on the front, when war came in 1914. On the outbreak of war he was called up and promoted to Lieutenant Colonel to command the 1/5th Leicester battalion and served on the Western Front until 1917 where he was wounded twice. This was to be the culmination of a distinguished service as a part time soldier. He was born in Bristol, the third of nine children and educated at Bristol Grammar School. His school records indicate that he was an all-rounder with a strong academic record and excelled at sport but also shone in other areas; he was a regular singer and was secretary of the school debating society. After graduating from the University of London and before arriving at Uppingham in 1897 he taught at Bradfield and Rossall.[3]

---

1 *Record of War Service 1914-1918: Officers Training Corps (Junior Division) Public School Officers and Other Members of the Staffs* (London: privately published, 1919), p. v.
2 *USM*, April 1919, pp. 117-119.
3 USA:, CH Jones: Notes by Major W F Howard-Jones.

His involvement in the school debating society is not surprising given the reputation he had at Uppingham for being a somewhat forceful personality. When the school was buying its boarding houses from the masters who had previously owned them, the negotiations after the war with Jones, to buy his house, Meadhurst, proved to be the most difficult. School legend has it that he threatened to refuse to sell and instead turn Meadhurst into a girls' school if his asking price was not met but, his bluff was called and an agreement was reached. His letters suggest he had vulnerabilities and concerns but hid this by displaying a single mindedness. It was through this single mindedness that he showed himself to be an excellent corps commander and an important figure in the formation of the government's scheme for a national OTC. Before he had arrived at Uppingham he had already developed a reputation for his work with the cadet corps at Bradfield. An undated newspaper report discusses a visit by Jones to Leamington College in which he had given a fencing exhibition which had led to the establishment of a 'large and enthusiastic class at that school.'[4] Today, this appears to be anachronistic but at the time of his visit there was great concern about the swordsmanship of British officers and a desire to make sure public schoolboys had the opportunity to develop these skills. Jones's visit to Leamington was probably been at the request of his brother, Edgar Montague Jones. Edgar was a member of the Leamington Volunteers and a teacher at the school; in 1898 he became the commanding officer of its newly formed Cadet Corps. Its formation was viewed as a great success and initially 58 boys had joined it with only 12 eligible boys declining to join.[5] In 1898, Herbert (as Charles was known to his family) also became commanding officer of the Uppingham Cadet Corps. Both Herbert and Edgar had a long involvement in the Volunteer movement and schoolboy soldiering. From letters written by Herbert to Edgar and other material it is possible to gain an understanding of Herbert's role in developing military training for public school boys.

Both Herbert and Edgar became leading figures in the OTC; Edgar became Secretary of the Junior OTC Club and was awarded the OBE, for his services to the OTC, and the Territorial Decoration (TD). In 1902 Edgar was appointed Headmaster of St Albans School where he set up an OTC contingent. Just as single minded as his brother, he went off to war in 1914 as a Major in the Hertfordshire Regiment, a Territorial unit, without informing the St Albans School Governors. It was only at the insistence of the Board of Education that he returned to the school in 1916 where he became involved with its OTC again.[6] Like his brother Herbert he served in the Volunteers and their successor body the Territorials. Herbert was commissioned into the Leicester Volunteers in March 1899 and within a year took leave of absence from Uppingham to serve in South Africa. This was part of the national response to the 'Black Week' of December 1899 when the British had been defeated by the Boers on three occasions. As previously discussed in Chapter 3, the defeats had created a sense of crisis and shattered the myth that the Empire was invincible.[7] The school, on the initiative of the Headmaster Selwyn, made its own response to the call from the government by introducing a shooting test for all boys (see Chapter 3). It is clear from Herbert's letters that he had a good relationship with

---

4   St Albans School Archive (SASA): E Montague Jones: Military Matters.
5   SASA:, E Montague Jones: Leamington College Formation of a Volunteer Cadet Corps.
6   SASA: E Montague Jones: Death of Major E. Montague-Jones.
7   Martin Stephen, *The Price of Pity: Poetry, History and Myth in the Great War* (London: Leo Cooper, 1996), p. 4.

Selwyn, corresponded regularly with him from South Africa and enjoyed his support.[8] Given this strong relationship, it is probable that Jones was closely involved in Selwyn's introduction of a shooting test. Within months of arriving in South Africa he was already writing to his brother promising to 'make himself heard' on the subject of school cadet corps.[9] He was also keeping himself up to date on developments for training public schoolboys dismissing Warre's scheme (see Chapter 3) as 'absurd.'[10] Edgar's letters to Herbert have not survived but it appears there was regular correspondence about training schoolboys with Herbert encouraging Edgar to meet with Selwyn who shared his interest in army reform.[11]

By January 1901 he was writing to Edgar with his ideas about how to improve the cadet corps. These revolved around making the corps a more interesting experience and improving the quality of the training; corps 'must have more than square drill.' All boys should be allowed to attend the shooting range and it must not be reserved for 'crack shots.' On wet days when outside exercises were not possible there could be lectures on subjects such as model building and knot tying. NCOs should only appointed if they had passed an examination. In the school library there should be a section for military books which would include technical references and infantry and cavalry drill. He proposed that schools should establish a military history prize only open to corps members. However, the corps was not to be a closed society; there should be a school corps committee which would include at least one representative of 'Non-corps people.' At its discretion the school corps should invite non-members to meetings. For example, a history master could be invited to talk about a famous battle or war. All this would not be possible unless the 'Schoolmaster Captain' made 'himself as efficient as possible.' These ideas were very much work in progress; he described them as 'high flown' and did not want to force them on people. For this reason, he told his brother the contents of the letter should remain confidential.[12]

The most important feature of Jones's ideas was that corps should be interesting and not just devoted to square bashing. A variety of activities were proposed, promotions should be earned through success in examinations and the corps should provide an education in military matters. His experience in South Africa had convinced him of the need to reform training for school boys. He was in regular correspondence with Selwyn who had kept him up to date with discussions at the HMC and Warre's proposals. He and Selwyn were of a like mind on the need for military reform and Selwyn, through his participation at the HMC, was in a position to play an important part in influencing the approach of public schools towards military training. It was not until 1906 that Jones received an official hearing for his views when on 15 November he gave evidence to the Ward Committee.

The Ward Committee (see Chapter 2) had asked him to provide written answers to a number of questions which had been sent to all the OTC commanders who had been invited to give evidence. From over 100 school cadet corps seven of their commanders had been invited to

8   SASA: E Montague Jones: Letters from C H Jones 9 June 1900, 10 September 1900 and 1 March 1901.
9   SASA: E Montague Jones: Letters from C H Jones 9 June 1900.
10 SASA: E Montague Jones: Letters from C H Jones 10 September 1900. See Chapter 1 for a brief account of the scheme proposed by the Eton Headmaster.
11 SASA: E Montague Jones: Letters from C H Jones 30 November 1900.
12 SASA: E Montague Jones: Letters from C H Jones 19 January 1901.

give evidence along with one public school headmaster (Reverend J Gow of Westminster). Of the seven school corps commanders four were from one of the top 10 providers of regular army officers (Eton, Haileybury, Rugby and Wellington); with one school corps commander representing a school also known as a significant provider of regular army officers, Bedford. Apart from Uppingham the only other school which had its corps commander called to give evidence was Stonyhurst, the leading Roman Catholic public school. The HMC was represented on the committee by Reverend David of Clifton College which was another of the top 10 providers of officers to the regular army. The inclusion of Jones was significant as he represented a school which did not traditionally supply a large number of regular army officers. He had fulfilled his promise to his brother that he would make himself heard on the subject of school cadet corps and he had established himself as an influential figure on the subject.

His own figures, provided to the committee, demonstrated the nature of Uppingham's military contribution. He stated that 65 of the 214 (30 percent) corps members he had inherited on becoming commander were serving in the forces. His own analysis, provided later, showed that only nine of them had become regular army officers, another 27 were officers in the Militia and Volunteers and a further 24 were serving in the ranks of the University Volunteers.[13] Jones tried to over-egg Uppingham's contribution because he was keen to demonstrate that the approach he had put in place to train the boys to be an officer was effective. The committee do not appear to have been taken in by Jones's exaggerated claims but its proposals for the OTC scheme show that it was strongly influenced by his approach. Of this he said:

> We train them all though with the idea of their eventually becoming officers, and we take them a good way along the course towards that end. They have, of course, to begin with drills in the ranks and then they become corporals and sergeants, and we then make them drill the company, set piquets and outposts, and develop them as far as possible in the duties of junior officers.

Although there was an hour's compulsory drill work most cadets attended a further three hours of voluntary classes to gain certificates of proficiency in subjects such as signalling. In addition some time was spent on at the shooting range each term.[14] Jones had developed the ideas he had begun in South Africa about providing interesting training into a coherent scheme. When compared to the evidence given by the other school corps commanders it is obvious that he had developed a far more progressive training scheme than they had. The final OTC scheme adopted proposals he had set out in his evidence; as Jones had suggested it was agreed with the HMC that schools would be paid by results according to the number of efficient cadets they produced.[15] Another of his proposals which was adopted was that boys should be given three years to decide whether they wished to join the Special Reserve or the Territorials.[16] Most significantly, the final plan for the OTC reflected the work Jones was already carrying out at Uppingham. The syllabus would be geared towards producing men whose proficiency would be that of a Second Lieutenant in the Volunteers; the award of Certificate A demonstrating that

---

13 *Ward Committee Evidence*, p. 32.
14 *Ward Committee Evidence*, pp. 30-32.
15 *Ward Committee Evidence*, pp. 31, 89.
16 *Ward Committee Evidence*, pp. 31, 88.

they had achieved this. The training would include drill, tactical handling of a section, shooting, parts of the army training manuals and semaphore signalling. Typically, Jones was clear and decisive in getting his proposals heard. His brother later said that the scheme for the OTC was agreed after the two brothers and Hoare of Haileybury went to see Haldane, the Secretary of State for War in 1907 to set out their proposals.[17] Baden Powell who had developed his own ideas about training after service in South Africa also attended the meeting; he was not pleased about the decision to adopt the OTC scheme and decided to set up the boy scouts to put his own ideas into practice.[18]

Historical discussions about the school present Jones as a militaristic figure who 'galvanised the corps into much more active life.'[19] There is no doubt that he invigorated the corps but it is obvious he did far more than this. From the time he was serving in South Africa he was developing his ideas about how to train public school boys to be officers. With the support of Selwyn, who took a keen interest in military reform, he developed a programme of training to achieve this. The final scheme for the OTC reflected the way he had developed training at the Uppingham corps as well as some of his specific proposals such as paying OTC contingents by results. The rapid expansion of the army after war broke out created an urgent need for junior officers to lead it. Much of the response to this had to be improvised and the basic training which OTC cadets had received made them a valuable source for junior officers. The integrated training under the direction of the War Office which he had envisioned meant that the army could draw on a supply of men who it knew had had the basic training that a junior officer required. The existence of this training scheme owed much to the vision and work of Jones at Uppingham. As already noted in Chapter Five, at the end of the war, the army indicated the importance that it attached to the OTC when in April 1919 the School Magazine reported the War Office had written to express its appreciation of the 'great work' carried out. The letter was clear that the OTC had been a valuable source of officers for the army. In its eyes the decision to form the OTC in 1908 was fully justified; in particular, the number of officers it had provided was a testament to the standard of training provided by the OTC and the particular emphasis on developing the powers of leadership in its cadets. Jones in his evidence to the Ward Committee had proposed that the OTC's syllabus should be geared towards men who were of sufficient quality to immediately become Second Lieutenants in the Volunteers (who by the time the OTC was formed had become part of the Territorials). By integrating the training of the OTC into that set down in existing schemes such as the Field Service Regulations the War Office found a practical way to effectively implement the vision of Jones.[20] Jones became the first CO of the Uppingham OTC contingent in 1908 but retired in 1910.[21] This was not the end of his involvement in the military. He remained a dedicated part-time soldier serving as a Territorial in the 5th Battalion of the Leicester Regiment as a Major and, as detailed above, served in the war until November 1917. He retired from the school in 1926 and went to Australia where he continued to lead an active life. In Australia his work included placing English public school boys in jobs. He died in 1953.[22]

17   SASA: E Montague Jones: Thirty Years as a Headmaster.
18   Nigel Wood-Smith (2015)'CHJ' E-mail (15 August 2015).
19   Matthews, *By God's Grace*, p. 244.
20   *USM*, April 1919, p. 94.
21   Matthews, *By God's Grace*, p. 245.
22   USA: Charles Herbert Jones.

140 A School in Arms

By June 1914 the OTC was 350 strong but the contingent was five officers under strength; it was not possible to find enough committed teachers with enough free time to meet the rapid expansion of the OTC in the years before the war. Immediately, on the outbreak of war Jones, his successor Shea and two other masters who were members of the Territorials or Special Reserve were called up for service.[23] Not counting those masters who were involved in the home front effort 26 teachers and staff served in the war. As discussed in Chapter 6 the Trustees were caught in a position between wishing to support the war effort and retaining a teaching staff which had an acceptable standard. This was not always easy and as the war went on manpower shortages in the army meant that teachers were called up despite the school's appeals to the Military Service Tribunal. A comparison with Tonbridge and Winchester (Table 16) suggests that the proportion of teachers from Uppingham with OTC experience who served is far higher than the other two similarly sized schools. In total, their contributions are broadly similar although the number of OTC officers Winchester provided to serve is surprisingly low for an 'army' school. Uppingham's higher OTC involvement is partially explained by the influence of Jones; after stepping down as CO of the OTC he remained as a teacher at the school and is likely to have been an influence on a number of OTC officers who joined the Territorials and the Special Reserve before the war and were immediately called up.

Table 16 Teachers who served in the Great War – Tonbridge, Uppingham and Winchester[24]

School	Boys at School August 1914	OTC Officers Serving in the War	OTC Officers Retained for Service at School	Other Teachers Serving in the War	Total
Tonbridge	436	6	8	10	24
Uppingham	450	12	9	5	26
Winchester	445	3	5	13	21

Jones as a leader of men had a strong influence on his fellow teachers but a decision to serve was not always an easy one. Frank Street, Housemaster of Fircroft, who was 43 when war broke out, was torn by a conflicting sense of duty to school and country. Once the severity of the threat to the country became obvious he enlisted. He received his commission in January 1915 and was killed leading his men on the Somme. His obituary in the School Magazine spoke of his 'modesty and lack of personal ambition.' It was 'a high sense of public duty' which led him to serve although he had retired as an OTC officer.[25] Despite the many reasons why he should not go he was quick to follow Jones out of the school to serve with the army. In speaking of the teachers who served and died the School Magazine emphasised their gentleness and sense of duty rather than a militaristic leaning. George Oberhoffer, a music teacher, whose father was born in Germany, volunteered in January 1915 and served with the 1st Public Schools

23   Matthews, *By God's Grace*, pp. 245-246.
24   Based on analysis of *Record of War Service 1914-1919: Officers Training Corps (Junior Division), Tonbridge School and the Great War of 1914-1918, Old Uppinghamians who served in H.M. Forces 1914-1919* and *Wykehamist War Service*.
25   *USM*, pp. 194-197 and *Record of War Service 1914-1919: Officers Training Corps (Junior Division)*, p. 176.

Battalion. He was shot through the head on 18 February 1916.[26] Of him, his obituary in the School Magazine said:

> If ever there was a man of peace it was George Oberhoffer. A passionate lover of nature, enthusiastic over his work, he did the small things of this life as if they were of the greatest importance, infusing an atmosphere of cheery optimism wherever he went...Can we doubt he took up his military duties (hateful as they must have been) with an enthusiasm less than that which he had brought to bear on his art in times of peace?[27]

Both Street and Oberhoffer had public school educations, Westminster and Ampleforth respectively. There is no information available on all the masters' education but it is likely many were public school educated from the information available. The obituaries chose not to present the teachers as heroic and chivalric knights, the values public school boys were said to be imbued with, but as men called away from their true vocation because they believed it was their duty. There were no obituaries for old boys who had died in the School Magazine, only for two of the three teachers who died. Glorification of death was not the school's way.

Uppingham was a school in arms because that was its duty. Some of the teachers who became officers in the school's OTC contingent such as H H Champion returned after previous service. Others took up the responsibility for the first time including Owen, the Headmaster from 1916, for the first time. In this capacity he was under the command of the Director of Music, Major Sterndale Bennett. Owen, during his time at the school developed a reputation for being a martinet so this relationship must have been an interesting one although no details of how it worked in practice have been found. Sterndale Bennett was not just involved in the school's OTC. In the early stages of the war he acted as a recruiting officer for the Artist's Rifles, later he arranged a course for OTC COs and during the war attended nine training courses.[28] Unlike today, there was no separation between music and military. All parts of society were dedicated to meeting the threat to the Empire. A music mistress, Elsa West, became a VAD and worked as a "Music Sister" at St Dunstans, founded to provide rehabilitation, training and lifelong support to those blinded in the Great War, before going to work in France as a musician with Lena Ashwell's concert parties. Ashwell was a suffragist who pressed the War Office to allow parties to entertain the soldiers in France with concerts and plays instead of the somewhat lower brow entertainment the men had created for themselves.[29]

The role of teachers in the Great War is often forgotten and under researched. Only in recent years has more research been carried out. In the case of Uppingham, Jones, its leading part-time soldier is often seen by later generations as a slightly absurd militaristic figure. His importance

26 *The Pipeline*, (February 1915), p. 15 and p. 18.
27 *USM*, (March 1916), pp. 47-48.
28 *Record of War Service 1914-1919: Officers Training Corps (Junior Division)*, p. 178.
29 *Daily Telegraph* Lena Ashwell: the woman who brought music to WW1 trenches <http://www.telegraph.co.uk/history/world-war-one/10757403/LenaAshwell-the-woman-who-brought-music-to-WW1-trenches.html> (accessed 27 May 2016). A Suffragist was a person advocating the extension of the suffrage to especially women but did not support violent action. Ashwell was a member of the Actresses Franchise League AFL (1908) which neither supported nor condemned militancy. Spartacus Educational British History, <Women's Suffrage> Lena Ashwell <http://spartacus-educational.com/WashwellL.htm> (accessed 14 October 2016).

in establishing the OTC has, to date, been little appreciated. Its value would be seen in the early years of the war when the army had to improvise in its recruitment of junior officers to lead a rapidly expanding army. His enthusiasm and leadership is shown in the number of OTC officers who left immediately to serve. The service of the teachers was one which arose out of a strong sense of duty. It was often a difficult choice to make but as with the rest of the country it was one that all parts of the teaching community made to meet a threat to the country. The defeat of this threat would be remembered in a variety of different ways after the war.

10

Laying Down Arms

Popular opinion often arrives at a point of view about an event in history which ignores the nuances and the context, which results in a grossly simplified perception of the event. The end of the Great War and how people responded to it is not immune to this trend. Rather as the beginning of the war is mistakenly thought of as in cheering crowds so too the predominant image of the public response to the end of the war is the cheering crowds. Remembrance of the war is often thought of in terms of the memorials to the in the towns and villages in Britain, the services which take place around in November them and the accompanying two minute silence. There were, understandably, cheering crowds in Britain and France on 11th November 1918 but it must also be remembered many men were serving with the armed forces throughout the world and their response was often different. The aftermath of the war is often thought in terms of the maimed and the psychologically damaged. This chapter will examine the response of Uppingham and those connected with it to demonstrate there was far more to the end of the war and its aftermath than these stereotypes represent.

There was a common agreement within the country that the sacrifices of the war needed to be marked. This was carried out in a variety of ways and the many different ways this was done indicates the variety in how families and organisations wished to remember those they had lost. Others wished to give thanks for the safe return of their sons, fathers and brothers. Different public schools varied in the nature of their war memorials and the style of the memorial books they produced about their old boys who had died. Of those who returned from the war some were maimed or damaged in other ways. Some would suffer for many years and die of the wounds they had sustained many decades later. Others would be unable to cope with life in a country at peace while others who had suffered terrible injuries were able to make a deep impact in their chosen areas. But many people also returned and successfully continued their lives, yes deeply affected in mind and body by their experiences but determined to remember their lost friends and family in their everyday lives.

Responses to the End of the War

At Uppingham, the end of the war was greeted with joy but surprise in November 1918's School Magazine.

> At last! After more than four years of waiting! The magic words "Victory and Peace" have reached us finally as in a dream. How are the mighty fallen! How unexpected is this debacle of the Prussian Empire, and the defeat of militarism and hope of world-domination. Only last March we were staring apparent disaster in the face, and now we are at peace! How many of us who came back to school in September, expected it or even dared to hope for it? And now we have got it as final a victory as we ever wished for. Praise be to God!

In March 1918 the German Spring Offensive, in the eyes of the British population, seemed to be a serious threat and that Britain and her allies were in serious trouble. This perception turned out to be misguided and this final offensive by the Germans was the last desperate throw of a fatally wounded empire. The misconception arose partly because BEF HQ in early 1918 had detached itself from the press and had failed to correct the perception the British army was being routed.[1] In September when the school returned from its holidays the 100 days offensive which would lead to victory had only opened on 8 August at the Battle of Amiens and it was not obvious that victory was in sight.

The report of how the school responded to news of the armistice in the magazine reflects a sense of elation at the news. News did not reach Uppingham until 55 minutes after the armistice had come into effect; something a little difficult to understand in an age of social media and instant communication. The school shared, like the vast majority of Britain's population, a sense of jubilation on Armistice Day. The chapel bell was rung, classrooms were emptied out and the school assembled for a brief service of thanksgiving. This was immediately followed by a school gathering on the green for the raising of the Union Jack and the singing of the National Anthem. A ceremony repeated in the market place as the school joined the town to share in the celebrations. Not surprisingly, there was no more work that day and, at an impromptu concert in the evening, the Headmaster announced there would be no early school the following day. He also announced that the drill and detention lists had been torn up; an announcement which was greeted with loud cheering![2]

The sense of elation and rejoicing was not shared by all. Vera Brittain, who had lost three men from Uppingham close to her, on Armistice Day, felt only a sinking heart as she passed through the celebrating crowds. She was washing dressing bowls when she heard the maroons go off, she wrote: 'And as I dried the bowls I thought; 'It's come too late for me.'[3] For those at the front there was often not the same sense of celebration; many OUs serving with the armed forces only experienced a sense of anti-climax if not frustration with the celebrations at home. Arthur Lee, serving with the BEF general staff was ambivalent about the armistice saying the whole thing left him cold. Laurence Carr told his wife in a letter on 15th November 1918 that in France they were fed up with the attitude of the population noting 'it is not peace'.[4] Even those who met civilians celebrating being liberated on 11th November had mixed feelings. Robert Creighton Seymour Aitken, 1900 to 1903, wrote to his Aunt Meta from the village of Herchies

---

1   Stephen Badsey, 'Haig and the Press,' in Brian Bond and Nigel Cave (eds) *Haig: A Reappraisal 70 Years On*, (Barnsley: Leo Cooper, 1999), p. 90.
2   *USM*, November 1918, pp. 219-221.
3   Brittain, *Testament of Youth*, pp. 422-424.
4   LHCMA: GB 0099 KCLMA Carr: Papers of Lt Gen Laurence Carr and Lee Papers. Carr like Lee is identified by Robbins as a war manager.

in Belgium describing a reception which included being cheered and bombarded with flowers. Aitken recorded the extremely odd experience, for an Englishman, of being kissed by a man! However, he also remarked that the death of a man shot through the heart took 'the gilt off a bit.' The end of the war was rather like leaving school. He was pleased but not sure of the future.[5]

By July 1919 the atmosphere of celebration had vanished and the School Magazine took a more subdued approach noting that the signing of the Versailles Treaty was greeted with none of the sudden joy of the armistice. A pre-war feeling had returned and Annual Camp had not taken place so that: 'we may forget for a season the troubles of militarism…It is the future now which is our immediate concern.' In the same edition it was reported that the Memorial Service had taken place on 6th July. Reflecting the more subdued attitude there was no report on the service or the sermon preached. The Memorial Service was not the last act of remembrance; there were reports about the dedication of the chapel on 16th October 1921 and the opening of the Memorial Halls in the July 1924 edition. However, by July 1919 the magazine's tone had changed and in its attitude the school was no longer at war.[6]

The School's Memorial

It is often thought that individual schemes for remembrance set out to remember the dead. The history of Uppingham's memorial shows that the purpose of a memorial could evolve in terms of what was being remembered and that it often had a practical use and was not just a symbol of remembrance. In 1917 the school started to plan for how it would honour its fallen; the July 1917 magazine had announced a proposal for a memorial fund with two aspects to it which were to show the school's gratitude: 'to the fallen should be marked not only by a great memorial which shall stand for all time but also by the offer of practical assistance to their sons.'

An education fund was to help with grants for boys whose fathers had died or needed assistance because of the war, there were plans for a memorial in the chapel and the building of a memorial quadrangle which would include a new hall and room for new classrooms. It was an ambitious scheme and the committee which was responsible for raising the funds set a target of £50,000.[7] In today's terms simply using a simple measure of inflation this is the equivalent of £2.5 million but such an ambitious building project would now be more likely to cost in the region of £10 million. Many other schools, such as Wellington, fell short of what their original appeal had asked for. In the difficult economic conditions after the war Uppingham was able to raise the funds to pay for the plans set out in 1917 (although just short of the £50,000 target). Owen followed the example of Selwyn (with his plans for the building of a combined concert hall and gym for the Boer War memorial) and took the opportunity to use the desire to remember the sacrifice of OUs by proposing much needed improvements at the school. His drive and ambition enabled the school to succeed where many other schools failed.

The ownership of the school's boarding houses was predominantly in private hands and this had created two serious problems. The house masters taught at their own houses spread throughout the town and this was a highly inefficient exercise with a great deal of time taken as

---

5   Aitken (2015), 'First World War Letter'. E-mail (28 April 2015).
6   *USM*, July 1919, pp. 153-154, *USM*, December 1921, pp. 233-240 and *USM*, July 1924, pp. 113-123.
7   *USM*, July 1917, pp. 94-97.

boys moved between lessons.⁸ The other problem for Owen was that his choice of housemaster, when one retired, was constrained to those who could afford to buy or rent the house, many of the houses were owned by the original builders. The need to deal with this was becoming more urgent as, by 1914, governors in many schools were starting to buy the privately owned houses at their schools.⁹ The appeal gave Owen the opportunity to partly solve this problem by making it possible to build extra classrooms on the school's central site making it no longer necessary to have lessons in the houses but it would take a separate scheme to bring all the houses into the school's ownership.¹⁰

When the appeal was originally announced in 1917 it was stated that the announcement was for information only and that no appeal would be made until the war had ended.¹¹ On 2 April 1918 the school wrote to old boys and other friends to say that after 'strong representations' by many OUs and because of the 'altered war conditions' it had been decided to launch the appeal.¹² Matthews, the historian of the school, was puzzled by this as the announcement came under two weeks after the launch of the German Spring Offensive; it did not strike him as a good time to launch an appeal.¹³ The announcement, however, said that all funds raised would be invested in 'Patriotic Funds' such as government war loans. The announcement reflects the sense of concern about the German offensive and a keen desire to support the government in its efforts to avoid defeat. So the appeal became more than a memorial to the dead but also a means to give financial support to the war. As previously noted, the nation had gone to war because it believed it needed to protect its way of life from a serious threat. Constructing a memorial to those who had fought and died was linked to the importance of the cause. Without supporting the country through such means as investing in patriotic funds the sacrifice of OUs would be significantly devalued. Every effort needed to be made to first support the cause for which they were fighting. The pressure to launch the appeal and invest in patriotic funds should be seen in this light.

This was not the last change to the details and purpose of the appeal. In the initial proposals a monument to the dead had been proposed but by 1920, when £33,000 had been raised, it was agreed that instead a shrine would be erected in the chapel.¹⁴ By 1919 Owen had modified the intention from being just one to honour the dead to a wider purpose. At the 1919 speech day, the first since 1914, he announced that although the appeal would 'first and foremost' be a memorial to 'the fallen' it would also be far more than that. It would also commemorate all those who had played their part in the war: 'The men who left their homes, their friends, their business and hazarded all for the greatest things for which a nation ever took up arms; and further it would commemorate those Old Boys who though prevented from active service, yet played their part in the national service.' Owen was keen to emphasise the idea of a school in arms as much marking the sacrifice of those who had lost their lives. Whether he intended it or not, an effect had been that parents who had boys in the school in 1919 had been some of the

8   Matthews, *By God's Grace*, p. 148.
9   Seldon and Walsh, *Public Schools and The Great War*, p. 17.
10 Matthews, *By God's Grace*, pp. 151-152.
11 *USM*, July 1917, p. 97.
12 *USM*, May 1918, p. 78.
13 Matthews, *By God's Grace*, p. 147.
14 Matthews, *By God's Grace*, pp. 147-148.

most generous donors; donations made, he said, in thanks for their sons not having to 'make the great sacrifice.'[15]

Like many memorials the shrine in the chapel was designed to be noble and uplifting while at the same time tragic and unendurably sad.[16] The shrine which was dedicated on 16 October 1921 is in the form of a small octagonal addition on the south side of the building. Around the top of the shrine were eight sentences from the bible which had been selected by E W Hornung, OU and author of *Raffles*. The sentences emphasise the uplifting nobility of those who had died; two of the sentences are "With perfect heart they offered willingly to the Lord" and "Make them to be numbered with Thy Saints in glory everlasting." The tragedy is represented by the 21 panels with the names on them of the OUs known to have died. The shrine was dedicated by the Bishop of Southampton, an OU, who also preached the sermon. It was a sermon which did not attempt to make those who had died into saints making a glorious sacrifice. The parallel he drew to Christian life was that service to God was not 'easy or cheap.' For him there was no romanticised vision of chivalric service.[17] Such a view is not surprising when one considers how the School Magazine throughout the war avoided commentary about the glorious sacrifice made by OUs. While Uppingham remembered those who had died its approach when compared with other public schools was far more understated in the way it remembered the OUs who had died. Leading schools such as Harrow, Winchester and Rugby produced multi-volume memorial books of all their old boys who had died often consisting of eulogies about the qualities of the men killed. Smaller schools such as Downside and St Georges, Harpenden also produced similar memorials with eulogies for those who had died. In many cases these were sold to raise money for the schools' memorial funds. In contrast to these more romanticised rolls of service Uppingham produced one which listed those who served with the briefest of details about each OU. Uppingham was not the only school to use its memorial fund for practical purposes; St Albans built a swimming pool while Bedales built a new library but others such as Shrewsbury Winchester and Clifton built memorials to the dead. At many schools there appears to have been a great deal of rancour in discussions about what was an appropriate memorial with older generations favouring a memorial while the younger generally favoured something which would benefit future generations.[18] Owen as a young man favoured the latter approach. He was probably helped in achieving this by the precedent of the Boer War commemoration and a pressing need to modernise the school.

Individual Memorials

Memorials were not just established after the war; in 1916 Mansel Copse on the Somme had been named after Spenser Mansel-Carey, 1907 to 1913, who had been killed there in February 1916.[19] On the home front street memorials were established in towns as diverse as St Albans and Wolverhampton. Most official town and village memorials were constructed supported by

---

15   *USM*, July 1919, pp. 182-183.
16   Jay Winter, *Sites of Memory Sites of Mourning* (Paperback edition, Cambridge: Cambridge University Press, 1996), p. 85.
17   *USM*, December 1921, pp. 234-240.
18   Seldon and Walsh, *Public Schools and The Great War*, pp. 194-198.
19   *The Tiger*, January 2013, p. 4.

appeals launched at the end of the war. However, there were exceptions and a few were dedicated before the end of the war such as the memorial at Hallaton in Leicestershire. Dedicated in April 1918 it was paid for by Mrs Effie Elizabeth Bewicke mainly in memory of her nephew the OU George Bewicke, 1911 to 1913, who had been killed in action in 1916. The Bewickes were the local landed family and on the north side of the column is carved the family motto 'Libertas et Natalie Solum' which is translated as 'For Freedom and Country'.[20] The family motto is an illustration of the values which inspired many OUs to fight and was reflected in many memorials both at the school and for individuals. When considering memorials for OUs who lost their lives it is apparent that there is a great deal of diversity in their nature. They range from memorial windows and plaques in churches to generous gifts of facilities in memory of the fallen.

Memorials were not just established for those who had died, as discussed earlier in this chapter many parents of boys at Uppingham supported the school appeal in thanks for their boys not needing to serve, similarly some OU parents gave thanks for the safe return of sons. One OU who fell into this category was William Stuart Rollo, 1901 to 1903 whose parents paid for a window in St Mary the Virgin at Waterloo Park, Liverpool. The window gave thanks for the safe return of William and his brother Brigadier-General George Rollo who had been educated at Rugby. The stained glass window had two lights each with a figure, St Michael in the left one and a female figure of peace in the right light.[21] The images give thanks for the defeat of evil and the return to peace. St Michael is a patron saint of the armed forces as in the Book of Revelations he leads God's armies against Satan's forces.

A number of memorials to OUs have a similar Christian theme of chivalry which it is believed public schoolboys were imbued with. The memorial window for John Gleed, 1912 to 1916, and his brother-in-law features both men dressed in armour. Made up of three lights it placed Christ at the centre with each man dressed in armour in the light on either side. The Christian theme is reinforced in Gleed's light with the RFC motto 'Per Ardua ad Astra' (Through adversity to the stars).[22] Gleed was killed near Ypres in July 1917 while flying over enemy territory. These images of Christianity and chivalry had many different variations. Frederick Marriot, 1908 to 1912, is remembered in a window at St Mary's in Cotesbach, Leicestershire together with his brother Hugh who also lost his life in the war and their father, Charles. The window consists of three panes with Christ surmounted by a dove at the centre. On the left hand side St George is depicted surmounted by a rose and on the right St Martin (patron saint of soldiers) surmounted by a lily.[23] The use of Christ in stained windows together with other saints and knightly images depicted a belief that those who had lost their life had been fighting a noble cause. Using St George a knight and the patron saint of England particularly reinforced this image. Disillusionment about the war only became more prevalent in the 1930s and even then few believed that the

20 Leicestershirevillages.com Hallaton A History of Hallaton War Memorial <http://www.leicestershirevillages.com/hallaton/ahistoryofhallatonwarmemorial.html> (accessed 10 June 2016).
21 Imperial War Museums Brig Gen G Rollo Cmg DSO And Capt W S Rollo MC <http://www.iwm.org.uk/memorials/item/memorial/15868 (accessed 9 June 2016)> and Grace's Guide George Rollo <http://www.gracesguide.co.uk/George_Rollo_(d.1945)> (accessed 9 June 2016.
22 Norman T Wills, *Fenland Churches and People between Spalding & Long* Sutton (Long Sutton: Privately published, 1988), p. 7.
23 War Memorials Project War Memorials in Cotesbach <http://www.leics.gov.uk/warmemorials_cotesbach.htm> (accessed 11 June 2016).

Great War had been pointless.²⁴ In the years after the war it was often the practice for memorials to bear phrases from the classics. The plaque dedicated in All Saints, Pavement, York to the memory of Stephen Jalland, 1903 to 1906, ends with the words 'Pulchrum est Pro Patria Mori' ('It is a beautiful thing to die for one's country' more usually written as 'dulci et decorum est pro patria mori').²⁵ Although many memorials had themes of Christianity and chivalry it would be a mistake to stereotype all OU memorials in this way. W Vaughan Sculthorpe's memorial, 1905 to 1910, has a simpler dedication from his parents: 'You were our pride / we dreamed great things for you / God intervened and so the dream came true" / Father and mother.'²⁶

Not all OUs were remembered through the erection of monuments and plaques. Collings-Wells, winner of a VC, is commemorated in a number of places including some which are near Caddington Hall, Bedfordshire where his parents lived at the start of the war. The most significant of these is the Collings-Wells Memorial Hall in Caddington which was opened by his brother Russell in 1935.²⁷ The idea of a hall had first been proposed in 1919 but it was not until 1928 that the vicar, Francis Greaves, initiated the fund raising and decided to dedicate it to the memory of Collings Wells, a former church warden. The family had erected other memorials to him in local churches but the hall was paid for by public subscription.²⁸ Gifts and memorials which were dedicated to the future good of the community were not just funded by public subscription. There are a number of examples where the relatives of deceased OUs made significant gifts for the benefit of the community. These gifts reflect a different approach before the welfare state existed. Philanthropy was far more prevalent than it is today and it was more common for the affluent to make gifts to benefit their communities and especially the less well off. While those making these gifts believed it was important to honour the sacrifice of OUs they also made them because they considered it was their duty to support their local community.

An example of this type of gift is the alms houses at Edwalton on the outskirts of Nottingham. These were erected by Oliver Hind, a local solicitor, whose family lived at Edwalton Hall, and opened in 1927. The plaque at the entrance states that it was built by Jesse Hind partly in memory of two OUs killed his brother Lieutenant Colonel Laurence Hind, 1892 to 1896, and a nephew Trooper Oliver Hind, 1899 to 1902. Oliver Hind had lost his only son in the war and had devoted a considerable amount of his resources and time to the care of wounded servicemen after the war. The Hind family was also closely associated with the Sherwood Foresters in which Laurence was a Lieutenant Colonel when he was killed on the first day of the Battle of the Somme. In the years before the war the family had also been involved with philanthropy and the alms houses were a natural extension of this approach.²⁹ The late nineteenth century

---

24 David Reynolds, *The Long Shadow* (Paperback edition London: Simon and Schuster, 2013) p. 207.
25 York and the Great War York – Jalland Memorial <http://yorkandthegreatwar.com/York-Jalland-Memorial> (accessed 11 June 2016) I am grateful to Alison Summerskill for the information on the use of Latin.
26 Leicester War Memorials <http://www.leics.gov.uk/leicester_war_memorials_v3.pdf> (accessed 11 June 2016).
27 Bedford Borough Council Caddington John Stanghope Collings-Wells VC DSO <http://www.bedfordshire.gov.uk/CommunityAndLiving/ArchivesAndRecordOffice/CommunityArchives/Caddington/JohnStanhopeCollingsWellsVCDSO.aspx> (accessed 13 June 2016).
28 Peter Graham (2016) Collings Wells E-mail (13 June 2016).
29 Leicestershire Antills and Connected Families HIND, Sir Jesse William Kt, DL, MA <http://antill.org.uk/getperson.php?personID=I4673&tree=tree1> (accessed 13 June 2016).

and early twentieth century saw the decline the aristocracy and landed gentry who had seen it as their duty to raise forces in times of war and support good works. These social classes had been replaced in influence by the professional and commercial classes (the background of many Uppingham parents) who had started to assume the roles of supporting the army and philanthropy. Provision of support for former servicemen was a theme in many of the gifts made in memory of OUs. Tower Hill at Westfield War Memorial Village near Lancaster was built in memory of Thomas Storey Inglis Hall, 1900 to 1901 who had been killed in Mesopotamia. It was one of 20 bungalows built as part of the first phase of the village which were intended for amputees. The land for the village had been given by the Storey family into which Hall had married. The Storeys a family of local industrialists were well known for their philanthropy. They were also well known for their support for the local Territorial battalion, the 5th King's Own, and the family's business had provided one company for it for many years. The original scheme for Westfield had relied on government funding but this was not forthcoming. The government was not keen on segregating former servicemen in special villages preferring to integrate them. It was also under considerable financial pressure after 1918 and its priority was to cut expenditure to deal with the large deficit created by the war. As noted above, there was no welfare state and the government felt the system of the poor and needy being supported by charities should continue. Undeterred a local committee of the great and good was set up to persuade individuals to subscribe for a bungalow at £500 each. When the time came to honour these pledges most of the money expected was not forthcoming. The Storeys stepped in and paid for most of the accommodation; Tower Hill was paid for by Hall's widow and was named after their house in Cumbria. Despite many problems the village continues to provide accommodation for former servicemen.[30] The connection between philanthropic giving and support can also be seen in the gift of Ryton Towers to the army as a convalescent hospital by the OU Lieutenant Colonel Charles Harrie Innes Hopkins, 1871 to 1876 who ran a shipping firm. Both of Hopkins's sons, one an OU, were killed in the war and he was also the founder of the Tyneside Scottish Brigade which was part of the New Army formed by Kitchener in 1914. It was natural for Hopkins that support for the military and philanthropy should run hand in hand.

Today, support for both the military and philanthropy may seem a little hard to understand but it was typical of many wealthy men in the years before the Great War. They saw it as their duty to support the raising of forces for their country when it was at war but also had a *noblesse oblige* towards those less well off than them. Gifts could also have a wider purpose than just sorting the needy and were designed to support the community such as providing cultural facilities. Leigh Tolson gave his home Ravensknowle Hall to Huddersfield Corporation so that it could become the town's museum. He was an industrialist but also an antiquarian and local historian and had made the gift in memory of his two nephews both who were killed in the war. One of these was an OU, Robert Huntriss Tolson, 1912 to 1915.[31] Although he may have planned to make the gift anyway by making this gift in memory of his nephews he also marked their sacrifice by making his home available for all to benefit from it. This was not the only museum gift made in memory of OUs. Ernest Marsh, a Quaker miller and collector gave 61

---

30   Martin Purdey University of Lancaster (2016) 'Tower Hill Westfield Village', Telephone Conversation 14 June 2016.
31   Kirklees Council The Story of Tolson <https://www.kirklees.gov.uk/leisure/museumsGalleries/tolson/tolsonStory.aspx> (accessed 13 June 2016).

pieces of Martin Brothers stoneware to the V and A museum in memory of his OU son Francis, 1910 to 1914.³² Ernest Marsh was a benefactor to the arts and over the years this was one of many gifts he made to different collections.³³ As with many of the gifts made in memory of OUs who were killed they were part of a wider scheme of gifts for the public benefit.

Other gifts included those from OUs who had been killed and had left legacies to institutions with which they had been associated. Vere Currey of the Suffolk Regiment, 1899 to 1901, was killed in October 1915 at the Battle of Loos. A man of considerable intellect he was also a gifted linguist and a professional soldier. In his will he left a substantial legacy to his regiment's Old Comrades Association as well as his substantial collection of military books to the Regiment.³⁴ His parents presented the Currey Cup to the regiment which became a shooting trophy.³⁵ Another gift for an institution with which an OU was closely associated with was the Uppingham School Assistant Masters Gaffikin Fund. This was set up with funds from the will of George Gaffikin, 1900 to 1905, as well as friends and family and still exists today to contribute to teachers' further studies and development; today, the fund is still used for this purpose.³⁶

The story of Gaffikin demonstrates how commemoration and remembrance could also serve more political purposes. He was the son of a Belfast Linen Merchant and was killed on the first day of the Somme. Gaffikin was seen falling by fellow OU Frank Thornely (see Chapter 5) who spoke of his men going 'mad' because 1st July was the anniversary of the Battle of the Boyne.³⁷ This sense of identity with Ulster's cause was reinforced by his battalion wearing orange shoulder badges.³⁸ There are many and varying accounts of Gaffikin's involvement including one which has him waving an orange sash over his head shouting out references to the Boyne.³⁹ It appears there was a febrile atmosphere within at least some elements of the 36th Ulster Division on that day. In Ulster the first day of the Somme forms a significant part of legend about its identity. This is partly explained by 1916 also being the year when the Easter Rising took place in Dublin and as a result the actions on the Somme has been presented as Ulster fighting to defend the United Kingdom in contrast to the Southern Irish. This of course is a misrepresentation; many Southern Irishmen fought bravely for the British Empire during the war. Within Ulster, however, there was a desire to celebrate the action of men such as Gaffikin in support of Ulster. It was an approach which Thornely unwittingly became part of. In the picture *Battle of the Somme: The Attack of the Ulster Division* by J P Beadle he is depicted as the officer leading the attack. After being wounded in the assault he recuperated at his father's house in Newbury and was asked to advise on and pose for the picture. Beadle was based in London and Thornely was staying close enough to meet him there. Subsequently Belfast City Council purchased the

32 V & A Search the collection <http://collections.vam.ac.uk/item/O77944/jug-martin-robert-wallace/> (accessed 14 June 2016).
33 Christopher Jordan and Steering Taste, *Ernest Marsh. A study of private collecting in England in the early 20th Century* (University of the Arts London Camberwell College of Arts, 2007).
34 Mark Forsdike (2015) 'Currey Cup' E-mail, 26 July 1915.
35 Gwyn Thomas (2015) 'Vere Fortrey Currey' E-mail, 19 August 2015.
36 J P Rudman (2016) 'Major George Horner Gaffikin' E-mail, 6 January 2016.
37 SA, Thornely Letters, Letter to Mother, 6 July 1916 and Thornely Letters, Letter to Father 7 July 1916.
38 Discussion with Nick Thornely, 24 February 2016.
39 Middlebrook, *The First Day on the Somme*, p. 175.

picture which now hangs in the City Hall. It forms an important part of the story of Ulster's involvement at the Somme. In a sign of changing times the picture was used on a postage stamp in Eire on the ninetieth anniversary of the Somme in 2006. Ironically, Thornely's involvement with Ulster was only a passing one. He had visited Ulster when he had enlisted in 1914 but after the war never returned to Ireland but still became part of the semi-official history of the Ulster Division's heroic assault on 1t July.[40] This has to be the most unusual of all the various acts of commemoration involving OUs, which followed the Great War.

OUs After the War

After the war many OUs returned to their pre-war occupations while those who had not worked before the war started new careers. Thornely became a cotton broker (the family business in Liverpool) in Bombay and returned to England in 1944 before Indian independence.[41] Malcolm Campbell, 1899 to 1902, returned to his motor racing career and was later knighted. For others the consequences of the war were more serious. Some never recovered from their war wounds and eventually died from them. Edward Gibson, 1904 to 1906 died of them in March 1926. James Sydney La-Fontaine, 1907 to 1912, who came from a long established family in Smyrna in the Ottoman Empire in one of the many ironies of war was severely wounded at Gallipoli and died in 1932 from his wounds which never healed.[42] These and other men such as Geoffrey Northrop, 1906 to 1910, who died of his wounds in January 1922 would find no place on official memorials for which the cut-off date was 31 August 1921 for those who had died of their wounds. Others found the process of adapting to life after the war too much. Colonel Hugh Westmacott, 1881 to 1883, shot himself through the heart in January after 1920 after 'repeated disappointments' in his efforts to find work. In his suicide note he said 'I have reached the limit of my endurance. The outlook for the future fills me with despair.'[43] He had tried to exercise the qualities of independence and initiative after the war but had failed to achieve what he considered to be success and despair had consumed him.

To balance personal stories of despair there are others which tell of OUs who, despite tremendous adversity, lived fulfilled lives after the war. The most remarkable of these stories is that of Godfrey Robinson, 1911 to 1915. Commissioned into the Royal Field Artillery he won an MC and was blinded when acting as a forward observation officer. Although he was unconscious his signaller, in an act typical of the relationship between officers and their men, insisted he was taken to a field hospital. He remained unconscious for three weeks and lost his hearing, his sense of smell and eyesight. In a piece of innovative medicine his hearing was restored by a skin transplant. When his family lost touch with him, his mother and two sisters travelled in a chauffeur driven car looking for him. This was an action typical of his family's resolute approach to life and he was no different as he took up work in 1920 in the family business and the Hull Institute for the Blind. In the latter role he made a significant contribution to the welfare of the blind by setting up workshops for them. From 1938 he was Chairman of the National Institute

---

40 Discussion with Nick Thornely, 24 February 2016.
41 Discussion with Nick Thornely, 24 February 2016.
42 Family Records – a short history of the La Fontaine family <http://levantineheritage.com/book1.htm> (accessed 14 June 2016).
43 *The Morning News Wilmington Delaware*, 3 February 1920, p. 13.

for the Blind and under his leadership it received a Royal Charter. He was awarded the CBE for his work for the welfare of the blind. A brief summary such as this can only touch on his achievements and his spirit and independence are best illustrated by a couple of anecdotes from his family. Throughout his business career he regularly travelled to London on the train with another blind man connected with St Dunstans, the charity for blind servicemen. During the journeys they played chess together without a board calling out the moves and memorising the positions of all the pieces in their heads. Godfrey also had one of his gardeners teach him how to prune and pick apple and pear trees in his orchard. This he was able to do at any time of day or night and he found it a great source of relaxation. He was a man who continued to inspire loyalty throughout his life; at his memorial service in 1962 a Kings Cross porter introduced himself to the family. He had always met the Hull Pullman to ensure Godfrey was safely taken to the taxi rank. Godfrey died in 1961 from his war wounds; as part of his work he had flown to Russia to advise on blind welfare, especially for blind servicemen. The effect of flying at high altitudes led to a series of blackouts caused by the pressure on his weakened skull.[44] At his funeral on 22 December 1961 the Bishop of Hull in his address said of him 'he conquered his disability in a wonderful way, and was spared to give a considerable life of service to the community, because of his wonderful spirit, his integrity, and his great-heartedness.'[45]

Godfrey Robinson is an inspiring memorial to those who made considerable for their country and survived. He lived with his disabilities displaying independence and initiative. It was perhaps because he believed in what he had fought for that he was inspired to help others who had suffered in the war. His approach to life demonstrates the dangers of being too fixed in one's ideas about the consequences of the Great War. Many of the gifts in memory of dead OUs arose from a desire to serve the country by people who were philanthropists but also believed in the need to defend their country and were closely associated with the Territorials. Remembrance through images of chivalry also reflected this duty to defend one's country even if some commemorations such as that involving Thornely were a little unexpected. As demonstrated by the purpose of the school's memorial hall the acts of remembrance were as much for those who had died as for those who served and survived. Marking the contribution of OUs within the Great War was part of a movement within the whole country. Twenty-one years after the end of the Great War in 1939 OUs would once again be called to defend their country.

---

44 I am grateful to the Robinson family and particular Hugh, OU, for providing me with much of this information.
45 *The New Beacon: The Magazine Of Blind Welfare*, 25 January 1962, p. 13.

11

Taking Up Arms Again

The Armistice of 1918 was not the end to total war in the twentieth century and scarcely 20 years later another generation of Public School Boys would be called to serve as Nazi Germany triggered the Second World War with its invasion of Poland. The purpose of this chapter is not to provide a brief summary of the school's involvement in the Second World War as there is a great deal more work to be done to gain a better understanding. This chapter discusses the role of those OUs who saw service in the Great War and contributed to the war effort in various capacities during the Second World War. Like many aspects of the Second World War Uppingham's involvement in it is under researched such as whether OUs OTC background once again made them attractive to the army as officer cadets. It is not known how many OUs served in the war although a roll of honour produced in August 1945 stated that approximately 1,600 served in Europe and that it was estimated that a further 400 had served in the Far East. Most aspects of the school's involvement need considerable further research the fruits of which will merit a book in their own right. The involvement of those OUs who served in the Great War and went on to do the same in the Second World War in various capacities offers some insights into the limits of an Uppingham education. Consideration needs to be given to the contribution of those who fought in the Great War and were young enough to serve in the Second World War. By examining a sample of these men and their contribution the limits of an Uppingham education can be better illustrated. This is particularly well illustrated when the service of OUS at the senior levels of the army in the Second World War is examined.

Of those OUs who served in the armed forces in the Great War 205 (nine percent of those who served between 1914 and 1918) are known to have to served again in the Second World War. It was mainly a new generation of OUs who served their country between 1939 and 1945. Conscription had been introduced before war broke out so there was no dramatic rush to volunteer as there had been in 1918. The school OTC had continued to exist between the wars so it is not surprising that a large number of OUs once again became officers. Many of the civilian OUs who became officers volunteered but conscription meant that the population as a whole waited to be called up rather than gathering outside the recruiting offices. Conscription meant that the government could allocate men and women where it thought best in the face of limits on available manpower. Not all men were called up for military service; a judgement was made as to where their skills and abilities were most needed so that the problems experienced by the munitions industry in the early part of the war were avoided. For example, many men who were working in food distribution were not allowed to serve as, with the introduction of rationing, management of food supplies was crucial. Instead, they were allowed to undertake voluntary roles such as that of a Special Constable. The government also made maximum use of those who could not serve to release men for service. Godfrey Robinson, discussed in the last chapter, took over the running of the family wholesale grocery business in Hull when his brothers left to join the armed forces. The government also drew on his extensive experience and co-opted him onto committees advising on food distribution. Not only did he provide practical support and leadership but also served as an inspiration in his capacity as Sherriff of Kingston-Upon-Hull, the city most damaged in the blitz, during the worst period of the bombing in 1941.[1]

The *School Roll* is more forthcoming about the contribution of civilian OUs to the war effort between 1939 and 1945 which is perhaps a recognition that in the Great War there had not been enough recognition of the efforts of all OUs. Like Robinson, some employed the expertise they had gained in civilian life, during the war. Harold Howitt (see Chapter 7) who by 1939 had become a prominent Chartered Accountant and was 52 in September 1939 used his business skills serving on the Air Council. Francis Johnston, 1907 to 1912, served in the Northumberland Fusiliers in the Great War and by 1939 was a ship owner and 47 years old; during the war he sat on government committees concerned with the requisition of shipping. Other OUs drew more closely on their Great War military experience and served in more defence related roles. Gilbert Dryland, 1896 to 1900, served as a Lieutenant in the RAMC in the Great War until he was invalided out and returned to his GP practice. In the Second World War he served with the Home Guard taking responsibility for the training of ambulance squads.[2] Lesley Hales Finch was also invalided out of the Sherwood Foresters in the Great War after being gassed but in the Second World War served as a Major in the Staffordshire Home Guard for which he was awarded an MBE in 1944.[3] One of the more unusual cases of civilian OU involvement in the Second World War was that of Gerald Ash, 1896 to 1901. Ash was a dentist and served in the RAMC during the Great War and was 52 in September 1939. In the Second World War he served as commander of the 2nd Group of the West Hampshire Auxiliary Unit.[4] The Auxiliary units were part of the Home Guard and were composed of both men and women, in the event of a German invasion they would have had the task of disrupting it by engaging in irregular warfare. These units were composed of the most able members of the Home Guard and consisted of men with military experience, while women with local knowledge, would appear to present no threat to an invader, their primary role was to gather information.[5] They have been mistakenly referred to as the British Resistance but if the Germans had been successful that task would have fallen elsewhere.

The threat of German invasion from 1940 onwards led to an escalation in the total war being waged by Britain. The school's educational ethos aimed to produce boys with independence, inquisitiveness and self-confidence which had made them equipped and prepared to take

---

1   I am grateful to Hugh Robinson, OU, for providing me with this information.
2   Obituary G W Dryland, M.B., B.Ch. *British Medical Journal* (12 March 1960), p. 808.
3   An Auction of Orders, Decorations, Medals and Militaria <https://www.dnw.co.uk/media/auction_catalogues/Medals%2019%20Jun%2013.pdf> (accessed 7 July 2016).
4   British Resistance Archive Hampshire Auxiliary Unit Group Commanders <http://www.coleshill-house.com/hampshire-auxiliary-units-group-commanders.php> (accessed 8 July 2016).
5   Stephen M. Cullen, *In Search of the Real Dad's Army: The Home Guard and the Defence of the United Kingdom 1940-1944* (Barnsley: Pen & Sword, 2011), pp. 39-41, 118-120, 184.

leadership roles in the Great War. At a time of national crisis the OUs who had served between 1914 and 1918 once again undertook the roles which called on these qualities. These qualities were attractive to the army and government who called on them when Britain remained as the only active enemy of Germany. Similarly, OUs in their work in civilian life had been successful because of their independence, inquisitiveness and self-confidence and men such as and these were attractive to the government when it sought civilian expertise to prosecute the war. However, these qualities were not always a guarantee of success as Trench and Regnart had demonstrated during the Borkum incident in 1910. This can be seen by looking at the military careers during Second World War of OUs who held senior command after serving in the Great War. There are five OUs Lethbridge, Carr, Barber, Horrocks and Dorman-Smith, who held positions of senior command in the Second World War and for whom a sufficient amount of biographical information is available.[6] Analysis of their careers demonstrates that while they displayed these qualities and this helped them to gain a senior rank it was not sufficient to guarantee success. In particular a comparison of the careers of Horrocks and Dorman-Smith demonstrates this well.

The main factor which affected the success of these men was an ability to fit into the team; in some cases this arose from their own shortcomings and in others even though they were admired were simply viewed as being the wrong man for the job (as Lake was in Mesopotamia see Chapter 8). Others had shortcomings but fitted well into their team and were viewed as being a success. Public school boys had been attractive to the army for a variety of reasons which included a belief that playing team games and an emphasis on taking rapid decisions was useful training for the battlefield. The way the game was played was also important with a stress on gentlemanliness from which followed a sense of responsibility and paternalism towards an officer's men.[7] While these factors remained important they were not as significant to the success of senior officers. All the senior officers discussed had some experience of fighting in the Great War but this too was not a crucial factor in their success.

Laurence Carr was one of the seven OU 'war managers' in the Great War identified by Robbins (see Chapter 8). After the war he had held a number of staff positions in the army and between 1939 and 1940 had been Assistant CIGS. In 1941 he became GOC of Eastern Command which was a highly important command as it was where the Germans were considered more likely to launch their invasion. Field Marshal Alan Brooke who had become CIGS late in 1940 appointed him to this command because he believed it required strategic and tactical flair. In his diaries Brooke says that he had great belief in Carr but he had proved not to have the right attributes for the job.[8] After Carr fell out with one of his subordinates who virtually refused to serve under him the CIGS was forced to move both officers.[9] Brooke continued to hold Carr in high esteem and it was a source of regret to him when in June 1944 when he met Carr to tell him he was being retired.[10] Brooke was a man of clear opinions about the abilities of individual

---

6 There are others such as Caunter for whom information is not readily available.
7 See Chapter 1 for a fuller discussion of this.
8 Alex Danchev and Daniel Todman (eds), *War Diaries 1939-1945: Field Marshal Lord Alanbrooke* (London: Wiedenfield and Nicolson, 2001), p. 148.
9 Nick Smart, *Biographical Dictionary of British Generals of the Second World War* (Barnsley: Pen and Sword, 2005).
10 Danchev and Todman (eds), *War Diaries*, p. 560.

senior officers and he did not hold everyone in high esteem. Being held in high esteem, however, was not enough and when problems arose in Eastern Command Brooke clearly believed that the way Carr had exercised his command was part of the problem and decided to remove him.

The qualities which arose from playing team games only took a man so far. A team requires that all the parts of it work together and at higher levels of command this becomes even more important; Carr had failed in this respect. An OU who worked well as part of a team was John Lethbridge, 1911 to 1914, who was a Royal Engineer and Chief of Staff to the 14th Army in Burma under General William Slim between 1944 and 1945. Slim had worked extremely well with Lethbridge's predecessor and held him in high esteem but in his memoirs said he was fortunate to have got Lethbridge as replacement. In his view, Lethbridge's success in the role was a combination of clarity of thought, an ability to get on with those who he worked with and his subordinates and a strong sense of humour.[11] Success in the jungles of Burma, against a tactically ferocious but operationally and strategically incompetent Japanese army, was based on a well organised and planned campaign which required close liaison with the RAF. In Slim's view, the way he worked with Air Commodore Gordon Vass was a model in how the army and air force should work together. Between them, they developed plans which included reconnaissance, air patrols, ground-air attacks, the dropping of supplies and bombardments. It was a logistically innovative campaign even more remarkable because the 14th Army operated on a shoestring budget. For the army Lethbridge had to develop complicated and detailed plans to prepare the army and execute each offensive. The success of the Burma campaign needs to be understood in the context of severe equipment and manpower shortages. It was a success heavily dependent on the management, planning and inter-personal skills of Lethbridge.[12] As important as his technical skills were Lethbridge's ability to fit in with others was crucial.

The ability to fit in was is crucial at senior levels of the military but there is an element of luck in this as this is heavily dependent on the personalities of those in command. Lethbridge got on well with Slim but every commander is different in their character. Slim differed from Montgomery in being modest, prepared to admit his mistakes and, as discussed above, prepared to praise those he commanded.[13] Working with Montgomery required different personality traits. Colin Barber, 1911 to 1915, had distinguished himself during his division's retreat across France and had been awarded the DSO. In 1944 he commanded a brigade during the Normandy landings and was promoted to command a division when his predecessor was wounded and remained in command as it advanced from Normandy to Germany between 1944 and 1945.[14] His division had a reputation for being extremely effective but his success was partly down to his ability to work with abrasive Montgomery and not to fall out with him.[15]

Montgomery played a significant part of the careers of the two most prominent Second World War generals, Brian Horrocks and Eric Dorman-Smith. Both men came to Uppingham in September 1909 the same term as Edward Brittain and Roland Leighton. At school they shared the same ambition of gaining commissions in the army. Both left Uppingham to go to

---

11   Field Marshal Viscount Slim, *Defeat into Victory* (Paperback edition, Pan: London, 2009), p. 445.
12   Slim, *Defeat into Victory*, pp. 471-475.
13   Smart, *Biographical Dictionary of British Generals of the Second World War*, p. 288.
14   Smart, *Biographical Dictionary of British Generals of the Second World War*, pp. 19-20.
15   Carlo D'Este. *Decision in Normandy: The Unwritten Story of Montgomery and the Allied Campaign* (Paperback edition, London: Classic Penguin, 2001), p. 239.

Sandhurst but in different circumstances; Dorman-Smith devoted himself to the study required to passing the entrance exams while Horrocks devoted himself to games. In the exams for 172 places Dorman-Smith finished 69th while Horrocks scraped in, last but one.[16] Both men passed their Certificate A exams while members of the OTC and in Horrock's case this was probably crucial. Passing Certificate A gave a candidate 200 marks towards his entrance examination which was probably enough to get him over the line.[17] Dorman-Smith graduated from Sandhurst at the first attempt finishing tenth in the exams while Horrocks was left to sit his exams again.[18] As at Uppingham Horrocks was noted for his prowess at games and not for his academic ability; he was a good games player, a good shot and a rebel. When he came to sit his exams again he was not confident of having done enough to earn a commission. He left Sandhurst in July 1914 and awaited his results but the outbreak of war on 4 August 1914 meant the results became irrelevant and he was immediately given a commission.[19]

For Horrocks his experience of fighting was relatively short; in October 1914 he was wounded and taken prisoner at Le Maisnil near Lille.[20] After recovering from his wounds he spent most of the war trying to escape. Although he gained limited military experience he used the free time to learn French, German and Russian.[21] This was an early sign that he was able to impose himself academically. By contrast Dorman-Smith spent the whole war with the army. He was wounded on a number of occasions fighting on the Western Front and spent a significant period in training roles. By 1918 he had started to develop his views on the need for army reform.[22] In 1924 Dorman-Smith successfully applied to become an instructor at Sandhurst, in 1927 he passed the entrance exams, with full marks, for the Staff College at Camberley where the elite of the British Army was trained.[23] The qualities of independence, inquisitiveness and self-confidence which Uppingham aimed to produce had been displayed in his rapid rise. This was not enough for long term success and at Staff College he developed a contempt for and clashed with Montgomery who was the senior lecturer. Both men believed the army was in need of reform but had completely different ideas about what was required.[24] On graduating in 1928 he publicly burnt his lecture notes, an action which was not guaranteed to earn the goodwill of others. When he came under Montgomery's command in the 1942 Western Desert Campaign the antagonism which had developed between them would count against him. His inability to appreciate the need to get on with others would ultimately be his downfall.

Horrocks, in contrast to Dorman-Smith, spent the first half of the 1920s bored with the training he was being given and pursuing his sporting interests. He took up the modern pentathlon excelling in national events and earning selection for the 1924 Olympics team. The intervention of his father who had served in the RAMC led to a change in his attitude. His father gently pointed out that he would soon be too old to attend Staff College and without

---

16   Greacen, *Chink*, p. 21.
17   *Regulations for the OTC*, p. 22.
18   Greacen, *Chink*, p. 27.
19   Philip Warner, *Horrocks: The General Who Led from the Front* (Paperback edition London: Sphere, 1985), pp. 6-7.
20   Warner, *Horrocks*, p. 14.
21   Warner, *Horrocks*, p. 19.
22   Greacen, *Chink*, p. 51.
23   Greacen, *Chink*, p. 96.
24   Greacen, *Chink*, pp. 99-102.

passing its course he had no chance of achieving high command. Horrocks followed this advice and, perhaps for the first time, worked hard to pass the entrance exam. He sat the exam in 1927 successfully but his marks were not high enough to gain immediate entrance and he needed a nomination to do so. At his father's suggestion he undertook specialist courses and was admitted to the two year staff college course in 1931. From that point on his career took a new direction with Staff College being followed by a series of prestigious appointments.[25]

In May 1940 he was rushed out to take up a new appointment in command of the Second Battalion of the Middlesex Regiment when the Germans invaded France and the Low Countries. It was at this point that he first encountered Montgomery who was his new divisional commander. Montgomery had a reputation as being an awkward character and Horrocks viewed working with him with trepidation but from the start there was none of the animosity that characterised Montgomery's relationship with Dorman-Smith. During his short period in France he also met Brooke, later CIGS.[26] Throughout the war he would enjoy excellent relations with both men in contrast to Dorman-Smith's relationship with them. Although Dorman-Smith was full of ideas about fighting the war Brooke did not trust him; noting that although Dorman-Smith had many ideas only a few of them were good ones. He blamed the influence of Dorman-Smith on Auchinleck for the latter's failure as a commander in the North African desert in 1942.[27] When Montgomery took command in 1942 he swiftly removed Dorman-Smith describing him as a 'menace.'[28] From that point on Dorman-Smith's military career was in terminal decline and he retired before the end of the war. His personality was his biggest problem and he was extremely adept at falling out with the wrong people.[29] His abrasive personality means that he has received less credit than he deserves. The quality of his advice to Auchinleck was a significant factor in Rommel's advance being halted at the First Battle of El Alamein in July 1942 but this has been overshadowed by Montgomery's victory at the Second Battle of El Alamein.

Unlike Horrocks his self-confidence was a barrier to him getting on with others. At Uppingham he had poured scorn on team games and only enjoyed playing fives in contrast to Horrocks who was a keen participant in all team games.[30] Although the playing of games was a severe impediment to his early military career it appears to have helped him develop the essential social skills to rub along with others as his career progressed. It was an essential trait that Dorman-Smith lacked. As Dorman-Smith left the desert Horrocks was summoned by Montgomery to command 13 Corps. He played an important role in the victory at the Second Battle of El Alamein (described by Churchill as the end of the beginning for the British in the Second World War) in October and November 1942. Ironically, part of the success was based on Auchinleck demonstrating the Germans were not invincible at First El Alamein and the preparation that he'd put into readying and training the Army.[31] Although severely wounded in June 1943 which kept Horrocks out of action for a year Montgomery recalled him as soon as he

---

25 Alan Shepperd, 'Horrocks', in John Keegan (ed) *Churchill's Generals* (Paperback edition, London: Warner, 1992), pp. 228-230.
26 Warner, *Horrocks*, p. 51-53.
27 Danchev and Todman (eds), *War Diaries*, pp. 224-225.
28 Stephen Brooks (ed), *Montgomery and the Eighth Army* (London: Army Records Society, 1991), p. 20.
29 Bidwell and Graham, *Fire-Power*, p. 243.
30 Greacen, *Chink*, p. 18.
31 Warner, *Horrocks*, p. 79.

was fit to take part in the later stages of the Battle of Normandy and the advance into Germany. Montgomery's view of Horrocks contrasted with that he held of Dorman-Smith; among the praise he heaped on Horrocks in his diary he described him as 'a really good soldier.'[32]

It's important not to turn Horrocks into some sort of military saint. At times he was lucky and he never reached the highest rank of the British army; that would have been beyond his capabilities. He made mistakes during the advance of 1944 to 1945, especially in Operation Market Garden and the advance to Arnhem. He had his critics too; one of whom said that he made up for his stupidity with his gregarious personality. In particular, he was accused of avoiding responsibility for his mistakes in Market Garden by openly admitting to them.[33] However, he was not the only Second World War General to take this approach. Slim also followed an approach of admitting to his errors in his memoirs, *Defeat into Victory*. In contrast Montgomery in his memoirs followed an approach of taking as much credit as possible and placing the blame for failures on others; as a result, he has been the subject of far more criticism.

The position of senior commander leaves one more exposed to criticism. Some such as Montgomery and Dorman-Smith as a result of their abrasive personalities attracted it more easily than the more personable Slim and Horrocks. It demonstrates that the qualities of independence, inquisitiveness and self-confidence which Uppingham aimed to develop in its boys were important in the development of senior officers. However, these qualities were not sufficient for success at the highest levels of the army. Both Carr and Lethbridge demonstrated these qualities and were highly regarded by their superiors but each demonstrated in contrasting ways the importance of being able to fit in. Carr's abrasiveness led to him being relieved of his command while Lethbridge was a success partly because of his ability to get on with both officers at his own rank and his subordinates. It is noticeable that one of the OUs who served as a senior officer, Horrocks gained little fighting experience in the Great War and had an undistinguished early career in the army but became a highly respected commander in the Second World War. Above all, it demonstrates that as much as Uppingham's contribution to the Great War was unique so was its contribution between 1939 and 1945. It is a topic, as was noted at the start of this chapter, which needs a detailed study in its own right.

32 Brooks (ed), *Montgomery and the Battle of Normandy*, p. 95.
33 John Buckley, *Monty's Men: The British Army and the Liberation of Europe* (London: Paperback Edition, Yale University Press, 2014), pp. 35-36.

Conclusion

Vera Brittain's *Testament of Youth* remains a powerful and moving account 80 years after it was first published. Her account, however, is not just an account about the death of four men she was very close to; it is also an account of how she recovered from despair after the war. In the same way that it is a limited view to think of Brittain's account solely about being of loss it is unhelpful to see her book as reflecting Uppingham's participation in the Great War; that was not her intention. The aim of this book has been to attempt to explain the contribution of the school and its old boys, the skills contributed to the war effort and why nearly all of them believed in the cause they fought for. The involvement of the school in the Great War was complex and multifaceted.

In the years leading up to 1914 many in Britain were concerned about the threat of Germany. There were good reasons to be concerned. The expansion of a large German navy out of proportion to the requirements of its own empire was of great concern to the British. Britain had a navy to protect its trading links with its empire and the rest of the world. The expansion of the German navy was taking place, it was believed, to threaten Britain. The majority of the British population feared German domination of Europe and believed that would be a disaster. It was a view that, not surprisingly, continued to be held by the British during the war and for a considerable time afterwards. Many OUs volunteered because they believed that Germany needed to be resisted as a threat to the British way of life. To many today this is a view that is difficult to understand but hindsight must be put to one side and the involvement of those connected with the school needs to be understood as the genuinely held belief of the vast majority of OUs and staff. Volunteering to fight was for most OUs their patriotic duty and it is not for us to pity them for this genuinely held view. The British Empire was under threat and they believed it was their duty to defend it.

It has been suggested that public schools engendered a spirit of militarism within their boys. This is an accusation that has, in particular, been levelled at Thring's successor Selwyn. His introduction in 1900 of a compulsory shooting test has been depicted by some as a pointless militaristic act. This is patently untrue. Selwyn was, instead, responding to national concerns following the 'Black Week' in the second Boer War (1899-1902). The government had made an appeal for volunteers to serve in South Africa. Selwyn was keen that the school be seen to be responding to the sudden awakening within Britain that the empire was not invulnerable. As the government was seeking men who had musketry skills, the introduction of a shooting test for its boys was an excellent way of demonstrating Uppingham's practical support for the government's appeal. The enthusiastic response of both town and school to the visit of Lord Roberts, believed by the general public to be the architect of the victory in South Africa, in March 1905 to open the Boer War memorial demonstrates school and public attitudes were closely related. Despite this concern in the years leading up to 1914 there was not an overtly militaristic response by the population and within it there was an ambivalent attitude towards compulsory military service. Although the introduction of the OTC with its training and approach co-ordinated by the War office led to an increase in the number of OUs getting commissions in the regular army this is more of a reflection of the army's realisation that it needed to recruit cadets from a wider social base. The percentage of entrants gaining commissions rose from under one percent to a peak just under 12 percent following the introduction of the OTC but Uppingham was never a leading provider of officers for the regular army. Many more boys took up careers in business and the professions. OTC membership in the years leading up to the war was never compulsory and the proportion of boys who were members only grew alongside rising concern about the threat of Germany, especially after 1911.

Although Selwyn may have been reflecting the national mood when he introduced compulsory shooting tests this did not guarantee him success. While he was Headmaster the cult of games got out of control and led to a decline in moral standards at the school. There was a great deal of parental concern about this and it led a decline in the number of boys at the school which was the underlying reason for Selwyn's departure. Traditional theories about public schools have suggested that the combination of games and classics made public schools attractive to parents but their response to Selwyn shows that other factors were just as important. Parents were more interested in their sons gaining the status of a gentleman which could be achieved through the passing of exams for bodies such as the civil service, army and the professions. While the playing of games was attractive to the army at Uppingham and other public schools there was a conflict for athletes who usually preferred to spend their spare time training rather than participating in the OTC. The scope for boys being influenced by the deeds of military heroes in the classics was limited as many had a minimal exposure to Latin while they concentrated on the moderns. At Uppingham there was more to school life than the classics and games with music playing a prominent part in its daily life; Edward Brittain was a gifted musician but a less able games player but still was keen to sign up in 1914 as soon as he could. Not all boys were happy at Uppingham but many still willingly volunteered. The influence of Uppingham on boys and their attitude to war has been overstated but the existence of bodies of the OTC gave them a way of responding to the threat from Germany and in doing so they reflected the same concerns within wider society. The school's educational ethos aimed to produce boys with independence, inquisitiveness and self-confidence. This would make OUs attractive to the army when war came but as the spies Regnart and Trench demonstrated these qualities were not always a good thing. The incident at Borkum demonstrated that if poor judgement was exercised severe problems could arise and a result Trench ended up in a German fortress. The clumsiness of the way the spying mission was conducted does not detract from the fact it was undertaken because there were serious tensions in the relationship between Germany and Britain. The interest of the Admiralty in the facilities at Borkum demonstrates that those in positions of responsibility shared the concerns of the wider population about Germany.

The Great War was chaotic and it is not surprising that more information has come to light about OUs who served since the war's conclusion. It is possible to identify 2,343 OUs who were in military service during the war. There is some evidence to suggest that at least 2,500 served but the records which support this claim have not survived. In the years before the war the vast majority of OUs who fought had led a civilian life. No more than one fifth of OUs served in the Territorials or Special Reserve but even then they led a predominantly civilian life. Many but not all OUs had experience of serving in the OTC or its predecessor, the Rifle Corps, but they were not a group of men who actively sought war. Most were concerned about the threat of Germany but the majority had no significant military experience outside the school before the war started. When war came they believed it was their duty to serve their country and empire against the threat to it. For them it was the right thing to seek a commission; in the early months of the war there was a backlog while applications for commissions were processed but they still volunteered. It was a reflection of the school's philosophy which stressed a strong sense of duty, leadership skills and taking responsibility. Thring's educational philosophy promoted independence, inquisitiveness and self-confidence in boys; they were also the skills required for leadership in the armed forces. The rapid expansion of the army meant that there was a greatly increased need for officers. The expansion also meant that there was an increased demand for a variety of different skills needed for a modern army. These included legal skills in the management of discipline, medical skills in the treatment of men, technical skills to run the railways and business skills in areas such as logistics. These were skills which OUs from a wide variety of age groups could provide. The Army, as it rapidly expanded, could no longer rely on the schools it had predominantly relied on to supply its officers. The training provided by the OTC provided the basic skills to rapidly give commissions to many young OUs but the wider age range of OUs who volunteered suggests there were many more that had a background attractive to the army. As many in the country took up arms to fight Germany so too did many OUs. There was no standard public school response and Uppingham's response was unique and influenced by its ethos and the backgrounds of its old boys.

Britain became a nation in arms between 1914 and 1918 with all parts of the country involved; at the same time Uppingham became a school in arms. Uppingham's evolution to a school in arms took some time. The government had given little thought to how the country's economic resources would be deployed in war. It is not surprising that the school devoted its initial efforts to supporting the military effort when in the early stages of the war the government's main focus was on Kitchener's call to arms. There were limits to the school's support for the war effort, however, and after the departure of several teachers in 1914 it became far more reluctant to release them for military service. It was only slowly that the school's efforts were developed so that it played its part on the home front. The school turned over the metal and carpentry shops to producing goods to support the military effort. Boys were made available to work on local farms and Harvest Camps were held during the summer holidays of 1917 and 1918. When compared to other schools such as Oundle, Uppingham's commitment to the home front was slower and less substantial. Uppingham, unlike other schools, did not seek to glorify the deeds of its old boys. There were no glowing obituaries for OUs who died; the School Magazine confined itself to listing the old boys who had died. A similar approach was taken to the reporting of medals and honours given to OUs. The magazine's main way of reporting the involvement of OUs was by publishing accounts from them of their involvement in the war effort. The nature of total war meant that despite their commitment to volunteering not all of OUs were allowed to serve on the front line. Those with particular expertise found themselves working in industry. Others, too old to serve, provided expertise in matters such as shipping. The involvement of OUs on the home front has been little discussed but was significant. Much as it is necessary to look beyond those who died to understand the school's military involvement so it is necessary to look at the involvement of OUs on the home front to understand that they were involved in many aspects of the total war fought between 1914 and 1918.

The medals and honours won by OUs reflect the quality of their involvement and was recognition of their qualities of independence, inquisitiveness and self-confidence. As a school Uppingham's old boys won an unusually high number of VCs especially when it is considered the school did not have strong army connections. It was to some extent a reflection of the school's philosophy which stressed a strong sense of duty, leadership skills and taking responsibility. Medals and honours were not just awarded for acts of bravery and gallantry. Especially, in the case of DSOs and MCs the awards reflected exceptional leadership skills. Leadership skills were not just exercised through acts of gallantry. Over two thirds of DSOs to OUs were for distinguished service and not a specific act of gallantry. Many MCs were awarded for good work which reflects the practical skills many OUs had developed at the school. Being mentioned in despatches was often earned as a result of skills acquired by OUs in their civilian occupations. Although OUs achieved substantial recognition it appears that medals were more easily won by the old boys of some public schools than others. The stronger the connection to the army by the school the better their old boys appear to have done.

Uppingham's lack of status as an army school is reflected in the lower number of senior commanders compared to the top 10 army schools it contributed to the war. However, a study of those OUs who became senior commanders does throw light on the complexities of senior command and how the British army became an organisation capable of winning the war. The initial stages involved improvisation to cope with the rapid expansion of the army. Retired OU army officers found themselves being 'dugout' for senior roles. Necessity often meant they were placed in posts where they were not best suited. Others found themselves with a new superior who had different ideas about what sort of man he wanted in the post and was made a scapegoat for failure. In Lake's case his successor was given the resources he was denied. Most importantly, however, the story of senior OU commanders shows how the lessons of evolving a mass army from a small highly professional one were learned. As the career of the OU, Vaughan, demonstrates the army developed by 1918 into the highly effective machine which helped win the war.

Uppingham, as a school in arms, was not just about the contribution of its old boys and pupils to total war and the school's teachers too made a significant contribution which is not fully understood. The contribution of teachers tends to be told with the context of the public schools they themselves attended. At Uppingham it appears that it was able to provide a significant number of teachers with OTC experience and therefore make them suitable officer material. Teachers did not necessarily serve because they were militarists; Street was torn between his sense of duty to both school and country while Oberhoffer was known as a man of peace. One teacher, C H Jones, stands out as the most significant in the contribution of the school's teachers. As an excellent commander of the OTC he made an important contribution to the training of the young men from the school who would become officers. This was based on ideas he had started to develop while serving in South Africa during the Boer War. His influence went beyond the military training of boys at Uppingham and his ideas played a strong part in the scheme for the OTC. Throughout the war but especially in its early stages the OTC was an important source of officers for Kitchener's army.

The end of the war was seen by the School Magazine as a time to return to normality and look to the future. This was a common view but the country wished to remember and give thanks as well. The concept of what the school was giving thanks for evolved from the initial one set out when the initial memorial scheme for the school was launched. Initially, it was seen as thanksgiving for those who had died but over time it evolved into one for all OUs involved in the war. As with the Boer War memorial the scheme had a practical element to it as it was used as an opportunity to improve the facilities at the school. Individual memorials for OUs in many cases were practical and designed to help the wider community going far beyond far beyond the building of monuments and the erection of plaques. OUs responded to the end of the war and its effects in a wide variety of ways. For some it proved too much and they took their own lives while others who had suffered terribly set aside adversity to work to improve the lives of others. Within all the discussion about the remembrance and the effects of war it must be remembered many OUs returned to civilian life and got on with their lives unscarred.

As a footnote to the efforts of Uppinghamians in the First World War the Second World War saw a significant number of OUs who had served in the Great War once more respond to their sense of duty and serve their country. The ways they did this varied; some were in the forces again, some lent their expertise to the government and others carried out other volunteer activity such as joining the Home Guard. However, a new generation of OUs made up the bulk of the old boys who served in the Second World War and this requires a separate account. For those OUs who had served in the Great War and held senior commands between 1939 and 1945 the experience they gained and the qualities of independence, inquisitiveness and self-confidence were not sufficient to guarantee success. The qualities and experience which OUs attractive as junior officers were not such important factors at more senior levels. A wider range of skills and attributes were called for as the cases of Dorman-Smith and Horrocks demonstrate. The experiences of OUs in the Second World War show that the school's involvement in both wars differed between them. Uppingham's involvement in the Great War was unique.

Uppingham's involvement in the Great War cannot simply be understood in terms of loss and futility. Those who went off to serve their country did so out of a sense of duty to protect their country and it was not indoctrination that led them to do so. Their views reflected a wider concern about Germany in the years leading up to war. As public school boys, their status as gentlemen made them ideal candidates to be junior officers leading men into action. In addition to this, the school's educational ethos aimed to produce boys with independence, inquisitiveness and self-confidence and as a result they were equipped and prepared to take leadership roles in the Great War. It was not just the younger OUs who served; old boys from a variety of backgrounds and ages provided skills to the country as it prosecuted total war. The school and its boys made their own contribution to waging total war. The school and its old boys were part of a nation in arms and did not consider themselves to be victims. It is in emphasising these factors that this book has set out to provide a fuller understanding of the school's involvement in the Great War. It is as a school in arms that Uppingham's involvement in the Great War needs to be understood.

Appendix I

Record of Service for Old Uppinghamians

Surname	Initials	Honours and Awards	Died on Service	Rank	Service	T/SR etc.
AARONS	F L F			Cadet OTC	Cambridge University	
ABEL	J D		26/03/1918	Second Lieutenant	Seaforth Highlanders	
ACTON	H L B			Brevet Colonel	Indian Army (Retired) Assistant Provost Marshal	
ADDINGTON	G W		01/12/1917	Second Lieutenant	Durham Light Infantry	
ADDINGTON	J S			Lieutenant	Guards	
AGNEW	Q G K (D S O)			Lieutenant Colonel	Royal Scots Fusiliers	
AITKEN	J G			Not Known	RASC	
AITKEN	R C S			Major	Cameronians (Scottish Rifles)	T
AIZLEWOOD	J A	MC and Bar, Mentioned in Despatches		Captain	4th Dragoon Guards (Royal Irish)	
AIZLEWOOD	L P	MC, AFC	29/09/1918	Major	Royal Air Force	
AKROYD	H C			Major	Kings Own Yorkshire Light Infantry	
ALBERY	B J			Lieutenant	RNVR	
ALBERY	I J	MC, mentioned in despatches		Major	Yeomanry	T
ALDER	S		02/04/1917 (listed as missing in The Times)	Lieutenant	Sherwood Foresters and RAF	POW
ALDERSEY	R P			Captain	East Surrey Regiment	T
ALEXANDER	C H	CBE, Mentioned in despatches		Brigadier General	Royal Field Artillery	
ALEXANDER	E			Captain	Royal Marines	
ALEXANDER	E A S			Lieutenant	Irish Guards	
ALEXANDER	H		17/10/1915	Second Lieutenant	Grenadier Guards	
ALEXANDER	J E S			Flight-Lieutenant	RAF	

Appendix I

Surname	Initials	Honours and Awards	Died on Service	Rank	Service	T/SR etc.
ALEXANDER	W L			Lieutenant	RNVR	
ALEXANDER	R G	MC, mentioned in despatches (3 times)		Captain	11th Lancers (Indian Army)	
ALLAN	A C			Second Lieutenant	Middlesex Regiment	
ALLEN	G W	Mentioned in Despatches		Captain	Leicestershire Regiment	
ALLEN	H B			Lieutenant	Royal Field Artillery	T
ALLEN	P			Major	Northants Regiment	
ALLEN	W R		11/03/1919	Captain	Royal Army Medical Corps	
ALMACK	E P		25/01/1916	Captain	Royal Horse Artillery	
AMBLER	M J			Lieutenant Colonel (Acting)	14th Hussars attd. RAF	
AMBROSE	W G	MC		Captain	Cheshire Regiment, Nigerian FF	
ANDERSON	C F E		09/01/1918	Cadet OTC	The Queen's (Royal West Surrey Regiment)	
ANDERSON	G			Lieutenant	Life Guards attd. Indian Army (Skinner's Horse)	
ANDERSON	K	MC, mentioned in despatches (3)		Lieutenant Colonel	Royal Field Artillery	T
ANDERSON	V L			Lieutenant	RAF, formerly South West Africa Imperial Light Horsemen and Argyll and Sutherland Highlanders	
ANDREWS	M			Private	American Army	
ANNAN	J G			Captain	Royal Field Artillery	
ANNAN	R			Lieutenant	Royal Engineers	T
ANNS	H F	Mentioned in despatches		Captain	London Regiment and RAF	
APPLEBY	D			Captain	Welsh Regiment	
ARCHER	C K			Lieutenant	King's African Rifles	
ARCHER	H D			Captain	Honourable Artillery Company (&RHA)	
ARCHER	H de B	MC, Croix de Guerre (Belgian)		Captain	Royal Field Artillery	T
ARCHER	J C	MC		Captain	Royal Engineers	
ARCHER	J F			Major	King's Own Yorkshire Light Infantry	
ARCHER	R H		27/12/1917	Second Lieutenant	Northumberland Fusiliers	
ARMSTRONG	Cecil A			Lieutenant	RASC	
ARMSTRONG	Charles A			Captain	Royal Horse Artillery	T
ARMSTRONG	G D			Lieutenant	Royal Horse Artillery	T
ARMSTRONG	J	Mentioned in despatches (2)		Captain	Royal Field Artillery	
ARMSTRONG	R K			Lieutenant	Worcestershire Regiment	
ARNOLD	A H		30/12/1916	Captain	West Yorkshire Regiment (Prince of Wales's Own)	

Surname	Initials	Honours and Awards	Died on Service	Rank	Service	T/SR etc.
ASH	B C		20/09/1914	Lieutenant	Sherwood Foresters (Notts and Derby Regiment)	
ASH	B N			Captain	RAMC	
ASH	F H	Croix de Guerre		Lieutenant	4th Hussars	
ASH	G B			Captain	RAMC	
ASH	O A			Lieutenant	Royal Garrison Artillery	SR
ASH	P C M			Captain	Post Offfice Rifles London Regt	T
ASHTON	C C G	OBE, Mentioned in Despatches (2), Greek Military Cross, Russian Order of St Vladimir		Lieutenant Colonel	East Surrey Regiment	
ASHTON	F H			Sub-Lieutenant	Royal Navy	
ASHTON	J A			Lieutenant	Lancashire Hussars	T
ASHTON	Sir R P			Major	General List	TFR
ASSER	V (D S O)	CMG, Mentioned in Despatches (4) & Brevet		Lieutenant Colonel	Royal Artillery	
ATKINS	H De C		10/10/1915	Lieutenant	Durham Light Infantry	
AULD	W	Mentioned in Despatches		Lieutenant Colonel	Highland Light Infantry	
AUSTIN	F C			Major	North Staffordshire Regiment	
AUSTIN	G E			Captain	Royal Inniskilling Fusiliers	
AVERDIECK	G G		14/09/1916	Lieutenant	Rifle Brigade	
AVERDIECK	G U			Second Lieutenant	Lancers	
AYLWIN	W E	MC		Captain	Bedfordshire Regiment	
AYTOUN	R M G	Mentioned in Despatches	27/08/1914	Lieutenant	Argyll and Sutherland Highlanders	
BACK	P G			Captain	Norfolk Regiment	T
BADGERY	T S M			Lieutenant	Royal Field Artillery	
BAGENAL	P H E	DCM		Corporal	RAMC	
BAGNALL	A H	OBE		Captain	Remounts Department	
BAGNALL	C E			Major	Essex Regiment	Reserve of Officers
BAGNALL	E W			Captain	RASC	
BAGNALL	H G			Captain	Royal Garrison Artillery	
BAGSHAWE	H V	CBE, DSO, Mentioned in Despatces		Lieutenant Colonel	RAMC	
BAILEY	C M		03/08/1917	Second Lieutenant	Royal Flying Corps	
BAILEY	D F		23/04/1917	Sub-Lieutenant	Royal Naval Volunteer Reserve	
BAILEY	C V			Captain	South Staffordshire Regiment	
BAILEY	G S			Lieutenant	Manchester Regiment	

Appendix I 169

Surname	Initials	Honours and Awards	Died on Service	Rank	Service	T/SR etc.
BAILEY	L N H			Lieutenant	Royal Engineers	T
BAKER	H G A			Captain	Labour Corps	
BAKER	J L		14/12/1915	Second Lieutenant	Royal Field Artillery	
BAKER	O T			Lieutenant	2nd Rhodesia Regiment BE Africa	
BALDWIN	C E H			Second Lieutenant	Royal Garrison Artillery	
BALLOCH	H C		02/06/1915	Second Lieutenant	Gordon Highlanders	
BALLY	E D	OBE		Major	Somerset Light Infantry	
BAMFIELD	W H			Second Lieutenant	Royal Welsh Fusiliers	
BAMFORD	E S		23/04/1915	Captain	York and Lancaster Regiment	
BAMFORD	C			Major	Royal Engineers	T
BAMFORD	C A	Mentioned in Despatches, Brevet		Major	Leicestershire Regiment	
BANCROFT	N		16/06/1916	Second Lieutenant	Cheshire Regiment	
BANCROFT	W			Captain	Royal Welsh Fusiliers	
BANKS	J		17/08/1917	Gunner	Royal Garrison Artillery	
BANKS	E H			Captain	Cheshire Regiment	
BANKS	G F H	Mentioned in Despatches		Lieutenant	Middlesex Regiment	
BANKS	P			Captain	Royal Field Artillery	SR
BARBER	J C		16/06/1915	Second Lieutenant	The King's (Liverpool Regiment)	
BARBER	C M			Captain	Queen's Own Cameron Highlanders	
BARBER	J C		16/06/1915	Second Lieutenant	The King's (Liverpool Regiment)	
BARBER	K			Driver	RAMC	
BARBER	W G			Lieutenant	RASC	
BARBER	W L			Lieutenant	Leicestershire Regiment	
BARCHARD	D M	Mentioned in Despatches (2)		Captain	Royal Welsh Fusiliers	POW
BARCLAY	H J			Captain	Somerset Light Infantry	T
BARDSWELL	H A		30/11/1917	Second Lieutenant	The King's (Liverpool Regiment)	
BARFORD	W G			Captain	Royal Field Artillery	T
BARKER	C R			Lieutenant	Royal Field Artillery	T
BARKER	K E M			Captain	Cambridgeshire Regiment	T
BARNSLEY	A A		25/10/1914	Captain	Lancashire Fusiliers	
BARNSLEY	G			The Rev.	CF (4th Class)	
BARRON	G H A			Lieutenant	Nottinghamshire Yeomanry, Scottish Horse and Machine Gun Corps	T
BARROW	H A J se S			Indian Cadet	RMC, Camberley	

Surname	Initials	Honours and Awards	Died on Service	Rank	Service	T/SR etc.
BARTHOLOMEW	J			Captain	Royal Garrison Artillery	T
BASCOMBE	C R		10/10/1917	Second Lieutenant	Royal Flying Corps	
BASS	K C J G			Second Lieutenant	Royal Flying Corps & RAF	
BASSET	F M	OBE		Major	Bedfordshire Regiment	
BATES	R P		10/03/1915	Lieutenant	Devonshire Regiment	
BATEMAN-FOX	H			Captain	London Regiment	T
BATTEN	J F	MC, Mentioned in Despatches		Captain	Royal Field Artillery	
BATTEN	S A H	Mentioned in Despatches		Lieutenant	Royal Engineers	
BAXTER	F B			Lieutenant	Royal Engineers and RAF	T
BAXTER	J B			Major	Leicestershire Regiment	
BAXTER	J F			Lieutenant	Royal Field Artillery	
BAYLEY	A E		24/04/1915	Private	Canadian Infantry	
BAYLEY	R M	Mentioned in Despatches, Croix de Guerre		Lieutenant	Royal Navy	
BEACHCROFT	P M	OBE, Mentioned in Despatches		Major	Royal Field Artillery & RAF	
BEADON	A E			Lieutenant Colonel	APD	
BEADON	H C			Captain	RASC	
BEALE	L A H			Lieutenant	Royal Engineers	
BEATSON	W W G		18/07/1916	Second Lieutenant	Royal Flying Corps	
BEAUCHAMP	M H			The Rev.	CF	
BEAUMONT	G	MC and bar		Major	Kings Own Yorkshire Light Infantry	T
BECHER	R F R	Mentioned in Despatches		Captain	Cameronians	
BECK	B	MC	18/08/1916	Captain	The King's (Liverpool Regiment)	
BECK	E W T	DSO, MC, Mentioned in Despatches (4)		Major	Royal Fusiliers & RAF	
BECKER	H T M			Second Lieutenant	Suffolk Regiment	T
BEDFORD	S H		01/07/1916	Second Lieutenant	Royal Berkshire Regiment	
BEDFORD	R A			Private	Royal Fusiliers	
BEDWELL	E P			Not Known	RNVR	
BEDWELL	F C	MC, Meantioned in Despatches (2), Brevet, Croix de Guerre, Order of St. Maurice and St. Lazarus		Captain Brevet Major	West Yorkshire Regiment (Prince of Wales's Own)	
BEER	A H	MC	21/04/1918	Lieutenant	Royal Field Artillery	T
BEER	S W			Cadet	King's Liverpool Regiment	

Appendix I   171

Surname	Initials	Honours and Awards	Died on Service	Rank	Service	T/SR etc.
BEETON	E C			Major	Royal Sussex Regiment	T
BEHRENS	J H			Lieutenant	West Yorkshire Regiment (Prince of Wales's Own)	T
BELK	T B			Second Lieutenant	Royal Field Artillery	T
BELL	A			Lieutenant	Northern Fusiliers	
BELL	H S (DSO)	CMG, Mentioned in Despatches (3)		Lieutenant Colonel	Royal Field Artillery	T
BELL	John			Captain	Ayrshire Yeomanry	T
BELL	K P	MC		Second Lieutenant	Royal Field Artillery	T
BELL	W A			Lieutenant	Royal Field Artillery	
BELLINGHAM	R K			Captain	Welsh Regiment	
BENGOUGH	G C			Second Lieutenant	Rifle Brigade	
BENGOUGH	H G			Cadet	Infantry	
BENNETT	H		14/11/1914	Captain	3rd Queen Alexandra's Own Gurkha Rifles	
BENNET	S			Second Lieutenant	Norfolk Regiment	
BENNETT	C K			Not Known	South African Forces	
BENNETT	N R O G			Rev.	CF	
BENNING	M S		01/11/1914	Lieutenant	East Surrey Regiment	
BENNION	C F			Captain	Royal Horse Artillery	T
BENTLEY	H M	Mentioned in Despatches		Captain	Lancashire Fusiliers and RAF	T
BERISFORD	F	Mentioned in Despatches		Captain	Durham Light Infantry	
BERNHARD	J E		01/12/1918	Private	Duke of Wellington's (West Riding Regiment)	
BERNHARD	H A			Lieutenant	Royal Field Artillery	
BERRY	T G			Captain	York and Lancaster Regiment	
BEVEN	D			Lieutenant	Leicestershire Regiment and Machine Gun Corps	T
BEWICKE	C G		26/07/1916	Lieutenant	Welsh Regiment	
BEYTS	L S			Captain	Lancashire Fusiliers	
BICKET	M			Lieutenant	Sherwood Foresters (Notts and Derby Regiment)	SR
BICKET	L P			Second Lieutenant	Royal Field Artillery	
BICKET	T B	MC		Captain	Royal Field Artillery	T
BICKNELL	A	MC, Brevet		Captain Brevet Major	Gloucestershire Regiment	T
BIDDOLPH	N	Mentioned in Despatches		Captain	Royal Scots	POW
BILLINGTON	E	MC, Mentioned in Despatches		Lieutenant	Cheshire Regiment	

Surname	Initials	Honours and Awards	Died on Service	Rank	Service	T/SR etc.
BILLINGTON	G M			Second Lieutenant	Royal Garrison Artillery	
BINDLOSS	E H	MC, Croix de Guerre		Captain	Royal Field Artillery	
BIRCH	A L			Major	Buckinghamshire Yeomanry	T
BIRLEY	P L			Air Mechanic	RAF	
BIRLEY	M			Lieutenant	West Yorkshire Regiment (Prince of Wales's Own)	
BIRT	D T			Lieutenant	RAMC	
BISHOP	C G	DSO, Mentioned in Despatches	30/10/1917	Major	Royal Engineers	T (POW)
BISHOP	J F			Lieutenant	Sherwood Foresters (Notts and Derby Regiment)	POW
BLACKBURN	L O G			Major	RASC	
BLACKBURN	R W			Cadet	Leeds University OTC	
BLACKIE	W G			Second Lieutenant	Royal Field Artillery	T
BLADWORTH	K T			Private	Honourable Artillery Company	
BLAKE	A L			Captain	Somerset Light Infantry	T
BLEW	A S			Lieutenant	RASC	
BLEW	C L			Major	Worcestershire Hussars (Attached Worcestershire RegimenT)	
BLEW	E W			Private	Royal Fusiliers	
BLUMER	J		26/09/1916	Second Lieutenant	Royal Field Artillery	
BLYTHE	R A			Not Known	65th Division Canadian Contingent	
BOLLAND	T J		09/05/1915	Major	The King's (Liverpool Regiment)	
BOLUS	G W		11/03/1916	Rifleman	Rhodesia Regiment	
BOND	D H			Second Lieutenant	RASC	
BONSOR	A J			Captain	Royal West Kent Regiment	
BOOTH	P J	MC	02/03/1920	Lieutenant	Royal Scots Fusiliers	
BOOTH	C H B	MC		Captain	RAMC	
BOOTH	C V			Lieutenant	Suffolk Regiment	
BOOTH	H	MC, Mentioned in Despatches		Major	3rd Hussars	SR
BOOTHBY	J C			Second Lieutenant	Sherwood Foresters (Notts and Derby Regiment)	
BORRER	J M		09/09/1917	Lieutenant	Royal Sussex Regiment	T
BOSTON	H G			Flight Commander	RAF	

Appendix I 173

Surname	Initials	Honours and Awards	Died on Service	Rank	Service	T/SR etc.
BOSTON	L	MC, Mentioned in Despatches	06/05/1916	Lieutenant	West Yorkshire Regiment (Prince of Wales's Own)	
BOSWORTH	L O	OBE, MC, Mentioned in Despatches (2)		Captain	Intelligence Corps	
BOTHAMLEY	H W H			Lieutenant	Royal West Kent Regiment	
BOTTOMLEY	G G D			Lieutenant	Queen's Royal West Surrey Regiment	
BOUCH	F C			Second Lieutenant	RASC	
BOUCHER	H E	MC		Lieutenant	Royal Field Artillery	T
BOURKE	E G W		16/06/1915	Captain	King's Royal Rifle Corps	
BOURKE	U H			Not Known	East African Regiment MGC	
BOUSFIELD	J S			Lieutenant	East Lancashire Regiment	
BOUVERIE	H P			Captain	5th Dragoon Guards	
BOWER	C W			Surgeon-Lieutenant	Royal Navy	
BOWER	H J			Captain	RAMC	
BOWIE	D A J			Second Lieutenant	Royal Field Artillery	
BOWLY	G R M			Lieutenant	Royal Warwickshire Regiment	
BOWMAN	W P		17/10/1916	Lieutenant	Royal Flying Corps	
BOYD	G W			Lieutenant	Royal Field Artillery	T
BRADDELL	C F	Mentioned in Despatches		Lieutenant	RASC	
BRADLEY	C C			Captain	Royal Fusiliers	
BRADLEY	J B			Sergeant	Royal Engineers	T
BRADLEY	M G			Captain	Middlesex Regiment	
BRAHAM	D C	Croix de Guerre		Second Lieutenant	Queen's Royal West Surrey Regiment	
BRAHAM	J E	Mentioned in Despatches (3)		Captain	Royal Garrison Artillery	
BRAILSFORD	C H			Lieutenant	Royal Field Artillery	T
BRAND	H D F			Captain	RAMC	
BRANDON	A C		21/01/1916	Captain	Hampshire Regiment	T
BRANDRETH	L	Mentioned in Despatches	06/06/1915	Major	Royal Fusiliers	
BRAY	G	MC		Lieutenant	Royal Engineers	T
BREWILL	L C			Captain	Sherwood Foresters (Notts and Derby Regiment)	T
BREWIS	A P	Mentioned in Despatches	01/06/1917	Captain	Northumberland Fusiliers	
BREWIS	J A G		29/04/1917	Lieutenant	Royal Flying Corps	
BREWIS	N H			Cadet	RAF	
BRIGGS	C		20/09/1917	Private	Royal Fusiliers	
BRIGGS	C B	MC		Lieutenant	Royal Engineers	

Surname	Initials	Honours and Awards	Died on Service	Rank	Service	T/SR etc.
BRIGHT	A V		07/06/1917	Lieutenant	Sherwood Foresters (Notts and Derby Regiment)	
BRIGHT	T B			Second Lieutenant	Royal Garrison Artillery	T
BRITTAIN	E H	MC	15/06/1918	Captain	Sherwood Foresters (Notts and Derby Regiment)	
BROAD	A E	MC, Mentioned in Despatches	02/03/1916	Lieutenant	Dorsetshire Regiment	
BROAD	A M			Second Lieutenant	Royal Fusiliers	
BROAD	P G			Captain	Royal Engineers	
BROADBENT	E R	MC, Mentioned in Despatches	31/10/1918	Major	8th (King's Royal Irish) Hussars	
BROADBENT	H G			Second Lieutenant	Royal Engineers	
BROADLEY	W W B			Captain	East Yorkshire Regiment	SR
BROCK	G S		07/10/1918	Captain	Indian Medical Service	
BRODIE	P W		18/11/1918	Captain	Royal Air Force	
BROMET	W G H			Second Lieutenant	Royal Field Artillery	
BROOK	R J	DSO, Mentioned in Despatches		Lieutenant Colonel	Royal Canadian Regiment	
BROOK	R W			Private	Northants Regiment	
BROOKS	L W		25/09/1915	Lieutenant	West Yorkshire Regiment (Prince of Wales's Own)	SR
BROOKSBANK	J L			Second Lieutenant	Machine Gun Corps (Infantry)	
BROOKSBANK	W E H			Lieutenant	Rifle Brigade	
BROOME	F C	DFC		Flight Lieutenant	RAF	
BROSTER	W O			Lieutenant	Royal Field Artillery	
BROWN	A W S		18/08/1916	Lieutenant	Rifle Brigade	
BROWN	H M		09/04/1916	Second Lieutenant	East Lancashire Regiment	
BROWN	R W		09/04/1917	Captain	Wiltshire Regiment	
BROWN	P W	CMG, DSO, Brevet, Mentioned in Despatches (6)		(Temporary) Brigadier-General, Brevet Lieutenant Colonel	Gordon Highlanders	
BROWN	R L			Second Lieutenant	Royal Field Artillery	
BROWN	T E			Not Known	RASC	
BROWNE	B			Captain	Corps of Military Accountants (Railway Transport Officer)	
BROWNE	O P			Lieutenant	RNVR	
BROWNE	T B			Lieutenant	5th Dragoon Guards	

Appendix I 175

Surname	Initials	Honours and Awards	Died on Service	Rank	Service	T/SR etc.
BROWNING	C S		10/12/1916	Captain	129th Duke of Connaught's Own Baluchis	
BRUCE	A H			Not Known	RAF	
BRUCE-LOW	H	MC and Bar		Captain	RAMC	
BRUFORD	G W B			Cadet	RAF	
BRUMELL	A E V	MC, Mentioned in Despatches		Captain	Northumberland Hussars	T
BRUNT	F H G			Lieutenant	Royal Field Artillery	T
BRUTY	W G	Mentioned in Despatches		Captain	County of London Regiment	
BRYAN	N T			Second Lieutenant	Royal Field Artillery	
BRYNING	E A			Captain	Royal Field Artillery	
BRYSON	G L U		30/07/1916	Captain	Royal Warwickshire Regiment	
BRYSON	O C	MC, Albert Medal, DFC		Lieutenant	Dorset Yeomanry (Attd RAF)	
BUCKTON	G N			Lieutenant	1/10 Jats (Indian Army)	
BULKELEY	L A H		10/04/1918	Captain	Royal Army Medical Corps	
BULLEN-SMITH	C J			Lieutenant	Nottinghamshire Yeomanry	T
BULMAN	P			Colonel	Deputy Army Adjutant General	
BUNCE	H P		05/10/1916	Second Lieutenant	North Staffordshire Regiment	
BUNNING	A E			Not Known	Australian Expeditionary Force	
BURDER	G E L			Lieutenant	Royal Garrison Artillery	
BURGOYNE-JOHNSON	G H			Lieutenant	Durham Light Infantry	
BURLISON	J C	Mentioned in Despatches (3)		Captain	RNVR Machine Gun Corps (Infantry)	
BURMAN	W F	MC		Captain	Suffolk Regiment	
BURN	R W			Second Lieutenant	Scots Guards	
BURN	S A			Captain	RAMC	
BURNABY	H B (D S O)	Mentioned in Despatches	08/09/1916	Lieutenant Colonel	The Queen's (Royal West Surrey Regiment)	
BURNAND	R F	OBE, Mentioned in Despatches		Major	Machine Gun Corps (Infantry)	T
BURNAND	R M	MC		Second Lieutenant	RAF	
BURNE	N O		27/10/1917	Lieutenant	40th Pathans	
BURNE	N A K	Mentioned in Despatches (2)		Lieutenant Colonel	Indian Army	
BURRARD	S G (Sir)			Colonel	Royal Engineers	
BURRELL	W (K C S I_		18/11/1914	Lieutenant	Royal Naval Volunteer Reserve	
BURRELL	G G			Lieutenant	Royal Navy (RNVR)	
BURRELL	T M			Lieutenant	Highland Light Infantry	T

Surname	Initials	Honours and Awards	Died on Service	Rank	Service	T/SR etc.
BURTON	H C			Sub-Lieutenant	Royal Navy	
BUTLER	G W			Lieutenant	King's Own Yorkshire Light Infantry	
CAITHNESS	Earl of	CBE, Mentioned in Despatches		Lieutenant Colonel	Gordon Highlanders	T
CALDECOTT	J L	Mentioned in Despatches	09/09/1914	Lieutenant	Royal Garrison Artillery	
CALLARD	S E		23/04/1915	Second Lieutenant	East Yorkshire Regiment	
CALLARD	E M R			Not Known	Malay Rifles	
CALLARD	N L			Lieutenant Colonel	South Lancashire Regiment	SR
CAMERON	D H	OBE		Brigade Major	RAF (Retired Major Indian Army)	
CAMERON	G F			Second Lieutenant	Cameronians (Scottish Rifles)	
CAMPBELL	A C C	OBE, Mentioned in Despatches (2)		Major	RASC	T
CAMPBELL	M			Captain	Royal Flying Corps	
CAMPION	F E			Lieutenant	Royal Engineers	SR
CANDLER	A P			Lieutenant	London Regiment	T
CANDLER	W H			Lance Corporal	Royal Sussex Regiment	
CANE	A S	DSO, OBE, Mentioned in Despatches (4)		Major	RAMC	
CANE	L B			Major	RAMC	
CANNY	J C M (DSO)	CBE, Mentioned in Despatches(2), Brevet		Lieutenant Colonel	RASC (& Royal Munster Fusiliers)	
CARDER	C D			Major	Royal Field Artillery	T
CAREY	W H			Captain	RASC	
CARKEET-JAMES	C A			Cadet	RMA (Woolwich)	
CARLYON	H M T			Lieutenant	Royal Field Artillery	
CARPENTER	G			Second Lieutenant	RAF	
CARR	S T		27/09/1916	Lieutenant	Manchester Regiment	
CARR	G P			Cadet	Royal Field Artillery	
CARR	L	OBE, DSO, Brevet, Mentioned in Despatches (5)		Major	Gordon Highlanders	
CARR	P			Lieutenant	Not Known	
CARSON	H R			Lieutenant	RNVR	
CARTER	A B			Second Lieutenant	Indian Army (Attd 35th Sikhs)	
CARTER	F W			Captain	County of London Yeomanry	T
CARTER WOOD	J A		01/02/1915	Second Lieutenant	Coldstream Guards	
CARTHEW	T W C	DSO, Mentioned in Despatches(3), Croix de Guerre		Major	Bedfordshire Regiment & RAF	

Surname	Initials	Honours and Awards	Died on Service	Rank	Service	T/SR etc.
CARVER	M D	AFC		Flight Lieutenant	RAF	
CARVER	W H			Major	East Yorkshire Regiment	
CASSON	J F R			Not Known	South African Forces	
CASTLE	D			Lieutenant	Cameronian Scottish Rifles)	
CASTLE	E			Assistant Paymaster	RNVR, RND	
CASTLE	T			Major	East Surrey Regiment	T
CATLOW	E S			Captain	South Lancashire Regiment	T
CAUNTER	R L L		18/12/1916	Second Lieutenant	Gloucestershire Regiment	
CAUNTER	J A L	Brevet		Captain, Brevet Major	Gloucestershire Regiment	POW Escaped
CAUSTON	G T	Mentioned in Despatches		Captain	RASC	
CAUSTON	L J			The Rev.	CF	
CAUSTON	R H			Captain	Royal Berkshire Regiment	
CAWLEY	J D			Lieutenant	Royal Field Artillery	
CHADWICK	A R			Company Quartermaster Sergeant	Manchester Regiment	
CHADWICK	H			Captain	RAMC	
CHADWICK	R	MC, DCM		Lieutenant	RAF	
CHAFFERS	N B	MC, Mentioned in Despatches		Captain	Duke of Wellington's (West Riding Regiment)	T
CHALONER	R G H		03/04/1917	Captain	Wiltshire Regiment	SR
CHAMBERLAIN	D A			Lieutenant	RAMC	
CHAMBERS-HUNTER	C A		01/04/1916	Second Lieutenant	Gordon Highlanders	SR
CHAPMAN	H R		27/06/1915	Major	Durham Light Infantry	
CHAPMAN	J			Not Known	Duke of Wellington's (West Riding Regiment) and Royal Engineers	
CHAPPLE	G L			Captain	East Surrey Regiment	T
CHARLTON	J M	Mentioned in Despatches	01/07/1916	Captain	Northumberland Fusiliers	
CHARNAUD	C A H			Lieutenant	RNVR	
CHARLTON	R	MC		Captain	South Staffordshire Regiment	
CHECKLAND (BEAUMONT-CHECKLAND)	B M		17/08/1917	Lieutenant	West Somerset Yeomanry	T
CHESTER	L C B		04/04/1918	Second Lieutenant	Lancashire Fusiliers	
CHEYNE	J L	MC and Bar, Mentioned in Despatches		Captain	16th Lancers	
CHIPMAN	R B		20/07/1916	Lance Corporal	Cameronians (Scottish Rifles)	
CHRISTMAS	D V		23/10/1915	Lieutenant	Suffolk Regiment	T

Surname	Initials	Honours and Awards	Died on Service	Rank	Service	T/SR etc.
CHRISTOPHERSON	A B			Lieutenant	Welsh Regiment	
CHRISTOPHERSON	C B	Mentioned in Despatches		Captain	Welsh Regiment	
CHRISTOPHERSON	I			Second Lieutenant	Royal Garrison Artillery	
CHRISTOPHERSON	K			Captain	The Buffs (East Kent Regiment)	
CHRISTOPHERSON	N C	MC, Mentioned in Despatches		The Rev.	CF (4th Class)	
CHURCH	G W	MC	03/05/1917	Second Lieutenant	The Buffs (East Kent Regiment)	
CLAPPERTON	C R			Lieutenant	Royal Garrison Artillery and RAF	T
CLARK	A G			Captain	Highland Light Infantry	T
CLARK	A H	Mentioned in Despatches		Captain	Lincolnshre Regiment	T
CLARK	H M			Lieutenant	Royal Field Artillery	
CLARK	N M			Lieutenant	Highland Light Infantry	
CLARK	J			Lieutenant	Northumberland Fusiliers	
CLARK	W M			Captain	King's Own Scottish Borderers	
CLARKE	H Y C		23/04/1917	Second Lieutenant	South Wales Borderers	
CLARKE	D A	Mentioned in Despatches, MBE		Captain	South Staffordshire Regiment	T
CLARKE	F S			Lieutenant	Royal Field Artillery	
CLARKE	G P	MC		Major	Somerset Light Infantry	T
CLARKE	J C			Major	Lord Strathcona's Horse	
CLARKE	M L			Lieutenant	4th Infantry Brigade Australian Expeditionary Force	
CLARKE	M N			Major	RASC	
CLARKE	W F	OBE		Lieutenant-Commander	RNVR	
CLARKSON	A B	DSO, MC, Mentioned in Despatches		Major	Duke of Wellington's (West Riding Regiment)	
CLARKSON	W B	DSO, Mentioned in Despatches		Major	Royal Garrison Artillery	
CLAYTON	W F			Chief Petty Officer	RNVR	
CLEGG	R L		03/09/1917	Lieutenant	Royal Flying Corps	
CLEGG	E B			Captain	Lancashire Fusiliers	T
CLEGG	J H		04/06/1915	Captain	Manchester Regiment	T
CLEGG	W J	MC		Second Lieutenant	Queen's Own Yorkshire Dragoons	T
CLIFF	G T	Croix de Chevalier	10/02/1918	Major	3rd Dragoon Guards (Prince of Wales' Own)	
CLODE-BAKER	G E		01/07/1916	Lieutenant	London Regiment (London Rifle Brigade)	T
CLOUGH	F N			Major	Manchester Regiment	

Appendix I 179

Surname	Initials	Honours and Awards	Died on Service	Rank	Service	T/SR etc.
COALBANK	R M			Captain	RAMC	POW
COATES	W C			Captain	King's Royal Rifle Corps	
COBBOLD	F R			Corporal	Canadian Mounted Rifles	
COCKSHOTT	F G			Private	Saskatchewan Light Infantry	
COCKTON	J C			Lieutenant	Westmoreland and Cumberland Yeomanry	T
CODRINGTON	C W G H			Lieutenant	19th Hussars	SR
COHAN	C M			Engineer	Royal Navy (Transport)	
COHAN	E M		05/08/1914	Second Lieutenant	Royal Field Artillery	T
COHAN	H M		06/08/1919	Gunner	Royal Garrison Artillery	
COHAN	W M			Captain	Royal Field Artillery	
COHEN	A M			Captain	Royal West Kent Regiment	
COLE	L S		03/10/1915	Second Lieutenant	Cheshire Regiment	SR
COLE	N E F		05/10/1917	Lieutenant	The Buffs (East Kent Regiment)	
COLEMAN	P G	DSO, Mentioned in Despatches		Captain	Welsh Guards formerly North Staffordshire Regiment	T
COLLEY	W A		01/07/1916	Captain	York and Lancaster Regiment	
COLLIER	J			Not Known	RAF	T
COLLIN	E N T	Mentioned in Despatches		Captain	Sherwood Foresters (Notts and Derby Regiment)	T
COLLINGE	W R		07/08/1917	Lieutenant	The King's (Liverpool Regiment)	
COLLINGE	A			Lieutenant	Machine Gun Corps (Infantry)	
COLLINGS-WELLS	J S	VC, DSO, Mentioned in Despatches	27/03/1918	Lieutenant Colonel	Bedfordshire Regiment	T
COLLINS	J L			Captain	Lancashire Fusiliers	T
COLLINS	J W	MC, Croix de Guerre Ordre de L'Etoile Noire		Captain	Highland Light Infantry	T
COLLINS	M D			Private	RAMC	
COLLINS	S H	MC		Lieutenant	Royal Field Artillery	
COLLS	A B H			Lieutenant	Royal Garrison Artillery	
COLLYER	H O			Captain	Machine Gun Corps (Infantry)	
COMBER	T G			Commander	Royal Navy	
CONSTABLE	O C			Lieutenant	Worcestershire Regiment	
CONSTANTINE	H N	MC	27/05/1918	Captain	Yorkshire Regiment	T
CONSTANTINE	R A			Major	Yorkshire Regiment	T
CONSTANTINE	W W	MC		Major	Yorkshire Regiment	T

Surname	Initials	Honours and Awards	Died on Service	Rank	Service	T/SR etc.
COOK	G T R	CMG, DSO, Twice Mentioned in Despatches, Croix de Guerre	26/03/1918	Lieutenant Colonel	20th Hussars	
COOKE	G P		03/05/1915	Sub-Lieutenant	RNVR	
COOKE-HURLE	J A	Mentioned in Despatches		Major	North Somerset Yeomanry	T
COOPER	C F		05/09/1916	Major	Royal Field Artillery	
COOPER	A H	MC, Mentioned in Despatches		Captain	Essex Regiment	T
COOPER	H			Captain	Army Veterinary Corps	
COOPER	J C			Trooper	Northants Yeomanry	T
COOPER	R			Captain	Yorkshire Regiment	
COPE	G S			Second Lieutenant	Machine Gun Corps (Infantry)	
CORBETT	D B		03/07/1916	Second Lieutenant	Royal Irish Rifles	
CORRY	C L			Lieutenant	Royal Field Artillery	T
COSTER	H R			Second Lieutenant	Tank Corps	
COTT	A M			Captain	RAF	
COUPER	E E			Colonel	4th Gurkas	
COUPER	G R C			Lieutenant	Machine Gun Corps (Infantry)	T
COUPER	V A	KCB, CB, Mentioned in Despatches (4), Order of Danilo		Major-General	Not Known	
COURAGE	P M	MC and Bar, Mentioned in Despatches		Lieutenant	4th Dragoon Guards (Royal Irish)	
COURT	G B			Captain	Duke of Wellington's (West Riding Regiment)	T
COURTNEY	R W	Mentioned in Despatches (2), Brevet		Major, Brevet Lieutenant-Colonel	RASC, DAQMG	
COUSANS	G N		09/09/1916	Second Lieutenant	Royal Flying Corps	
COWAN	J O C		14/07/1916	Captain	Royal Scots	
COWELL	E J E			Lieutenant Colonel	Royal Fusiliers	SR
COWELL	G E M		30/12/1917	Major	Royal Field Artillery	
COX	G W		03/05/1917	Major	Royal Warwickshire Regiment	T
COX	N G			Second Lieutenant	RFC & RAF	
COX	P G A	DSO, Mentioned in Despatches (3), Legion of Honour, Croix d'Officier		Lieutenant Colonel	Royal Dublin Fusiliers formerly Rifle Brigade	
COXON	H			Gunner	Royal Field Artillery	
CRAIGMILE	H W C			Second Lieutenant	Seaforth Highlanders	

Surname	Initials	Honours and Awards	Died on Service	Rank	Service	T/SR etc.
CRAWLEY	A C			Captain	Provost Company	
CREE	J F		03/09/1918	Second Lieutenant	Northumberland Fusiliers	
CREIGHTON	A B			Lieutenant	London Regiment	
CREWDSON	B F	Mentioned in Despatches		Lieutenant	Irish Guards	
CREWDSON	E	MC, Mentioned in Despatches (2)		Lieutenant	Royal Engineers	
CRISPE	L H			Not Known	RASC	
CROASDAILE	L			Major	Bedfordshire Regiment	
CROFT	B		10/11/1918	Captain	London Regiment (Artists' Rifles)	T
CROSBY	J C P		21/01/1918	Second Lieutenant	The King's (Liverpool Regiment)	
CROSBY	T H S		03/02/1918	Lieutenant	Royal Flying Corps	
CROSLEY	C	MC, Mentioned in Despatches	16/08/1915	Second Lieutenant	Royal Irish Fusiliers	
CROSTHWAITE	A R	DFC		Second Lieutenant	RAF	
CROSTHWAITE	J D	DSO, MC and Bar, Croix de Chavalier, Mentioned in Despatches (3)		Lieutenant Colonel	Royal West Kent Regiment	T (POW)
CROWDER	G C G			Trooper	Dragoon Guards	
CROWE	D M	MC		Major	Malay Regiment	
CROWTHER	C T B			Lieutenant	Royal Engineers	
CRUTCH	J H			Lieutenant	RAF	
CULL	A T		11/05/1917	Captain	Royal Flying Corps	
CULLEN	J G C			Lieutenant	Royal Field Artillery	T
CUMMING	F K		23/10/1918	Second Lieutenant	Black Watch (Royal Highlanders)	
CUMMING	R S			Cadet	Guards Cadet School	
CUNNINGHAM	C C F		19/08/1916	Captain	Argyll and Sutherland Highlanders	
CURREY	V F		13/10/1915	Major	Suffolk Regiment	
CURTIS	P P	MC, Mentioned in Despatches		Captain	15th Hussars	
CUTBILL	E H E			Lieutenant	RAF	POW
CUTTS	T B		20/07/1916	Captain	Sherwood Foresters (Notts and Derby Regiment)	
DACRES	L S L		20/04/1919	Captain	Indian Army Reserve of Officers	
DAGLISH	G G			Lieutenant-Commander	RNVR	
DAGLISH	J W		14/02/1916	Lieutenant	Durham Light Infantry	
DAGLISH	R S			Lieutenant	King's Liverpool Regiment	
DALE	G F			Lieutenant Colonel	2nd Dragoon Guards	

Surname	Initials	Honours and Awards	Died on Service	Rank	Service	T/SR etc.
DALISON	J P	Mentioned in Despatches		Lieutenant Colonel	Royal West Kent Regiment	
DALY	D	DSO, MC, Mentioned in Despatches (4)		Major	Royal Horse Artillery	
DALY	S O			Captain	London Regiment	
DALZIEL	G N C	Mentioned in Despatches		Captain	London Regiment	
DANIEL	A C E			Captain	Norfolk Regiment	SR
DANIEL	T W	DSO and Bar, MC, Mentioned in Despatches		Major, Acting Lieutenant Colonel	Sherwood Foresters (Notts and Derby Regiment)	
DANIEL	V E T	MC		Lieutenant	Royal Field Artillery	
DANIELL	V S			Captain	Scots Guards	
DARBYSHIRE	L C		31/07/1917	Lieutenant	Canadian Infantry	Can. Militia
D'ARCY-IRVINE	C W		06/08/1915	Captain	Leinster Regiment	
DARKE	E			Lieutenant	Sherwood Foresters (Notts and Derby Regiment)	
DARLEY	C H			Second Lieutenant	Royal Field Artillery	
DARLING	J A			Lieutenant	King's Own Scottish Borderers	
DAUKES	A H		07/08/1915	Lieutenant Colonel	South Staffordshire Regiment	
DAVENPORT	T L		27/04/1917	Second Lieutenant	Royal Field Artillery	T
DAVENPORT	C M	Mentioned in Despatches		Captain	Royal Field Artillery	
DAVENPORT	E			Captain	Royal Engineers	T
DAVEY	A			Captain	Herefordshire Regiment	T
DAVIES	H L	Mentioned in Despatches	25/10/1914	Lieutenant	Royal Horse Artillery	
DAVIES	D B			Second Lieutenant	Welsh Guards	
DAVIES	G F			Captain	Gloucestershire Regiment	
DAVIES	S N			Captain	London Regiment	T
DAVIES	T M			Captain	RoyalSussex Regiment and Royal Garrison Artillery	T
DAVIES-COLLEY	T H			Lieutenant Colonel	Manchester Regiment	T
DAVIS	J B S			Not Known	South Lancashire Regiment	
DAVY	D H			Lieutenant	Wiltshire Yeomanry	T
DAWSON	E N			Lieutenant	Royal Field Artillery	
DAWSON	I			Second Lieutenant	Royal Field Artillery	
DE BRISAY	A C D			Lieutenant	Lincolnshire Regiment	T
DE CORDOVA	M R			Captain	RASC	T

Appendix I   183

Surname	Initials	Honours and Awards	Died on Service	Rank	Service	T/SR etc.
DE PASS	C A		22/03/1918	Second Lieutenant	Tank Corps	
DE PASS	F P C			Captain	RASC	
DE PIERRES	E N		16/09/1917	Lieutenant	Royal Field Artillery	
DE PLEDGE	E K		03/06/1916	Captain	West Yorkshire Regiment (Prince of Wales's Own)	
DEANE	C H	MC, Mentioned in Despatches		Major	RAOC	
DEARDEN	J			Not Known	P.S.B. Royal Fusiliers	
DELMEGE	C H			Major	21st Lancers	
DENMAN-JUBB	C O		24/08/1914	Captain	Duke of Wellington's (West Riding Regiment)	
DENNING	W F			Major	Duke of Wellington's (West Riding Regiment)	T
DENT	B W			Lieutenant	Royal Garrison Artillery	
DENT	R St. A		17/11/1916	Sergeant	South African Infantry	
DESPREZ	C C S			Captain	Royal Marine Light Infantry	
DEUCHAR	A G		22/11/1917	Captain	Royal Flying Corps	
DEUCHAR	E C	MC		Lieutenant	Northern Fusiliers	
DEVONSHIRE	C H			Lieutenant	Indian Army Reserve of Officers	
DEVONSHIRE	E R			Captain	Lincolnshire Regiment	
DEWHURST	M S			Second Lieutenant	King's Royal Rifle Corps	
DICKENSON	W C			Lieutenant Colonel	Royal Engineers	Reserve of Officers
DICKINSON	D C C		28/08/1918	Second Lieutenant	South Wales Borderers	
DICKSON	W T		09/07/1916	Captain	Royal Inniskilling Fusiliers	
DICKSON	T C H	MC		Major	Royal Dublin Fusiliers attached Royal Inniskilling Fusiliers	
DINGLE	C E J			Lieutenant	RAF	
DINSMORE	J F			Second Lieutenant	Royal Horse Artillery	
DINN	H K			Lieutenant	King's Royal Rifle Corps	
DIXON	A M			Major	Royal Field Artillery	T
DIXON	C			Lieutenant	Royal Engineers	T
DIXON	J B			Not Known	Royal Fusiliers	
DIXON	J S D			Lieutenant	Argyll and Sutherland Highlanders	
DIXON	P E			Colonel	Royal Engineers	Reserve of Officers
DIXON	R L			Lieutenant	Royal Field Artillery	
DIXON	R S	DSO, MC		Major	Highland Light Infantry	
DIXON	W G	MC		Lieutenant	Coldstream Guards	
DOBELL	G			Captain	South Wales Borderers	T
DORE	G L H			Lieutenant	RAF	

Surname	Initials	Honours and Awards	Died on Service	Rank	Service	T/SR etc.
DORMAN-SMITH	E E	MC, Mentioned in Despatches (2)		Captain	Northumberland Fusiliers	
DOUGLAS	A L			Private	London Scottish	
DOUGLAS-HAMILTON	H E S			Lieutenant	Black Watch (Royal Highlanders)	
DOW	W		19/12/1915	Second Lieutenant	Cameronians (Scottish Rifles)	T
DOWSON	H	MC	15/09/1916	Captain	King's Royal Rifle Corps	
DOWSON	J B			Captain	Worcestershire Regiment	T
DOWSON	L			Lieutenant	Divisional Cyclists Company, East Anglian Division	
D'OYLY	C T			Captain	Royal Field Artillery	
DRAFFEN	G W			Second Lieutenant	Not Known	
DRAKE	T			Not Known	Hertfordshire Yeomanry	
DRAKE-BROCKMAN	F H			Lieutenant	The Buffs (East Kent Regiment)	
DRAKE-BROCKMAN	W			Lieutenant	City of London Regiment	
DRUCE	L M			Sub-Lieutenant (Paymaster)	RNVR	
DRUMMOND	C A			Captain	County of London Yeomanry	T
DRYLAND	G W			Lieutenant	RAMC	
DU CANE	H J (M V O, C B)		15/06/1916	Brigadier General	General Staff	
DUDLEY	C L		04/06/1915	Second Lieutenant	Manchester Regiment	
DUFF	D T			Lieutenant	Royal Engineers	
DUNCAN	D A			Second Lieutenant	Royal Engineers	
DUNDAS	G W S			Captain	Rifle Brigade	
DUNN	G M		23/02/1917	Second Lieutenant	Duke of Wellington's (West Riding Regiment)	
DUNN	P M		03/02/1917	Captain	Royal Welsh Fusiliers	
DUNN	B M	MC, Mentioned in Despatches, Croix de Guerre		Captain	Welsh Regiment	
DUNN	P D W	Mentioned in Despatches		Captain	Lancashire Fusiliers	
DUNN	R M			Lieutenant	Machine Gun Corps (Infantry)	
DUNNING	J D			Lieutenant	10th Australian Contingent	
DUNNING	J S			Sapper	Canadian Expeditionary Force	
DURHAM	J C			Lieutenant	Suffolk Regiment	
DURIE	J A	MC, Brevet, Mentioned in Despatches		Major	Black Watch (Royal Highlanders)	
DURLACHER	P A	MC	12/05/1918	Lieutenant	Machine Gun Corps (Infantry)	

Appendix I 185

Surname	Initials	Honours and Awards	Died on Service	Rank	Service	T/SR etc.
DURNFORD	G E J	DSO, Brevet, Mentioned in Despatches (3)		Lieutenant Colonel	Royal Engineers	
DURRELL	T C V			Lieutenant	Royal Field Artillery	
DURST	A	Mentioned in Despatches		Lieutenant	Royal Engineers	
DUSGATE	R E		19/12/1917	Second Lieutenant	Royal Flying Corps	
DUST	F W	MC	23/04/1917	Major	Royal Field Artillery	T
DYER	C R			Colonel	Middlesex Regiment	Reserve of Officers
DYER	G E			Second Lieutenant	Royal Horse Artillery	T
DYER	I R			Lieutenant	Dorset Regiment	SR
DYSON	J S			Second Lieutenant	Royal Field Artillery	
DYKE-DENNIS	H V T	Mentioned in Despatches		Lieutenant	Royal Engineers	SR
EADIE	P			Lieutenant	Royal Engineers and RAF	T
EARL	F D			Captain	Oxford and Bucks Light Infantry	T
EASTMAN	H C W			Lieutenant	Royal Artillery	
EATON	H R	OBE, Mentioned in Despatches		Captain	Manchester Regiment	T
EATON	T R	OBE		Captain	Manchester Regiment	
ECCLES	J H			Captain	King's Liverpool Regiment	
ECKENSTEIN	K E	Croix de Guerre, Ordre de la Couronne Belgique		Medecin Aide-Major (1st Class)	French Army	
ECKENSTEIN	T C	MC		Captain	South Lancashire Fusiliers	
EDELL	I J	MC		Lieutenant	Royal Field Artillery	T
EDGE	L			Bombadier	Honourable Artillery Company	
EDGE	R W			Lieutenant	Leicestershire Regiment	
EDGINTON	H	Mentioned in Despatches		Major	RASC	
EDMONDSON	J D	MC		Captain	King's Liverpool Regiment	
EDWARDS	J H		07/01/1917	Lieutenant	Durham Light Infantry	
EDWARDS	L			Captain	Northumberland Fusiliers	T
EDWARDS	M W			Second Lieutenant	RAF	
EDWARDS	T T			Private	Duke of Wellington's (West Riding Regiment)	
EGGAR	A T E	Mentioned in Despatches		Captain	RAF	
EILOART	C H		26/09/1918	Second Lieutenant	Irish Guards	

Surname	Initials	Honours and Awards	Died on Service	Rank	Service	T/SR etc.
EILOART	F O		03/05/1917	Captain	London Regiment (Royal Fusiliers)	T
EILOART	F R	MC		Lieutenant	Royal Garrison Artillery	
EILOART	R E			Second Lieutenant	Irish Guards	
ELBPORNE	C C			Lieutenant	Sherwood Foresters (Notts and Derby Regiment)	
ELGER	E G (D S O)	Mentioned in Despatches (2)		Major	Somerset Light Infantry	
ELKINGTON	A D	Mentioned in Despatches		Major	Royal Warwickshire Regiment and Machine Gun Corps	T
ELLIMAN	B A			Lieutenant	RNAS and RAF	
ELLINGER	M R			Second Lieutenant	Sherwood Foresters (Notts and Derby Regiment)	
ELLISON	J M			Lieutenant	Royal Field Artillery	T
ELLISON	W J	Mentioned in Despatches		Captain	Royal Field Artillery	
ELTON	H C			Second Lieutenant	Royal Field Artillery	
ELTON	H G			Captain	Manchester Regiment	T
EMSLEY	J A		01/12/1918	Major	West Yorkshire Regiment (Prince of Wales's Own)	T
ENNOR	F H			Lieutenant	Grenadier Guards	
ENTWISLE	E			Lieutenant	Royal Field Artillery	T
ENTWISLE	E A			Second Lieutenant	Royal Field Artillery	T
ENTWISLE	F W	MC, Mentioned in Despatches		Captain	Manchester Regiment	T
ESCOMBE	R D			Lieutenant	Royal Engineers	
ETCHES	C E	OBE, Mentioned in Despatches		Major	Royal Warwickshire Regiment	Reserve of Officers
EVANS	G	DSC		Captain	Royal Marine Artillery	
EVANS	M W H			Captain	RAF	
EVANS	W K	CMG, DSO and Bar, Mentioned in Despatches (8)		Brigadier General	Manchester Regiment	
EVERETT	A G			Lieutenant	Royal Field Artillery	
EVERITT	S O	OBE, Mentioned in Despatches		Captain (Staff)	Leicestershire Regiment and RAF	
FABER	H G	Mentioned in Despatches		Major	Durham Light Infantry	T
FAIR	G P C		01/07/1916	Second Lieutenant	Somerset Light Infantry	
FAIRCLOUGH	J D			Lieutenant Colonel	South Lancashire Regiment	T
FALK	H	Mentioned in Despatches, Order of White Eagle (5th Class)		Major	Indian Medical Service attached 6th Gurkas	

Appendix I   187

Surname	Initials	Honours and Awards	Died on Service	Rank	Service	T/SR etc.
FALK	O F			Lieutenant	The Buffs (East Kent Regiment)	
FARLEY	C F	MC		Captain	4th Dragoon Guards (Royal Irish)	
FARLEY	F D			Lieutenant	Leicestershire Regiment	
FARLEY	R L	OBE		Major, Acting Lieutenant Colonel	Reserve Regiment of Cavalry and R A F	
FARMILOE	G F		26/06/1917	Second Lieutenant	Honourable Artillery Company	T
FAWCETT	L G F E		06/11/1917	Captain	Royal Scots Fusiliers	T
FAWCETT	R H		26/04/1915	Second Lieutenant	Bedfordshire Regiment	
FAWCUS	J G			Lieutenant	Royal Berkshire Regiment	
FAWCUS	L R			Second Lieutenant	Indian Cavalry	
FAWKES	W H	MC		The Rev.	CF (4th Class)	
FEARNLEY	C C			Cadet	Royal Field Artillery	
FEATHERSTONE	E	MC		Captain	Middlesex Regiment	
FEATHERSTONE	O			Lieutenant, ADC to the Governor of Bengal	Queen's Royal West Surrey Regiment	
FEILDEN	O H		29/09/1917	Captain	Leicestershire Regiment	T
FENN	H F	DSO, Mentioned in Despatches (3)		Lieutenant Colonel	Lancashire Regiment	
FENWICK	A	Mentioned in Despatches		Sergeant	EA Mechanical Transport	
FENWICK	G E			Lieutenant	Northumberland Fusiliers	
FENWICK	O F			Second Lieutenant	Royal Field Artillery	
FENWICK	N P			Not Known	Ross's Scouts, German East Africa	
FERGUS	A M H			Lieutenant	Seaforth Highlanders	
FIELD	H D		28/09/1917	Captain	Royal Army Medical Corps	
FIELD	S			Captain	Machine Gun Corps (Infantry)	
FIELD	S H		31/07/1917	Second Lieutenant	South Lancashire Regiment	
FIELDHOUSE	B			Lieutenant	RAF	
FILLINGHAM	A	MC		Major	Royal Field Artillery	
FINCH	H N			Lieutenant	Norfolk Regiment	T
FINCH	L H		Mentioned in Despatches	Captain	Sherwood Foresters (Notts and Derby Regiment)	T
FINDLAY	H	CBE, Brevet, Mentioned in Despatches (2)		Major, Brevet Lieutenant-Colonel	The Buffs (East Kent Regiment)	
FINLAY	J P			Lieutenant	South Lancashire Regiment	

Surname	Initials	Honours and Awards	Died on Service	Rank	Service	T/SR etc.
FINLINSON	N			Second Lieutenant	Royal Field Artillery	
FIRTH	L G			Captain	Royal Field Artillery	
FISHER	C L			Lieutenant	Royal Field Artillery	
FISHER	E			Lieutenant	Durham Light Infantry	T
FISON	R			Cadet	Royal Field Artillery	
FITZ-HENRY	C B	Mentioned in Despatches		Major	7th Hussars	
FITZGERALD	E W	MC		Captain	Royal Engineers	
FITZGERALD	J F			Staff-Sergeant Major	RASC	
FLETCHER	J H B		13/05/1915	Lieutenant	London Regiment	
FLINT	W F			Not Known	British Red Cross BEF	
FORBES	A. H. D'E	MC		Lieutenant	East Surrey Regiment	
FORBES	A H			Lieutenant	Grenadier Guards	
FORBES	C S			Captain	US Infantry	
FORDE	F A			Lieutenant	9th Lancers (Attached)	
FORDE	F C			Major	East Surrey Regiment	T
FORDHAM	H J			Lieutenant	Hertfordshire Yeomanry	
FORREST	C E DSO		22/11/1915	Major	Oxford and Bucks Light Infantry	
FORREST	G A			Lieutenant	Princess Patricia's Light Infantry, RASC & RFC	
FORRESTER	R D			Second Lieutenant	RAF	
FORSELL	A R		14/10/1915	Lieutenant	Leicestershire Regiment	T
FORSTER	C J		21/07/1917	Lieutenant	Royal Field Artillery	
FOSBERY	F C W			Second Lieutenant	Not Known	
FOSTER	G B	Mentioned in Despatches		Major	Lincolnshire Yeomanry	T
FOSTER	P			Captain	Royal Garrison Artillery	T
FOSTER	P B			Captain	Royal Horse Artillery	T
FOSTER-IRVINE	E			Major	Royal Garrison Artillery	SR
FOTHERGILL	G A			Lieutenant	RAMC	
FOWKE	G H S			Captain	Gordon Highlanders	POW
FOWKE	L A	Mentioned in Despatches		Lieutenant	Leicestershire Regiment	
FOX	H B			Captain	London Regiment	
FRANCIS	J		02/06/1915	Captain	Royal Warwickshire Regiment	T
FRANCIS	R F			Not Known	YMCA	
FRANKLIN-SMITH	N C			Lieutenant	Reserve Regiment of Cavalry	
FRASER	H H		27/05/1918	Lieutenant	Yorkshire Regiment	
FRASER	A C			Captain	Royal Field Artillery	T
FRASER	D C			Captain	Royal Field Artillery	T
FREELAND	P			Lieutenant	Royal Fusiliers	
FREELAND	R B			Flight Lieutenant	RAF	

Appendix I 189

Surname	Initials	Honours and Awards	Died on Service	Rank	Service	T/SR etc.
FREEMAN	E		03/03/1916	Major	Royal Welsh Fusiliers	
FREEMAN	E R			Captain	Royal Welsh Fusiliers	
FREEMAN-COHEN	F H			Second Lieutenant	RASC	
FROST	E L		16/06/1915	Lieutenant	South Lancashire Regiment	
FRY	J L	MC		Captain	Royal Field Artillery	T
FUGE	T L M	Mentioned in Despatches		Lieutenant	Indian Army attached King George's Own Pioneers	
FULFORD	J H			Private	Durham Light Infantry	
FULTON	F F			Cadet	Infantry	
GAFFIKIN	G H	Mentioned in Despatches	01/07/1916	Major	Royal Irish Rifles	
GAGE-BROWN	J D			Captain	Somerset Light Infantry	T
GAIRDNER	J F R			Major	RAMC	
GALLON	R D			Lieutenant	Northumberland Fusiliers	
GALLOWAY	J M	OBE		Major	Royal Field Artillery	T
GALLOWAY	R C	Mentioned in Despatches, Brevet, Ordre de l'Etoile notre		Captain Brevet Major	Royal Scots Fusiliers	T
GALLOWAY	T L			Major	Queen's Own Glasgow Yeomanry	T
GAMBLE	C L	Croix de Guerre		Lieutenant Acting Commander	RNVR	
GAMBLE	V F			Lieutenant	Royal Field Artillery	
GAMMELL	J R	MC		Lieutenant	Royal Engineers	
GAMON	S P		23/03/1918	Captain	Royal Flying Corps	
GARDINER	R			Second Lieutenant	Royal Field Artillery	
GARDNER	A T G	MC, Mentioned in Despatches		Captain	Royal Field Artillery	
GARDNER	H E			Second Lieutenant	Northumberland Fusiliers	
GARDNER-WATERMAN	A			Major	Royal Field Artillery	
GARNETT	C			Not Known	British Red Cross Attached RAMC	
GARNETT	J C			Second Lieutenant	West Yorkshire Regiment (Prince of Wales's Own)	T
GARNETT	R C			Lieutenant	Duke of Lancaster's Own Yeomanry	T
GARNETT	R T	Mentioned in Despatches		Lieutenant	Royal Garrison Artillery	
GARNIER	A P	MBE, MC, Mentioned in Despatches (2), Order of Kara-George (4th Class)		Captain (Staff)	Northumberland Fusiliers	

Surname	Initials	Honours and Awards	Died on Service	Rank	Service	T/SR etc.
GARRATT	G H			Major	Border Regiment	
GARROD	R P		22/05/1915	Second Lieutenant	London Regiment (City of London Rifles)	
GARVEY	I H	MC	20/02/1917	Captain	Connaught Rangers	SR
GASCOIGNE	H			Lieutenant	Worcestershire Regiment	
GASKELL	Humphrey			Second Lieutenant	Reserve Regiment of Cavalry	
GASKELL	G N	MC		Lieutenant	Royal Field Artillery	
GATES	C E			Lieutenant	Royal Garrison Artillery	POW
GAUSSEN	A W D		17/05/1915	Captain	Highland Light Infantry	
GAUSSEN	J R (D S O)	CMG, Mentioned in Despatches (2)		Lieutenant Colonel	Indian Army (Skinner's Horse)	
GAVIN	W			Lieutenant	RNVR	
GAYMER	B P	Mentioned in Despatches		Lieutenant	Royal Engineers	
GEARY-SMITH	A		07/08/1915	Captain	West Yorkshire Regiment (Prince of Wales's Own)	
GEMMELL	K A		16/06/1915	Lieutenant	The King's (Liverpool Regiment)	
GEMMELL	S S		21/03/1918	Second Lieutenant	Cameron Highlanders	
GEMMELL	A A	MC, Mentioned in Despatches (2)		Captain	Cameron Highlanders	
GEOGHEGAN	W G R		13/04/1917	Second Lieutenant	Royal Inniskilling Fusiliers	SR
GEORGE	P A			Captain	RASC	
GIBBS	G F			Second Lieutenant	Worcestershire Regiment	
GETHING	G			Second Lieutenant	South Lancashire Regiment	
GIBBES	F G V			Not Known	King Edward's Horse	
GIBBONS	R	MC and bar, Croce di Guerra		Captain	Devon Regiment	
GIBBONS	W G B (The Reverend)			Chaplain	South African Defence Force	
GIBSON	C O P	MC, Mentioned in Despatches (2)		Captain (Staff)	Northern Fusiliers	T
GIBSON	E M			Second Lieutenant	Cheshire Regiment	POW
GIBSON	J C			Not Known	U P Horse (India)	
GILL	A O			Private	Gordon Highlanders	SR
GILL	H L O	MC		Lieutenant	Gloucestershire Regiment	
GILLOTT	G S			Corporal	Engineers Unit, RND	
GILLOTT	J S			Lance Sergeant	City of London Yeomanry	T
GILPIN	E H		21/03/1918	Captain	Durham Light Infantry	T
GLADSTONE	B H			Lieutenant	Black Watch (Royal Highlanders)	T

Appendix I 191

Surname	Initials	Honours and Awards	Died on Service	Rank	Service	T/SR etc.
GLADSTONE	T A			Flight Lieutenant	RAF	
GLAISBY	K		01/11/1917	Lieutenant	Royal Field Artillery	T
GLEED	J V A		07/07/1917	Second Lieutenant	Royal Flying Corps	
GLEED	R W B			Cadet	RAF	
GLOVER	R B G	Mentioned in Despatches	05/11/1915	Captain	London Regiment	T
GLOVER	J M A	Mentioned in Despatches (2)		Captain	Tank Corps and Staff	
GLOVER	M A			Private	Liverpool Regiment	
GLOVER	W H			Captain	King's Liverpool Regiment	T
GLOVER	W R	CMG, DSO, Mentioned in Despatches		Lieutenant Colonel	London Regiment	T
GODFREY	H C			Second Lieutenant	East Yorkshire Regiment	
GOLD	C R	DSO, Mentioned in Despatches	21/11/1917	Captain	Derbyshire Yeomanry	
GOODE	C H			Lieutenant	Royal Field Artillery	
GOODYEAR	E T P			Captain	Royal Field Artillery	T
GORDON	G A			Lieutenant	Reserve Regiment of Cavalry	
GORRINGE	C R M	Mentioned in Despatches		Lieutenant	Imperial Camel Corps	
GOSLING	E C			Lieutenant	Bermuda Militia Artillery	
GOSSAGE	A W	MC		Captain	Royal Field Artillery	T
GOSSAGE	A F W	MC		Captain	17th Lancers	T
GOSSAGE	W H W			Second Lieutenant	1st Royal Dragoons	
GOTTO	C C			Lieutenant	RASC	
GOTTO	R P C	OBE		Captain	RASC	
GOURLAY	D W			Cadet	Royal Military College, Camberley	
GOVER	C N	MC		Lieutenant Colonel	RAMC	
GRACIE	A B	Mentioned in Despatches (2)		Captain	Northumberland Fusiliers	T
GRAHAM	J R B			Not Known	Canadian Contingent	
GRANGER	H R			Captain	Royal Field Artillery	T
GRANT-DALTON	S	DSO and Bar, AFC, Mentioned in Despatches (3), Order of the Nile (4th Class)		Lieutenant Colonel	Yorkshire Regiment and RAF	
GRANT-PETERKIN	M H			Lieutenant	Indian Army	
GRAVES	A P			Lieutenant	2nd Life Guards	

Surname	Initials	Honours and Awards	Died on Service	Rank	Service	T/SR etc.
GRAY	D D	Mentioned in Despatches (2), Order of the Crown, Chevalier and Croix de Guerre (Belgium)		Major	Royal Garrison Artillery	T
GRAY	J E B	DSO		Captain	Rifle Brigade	
GRAY	L A			Private	RASC	
GREEN	C C			Private	London Regiment	
GREEN	G R	MC		Lieutenant	Grenadier Guards	
GREEN	R H			Lieutenant	General List	
GREEN	W T W	MC		Captain	Manchester Regiment	
GREENALL	G V	MC, Mentioned in Despatches (2)		Captain	Royal Field Artillery	SR
GREENER	C H			Not Known	Not Known	
GREENHILL	T W	Mentioned in Despatches	11/02/1916	Lieutenant	4th Dragoon Guards (Royal Irish)	
GREENLEES	M C			Lieutenant	RNVR	
GREENLEES	R C			Captain	Argyll and Sutherland Highlanders and RAF	
GREENLEES	T			Lieutenant	Argyll and Sutherland Highlanders	
GREENWELL	T W M		19/07/1918	Lieutenant	Northumberland Fusiliers	T
GREENWELL	P S			Lieutenant	Durham Light Infantry	
GREENWOOD	B P			Captain	RAF	
GREENWOOD	F B			The Rev.	CF (4th Class)	
GREENWOOD	J J G	Mentioned in Despatches		Second Lieutenant	West Yorkshire Regiment (Prince of Wales's Own)	
GREENWOOD	R N	MC, Mentioned in Despatches		Major	Cheshire Regiment	SR
GREG	H S			Captain	Manchester Regiment	
GREGSON	D S L			Cadet	Indian Army	
GREGORY	A E			Gunner	Royal Field Artillery	
GREGORY	F			Major	Loyal North Lancashire Regiment and Tank Corps	
GREGORY	G R			Lieutenant	Royal Army Ordnance Corps	
GREGORY	H G			Lieutenant	RAOC	
GREGORY	J V	MC and Bar		Captain	Northumberland Fusiliers	
GREY-JONES	E			Not Known	RAF	
GRESHAM	S R			Second Lieutenant	Royal Fusiliers	
GRIERSON	A G W			Major	Royal Marine Light Infantry	
GRIERSON	Sir R G W Bart.			Captain	King's Own Scottish Borderers	T
GRIFFIN	R P	Mentioned in Despatches		Lieutenant	Royal Engineers	

Appendix I   193

Surname	Initials	Honours and Awards	Died on Service	Rank	Service	T/SR etc.
GRIFFIN	W P			Lieutenant	Sherwood Foresters (Notts and Derby Regiment)	
GRIFFITHS	G H			Lieutenant	Leicestershire Regiment	T
GRIGG	R M			Captain	Hampshire Regiment	T
GRIGG	R L			Captain	West Yorkshire Regiment (POW) & Royal Engineers	
GRIGG	R S			Major	Machine Gun Corps (Infantry)	
GRIMSDALE	E M			Lieutenant	Royal Horse Artillery	T
GRIMWADE	E L			Not Known	Public School Battallion	
GRINLEY	G C	Mentioned in Despatches (2)		Captain	Royal Field Artillery	
GROGAN	J H	Mentioned in Despatches		Captain	Border Regiment	
GROVES	E J	DSO, MC, Mentioned in Despatches (4)		Captain	Cheshire Regiment	
GROVES	J O			Flight Lieutenant	RAF	POW
GROVES	K G	Mentioned in Despatches		Captain	London Regiment	T
GUIMARAENS	P F F			Lieutenant	RAOC	
GUINNESS	O C	OBE		Captain (Staff)	Worcestershire Regiment	
GUNNING	J E			Major	Royal Irish Rifles	
GWYER	H L			The Rev.	CF	
GWYNNE	E C		19/10/1918	Second Lieutenant	US Army	
HACKFORTH-JONES	A	Mentioned in Despatches	08/08/1918	Lieutenant	Gloucestershire Regiment	
HACKFORTH-JONES	M C			Lieutenant	Royal Scots Fusiliers	
HACKFORTH-JONES	O H	MC		Captain	Royal Field Artillery	T
HADLEY	R B		31/10/1914	Lieutenant	South Wales Borderers	
HADWEN	E H			Cadet	RAF	
HAGGAS	J E			Second Lieutenant	15th Hussars	
HAGGAS	G E			Cadet	Infantry	
HAGUE	W J			Private	RAMC	
HAINING	R H	DSO, Brevet, Mentioned in Despatches (5)		Lieutenant Colonel	Royal Field Artillery	
HALE	A M			Not Known	Royal Flying Corps and RAF	
HALE	E N	Mentioned in Despatches		Captain (Staff)	Black Watch (Royal Highlanders)	
HALE	J			Surgeon-Lieutenant	Royal Navy	
WHITE	A H			Captain	RAF	
HALL	A B		03/05/1917	Lieutenant	Army Cyclist Corps	
HALL	J L			Not Known	RFC	

Surname	Initials	Honours and Awards	Died on Service	Rank	Service	T/SR etc.
HALL	T S I		11/04/1916	Second Lieutenant	King's Own (Royal Lancaster Regiment)	T
HALL	R			Lieutenant	Lancashire Fusiliers	T
HAMILTON	G		26/11/1917	Lieutenant	Scots Guards	
HAMILTON	J S			Captain	Royal Irish Fusiliers	
HAMLYN	H W			Lieutenant	Devonshire Regiment	
HAMLYN	W A			Lieutenant	Machine Gun Corps (Infantry)	
HAMMOND	J E			Captain	Middlesex Regiment	
HANNAY	G M	DSO, Mentioned in Despatches (3), Brevet		Major	Royal Scots Fusiliers	
HARDING	C H	Mentioned in Despatches		Major	Gloucestershire Regiment	
HARDMAN	R C			Lieutenant	East Surrey Regiment	
HARDMAN	R H			Second Lieutenant	RAF	
HARGREAVES	R			Captain	RAMC	
HARKESS	W			Lieutenant	Royal West Surrey Regiment and RASC	
HARMAN	J A		17/11/1917	Lieutenant	RFC	
HARMAN	E			Second Lieutenant	Rifle Brigade	
HARMER	R T			Captain	Royal Engineers	
HARMER	W D			Captain	RAMC	
HARPER	K B			Second Lieutenant	Royal Marines	
HARRISON	C C		20/09/1914	Lieutenant	Worcestershire Regiment	
HARRISON	C G	MC	26/09/1918	Second Lieutenant	South Lancashire Regiment	
HARRISON	D G		26/09/1917	Private	Middlesex Regiment	
HARRISON	A M L	MC		Major	4th Gurkas	
HARRISON	F			Major	King's Liverpool Regiment	
HARRISON	F C			Lieutenant	Duke of Cornwall's Light Infantry	
HARRISON	G			Cadet	Royal Navy	
HARRISON	H			Second Lieutenant	Royal Dragoons	
HARRISON	R F			Captain	Northumberland Fusiliers	T
HARRISSON	J A E			Cadet	Infantry	
HARRISSON	L G E			Lieutenant	RASC	
HARTLEY	F W			Lieutenant	RAMC	
HARTLEY	S			Captain	Worcestershire Regiment	
HARTMANN	F W			Captain	Royal Engineers	
HARTNOLL	W J			Lieutenant	West Yorkshire Regiment	
HARTOPP	E L			Lieutenant	Worcestershire Regiment	SR
HARVEY	H			Assistant-Paymaster	RNVR	

Surname	Initials	Honours and Awards	Died on Service	Rank	Service	T/SR etc.
HASLAM	S F O'G			Sub-Lieutenant	RNVR	
HASTINGS	G A			Private	Hong Kong Volunteers	
HASTINGS	G L	MC		Captain	7th Dragoon Guards (Princess Royal's)	
HASTINGS	J			Captain	Not Known	
HATTON	G C			Lieutenant	Royal Garrison Artillery	
HAWKINS	C R G			Lieutenant	Northants Regiment	
HAWKSLEY	T E			Second Lieutenant	Grenadier Guards	
HAWLEY	A E	MC		Lieutenant	Leicestershire Regiment	T
HAWTREY	H C	CMG, DSO, Brevet, Mentioned in Despatches (2)		Lieutenant Colonel	Royal Engineers	
HAYNES	C D			Second Lieutenant	Royal Garrison Artillery	
HAYTER	G K H	Mentioned in Despatches		Lieutenant	Royal Field Artillery	
HAYTON	L M			Not Known	RAF	
HEAD	C W B			Bombadier	South African Artillery	
HEAD	W G H	Mentioned in Despatches		Major	East Yorkshire Regiment	
HEADINGTON	A H		27/11/1917	Captain	Berkshire Yeomanry	T
HEALEY	R E H		22/07/1916	Lieutenant	Queen's Own (Royal West Kent Regiment)	
HEALEY	A J			Lieutenant	Royal Engineers	
HEAP	G W			Second Lieutenant	Lancashire Fusiliers	
HEARN	E R			Lieutenant	Indian Army	
HEARN	G W R			Captain	South Staffordshire Regiment	
HEARSEY	L D W	MC		Lieutenant	Indian Army Reserve of Officers	
HEATH	G		10/08/1915	Captain	Cheshire Regiment	T
HEATH	G N	DSO and Bar, Mentioned in Despatches (2)		Colonel	Cheshire Regiment	
HEBBLETHWAITE	C J		07/04/1915	Lieutenant	General List	
HEBERT	A			Major	Royal Garrison Artillery	
HECHT	A P			Second Lieutenant	Royal Fusiliers	
HEDDERWICK	G		22/09/1916	Second Lieutenant	RFC	
HEDDERWICK	N S	MC		Lieutenant	15th/19th Hussars	
HEDLEY	E W			Captain	RAMC	T
HEDLEY	G			Captain	Royal Engineers	T
HEDLEY	I M	Mentioned in Despatches		Captain	17th Lancers	T
HEDLEY	J P			Captain	RAMC	T
HEDLEY	W	DSO, Mentioned in Despatches (2)		Major	Royal Garrison Artillery	T

Surname	Initials	Honours and Awards	Died on Service	Rank	Service	T/SR etc.
HEMMANT	T			Sergeant	Australian Tunnellers	
HEMINGWAY	F S			Second Lieutenant	Gordon Highlanders	
HEMINGWAY	P C			Lieutenant	Sherwood Foresters (Notts and Derby Regiment)	
HEMINGWAY	R L L			Not Known	Not Known	
HENDERSON	D F		09/08/1916	Captain	Royal Inniskilling Fusiliers	
HENDERSON	L D			Captain	Army Ordnance Department	
HENDERSON	V L	MC, Mentioned in Despatches		Lieutenant Colonel	Loyal North Lancashire Regiment	
HEPBURN	D H			Second Lieutenant	RAOC	
HEPBURN	J			Lieutenant	Natal Field Artillery	
HEPWORTH	G M			Captain	Royal Engineers	
HERBERT	A S	Mentioned in Despatches		Captain	Royal West Surrey Regiment	
HERBERT	C A			Not Known	Queen's Royal West Surrey Regiment	
HERBERT-SMITH	G M			Major	Machine Gun Corps (Infantry)	
HERDMAN	E C	Mentioned in Despatches		Captain	North Irish Horse	
HERDMAN	J K			Cadet	Edinburgh University OTC	
HERON-MAXWELL	J E B			Cadet	Infantry	
HERRON	W F	Mentioned in Despatches	03/04/1916	Lieutenant	4th Dragoon Guards (Royal Irish)	
HERRON	G F			Lieutenant	RNVR	
HESELTINE	H N			Second Lieutenant	Labour Corps	
HESS	H	Mentioned in Despatches	28/10/1916	Second Lieutenant	Middlesex Regiment	SR
HETT	A S			Lieutenant	RAF	
HEURTLEY	W A	OBE, Mentioned in Despatches(3)		Major	East Lancashire Regiment	
HEWETSON	H A C			Lieutenant	RASC (Motor)	
HEWITT	G A G		27/11/1917	Captain	York and Lancaster Regiment	T
HEWLETT	G			Second Lieutenant	RAF	
HEYN	F M			Driver	RAMC	
HEYWOOD	L J		20/07/1916	Private	Royal Fusiliers	
HEYWOOD	S		04/06/1915	Lieutenant	Manchester Regiment	T
HIBBERT	E H R			Major	Duke of Cornwall's Light Infantry	
HIBBERT	H B			Captain	King's Own Yorkshire Light Infantry	POW
HICK	E			Captain	Rhodesian Regiment, British East Africa	

Appendix I 197

Surname	Initials	Honours and Awards	Died on Service	Rank	Service	T/SR etc.
HICKING	F J		01/07/1916	Second Lieutenant	West Yorkshire Regiment (Prince of Wales's Own)	
HICKING	G G		01/07/1916	Lieutenant	York and Lancaster Regiment	
HICKING	H Y	MC		Captain	Canadian Expeditionary Force	
HICKLING	J C		11/04/1916	Second Lieutenant	Middlesex Regiment	
HILL	P A		23/04/1917	Captain	South Wales Borderers	T
HILL	A C	MC		Captain	Gloucestershire Regiment	
HILL	F E			Captain	Middlesex Regiment	
HILL	H O			Engineer-Lieutenant	Royal Navy	
HILL	O F			Captain	London Regiment	T
HILL	R F W	Mentioned in Despatches		Colonel	Devon Regiment	
HILL	T A			Lieutenant	Oxford and Bucks Light Infantry	
HILL	T A M	Mentioned in Despatches		Captain	Royal Engineers	SR
HILL	W N			Second Lieutenant	Northants Yeomanry	T
HILLMAN	L H		31/07/1917	Lieutenant	Rifle Brigade	
HIND	L A	MC, Mentioned in Despatches	01/07/1916	Lieutenant Colonel	Sherwood Foresters (Notts and Derby Regiment)	T
HIND	O A		03/11/1917	Trooper	Australian Light Horse	
HINDLEY-SMITH	G R			Lieutenant	RN	
HINDLEY-SMITH	J D			Captain	Royal Field Artillery	
HINE	N A W		01/02/1919	Lieutenant	West Yorkshire Regiment	
HIRD	F L	MC		Lieutenant	RAF	
HOBART	V E			Captain	42nd Royal Highlanders of Canada	
HOARE	G H R			Lieutenant	Ceylon Contingent and Grenadier Guards	
HOBSON	O E	Mentioned in Despatches	27/09/1918	Captain	Bedfordshire Regiment	
HOBSON	A J	MC		Lieutenant	Royal Field Artillery	
HODDING	H E	MC	08/11/1918	Lieutenant	Sherwood Foresters (Notts and Derby Regiment)	
HODGKINSON	R J			Lieutenant	King's Royal Rifle Corps	
HODGSON	B H			Captain	Rifle Brigade	
HODSON	H S			Captain	Staffordshire Yeomanry	
HOFFMAN	J A			Lieutenant	Duke of Wellington's (West Riding Regiment)	
HOLDEN	H S			Cadet	RAF	
HOLDER	N F			Lieutenant	Royal Warwickshire Regiment	

Surname	Initials	Honours and Awards	Died on Service	Rank	Service	T/SR etc.
HOLDSWORTH	H R			Captain	Duke of Wellington's (West Riding Regiment)	SR
HOLLAND	G F			Major	East Yorkshire Regiment	
HOLLAND	W	OBE		Captain	Royal Fusiliers	
HOLLIDAY	L B	Mentioned in Despatches		Major	Duke of Wellington's (West Riding Regiment)	
HOLLWAY	J C	Mentioned in Despatches	11/01/1917	Lieutenant Colonel	Royal Defence Corps	
HOLMES	R E		04/06/1918	Captain	Scots Guards	
HOLMES-KERR	D R			Corporal	Royal Sussex Regiment	
HOLROYD	C P			Major	Royal Welsh Fusiliers	SR
HOLT	L		11/03/1918	Captain	London Regiment	T
HOLT	G N			Captain	London Regiment	T
HOLT	N			Captain	Royal Lancaster Regiment	T
HOLT	W V			Lieutenant	Royal Engineers	
HOMER-DIXON	T F	DSO		Lieutenant Colonel, DAA and Quarter Master General	Lord Strathcona's Horse	
HOMER-DIXON	H E			Major	Lord Strathcona's Horse	
HOOLEY	B T	MC	28/10/1918	Major	Sherwood Foresters (Notts and Derby Regiment)	
HOOLEY	G B			Lieutenant Colonel	Royal Engineers	
HOOLEY	N J			Trooper	Derbyshire Yeomanry	T
HOOPER	C A	Mentioned in Despatches		Major	RFC and RAF	
HOOPER	R S			Captain (Staff)	Herefordshire Regiment	T
HOPE	B			Captain	Royal Defence Corps and BRRCS	T
HOPKINS	C R I		18/12/1914	Lieutenant	Cameronians (Scottish Rifles)	
HOPKINS	C H I			Lieutenant Colonel	Northumberland Fusiliers & Devonshire Regiment	
HORN	C A			Lieutenant	Middlesex Regiment	
HORNE	G B	MC, Mentioned in Despatches		Captain	Suffolk Yeomanry	T
HORNE	L F	MC		Major	Royal Field Artillery	
HORNUNG	E W			A.B.	Anti-Aircraft, RN Division	
HORRIDGE	J L		21/11/1918	Captain	Royal Air Force	
HORRIDGE	G B			Captain	Lancashire Fusiliers	T
HORRIDGE	W	MC, Mentioned in Despatches		Captain	Lancashire Fusiliers	T
HORROCKS	B G			Captain	Middlesex Regiment	POW
HORSFALL	C F		19/09/1916	Captain	Duke of Wellington's (West Riding Regiment)	T
HORSFALL	J D Sir			Captain	Duke of Wellington's (West Riding Regiment)	T

Surname	Initials	Honours and Awards	Died on Service	Rank	Service	T/SR etc.
HORTON	A H			Captain	King's Royal Rifle Corps	
HORTON	K			Captain	Wiltshire Regiment	
HOSE	J E			Not Known	RAF	
HOTBLACK	H S			Lieutenant	Royal Field Artillery	T
HOUGH	G F, The Rev.			CF	Royal Field Artillery	T
HOW	E R			Lieutenant	Royal Bucks Hussars	T
HOWARD	J C (Sir)			Captain	Lincolnshire Regiment	T
HOWORTH	H			Major (Staff)	Sherwood Foresters (Notts and Derby Regiment)	SR
HOWE	P	MC		Captain	West Yorkshire Regiment	
HOWELL-JONES	J H	CIE, DSO, Brevets (3), Mentioned in Despatches (6)		Lieutenant Colonel	Royal Military Academy	
HOWITT	A G			Captain	Royal Field Artillery	
HOWITT	F D			Lieutenant	RAF	
HOWITT	H G	DSO, MC, Mentioned in Despatches (3)		Major	Yorkshire Regiment	T
HOWITT	J A			Lieutenant	Royal Engineers	
HOWSON	G	MC, Mentioned in Despatches		Captain	4th Cavalry, Indian Army	
HOWSON	H G	MC		Captain	Royal Field Artillery	
HOYLAND	C E			Captain	General List	T
HUDDART	G W O			Captain	Yorkshire Regiment	T
HUDSON	A A			Captain	RAMC	
HUGGINS	C L	MC		Captain	3rd Hussars	
HUGHES	K K			Lieutenant	Royal Field Artillery	
HUGHES	R E			Not Known	Artists Rifles	
HULL	J H			Lieutenant	Essex Regiment	
HULSEN	W J			Corporal	Northumberland Yeomanry	T
HULTON-HARROP	F L			Captain	Shropshire Light Infantry	SR
HUMBERT	S F M	MC		Lieutenant	Royal Engineers	
HUME	G M		12/06/1915	Second Lieutenant	Royal Engineers	T
HUME	N H			Captain	Indian Medical Service	
HUMPHREYS	B			Lieutenant	York and Lancaster Regiment	
HUNT	E D C	MC and Bar		Captain (Staff)	Suffolk Regiment	
HUNT	G H			Captain	Shropshire Light Infantry	
HUNT	H R A	DSO, Brevet, Mentioned in Despatches (4), Croix de Chevalier		Major (Staff)	25th Punjabis	
HUNTER	G A			Lieutenant	RAF	

Surname	Initials	Honours and Awards	Died on Service	Rank	Service	T/SR etc.
HUNTER	W E			Lieutenant	Royal Field Artillery	POW
HUNTRISS	C J	MC, Mentioned in Despatches	01/07/1916	Captain	East Yorkshire Regiment	
HUNTRISS	G H			Lieutenant	Liverpool Regiment	
HUNTRISS	H E		17/05/1915	Captain	Bedfordshire Regiment	
HUNTRISS	W		23/10/1918	Lieutenant	Duke of Wellington's (West Riding Regiment)	
HUNTRISS	E M	MC, Mentioned in Despatches		Captain	Duke of Wellington's (West Riding Regiment)	
HURLBUTT	H			Lieutenant Colonel (Hon.)	Not Known	
HURFORD	D L	MC		Lieutenant	Royal Garrison Artillery	
HURLEY	C W	Mentioned in Despatches		Captain	RASC	
HURLEY	H A			Captain	London Irish Rifles	
HUNWICKE	R F			Lieutenant	RASC	
HURST	P G			Lieutenant	Lancashire Fusiliers	
HUTCHINSON	M M	Mentioned in Despatches		Lieutenant	Durham Light Infantry	
HUTCHISON	B O	Mentioned in Despatches (6)		Captain	7th Hussars	
HUTHWAITE	H Y	MC		Lieutenant	King's Own Royal Lancaster Regiment	T
ILLINGWORTH	C A			Lieutenant	Duke of Wellington's (West Riding Regiment)	
INGLIS	R C		29/06/1915	Lieutenant	South Wales Borderers	
INGLIS	H J	DSO, MC, Mentioned in Despatches (2)		Captain	South West Borderers	SR
INMAN	G H N			Sub-Lieutenant	RNVR	
INMAN	R T			Petty Officer	RNVR	
INMAN	V H T			Lieutenant	Royal Field Artillery	
IRWIN	G R			Captain	Royal Irish Rifles	
IRWIN	H N	MC		Lieutenant	Gurka Rifles	
ISAAC	B A			Second Lieutenant	Cheshire Regiment	
ISHAM	H E M			Lieutenant	Royal Warwickshire Regiment	
IVATT	H G	Mentioned in Despatches		Captain	RASC	
JACKMAN	J			Lieutenant	RASC	
JACKSON	E C			Lieutenant	Canadian Engineers	
JACKSON	F I	Mentioned in Despatches		Lieutenant	South Lancashire Regiment	
JALLAND	S		09/08/1915	Lieutenant	East Yorkshire Regiment	
JAMES	H H	Mentioned in Despatches		Lieutenant	Manchester Regiment Attached RAF	
JAMES	M J	OBE		Second Lieutenant	RAF	
JAMES	R D L			Major	Royal Engineers (From Reserve of Officers)	

Appendix I

Surname	Initials	Honours and Awards	Died on Service	Rank	Service	T/SR etc.
JAMESON	F R W	DSO, MC and 2 Bars, Mentioned in Despatches (2)		Captain	Royal Engineers	
JAMIESON	A H M			Major	Royal Garrison Artillery	
JANION	A P			Lieutenant	6th Dragoon Guards	
JANION	J R			Not Known	Cape Mounted Rifles	
JAUNCEY	H C A		31/05/1916	Sub-Lieutenant	Royal Navy	
JEDDERE-FISHER	H C A			Major	Queen's Royal West Surrey Regiment	
JEFFERIS	A R			Captain	Royal Engineers	
JELF-REVELEY	A G R	Mentioned in Despatches (2)		Lieutenant Colonel	Royal Welsh Fusiliers	T
JENNINGS	A C			Second Lieutenant	Royal Engineers	
JENNINGS	A L N	Mentioned in Despatches		Captain	Machine Gun Corps (Infantry)	
JENNINGS	F N	MC, Croix de Guerre, Mentioned in Despatches		Captain	Royal Field Artillery	
JENNINGS	M R N	AFC, MC		Captain	RAF	
JESSOP	H W			Captain	West Yorkshire Regiment	
JESSOP	L A	DFC		Lieutenant	RAF	
JOHNS	T S			Captain	Royal Irish Rifles	
JOHNS	Sir W A	CB, Mentioned in Despatches	04/06/1918	Colonel	Attd. B.E.F., E.Africa	
JOHNSON	B A		26/05/1915	Private	London Regiment	
JOHNSON	H G E			Midshipman	RNVR	
JOHNSON	H A B			Lieutenant Colonel	26th King George's Own Light Cavalry (Indian Army)	
JOHNSON	H S			Lieutenant	Royal Field Artillery	
JOHNSON	K H			Captain	RASC	
JOHNSON	R E S	MC		Captain	Border Regiment	
JOHNSON	W D			Captain	The Buffs (East Kent Regiment)	POW
JOHNSTON	F B			Captain	Northumberland Fusiliers	T
JOHNSTON	G A			Lieutenant	Highland Light Infantry	
JOHNSTON	G L		04/10/1916	Major	Royal Field Artillery	
JOHNSTON	H M			Colonel	Indian Army, Assistant Adjutant, Quartermaster General	
JOHNSTON	J L			Second Lieutenant	Argyll and Sutherland Highlanders	
JOHNSTON	J T	Mentioned in Despatches		Major-General	Scottish Command	
JOHNSTON	J R			Captain	Cameronians (Scottish Rifles)	T
JOHNSTON	R L			Lieutenant	RAF	
JOHNSTON	O P			Lieutenant	Royal Field Artillery	

Surname	Initials	Honours and Awards	Died on Service	Rank	Service	T/SR etc.
JOHNSTONE-DOUGLAS	R S			Not Known	RNVR	
JOHNSTONE-DOUGLAS	W H G	Mentioned in Despatches		Captain	Staff, GHQ (Lanarks Yeomanry)	
JOLLIFFE	A H			Captain	Cheshire Regiment	T
JONES	D W C			Colonel	RAMC	T
JONES	E A O		18/09/1916	Second Lieutenant	London Regiment (Queen's Westminster Rifles)	
JONES	F T M			Captain	Leinster Regiment	
JONES	G T M	MC		Captain	Leinster Regiment	
JONES	I M	MC		Captain	Leinster Regiment	
JONES	O L D			Lieutenant	RASC	
JONES	R T T			Captain	London Regiment	T
JONES	W C			Driver	RAMC	
JORGENGENSEN	C R E			Captain	Royal Irish Regiment	
JOSE	E S			The Rev.	CF	
JOWITT	T M C			Private	Yorkshire Regiment	
JOYNSON	G A W			Driver	RAMC	
JOYNSON	H G G			Lieutenant	Royal field Artillery and RAF	
JOYNSON	K B			Lieutenant	Indian Army	
KARPELES	A R			Lieutenant	Northumberland Fusiliers	
KAY	A S			Lieutenant	Royal Garrison Artillery	SR
KAY	C S			Lieutenant	RASC	
KEATES	W			Lieutenant Colonel	Suffolk Regiment	
KEATINGE	H P	Mentioned in Despatches		Not Known	Not Known	
KELLIE	L L		01/02/1917	Second Lieutenant	Royal Field Artillery	
KELLY	J U	DSO, Mentioned in Despatches		Captain	Wiltshire Regiment and RAF	
KENDALL	J L		11/11/1914	Private	Scots Guards	
KENDERDINE	J H			Second Lieutenant	Royal Sussex Regiment and RAF	
KENDREW	A J	MC, Mentioned in Despatches		Captain	RAMC	
KENNARD	W A	DSO, Mentioned in Despatches (2)	30/10/1918	Major	13th Hussars	
KENNAWAY	R H			Captain	Devonshire Regiment	T
KENNEDY	J H	Mentioned in Despatches		Captain	Royal West Kent Regiment (from Reserve of Officers)	
KENNEDY	J R B			Lieutenant (Staff)	Royal Field Artillery	
KENNEDY	J S			Surgeon	RN	
KENT	A P			Captain	Not Known	
KENYON	A			Lieutenant	Loyal North Lancashire Regiment	T

Surname	Initials	Honours and Awards	Died on Service	Rank	Service	T/SR etc.
KEPPEL	F G			Captain	Norfolk Regiment	
KERR	A D G O		03/08/1916	Second Lieutenant	Middlesex Regiment	
KERR	C M			Cadet	Royal Garrison Artillery	
KERSHAW	N			Lieutenant	Lanakshire Yeomanry	T
KEYSER	R N		22/08/1917	Lieutenant	Royal Flying Corps	
KIDD	H J			Second Lieutenant	Royal Field Artillery	SR
KILNER	C G C			Major	Duke of Wellington's (West Riding Regiment)	T
KIMBER	G M			Second Lieutenant	13th Hussars	
KIMMOND	D C			Second Lieutenant	RAF	
KINDER	H F A			Lieutenant	Royal Engineers	
KING	P N			Captain	Duke of Wellington's (West Riding Regiment)	
KING	R B			Lieutenant	Argyll and Sutherland Highlanders	T
KING	W B R	OBE, Mentioned in Despatches (2)		Captain	Royal Welsh Fusiliers	
KINGERLEE	C H			Captain	Royal Berkshire Regiment	
KINGERLEE	S J			Lieutenant	Machine Gun Corps (Infantry)	
KING-HARMAN	L M			Lieutenant	Rifle Brigade	
KINGSTON	N A			Lieutenant	RASC	
KINMOND	D C			Second Lieutenant	RAF	
KIRKBRIDE	J K			Lieutenant	Sherwood Foresters (Notts and Derby Regiment)	POW
KIRKPATRICK	H P (DSO)			Major	16th Lancers (from Reserve of Officers)	
KIRKPATRICK	Y J			Not Known	RFC & RAF	
KIRKPATRICK	J C G			Captain	North Irish Horse	
KITCHING	H E	MBE, Mentioned in Despatches (2)		Captain	Durham Light Infantry	
KITCHING	J P S			Lieutenant	Inniskilling Dragoons	
KNAGGS	V St. G		12/08/1918	Lieutenant	Royal Field Artillery	
KNAGGS	G			Captain	Royal Inniskilling Fusiliers	SR
KNIGHT	P C		01/07/1916	Second Lieutenant	Somerset Light Infantry	
KNIGHTS SMITH	B A		05/09/1915	Second Lieutenant	Rifle Brigade	
KNIGHTS SMITH	P A		12/04/1918	Lance Corporal	Bedfordshire Yeomanry	
KNOX	R F			Lieutenant Colonel	Royal Engineers	
LA-FONTAINE	C W			Second Lieutenant	Rifle Brigade	

Surname	Initials	Honours and Awards	Died on Service	Rank	Service	T/SR etc.
LA-FONTAINE	E L	MBE, Mentioned in Despatches (2)		Captain	Special List, British Mediterranean Expeditionary Force (Intelligence Corps)	
LA-FONTAINE	J S			Interpreter	Formerly Sub-Lieutenant RND	
LA-FONTAINE	S H	DSO, MC		Captain	Intelligence Officer, British Easr Africa	
LAING	J G		03/10/1918	Major	London Regiment (Artists' Rifles)	
LAIDLAW	F F			Captain	RAMC	
LAKE	A H			Lieutenant	Royal Field Artillery	T
LAKE	B C	DSO, Mentioned in Despatches (2), Cavalier of Crown of Italy		Major	King's Own Scottish Borderers	
LAKE	E L D			Major	Suffolk Regiment	T
LAKE	H W	MC		Lieutenant	Coldstream Guards	
LAKE	Sir P H N (KCB, KCMG)			Lieutenant-General	Not Known	
LAKE	R D	DSO, Mentioned in Despatches		Major (Staff)	Northants Regiment	
LAMB	R E			Lieutenant	RASC	
LAMB	R P			Captain	Rifle Brigade and RAF	
LAMONBY	L	DSO, Mentioned in Despatches (2)		Major	Dorset Regiment	T
LANCASTER	S			Captain	Dorset Regiment	
LANDER	T E	MC		Lieutenant	Highland Light Infantry & RAF	POW
LANE	H J	Mentioned in Despatches		Lieutenant	Royal Garrison Artillery	
LANE	J A B	Mentioned in Despatches		Lieutenant	18th Hussars	
LANE	R G	Mentioned in Despatches		Lieutenant	Royal Garrison Artillery	
LANGLEY	A A			Captain	Gloucestershire Regiment	
LANGLEY	F O	MC, Mentioned in Despatches		Captain	South Staffordshire Regiment	T
LANGMEAD	L G N	MC, Mentioned in Despatches		Captain	Rifle Brigade	
LANGWORTHY	G			Major	Reseve Regiment of Cavalry	
LASCELLES	A M	VC, MC, Mentioned in Despatches	07/11/1918	Captain	Durham Light Infantry	
LASCELLES	P St J			Private	Artists Rifles	
LAST	F W			Lieutenant	Lincolnshire Regiment	
LATHAM	J	Mentioned in Despatches		Captain	King's Shropshire Light Infantry	
LAWES	T E		18/06/1917	Second Lieutenant	Suffolk Regiment	

Surname	Initials	Honours and Awards	Died on Service	Rank	Service	T/SR etc.
LAWLESS	N G H			Captain	RASC	
LAWS	P U	MC	20/09/1917	Captain	Sherwood Foresters (Notts and Derby Regiment)	
LAWSON	O H		17/03/1916	Major	26th Punjabis	
LAWSON	J O			Lieutenant	Northumberland Fusiliers	
LAZARUS	E L			Lieutenant	Worcestershire Regiment	
LAZARUS	K M	Mentioned in Despatches		Captain	Worcestershire Regiment	
LEACH	G de L	Albert Medal in Gold	03/09/1916	Second Lieutenant	Scots Guards	
LEACH	C de L	Chevalier of Order of the Redeemer, Mentioned in Despatches		Captain	Rifle Brigade	
LEACH	H E B	CB, CMG, Brevet, Mentioned in Despatches (2), Order of St Maurice and Saint Lazarus		Colonel, Temporary Brigadier-General	South West Borderers	
LEAKE	G A		29/08/1915	Second Lieutenant	Australian Light Horse	
LEAKE	F W			Lieutenant	Australian Imperial Force	
LECKY	F B			Major-General	Royal Artillery	
LEE	C		13/11/1916	Sub-Lieutenant	Royal Naval Volunteer Reserve	
LEE	A N	OBE, Mentioned in Despatches (3), Order of the Sacred Treasure (4th Class)		Lieutenant Colonel	Staff, GHQ (Sherwood Foresters)	T
LEE	J			Second Lieutenant	Cheshire Regiment	
LEES	A E			Major	Duke of Lancaster's Own Yeomanry	T
LEES	J			Captain	Royal West Kent Regiment	
LEGGATT	A F S	Mentioned in Despatches		Lieutenant Colonel	Royal Scots Fusiliers and King's Liverpool Regiment	
LEGGE	S F	Mentioned in Despatches (2)		Lieutenant Colonel	Deputy Assistant Quartermaster General	
LEIGHTON	R A		23/12/1915	Lieutenant	Worcestershire Regiment	
LENEY	B		30/10/1918	Cadet	Royal Field Artillery	
LENEY	C	DSO, Mentioned in Despatches (4)		Major	Royal Field Artillery	T
LENEY	R J B			Captain	RAMC	
LENNARD	E S R		14/09/1917	Second Lieutenant	Royal Flying Corps	

Surname	Initials	Honours and Awards	Died on Service	Rank	Service	T/SR etc.
LENNARD	E S	MC		Second Lieutenant	Machine Gun Corps (Infantry)	
LENNARD	J F W			Major	Royal Garrison Artillery	T
LESLIE	A			Lieutenant	Royal Field Artillery	T
LESLIE	K D			Second Lieutenant	Royal Irish Rifles	
LESLIE-SMITH	J L	MC		Captain	Border Regiment attached Gold Coast Regiment	
LETHBRIDGE	J S			Captain	Royal Engineers	
LEVY	L W			Captain	King's Liverpool Regiment & Cheshire Regiment	
LEWIN	R N S			Captain	Duke of Cornwall's Light Infantry	
LEWIS	A D			Second Lieutenant	Royal Engineers	
LEWIS	B G (DSO)	CB, Mentioned in Despatches (3)		Brigadier-General	Not Known	
LEWIS	D S	DSO, Brevet, Mentioned in Despatches (2)	10/04/1916	Lieutenant Colonel	RFC	
LEWIS	H	Brevet, Mentioned in Despatches (2)	01/07/1916	Lieutenant Colonel	37th Lancers (Baluch Horse)	
LEWIS	H V	DSO, MC and Bar, Mentioned in Despatches (3), Silver Medal of Crown of Italy		Captain	129th Baluchis	
LEWIS	J E			Petty Officer	RNAS (& then RAF)	
LEWIS	J F			Captain	RAF	
LEWIS	M A			Second Lieutenant	Royal Marines	
LEWIS	R F	Mentioned in Despatches, Order of White Eagle (5th Class)		Lieutenant	Punjab Cavalry	
LIDDELL	C G	CMG, CBE, DSO, Brevet, Mentioned in Despatches (6), Officer of the Crown of Italy		Major and Brevet Lieutenant Colonel	Leicestershire Regiment	
LIDDELL	E M	Mentioned in Despatches		Lieutenant Colonel	West Riding Regiment attached Royal West Kent Regiment	
LIEBERT (Later Lambert)	J B			Second Lieutenant	Royal Field Artillery	
LIMMER	G			Private	Honourable Artillery Company	
LINDBERG	O H			Captain	Northumberland Fusiliers	
LINDOP	K			Lieutenant	Devonshire Regiment	T
LINDSELL	R E			Lieutenant	Hong Kong Volunteers	

Surname	Initials	Honours and Awards	Died on Service	Rank	Service	T/SR etc.
LINDSELL	J	MC, Mentioned in Despatches		Captain	Loyal North Lancashire Regiment	
LINTON	R C			The Rev.	CF (4th Class)	
LITTLE	D L	MC		Second Lieutenant	Royal Field Artillery	T
LITTLEWOOD	R W S			Lieutenant	Rifle Brigade	
LIVEING	C H	CMG, DSO, Mentioned in Despatches (3), Legion of Honour, Croix d'Officier		Lieutenant Colonel	Royal Field Artillery	
LIVINGSTONE	T			Captain	RAMC	
LLOYD	H	DSO, MC, Mentioned in Despatches		Captain (Staff)	Northants Regiment	
LLOYD	L W			Lieutenant	Lancers	
LLOYD	R H			Second Lieutenant	Indian Army (Reserve of Officers)	
LLOYD	W N	CB, Mentioned in Despatches		Colonel	Assistant Quarter Master General	
LLOYD-JONES	J	MC, Mentioned in Despatches	11/03/1916	Captain	Yorkshire Regiment	
LOCKETT	G B	MC	04/11/1918	Lieutenant	Royal Field Artillery	
LOCKETT	G G			Lieutenant	Cheshire Yeomanry	T
LOCKETT	J			Lieutenant	Lancashire Hussars	T
LOCKHART	H		19/06/1915	Corporal	Royal Engineers	
LOCKHART	L A K			Lieutenant	Liverpool Regiment	
LONGMORE	C G		24/11/1918	Captain	Royal Field Artillery	T
LORD	E G	Mentioned in Despatches	25/06/1918	Second Lieutenant	Machine Gun Corps (Infantry)	
LORRIMER	J H			Lieutenant	RAF	
LOTZ	H C J			Not Known	London Regiment	T
LOUDAN	S M			Lieutenant	Royal Berkshire Regiment	
LOVERIDGE	S W			Lieutenant	Dragoon Guards	
LOW	D A			Major	Royal Engineers & RAF	SR
LOW	H B	MC and Bar, Mentioned in Despatches (3)		Major	RAMC	
LOWE	A H			Major	Oxford and Bucks Light Infantry	
LOWE	J B			Major	RAMC	
LOWE	J C M			Wing Commander	RAF	
LUCAS	W H			Lieutenant	Staffordshire Regiment	
LUDDINGTON	W J C			Lieutenant Colonel	East Lancs. Regiment	SR
LUDLAM	F	MC		Major	Royal Field Artillery	
LUMGAIR	R R M		19/04/1917	Captain	King's Own Scottish Borderers	T

Surname	Initials	Honours and Awards	Died on Service	Rank	Service	T/SR etc.
LUND	H K B			Second Lieutenant	Lancashire Fusiliers	
LUSHINGTON	H E C			Second Lieutenant	Indian Army Reserve of Officers	
LYLE	H d'O			Captain	Royal Welsh Fusiliers	
LYLE	H T (DSO)	CBE, Mentioned in Despatches		Lieutenant Colonel and Brevet Colonel	Royal Irish Fusiliers	
LYLE	O	OBE, Mentioned in Despatches (2)		Captain	Highland Light Infantry	
LYON	C G	Mentioned in Despatches		Major	East Riding Yeomanry	T
LYON	F T B			Captain	King's Liverpool Regiment	
LYON	W E	Mentioned in Despatches		Major	19th Hussars	
LYON-SMITH	G	Mentioned in Despatches		Lieutenant	Royal Field Artillery	T
LYON-SMITH	T	Mentioned in Despatches		Captain	Royal Field Artillery	
LYTHALL	A H			Not Known	Artists Rifles	
MACANDREW	C G			Captain	Ayrshire Yeomanry	T
MACASKIE	C F C	Mentioned in Despatches		Lieutenant	Essex Regiment attached Royal West Kent Regiment	
MACBEAN	F (CVO, CB)			Major-General	Indian Army	
MacDANIEL	F G V		20/11/1917	Lieutenant	Royal Munster Fusiliers	
MCDONALD	D H	Medal of Order of Crown of Italy		Second Lieutenant	Royal Engineers	
MACDONALD	N J			Surgeon Sub-Lieutenant	RNVR	
MACDOWELL	K M			Lieutenant	Royal Engineers	
MacINTOSH	J		23/07/1916	Second Lieutenant	Royal Warwickshire Regiment	
MacINTOSH	R C			Gunner	Royal Field Artillery	
MCIVER	I		10/08/1916	Lieutenant	Royal Field Artillery	
MACIVER	C R			Captain	Royal Engineers	
MACIVER	C I			Second Lieutenant	RASC	
MACIVER	J C			Sub-Lieutenant	RNVR	
MACIVER	W	Mentioned in Despatches		Captain	Special List (Late Nigerian Regiment)	
MACKENZIE	U K		08/09/1916	Captain	South African Infantry	
MACKENZIE	A C			Captain	Royal Warwickshire Regiment	T
MACKENZIE	D			Lieutenant	RASC	
MACKENZIE	H H			Lieutenant Colonel	Royal Artillery	
MACKENZIE	K D	Mentioned in Despatches		Lieutenant Colonel	RASC	
MACKENZIE	R C (CB, VD)	KBE, Mentioned in Despatches		Colonel	3rd Lowland Division	T

Surname	Initials	Honours and Awards	Died on Service	Rank	Service	T/SR etc.
MACKIE	J L		27/12/1917	Captain	Ayrshire Yeomanry	T
MACKIRDY	C D S		22/03/1918	Second Lieutenant	Hussars	
MACKIRDY	E M S			Captain	Royal Horse Guards	
MACKWORTH	P H	DFC		Captain	RAF	
MACLAREN	D			Captain	Border Regiment	T
MACLAREN	M			Lieutenant	RNVR	
MACLEAN	A G F			Lieutenant	Cameron Highlanders	
MACLURE	A F	Mentioned in Despatches		Lieutenant Colonel	Lancashire Fusiliers	T
MACMAIR	J L P			Captain	Royal Field Artillery	
MACNEE	D			Lieutenant	Yorkshire Dragoons	T
MACONCHY	F C (DSO)			Captain (From Reserve of Officers)	East Yorkshire Regiment	
MALAN	L N	Brevet, OBE		Lieutenant Colonel	Royal Engineers attached Indian Army	
MALING	G A	VC		Captain	RAMC	
MALLINSON	E A H		26/06/1918	Captain	East Lancs. Regiment	
MANN	C H D		30/09/1916	Second Lieutenant	Durham Light Infantry	
MANN	R L		21/12/1914	Lieutenant	7th Dragoon Guards (Princess Royal's)	
MANNOCK	R C			Captain	9th Gurkhas, Indian Army	
MANSEL-CAREY	S L M		24/02/1916	Second Lieutenant	Devonshire Regiment	
MANSEL-CAREY	D V M			Lieutenant	Devonshire Regiment	SR
MANSERGH	C J C		19/04/1918	Not Known	Australian Imperial Force	
MAPLES	E J S	MC		Captain	Lincolnshire Regiment	T
MAPPIN	W G			Lieutenant	Coldstream Guards	
MARKHAM	F W C			Lieutenant	Royal Fusiliers	
MARRIAGE	A W		28/04/1915	Rifleman	London Regiment	
MARRIOTT	F E		30/07/1915	Second Lieutenant	Rifle Brigade	
MARRIOTT	N C		17/08/1917	Captain	Leicestershire Regiment	
MARRIOTT	H C H			Captain	South Staffordshire Regiment	T
MARRIOTT	A J			Lieutenant	Royal Field Artillery	
MARSH	F B		05/10/1916	Second Lieutenant	The Queen's (Royal West Surrey Regiment)	
MARSH	J L	Mentioned in Despatches	16/10/1915	Captain	York and Lancaster Regiment	T
MARSH	W L			Lieutenant Colonel	RAF	
MARSHALL	D M			Lieutenant	Royal Navy	
MARSHALL	H	Mentioned in Despatches		Captain	Lincolnshire Regiment	
MARSHALL	H D			Major	Lincolnshire Regiment	T
MARSHALL	J D			Trooper	Calcutta Light Horse	

Surname	Initials	Honours and Awards	Died on Service	Rank	Service	T/SR etc.
MARSLAND	E K			Lieutenant	2nd Life Guards	
MARSTON	J E	DSO, MC, Mentioned in Despatches (2)		Major	Royal Artillery	POW (Exchanged)
MARTEN	E C			Captain	Rifle Brigade	
MARTIN	C F			Lieutenant	Royal Garrison Artillery	
MARTIN	F D		26/09/1917	Sergeant	Australian Infantry, A.I.F.	
MARTIN	G A K			Sapper	Royal Engineers	
MARTIN	J S		09/05/1915	Lieutenant	Royal Irish Rifles	
MARTIN	G N			Captain	Durham Light Infantry	
MARTIN	G N C	MC, Mentioned in Despatches (2)		Major	Royal Field Artillery	
MARTIN	O H			Lieutenant	RNVR	
MARTIN	R A			Lieutenant	RAF	
MARTIN	W H			Lieutenant	East Surrey Regiment	
MASON	G W		09/04/1917	Lieutenant	The King's (Liverpool Regiment)	
MATHER	N E		26/04/1915	Second Lieutenant	Northumberland Fusiliers	
MATHER	R C			Major	Manchester Regiment	
MATHEWS	H S		22/07/1916	Captain	Royal Warwickshire Regiment	
MATHEWS	A G			Major	Inns of Court OTC & Royal Garrison Artillery	T
MATHEWS	F R B			Second Lieutenant	Grenadier Guards	
MATHEWS	O L			Cadet	Royal Field Artillery	
MATHEWS	W F			Major	Royal Engineers	
MATHIESON	K R		01/11/1914	Lieutenant	Irish Guards	SR
MATTHEWS	W H			Not Known	Artists Rifles	
MATTHEY	G C H			Captain	RASC	
MAUFE	S B	Mentioned in Despatches	05/07/1916	Major	West Yorkshire Regiment (Prince of Wales's Own)	T
MAUFE	F W B	MC and Bar, Mentioned in Despatches		Captain	Royal Field Artillery	T
MAUFE	T H B	VC		Captain	Royal Field Artillery	
MAULE	E B		06/02/1917	Lieutenant	Royal Flying Corps	
MAURICE	D B (D S O)	CBE, Mentioned in Despatches		Lieutenant Colonel	Royal Berkshire Regiment	
MAWSON	C J			Lieutenant	Royal Field Artillery	
MAXWELL	H H		24/10/1918	Second Lieutenant	Cameron Highlanders	
MAY	E			Captain	Royal Garrison Artillery	SR
MAYALL	G	Mentioned in Despatches		Captain	Royal Horse Artillery	T
MAYDON	H C	Mentioned in Despatches, Order of the Nile (4th Class)		Captain	12th Lancers Attached Egyptian Mounted Infantry	

Appendix I   211

Surname	Initials	Honours and Awards	Died on Service	Rank	Service	T/SR etc.
MAYHEW	T G			Captain	Northumberland Fusiliers	
MCCLINTOCK	J H J			Captain	2nd Life Guards	
MCCLINTOCK	R le P	Brevet		Captain (Staff)	Not Known	
MCCONNELL	A A	MC		Lieutenant	Durham Light Infantry and RAF	
MCDOUGALL	A	DSO		Captain	County of London Yeomanry	T
McGEAGH	W M		10/02/1919	Lieutenant	South Lancashire Regiment	
MCGEAGH	J P			Captain	Nigerian Regiment	SR
MCGEAGH	G R D	MC		Lieutenant	RAMC	
MCGILLVRAY	A	Mentioned in Despatches		Captain	RAMC	T
MCGREGOR	R S			Captain	Norfolk Regiment	T
MACKENZIE	H J			Captain	Argyll and Sutherland Highlanders	
McKERGOW	R D W		21/09/1917	Second Lieutenant	Royal Flying Corps	
McLAREN	K		18/09/1918	Gunner	Royal Field Artillery	
MCMULLAN	H W			Second Lieutenant	Middlesex Regiment	
MCNEILL	J			Lieutenant	South Staffordshire Regiment	T
MEAKIN	K W G		16/05/1915	Second Lieutenant	North Staffordshire Regiment	T
MEAKIN	W K		15/08/1915	Captain	Bedfordshire Regiment	T
MEAKIN	L G			Second Lieutenant	RASC	
MEARES	C S		30/07/1916	Captain	Royal Fusiliers	
MEARES	D H	Mentioned in Despatches		Captain	Army Ordnance Department	
MEARES	R H			Private	Royal Engineers	
MEE	J T M			Captain	Suffolk Yeomanry	T
MELVILLE	C H	CMG, Mentioned in Despatches		Colonel	RAMC	
MELVILLE	J S			Colonel	Commancing 8th East Lancashire Regiment	
MERRIMAN	G		09/09/1914	Volunteer	Nyasaland Volunteer Reserve	
MERRIMAN	C F	MC		Lieutenant	Royal Artillery	SR
MERRIMAN	G W S			Private	Royal Fusiliers	
MERSON	R K			Captain	RAMC	
MICHAELSON	J			Lieutenant	Royal Fusiliers	
MICHELMORE	J E M		09/04/1918	Lieutenant	East Surrey Regiment	
MILBURN	W H			Major	Yorkshire Regiment	T
MILES	Sir C W Bart	OBE, Mentioned in Despatches		Captain	Somerset Light Infantry	
MILES	W H			Lieutenant	Somerset Light Infantry	T
MILLAR	R C		25/09/1915	Lieutenant	Seaforth Highlanders	

Surname	Initials	Honours and Awards	Died on Service	Rank	Service	T/SR etc.
MILLER	F C			Lieutenant	Royal Warwickshire Regiment	
MILLER	H F S			Second Lieutenant	King's Liverpool Regiment	
MILLER	R A T	Mentioned in Despatches		Captain	Royal Warwickshire Regiment	
MILLER	T E			Not Known	RAF	
MILLER-STERLING	A E S			Captain	Indian Army attached Gordon Highlanders	POW
MILLETT	H J C			Second Lieutenant	Queen's Own (Royal West Kent Regiment)	
MILNE	E C		28/10/1917	Second Lieutenant	Northumberland Fusiliers	
MILWARD	P H		07/12/1915	Captain	Rifle Brigade	
MIMS	C C			Lieutenant	Royal Field Artillery	
MIMS	F H	Mentioned in Despatches		Sub-Lieutenant	RNVR	
MITCHELL	E D			Lieutenant	Middlesex Regiment	
MITCHELL	E S	MC		Captain	Worcestershire Regiment	T
MITCHELL	G A		-	Not Known	Royal Norfolk Regiment	
MITCHELL	H	MC, Mentioned in Despatches		Captain	West Yorkshire Regiment	T
MITCHELL	H R			Captain	Worcestershire Regiment	
MITCHELL	J R	Mentioned in Despatches		Captain	RAMC	T
MITCHELSON	J K			The Rev.	CF	POW
MOERAN	E J S			Lieutenant	Norfolk Regiment attached West Yorkshire Regiment	
MONAGHAN	D L		24/11/1917	Captain	Tank Corps	
MONCTON	T C C			Lieutenant	Royal Field Artillery	
MONK	F H			Captain	Indian Army	
MONTEITH	W B R			Second Lieutenant	Royal Garrison Artillery	
MONTGOMERY	B R			Not Known	NZ Forces	
MOON	J	Mentioned in Despatches (2)		Lieutenant	Royal Field Artillery	
MOORE	Roger L	Mentioned in Despatches	20/12/1914	Lieutenant	Somerset Light Infantry	
MOORE	G	MC, Mentioned in Despatches		Captain	RAMC	
MOORE	H B	MC, Mentioned in Despatches (3), Belgian Croix de Guerre		Major (Staff)	Rifle Brigade	
MOORE	J de V			Captain	Royal Engineers	
MOORE	J L			Second Lieutenant	Royal Military College, Sandhurst	
MOORE	Robert L			Major	Royal Inniskilling Fusiliers	
MORETON (MACDONALD)	N C H	MC, Mentioned in Despatches	13/10/1915	Captain	King's Royal Rifle Corps	

Surname	Initials	Honours and Awards	Died on Service	Rank	Service	T/SR etc.
MORGAN	G Hamilton	Mentioned in Despatches	23/11/1917	Captain	Royal Welsh Fusiliers	
MORGAN	G Hungerford		15/08/1917	Lance Corporal	Canadian Infantry	
MORGAN	R C W		28/07/1917	Lieutenant	Royal Flying Corps	SR
MORLEY	C			Captain	Manchester Regiment	POW
MORRIS	C M			Lieutenant	128th Pioneers, Indian Expeditionary Force	
MORRIS	H			Lieutenant	RAF	
MORRIS	T R A	MC, Mentioned in Despatches		Captain	Gloucestershire Regiment	
MORRIS-EYTON	R E			Captain	Royal Field Artillery	T
MORRISH	J H	Mentioned in Despatches		Lieutenant	Royal West Kent Regiment	SR
MORRISH	R L			Lieutenant	Royal Garrison Artillery	
MORRISON	P D			Lieutenant	Royal Scots Fusiliers	
MORRISON	R K			Captain	King's Liverpool Regiment	T
MORTIMORE	C A	DSO, Brevet, Mentioned in Despatches (3), Legion of Honour, Croix de Chavalier		Colonel	Royal Field Artillery	
MORTON	C J			The Rev.	CF	
MORTON	E A		24/09/1918	Private	The Buffs (East Kent Regiment)	
MORTON	H J S			Captain	RAMC	SR
MORTON	R F S			Captain	RAF	
MOSER	H W		22/07/1916	Second Lieutenant	East Surrey Regiment	
MOSER	W W			Lieutenant	Border Regiment	
MOTT	C E			Captain	RASC	
MOTUM	E H	Mentioned in Despatches		Captain	Durham Light Infantry	T
MOUNTAIN	B			Lieutenant	RAMC	
MOYES	W B	MM	26/03/1918	Serjeant	The Queen's (Royal West Surrey Regiment)	
MOYES	E F			Squadron Commander	RAF	
MULLINER	A R	MC, Mentioned in Despatches (2)		Captain	8th Hussars	
MURDOCH	R	OBE, Mentioned in Despatches		Major	ASC	
MUNRO	G O G			Lieutenant	Seaforth Highlanders	SR
MUNTZ	G D E			Sub-Lieutenant	Royal Naval Reserve	
MURRAY	W A	DSO, Brevet, Mentioned in Despatches (2)		Lieutenant Colonel	Royal Horse Artillery	
MUSGRAVE	B	OBE, Mentioned in Despatches (2)		Major	Loyal North Lancashire Regiment	
MUSSON	T M B			Lieutenant	Royal Welsh Fusiliers	

Surname	Initials	Honours and Awards	Died on Service	Rank	Service	T/SR etc.
MYLNE	E L	MC	15/09/1916	Lieutenant	Irish Guards	
MYLNE	A F			Lieutenant	Worcestershire Regiment (attached Herefordshire Regiment)	
NALDER	J F			Flight Sub-Lieutenant	RAF	
NAPIER	W L		13/08/1915	Lieutenant Colonel	South Wales Borderers	
NAPIER	V J L	MC		Lieutenant	South West Borderers	
NEAME	A L C	OBE, Mentioned in Despatches (2)		Major (Staff)	Royal Engineers and RAF	
NEAME	E G			Lieutenant	East Surrey Regiment	
NEAME	G J	Mentioned in Despatches, Brevet		Captain, Brevet Major	The Buffs (East Kent Regiment) & Royal Engineers	
NEEDHAM	J O			Captain	152 Punjabis, Indian Army	
NEILD	W C	MC and Bar, Mentioned in Despatches		Captain	Essex Regiment	
NEILL	H S			Lieutenant	Staffordshire Yeomanry	T
NEILSON	A			Major	Yeomanry	
NEILSON	G C	Mentioned in Despatches (2)		Major	RAF	
NEILSON	G E			Lieutenant	Yeomanry	T
NEILSON	G M			Major	9th Lancers, Deputy Assistant Adjutant General	
NEILSON	J A			Captain	Ayrshire Yeomanry	T
NEILSON	J B			Major	Ayrshire Yeomanry	T
NEILSON	J F	DSO, Menrioned in Despatches, Order of St Vladimir (4th Class), Order of St Anne (2nd Class)		Major	10th Hussars	
NEILSON	William	DSO, Brevet		Lieutenant Colonel	4th Hussars and Derbyshire Yeomanry	T
NEILSON	W K			Lieutenant	Ayrshire Yeomanry	T
NELSON	A			Major	From Reserve of Officers	
NELSON	G S			Captain	Northumberland Fusiliers	
NELSON	W	Mentioned in Despatches		Captain	Royal Fusiliers	
NESHAM	H P	MC, Mentioned in Despatches (4)		Major	Royal Field Artillery	
NEVILL	C St. J		18/04/1918	Lieutenant	Royal Field Artillery	
NEVILL	G H			Lieutenant	Royal Garrison Artillery	T
NEVINSON	C R W			Private	RAMC	
NEW	F O W			Lieutenant	Leicestershire Regiment	

Appendix I   215

Surname	Initials	Honours and Awards	Died on Service	Rank	Service	T/SR etc.
NEWBIGGING	W P R (D S O)	CB, CMG, Brevet, Mentioned in Despatches (6)		Colonel	Manchester Regiment	
NEWBOLD	P		13/07/1916	Second Lieutenant	Queen's Own (Royal West Kent Regiment)	
NEWBOLD	C J	DSO, Mentioned in Despatches (3)		Lieutenant Colonel	Royal Engineers	
NEWBOLD	D (Sir)			Captain	Dorset Yeomanry (attached Cavalry Machine Gun Corps)	
NEWBOLD	E			Captain	Royal Garrison Artillery	
NEWBOLD	W	OBE, Mentioned in Despatches (3)		Major	Royal Garrison Artillery and Royal Engineers	
NEWMAN	K C H			Second Lieutenant	Royal Field Artillery	
NEWSHOLME	L W			Lieutenant	Loyal North Lancashire Regiment	
NEWSON	H A			Lieutenant	Royal Munster Fusiliers	POW
NEWTON	W T		01/07/1916	Lieutenant	North Staffordshire Regiment	T
NEWTON	F			Lieutenant	Royal Field Artillery	T
NEWTON	H L	DSO, Mentioned in Despatches		Major	Royal Field Artillery	T
NEWTON	L			Captain	RASC	
NEWTON-CLARE	H J	OBE, Mentioned in Despatches (3)		Major	R A F	
NEWTON-CLARE	W S	MBE		Lieutenant	RAF	
NICHOLSON	A G		10/08/1915	Lieutenant	Cheshire Regiment	T
NICHOLSON	E C	MC		Captain	Royal Berkshire Regiment	
NICHOLSON	G	MC, Mentioned in Despatches (3)		Captain	Hampshire Regiment	
NICHOLSON	G H			Lieutenant	Queen's Royal West Surrey Regiment and RAF	POW
NICHOLSON	J G	Mentioned in Despatches		Captain	Royal Field Artillery	
NICHOLSON	H W		13/10/1915	Captain	Lincolnshire Regiment	
NICHOLSON	L C	DSO, Mentioned in Despatches	02/11/1914	Lieutenant	Royal Berkshire Regiment	T
NICHOLSON	P C			Not Known	Not Known	
NICKOLS	H			Major	Royal Field Artillery	T
NIMMO	W L		26/07/1918	Second Lieutenant	Northumberland Fusiliers	
NOAKES	C J			Lieutenant	East Surrey Regiment	SR
NOCTON	W A			Lieutenant	Royal Field Artillery	
NORRIS	C S			Lance Corporal	1st Canadian Contingent	
NORRIS	E F		15/03/1918	Captain	Royal Flying Corps	
NORRIS	K A A		16/06/1916	Second Lieutenant	Queen's Own (Royal West Kent Regiment)	
NORRIS	S D			Captain	King's Liverpool Regiment	SR

Surname	Initials	Honours and Awards	Died on Service	Rank	Service	T/SR etc.
NORTHROP	G W			Captain	Royal Field Artillery	T
NORTHROP	J E		02/03/1917	Flight Sub-Lieutenant	Royal Naval Air Service	
NORTHROP	R			Captain	Royal Marine Light Infantry	
NORTON	T E G		20/04/1915	Second Lieutenant	East Surrey Regiment	
NORTON	R H			Lieutenant	Coldstream Guards	
NOWELL	H N			Lieutenant	Royal Horse Guards	
NOYES	C E			Major	Highland Light Infantry	
NUTTING	H B	Mentioned in Despatches		Captain	5th Cavalry Indian Army	
OLDREY	H C			Lieutenant	Royal Engineers	
ORD	G C			Private	Royal Fusiliers and RAF	
OLDREY	R J B		29/10/1914	Captain	4th Dragoon Guards (Royal Irish)	
OLVER	S C			Second Lieutenant	Royal Engineers	
OPENSHAW	E R			Captain	Somerset Light Infantry	T
ORFORD	L H			Cadet	RAF	
ORLEBAR	R C			Lieutenant	RAF	
OSBOURNE	B		11/11/1914	Lieutenant	15th (The King's) Hussars	
OVERTON	R E B			Lieutenant	Leicestershire Yeomanry	T
OWEN	H R			Lieutenant	Royal Field Artillery	
PACKARD	J E E	MC, Mentioned in Despatches		Major	King's Own attached King's Own Yorkshire Light Infantry	
PAGE	G F			Lieutenant	RAMC	
PALMER	Cedric			Lieutenant	Durham Light Infantry	
PALMER	Clayton	Mentioned in Despatches		Major	Army Ordnance Department	
PALMER	E B			Captain	Royal Scots Fusilliers	POW
PALMER	G			Lieutenant	Durham Light Infantry	
PALMER	G W			Major	Army Ordnance Department	
PALMER	P T			Captain	Northern Fusilliers	
PALMER	W L		08/05/1915	Second Lieutenant	Monmouthshire Regiment	T
PALMES	G C (D S O)			Major (Staff)	Not Known	
PALMES	G L (D S O)	Mentioned in Despatches		Captain (GSO)	Not Known	
PARK	A			Second Lieutenant	RAF	
PARK	R			The Rev.	CF (4th Class)	
PARKER	A P			Lieutenant	Royal Defence Corps	
PARKER	C P	OBE, Mentioned in Despatches		Captain (Staff)	Assistant Quarter Master General	
PARKER	F C F			Captain	Westmoreland and Cumberland Yeomanry	T

Surname	Initials	Honours and Awards	Died on Service	Rank	Service	T/SR etc.
PARKER	R G			Captain	East Lancs. Regiment	
PARKES	C E	Mentioned in Despatches		Lieutenant	Army Ordnance Department	
PARKES	E E			Major	RAMC	
PARKES	H R		28/05/1920	Captain	Royal Garrison Artillery	
PARRINGTON	N			Captain	West Yorkshire Regiment (Prince of Wales's Own)	
PARR	W W	MC	08/05/1917	Captain	Gloucestershire Regiment	
PARRY	D B	DSO, Mentioned in Despatches (4)		Lieutenant Colonel	5th Dragoon Guards and Machine Gun Corps	
PARSONS	W L	Mentioned in Despatches		Lieutenant Colonel	Army Ordnance Department	
PASKIN	G W			Second Lieutenant	Royal Engineers	SR
PATERSON-BROWN	A M			Second Lieutenant	RAF	
PATON	R M			Second Lieutenant	Royal Field Artillery	T
PATON	W A	Mentioned in Despatches		Second Lieutenant	Machine Gun Corps (Infantry)	
PATERSON	A E W			Second Lieutenant	Leicestershire Regiment	
PATERSON	R S			Midshipman	RNVR	
PATTRICK	A D		12/08/1915	Captain	Norfolk Regiment	
PAUL	A S			Captain	2nd Dragoon Guards (Queen's Bays)	
PAVEY-SMITH	A B	MC, Mentioned in Despatches		Major	RAMC	T
PAYN	R W		28/03/1918	Captain	Royal Engineers	
PAYNE	R S S			Lieutenant	RASC	
PEACHEY	H G	Mentioned in Despatches		Major	RASC	
PEACOCK	T G		25/09/1915	Lieutenant	Royal Berkshire Regiment	
PEARCE	G V		18/12/1914	Second Lieutenant	Royal Warwickshire Regiment	
PEARCE-JONES	G D			Lieutenant	Royal Field Artillery	SR
PEARSON	A G	DSO		Major	Royal Berkshire Regiment and Tank Corps	SR
PEARSON	C E			Captain	Special Reserve	
PEARSON	J E			Cadet	Royal Engineers	
PEARSON	L			Not Known	Artist's Rifles & RASC	
PEARSON	F		01/02/1917	Captain	Royal North Lancs Regiment	
PEASE-WATKIN	E H	DSO, Mentioned in Despatches (3)		Major	Royal Field Artillery	

Surname	Initials	Honours and Awards	Died on Service	Rank	Service	T/SR etc.
PEEL	E J R	CMG, DSO and bar, Mentioned in Despatches (4)		Lieutenant Colonel (Temporay Brigadier-General)	Royal Artillery	
PEEL	G N	Mentioned in Despatches		Not Known	RND	
PEERS	W H S			Private	Honorable Artillery Company	
PEILE	H G			The Rev.	CF (4th Class)	
PELHAM	C C A			Captain	Hussars & RAF	
PENDENNIS	H M			Second Lieutenant	Royal Welsh Fusiliers	
PENFOLD	J B		28/01/1916	Lieutenant	King's Own Scottish Borderers	
PERCIVAL	A F			Lieutenant	Royal Garrison Artillery	
PERRY	B H H	DSO, MC, Mentioned in Despatches (5), Brevet		Major	Royal Scots	
PERRYN	G H			Lieutenant	Royal Engineers	
PERSHOUSE	F S			Major	Royal Field Artillery	
PETERS	A	MC		Captain	Leicestershire Regiment	
PETLEY	L B			Cadet	RAF	
PHELPS	M P	Mentioned in Despatches		Lieutenant Colonel	Lincolnshire Regiment	
PHILCOX	C L	DFC		Captain	RAF	
PHILIPS	E A			Not Known	Reserve Regiment of Cavalry	
PHILLIPS	G F	CB, CMG, Mentioned in Despatches, Commander of the Order of the Redeemer, and of the Crown of Italy		Colonel	West Yorkshire Regiment (Prince of Wales's Own)	
PHIPPS	C L		14/08/1917	Lieutenant	Royal Flying Corps	
PICKERING	R E	Mentioned in Despatches (2)		Major	Queen's Royal West Surrey Regiment	
PICKERING	T		01/11/1915	Second Lieutenant	Gloucestershire Regiment	
PICKUP	W H		27/11/1918	Surgeon Lieutenant	Royal Navy	
PIGEON	H R			Lieutenant	RASC	
PILE	J W			Lieutenant	Royal Garrison Artillery	
PILGRIM	S A F		24/09/1918	Second Lieutenant	Tank Corps	
PINDER	A H			Captain	RAMC	
PINDER	T W	Mentioned in Despatches		Lieutenant Colonel	Rifle Brigade	T
PINNEY	J C D	Mentioned in Despatches		Major	(Formerly Indian Army) Staff	
PITCHER	J F			Sub-Lieutenant	RNVR	

Appendix I 219

Surname	Initials	Honours and Awards	Died on Service	Rank	Service	T/SR etc.
PLEWS	R H C	OBE, Mentioned in Despatches (2)		Major	RASC	
POLLOCK	A J A			Captain	Royal Scots Fusilliers	
Ponsford	F H S		03/10/1917	Lieutenant	King's Own Yorkshire Light Infantry	
POPE	R H L			Lieutenant	Royal Engineers	T
POPPLE	G M		26/06/1916	Second Lieutenant	Northumberland Fusiliers	
PORRITT	C A			Lieutenant	RASC	SR
PORTAL	A W			Lieutenant	Queen's Royal West Surrey Regiment	SR
PORTER-HARGREAVES	A H			Lieutenant	Northumberland Fusiliers	
POTTER	J W			Not Known	Anti-Aircraft Corps, RNVR	
POTTER	S L			Captain	Royal Marines	
POTTER	W A	DSO, Mentioned in Despatches		Lieutenant Colonel	RASC	T
POWELL	D W	DSO, Mentioned in Despatches		Major	Northamptonshire Regiment and RAF	
POWELL	H A			Lieutenant Colonel	RAMC	
POWELL	J M S			Private	Honorable Artillery Company and Royal Engineers	
POWELL	M		05/07/1917	Lieutenant	Royal Field Artillery	
POWELL	M C			Lieutenant-Commander	Royal Naval Reserve	
POWELL	M W			Cadet	London University OTC	
POWELL	T G		09/05/1915	Captain	Northamptonshire Regiment	
POWELL	V			Gunner	Royal Field Artillery	
POWLES	S H			Cadet	Royal Military Academy	
POWLETT	O R F W			Cadet	Royal Military College, Camberley	
PRATT	L H		25/09/1915	Second Lieutenant	London Regiment (London Irish Rifles)	T
PRICE	A R			Captain	Devonshire Regiment	T
PRICE	I C			Lieutenant	RASC	
PRICE	T W			Cadet	Infantry	
PRIDAY	A K	Mentioned in Despatches		Captain	Gordon Highlanders	
PRIDAY	T O			Captain	ADC on Staff, South Africa	
PRIDMORE	P M	MC	02/09/1917	Captain	Royal Warwickshire Regiment	
PRIESTLEY	A E			Lieutenant	Duke of Wellington's (West Riding Regiment)	
PRIESTLEY	H W			Major	London Regiment	T
PRIESTLEY	P W			Lieutenant	Bedfordshire Yeomanry	T
PRINGLE	R H	MC		Lieutenant	King's Own Scottish Borderers	

Surname	Initials	Honours and Awards	Died on Service	Rank	Service	T/SR etc.
PRIOLEAU	L H	MBE		Major	(Late) Manchester Regiment	
PUCKLE	B H	DSO, Mentioned in Despatches		Major	Welsh Regiment and Machine Gun Corps	
PUCKLE	F H			Captain	26th Punjabis	
PUCKLE	G H			Lieutenant	Indian Army (Reserve) Attached RAF	
PULLMAN	G C	OBE		Major	East Surrey Regiment	
PURSER	F D		27/12/1917	Lieutenant	Royal Naval Volunteer Reserve	
PYM	F L M	Mentioned in Despatches	02/07/1916	Lieutenant	Irish Guards	
QUICK	T S Q P			Lieutenant	Leinster Regiment	SR
QUINBY	F G			Lieutenant	RAMC	
RABONE	A B		01/07/1916	Captain	Royal Warwickshire Regiment	T
RADCLIFFE	E E			Captain	Duke of Wellington's (West Riding Regiment)	T
RAINE	A H			Lieutenant	Royal Engineers	T
RAMBAUT	B R R	Mentioned in Despatches		Captain	Royal Garrison Artillery	
RAMSAY	A P			Lieutenant	Royal Field Artillery	
RAMSAY	G W St C			Surgeon Sub-Lieutenant	Royal Navy	
RAMSAY	N B	MC, Mentioned in Despatches		Captain	Northumberland Fusiliers	T
RAMSBOTHAM	H	OBE, MC, Mentioned in Despatches (3)		Major	General List (Staff)	
RAMSBOTHAM	W H	Brevet		Major	West Yorkshire Regiment (Prince of Wales's Own)	
RANSOME	H F		14/11/1917	Lieutenant	Royal Army Medical Corps	
RATCLIFF	J E		19/10/1914	Lieutenant	Royal Warwickshire Regiment	
RAVEN	C E			The Rev.	CF	
RAVEN	E E			The Rev.	CF	
RAVEN	F G		24/03/1917	Captain	Royal Engineers	
RAVEN	C H R E		02/06/1919	Captain	Royal Air Force	
RAVEN	M O			Surgeon-Lieutenant	Royal Navy	
RAVENSCROFT	D	MC		Second Lieutenant	Royal Field Artillery	
RAWSON	G F			Lieutenant	RASC	
RAY	J E			Paymaster Lieutenant-Commander	Royal Navy Volunteer Reserve, Royal Naval Division	
RAY	M S			Not Known	East African Mounted Rifles	
RAYNER	G	Mentioned in Despatches (2)		Second Lieutenant	Royal Field Artillery	
RAYSON	J H K			Captain	Royal Field Artillery	

Appendix I 221

Surname	Initials	Honours and Awards	Died on Service	Rank	Service	T/SR etc.
REAVELEY	C T H			Captain	King's Shropshire Light Infantry	
REAVELEY	D F P			Second Lieutenant	Northumberland Fusiliers	
REAY	C T	Mentioned in Despatches		Brigadier-General	Staff	
REAY	J L			Not Known	Tank Corps	
REDDAWAY	H			Lieutenant	Royal Fusiliers	SR
REDFERN	S L		02/08/1917	Captain	The Loyal North Lancashire Regiment	T
REDMAYNE	G B	MM	31/03/1917	Driver	Royal Field Artillery	T
REES	E F			Lieutenant	Royal Field Artillery	
REEVES-SMITH	G		02/10/1915	Second Lieutenant	Royal Engineers	
REFORD	A D			Lieutenant	Canadian Mounted Rifles	
REGNART	C H	MC, Mentioned in Despatches		Major	Royal Marine Light Infantry	
REGNART	N S	MC, Mentioned in Despatches, Brevet		Captain (Brevet Major)	8th Hussars	
REID	J W			Second Lieutenant	Yorkshire Dragoons Yeomanry	T
REISS	P J	MC and Bar, MM		Captain	Bedfordshire Regiment	
REITH	R A			Lieutenant Colonel	(From Reserve of Officers) The Buffs (East Kent Regiment)	
RENSHAW	A H			Captain	Lanarkshire Yeomanry	
REVILLON	A J			Lieutenant	King's Royal Rifle Corps	
REYNOLDS	A			Sergeant	South African Mounted Rifles	
REYNOLDS	C H	DSO, MC		Captain	Royal Garrison Artillery	
REYNOLDS	S L	OBE		Major	RASC (Reserve of Officers)	
RICHARDS	G B			Captain	London Regiment & RASC	T
RICHARDSON	G P	Croix de Guerre		Major	Royal Garrison Artillery	
RICHARDSON	J R E			Cadet	RMC Sandhurst	
RICHARDSON	M B			Second Lieutenant	Sherwood Foresters (Notts and Derby Regiment)	
RICHARDSON	M N H			Captain	Royal Marines	
RICHARDSON	V	MC	09/06/1917	Lieutenant	Royal Sussex Regiment	
RICHMOND	A H R			Major	Royal Irish Rifles	
RICKARDS	G B	MC, Mentioned in Despatches		Captain	RFC & RAF	SR
RICKARDS	H W B		28/07/1917	Lieutenant	RFC	
RIDGWAY	H A		13/10/1915	Captain	North Staffordshire Regiment	T
RIDLEY	C A	MC, Mentioned in Despatches	01/07/1916	Second Lieutenant	Royal Fusiliers	

Surname	Initials	Honours and Awards	Died on Service	Rank	Service	T/SR etc.
RIGG	J W			Private	Devonshire Regiment	
RIGG	Samuel		25/03/1918	Major	Border Regiment	
RIGG	Stanley		21/06/1918	Second Lieutenant	Border Regiment	T
RILEY	R D			Rifleman	London Regiment	T
RILEY (Rev T)	T		05/08/1916	Captain	Royal Field Artillery	T
RITSON	J A S	DSO and Bar, MC, Mentioned in Despatches (4)		Major	Durham Light Infantry	T
RITSON	R			Captain	North Staffordshire Regiment	
ROBB	J			Lieutenant	RNVR	
ROBERTS	C L			Lieutenant	Machine Gun Corps (Infantry)	
ROBERTS	H A	MC		Captain	Royal Field Artillery	
ROBERTS	H M V			Not Known	Not Known	
ROBERTS	J T		20/07/1916	Second Lieutenant	The Queen's (Royal West Surrey Regiment)	
ROBERTS	K F			Captain (Staff)	Army Ordnance Department	
ROBERTS	T			Lieutenant	Sherwood Foresters (Notts and Derby Regiment)	
ROBERTSON	G H			Lieutenant	Liverpool Regiment	
ROBERTSON	J A T		30/12/1915	Lieutenant	Gurkha Rifles	
ROBERTSON-GLASGOW	R P			Lieutenant Colonel	Royal Scots Fusiliers	
ROBINSON	A C			Lieutenant Colonel	East Lancs. Regiment	T
ROBINSON	C			Lieutenant	South Staffordshire Regiment	T
ROBINSON	Claude			Not Known	Not Known	
ROBINSON	F			Lieutenant	Sherwood Foresters (Notts and Derby Regiment)	
ROBINSON	F B		03/07/1916	Captain	Sherwood Foresters (Notts and Derby Regiment)	T
ROBINSON	F D	Mentioned in Despatches		Lieutenant Colonel	East Lancs. Regiment	T
ROBINSON	G	MC		Lieutenant	Royal Field Artillery	T
ROBINSON	G J			Second Lieutenant	Tank Corps	
ROBINSON	J G			Captain	London Regiment	
ROBINSON	P D			Lieutenant	RN Brigade	
ROBINSON	P W			Captain	City of London Yeomanry	T
ROBINSON	S			Captain	Yorkshire Regiment	
ROBINSON	S A			Lieutenant	Border Regiment	
ROBINSON	T	MC, Mentioned in Despatches		Major	Royal Field Artillery	T

Surname	Initials	Honours and Awards	Died on Service	Rank	Service	T/SR etc.
ROBINSON	T A F	Mentioned in Despatches		Major	Royal Garrison Artillery	
ROBINSON	V P	Mentioned in Despatches		Lieutenant	Durham Light Infantry	
ROBSON	J S	Mentioned in Despatches		Major	Royal Artillery	SR
ROGERS	J A			Lieutenant	Royal Garrison Artillery	T
ROHDE	H T		12/04/1916	Captain	89th Punjabis	
ROLL	C H W			Cadet	Royal Military College, Camberley	
ROLLO	W S	MC, Brevet, Mentioned in Despatches		Major	Royal Engineers	T
ROME	R C	MC, Brevet, Mentioned in Despatches (2)		Major	Royal Field Artillery	
ROME	S G	OBE, MC, Mentioned in Despatches		Captain	Argyll and Sutherland Highlanders	
ROOK	R H	MC		Lieutenant	West Yorkshire Regiment (Prince of Wales's Own)	SR
ROPER	B F H			Captain	RASC	
ROSE	A A			Captain	Royal Engineers	T
ROSE	A E P			Not Known	Rifle Brigade	
ROSE	H A			Lieutenant	Royal Scots	T
ROSE-INNES	G Gregory			Major	London Regiment	T
ROSSITER	F M S			Captain	Royal Engineers	
ROTHERHAM	E			Captain	Royal Warwickshire Regiment	T
ROTHWELL	J			Captain	Royal Warwickshire Regiment	SR
ROUGHTON	T H	MC	24/03/1918	Captain	Lancashire Fusiliers	
ROUTH	H C E			Major	Royal Garrison Artillery	
ROUTH	W H F			Second Lieutenant	Somerset Light Infantry	
ROWE	C W D			Lieutenant Colonel	Northants Regiment	
ROWELL	G L S			Lieutenant	Royal Field Artillery	T
ROWLEY	G	MC and 2 Bar	15/10/1918	Captain	Cheshire Regiment	
ROYLE	J B		15/01/1917	Major	South Wales Borderers	
RYDER	W H		06/07/1917	Lieutenant	Royal Flying Corps	T
RYCOTT	H A	Mentioned in Despatches, Brevet		Captain (Brevet Major)	Northumberland Fusiliers	T
SALES	N		30/06/1918	Lieutenant	Royal Air Force	
SALES	W T			Second Lieutenant	AEF & King's Own Yorkshire Light Infantry	
SALISBURY	T H L			Lieutenant	RAF	
SALTER	G C T	MC	28/05/1918	Lieutenant	RAF	
SAMPLE	T			Second Lieutenant	Royal Field Artillery	T

Surname	Initials	Honours and Awards	Died on Service	Rank	Service	T/SR etc.
SANDAY	W D S	DSO		Captain	RAF	
SANDERSON	A J		02/05/1915	Captain	King's Own Scottish Borderers	
SANDERSON	J			Captain	London Regiment	T
SANDERSON	P C			Captain	1st Kumaru Rifles (Indian Army)	
SANFORD	D W	Mentioned in Despatches		Captain	Royal Engineers	
SATTERTHWAITE	W H	Mentioned in Despatches	07/06/1918	Captain	King's Own (Royal Lancaster Regiment)	T
SAUNDERSON	A E	Mentioned in Despatches		Surgeon	Royal Navy	
SAUNDERSON	D B	MC, Croix de Guerre		Major	Royal Engineers	
SAVILL	F E		09/02/1916	Lieutenant	9th (Queen's Royal) Lancers	
SAVORY	C H			Surgeon	Royal Navy	
SAVORY	K S	DSO and Bar, MC, Mentioned in Despatches (2), Croix de Guerre		Major	RAF	
SAVORY	R A	MC, Mentioned in Despatches		Captain	14th Sikhs	
SAWREY-COOKSON	G R			Captain	Gordon Highlanders	
SAWYER	G H	DSO and Bar, Croix de Guerre, Mentioned in Despatches (3)		Major	Royal Berkshire Regiment	
SCHIFF	M N		17/06/1916	Lieutenant	Scots Guards	T
SCHLESINGER	B E			Private	Queen's Westminster Rifles	
SCHOLEY	C H N		25/09/1915	Captain	Rifle Brigade	
SCOTT	H L	MC		Captain	King's Own Regiment	
SCOTT	H P F			The Rev.	Chaplain Royal Navy	
SCOTT	W S	MC and Bar, AFC, Mentioned in Despatches		Major	Lancashire Fusiliers and RAF	
SCOWCROFT	H E			Surgeon	Royal Navy	
SCRUTTON	A E	MC, Mentioned in Despatches		Captain	Tank Corps	
SCRUTTON	H U	MC, Mentioned in Despatches (2)	10/09/1916	Captain	Northumberland Fusiliers	
SCRUTTON	J A	MC, Mentioned in Despatches		Captain	Royal Engineers and Tank Corps	SR
SCULTHORPE	W V		08/06/1917	Second Lieutenant	London Regiment	
SEARLE	C S	MC		Lieutenant	Indian Army Attached Royal Berkshire Regiment	
SEARLE	V L S		22/06/1916	Second Lieutenant	Royal Field Artillery	
SECKEL	T M			Sergeant	Canadian Highlanders	

Surname	Initials	Honours and Awards	Died on Service	Rank	Service	T/SR etc.
SECKER	E H			Captain	Royal Field Artillery	
SECKER	J H	Mentioned in Despatches, Croix de Guerre		Captain	RFC & RAF	
SECRETAN	K			Major	RAF	
SECRETAN	N			Major	Royal Engineers	
SEDDON	A D			Major	The King's Own (Royal Lancaster Regiment)	T/POW
SEDDON	A E			Captain	Suffolk Regiment	
SEDDON	G N	MC		Lieutenant	Suffolk Regiment	
SEDDON	W D			Second Lieutenant	Inns of Court OTC	
SEDGWICK	F R	CMG, DSO, Mentioned in Despatches (2), Brevet		Lieutenant Colonel	Royal Field Artillery	
SELBY	M H			Not Known	Royal Artillery	
SELBY	R F			Cadet	Royal Field Artillery	
SELWYN	A P		18/05/1916	Lieutenant	11th King Edward's Own Lancers (Probyn's Horse)	
SELWYN	C W		17/05/1915	Second Lieutenant	Leicestershire Regiment	T
SELWYN	G			Lieutenant	Leicestershire Regiment	
SELWYN	J	Mentioned in Despatches (2)		Major	Royal Horse Artillery and RAF	
SENIOR	F G	Mentioned in Despatches		Captain	East Yorkshire Regiment	SR
SENIOR	H G		28/05/1918	Lieutenant	Manchester Regiment	
SETH-SMITH	D N			Captain	RAMC	
SETH-SMITH	G			Lieutenant	RASC	
SETH-SMITH	L M	MC, Mentioned in Despatches		Lieutenant	East African Transport Corps	
SEVER	C L M			Lieutenant	Royal Welsh Fusiliers	T
SEWELL	W A			Surgeon-Lieutenant	Royal Naval Brigade	
SHACKLE	C E			Lieutenant	RNVR and RAF	
SHARP	J S			Lieutenant	Highland Light Infantry	
SHARP	Harold			Lieutenant	East Surrey Regiment	
SHARP	Herbert			Second Lieutenant	Royal Fusiliers	
SHARP	H E			Lieutenant	King's Own Yorkshire Light Infantry	
SHARP	R			Lieutenant	Royal Engineers	T
SHARROCK	K S			Lieutenant	Royal Field Artillery	
SHAW	B H		22/01/1917	Second Lieutenant	Cheshire Regiment	
SHAW	R B			Lieutenant	Royal Field Artillery	SR
SHAW	R R S		01/07/1916	Lieutenant	North Staffordshire Regiment	T
SHAW	W C			Captain	RASC	

Surname	Initials	Honours and Awards	Died on Service	Rank	Service	T/SR etc.
SHAW	W W			Major	44th Merwara Infantry (Indian Army)	
SHENTON	G J H	MC		Lieutenant	Royal Horse Artillery	T
SHERBURN	J C			Captain	East Yorkshire Regiment	
SHEPHERD	D M			Captain	Devonshire Regiment	
SHIELL	D P	MC and Bar		Captain	Middlesex Regiment	
SHIPPARD	S S A			Lieutenant	Indian Army	
SHOLL	T H			Second Lieutenant	Royal Horse Artillery	T
SHOVE	R S			Captain	Royal Field Artillery	
SHUTE	G G			Not Known	Nigerian Field Force	
SHULDHAM-LEIGH	M S			Lieutenant	Queen's Royal West Surrey Regiment	
SIEVER	R B B	MC, Mentioned in Despatches (2)		Lieutenant	Royal Field Artillery and RAF	
SILBURN	L			Captain	RASC	T (POW)
SIMON	A W			Second Lieutenant	Royal Sussex Regiment	
SIMON	P B			Major	Royal Garrison Artillery	
SIMON	R de P			Lieutenant	Royal Field Artillery	
SIMOND	E C			Second Lieutenant	Royal Engineers	
SIMPSON	G C			Lieutenant	Royal Field Artillery	
SIMPSON	J			Second Lieutenant	Lancers and RAF	
SIMPSON	L (MVO)			Captain	King's Own Yorkshire Light Infantry	
SIMPSON	M C			Cadet	Royal Field Artillery	
SINCLAIR	J C			Lieutenant	Bedfordshire Regiment	
SINCLAIR	J N	DSO, Mentioned in Despatches (2)	24/03/1918	Lieutenant Colonel	Royal Field Artillery	
SINCLAIR	G D F			Captain	RASC	
SIVRIGHT	T B			Captain	Royal Dublin Fusiliers	
SKRINE	W V D	MC and Bar, Mentioned in Despatches		Lieutenant	York and Lancaster Regiment	T
SLADE	F W P			Lieutenant	RNVR	
SLATER	G H			Lieutenant	King's Royal Rifle Corps	SR
SLATER	W T		15/08/1917	Private	Canadian Infantry	
SLEIGH	R P			Second Lieutenant	Manchester Regiment	
SMALLEY	J D		15/03/1915	Lieutenant	Cambridgeshire Regiment	T
SMELT	W A C			Lieutenant	Essex Regiment	
SMETHAM	S J			Second Lieutenant	Royal Engineers & RAF	
SMITH	B W			Second Lieutenant	Royal Field Artillery	
SMITH	D			Captain	Border Regiment	T
SMITH	D V	DSO, Mentioned in Despatches (3)	13/04/1917	Lieutenant Colonel	Royal Fusiliers	T

Surname	Initials	Honours and Awards	Died on Service	Rank	Service	T/SR etc.
SMITH	E F			Captain	East Lancs. Regiment and South Lancashire Regiment	
SMITH	E P		02/05/1915	Colonel	Royal Field Artillery	
SMITH	G B			Lieutenant	Royal Field Artillery	T
SMITH	H F			Captain	Duke of Cornwall's Light Infantry	
SMITH	H N			Captain	Royal Warwickshire Regiment	POW
SMITH	H S		12/04/1917	Second Lieutenant	Royal Scots	
SMITH	H W (DSO)	Brevet, Mentioned in Despatches (2)		Lieutenant Colonel	Queen's Royal West Surrey Regiment	
SMITH	M P			Corporal	Royal Engineers	
SMITH	R A			Captain	Royal Field Artillery	T
SMITH	R H		30/07/1916	Second Lieutenant	The King's (Liverpool Regiment)	
SMITH	S H			Lieutenant	Royal Navy	
SMITH	S P H			Lieutenant	Royal Field Artillery	
SMITH	T			Captain	Grenadier Guards	
SMITH	W H			Captain	King's Own Yorkshire Light Infantry	T
SMITH	W N E	Mentioned in Despatches		Lieutenant Colonel	Royal Marines	
SMITHERS	M H W			Captain	Machine Gun Corps (Infantry)	
SMITHERS	R C W		16/08/1917	Captain	King's Own Yorkshire Light Infantry	
SMURTHWAITE	H			Captain	Royal Fusiliers	
SMYTH	A E			Lieutenant	Royal Berkshire Regiment	
SMYTH	E P			Major	RNVR attached RAF	
SMYTH	H L			Not Known	Middlesex Regiment	
SMYTH	J A			Medical Officer	VAD Hospital	
SMYTH	R A		27/09/1917	Major	Royal Inniskilling Fusiliers	
SNELL	H C			Captain	RAMC	T
SNELL	J A B			Surgeon-Lieutenant	Royal Navy	
SNOWDON	H F		06/10/1916	Lieutenant	London Regiment (Royal Fusiliers)	T
SOAMES	J H L			Captain	RASC	
SOMERVELL	A C	OBE, Mentioned in Despatches (2)		Major	RASC and Staff	
SOMERVELL	J G H			Lieutenant	Royal Wiltshire Yeomanry	T
SOMERVELL	L C	Mentioned in Despatches		Lieutenant	RAMC	
SOUTHERN	H		18/04/1916	Second Lieutenant	Indian Army Reserve of Officers	
SOUTHERN	N	MC		Major	Royal Field Artillery	T (POW)

Surname	Initials	Honours and Awards	Died on Service	Rank	Service	T/SR etc.
SOUTHERN	R W	Mentioned in Despatches		Captain	RASC	
SOWERBY	F D	Mentioned in Despatches	01/08/1916	Second Lieutenant	4th (Queen's Own) Hussars	SR
SPALDING	W B			Major	Royal Garrison Artillery	
SPEARMAN	H E J			Second Lieutenant	Royal Garrison Artillery	
SPEKE	H		12/08/1915	Major	Lancashire Fusiliers	
SPENCE	G O	DSO, Mentioned in Despatches (3)		Lieutenant Colonel	Durham Light Infantry	T
SPENCER	W			Captain	Royal Fusiliers	
SPRECKLEY	E P	Mentioned in Despatches		Captain	RASC	
SPRINGFIELD	E O	MC, Mentioned in Despatches		Major	Norfolk Regiment	
SPRINGFIELD	G P O		12/09/1914	Captain	2nd Dragoon Guards (Queen's Bays)	
SPRINGFIELD	H O	Mentioned in Despatches	05/08/1916	Second Lieutenant	Warwickshire Yeomanry	
SPRINGFIELD	G M O		01/04/1917	Not Known	Legion of Frontiersmen	
SPRINGFIELD	T O			Not Known	Remount Department	
SPURRIER	J M			Lieutenant	Royal Field Artillery	T
STANFORD	E F			Second Lieutenant	Honorable Artillery Company	
STANSFELD	J R E DSO	Mentioned in Despatches (4)	28/09/1915	Lieutenant Colonel	Gordon Highlanders	
STANSFIELD	G H			Captain	Royal Garrison Artillery	T
STAVEACRE	F W F			Lieutenant	Royal Field Artillery	T
STEDMAN	P B K		19/08/1916	Captain	London Regiment (Royal Fusiliers)	T
STEEDS	G G			Lieutenant	RASC	
STEEL	O S			Lieutenant	Gordon Highlanders	
STEIN	R H			Lieutenant	Welsh Guards	
STEPHEN	J G	MC		Captain	Highland Light Infantry	SR
STEPHEN	J H F		11/01/1917	Lieutenant	Highland Light Infantry	SR
STEPHENS	A C			Lieutenant	Cheshire Regiment	
STEPHENSON	Guy			Captain	Royal Engineers	
STEPHENSON	R	DSO, Mentioned in Despatches (3)		Lieutenant Colonel	South Staffordshire Regiment	
STEVENS	W A			Captain	RAMC	T
STEVENSON	C M			Captain	RAMC	
STEVENSON	H B	Mentioned in Despatches	06/08/1915	Captain	2nd Queen Victoria's Own Rajput Light Infantry	
STEWART	J	DSO, Mentioned in Despatches (4), Brevet		Brevet Lieutenant-Colonel, Major (from Reserve of Officers)	Black Watch (Royal Highlanders)	
STEWART	J A			Cadet	Glasgow University OTC	

Appendix I 229

Surname	Initials	Honours and Awards	Died on Service	Rank	Service	T/SR etc.
STEWART	R C		01/07/1916	Captain	York and Lancaster Regiment	
STIKEMAN	H F C			Major	Deputy Assistant Adjutant General, HQ Ottowa	
STIRLING	N E			Flight Lieutenant	RAF	
STITT	J H	MC		Captain	Gordon Highlanders	
STOBART	W E			Major (from Reserve of Officers)	5th Dragoon Guards	
STOCKER	C J	MC, Mentioned in Despatches (3)		Captain	Indian Medical Service	
STOKES	J W G			Lieutenant	Royal Garrison Artillery	
STONE	C C			Major	Berkshire Yeomanry	T
STONE	H C			Lieutenant	RNVR	
STONE	R			Lieutenant	Sherwood Foresters (Notts and Derby Regiment)	
STONEHAM	N C			Lieutenant	Leicestershire Regiment	T
STOREY	K C B		09/04/1917	Second Lieutenant	Royal Berkshire Regiment	
STORER	J Y		25/09/1915	Major	Lincolnshire Regiment	
STRAIN	L H	OBE, DSC, Mentioned in Despatches (2), Order of the Redeemer (4th Class)		Lieutenant Colonel	RAF	
STRANG	A R			Trooper	Wellington Mounted Rifles	
STRANG	J H D	Mentioned in Despatches		Captain	Yeomanry	T
STRANGE	The Rev. C			Captain	Loyal North Lancashire Regiment	
STRANGE	D	MC		Brigade Major	Border Regiment	SR
STRICKLAND	H T			Cadet	Infantry	
STRINGER	G E			Captain	Royal Field Artillery	T
STRINGER	G V	MC, Mentioned in Despatches		Lieutenant	Royal Field Artillery	T
STRINGER	H L	Mentioned in Despatches MBE		Lieutenant	Royal Engineers	T
STRONG	H R W	MC		Lieutenant	Middlesex Regiment	
STRONGITHARM	G			Major	Gloucestershire Regiment	T
STUART	J			Not Known	Mercantile Marine	
STYER	W H		03/11/1916	Private	London Regiment (Artists' Rifles)	T
STUDHOLME	L J M	Mentioned in Despatches	09/09/1916	Captain	Leinster Regiment	
STURGES	W E			Lieutenant Colonel	Northumberland Fusiliers	

Surname	Initials	Honours and Awards	Died on Service	Rank	Service	T/SR etc.
SUFFERN	C			Surgeon Sub-Lieutenant	RNVR	
SUFFLING	N A			Sub-Lieutenant	RN	
SUMMERS	G			Captain	Royal Engineers	
SUMNER	B A			Captain	RASC	
SUMNER	H N			Lieutenant	RNVR	
SUTCLIFFE	L P			Lieutenant	Royal Engineers	T
SUTTON-JONES	C G		11/09/1918	Flight Cadet	RAF	
SWAN	J H	MC, Mentioned in Despatches (2)		Captain	Northumberland Fusiliers	T
SWANN	L E			Lieutenant	RAF	
SWANSTON	H E			Captain	Royal Field Artillery	T
SWANWICK	F B			Lieutenant	Derbyshire Yeomanry	T
SWANWICK	R K		14/09/1914	Lieutenant	Gloucestershire Regiment	SR
SWETENHAM	R			Captain	East Surrey Regiment	
SWEET	R T	DSO, Mentioned in Despatches (4)	17/10/1918	Captain	7th Gurkha Rifles	
SWIFT	G H			Captain	Yorkshire Hussars	T
SWINDELLS	J			Captain	Lancashire Fusiliers	
SWINGLER	N H			Lieutenant	Sherwood Foresters (Notts and Derby Regiment) and Tank Corps	
SWORD	E S			Lieutenant	18th Hussars	
SWORD	F W		11/05/1917	Private	London Regiment (London Scottish)	
SWORDER	F R F			Major	Gordon Highlanders	
SYKES	A W		30/09/1917	Captain	York and Lancaster Regiment	
SYKES	F A			Lieutenant	Duke of Wellington's (West Riding Regiment)	T
SYKES	K	MC and Bar, Mentioned in Despatches (2), Croix de Guerre		Captain	Duke of Wellington's (West Riding Regiment)	T
SYKES	L G		22/03/1918	Second Lieutenant	Royal Flying Corps and Royal Field Artillery	
SYMES	H			The Rev.	CF (4th Class)	
SYMINGTON	A M C L			Lieutenant	Royal Field Artillery	
SYMONDSON	F S	MC, (Italian) Silver Medal for Valour		Lieutenant	RAF	
SYMONDSON	V F		13/11/1918	Lieutenant	RAF	
SYMONS	G G	MC		Captain	Cheshire Regiment	
SYMONS	H W	Mentioned in Despatches	19/11/1914	Captain	King's Own Yorkshire Light Infantry	
TAMPLIN	C H			Lieutenant	Dorset Yeomanry (attached to Russian Commission)	T

Appendix I 231

Surname	Initials	Honours and Awards	Died on Service	Rank	Service	T/SR etc.
TAMPLIN	G R	MC, Order of Crown of Roumania		Lieutenant	Royal Garrison Artillery	T
TANNER	O C R			Not Known	Public School Battalion, Royal Fusilers	
TAPPER	M J	MC		Major	London Regiment	T
TARR	F N		18/07/1915	Lieutenant	Leicestershire Regiment	
TARRY	M J			Lieutenant	Royal Field Artillery	T
TATHAM	G B	MC	30/03/1918	Captain	Rifle Brigade	
TATTERSALL	E H	DSO, Mentioned in Despatches (2)		Lieutenant (Staff)	5th Dragoon Guards	
TATTERSALL	G K			Cadet	Household Brigade, Officers' Cadet Battalion	
TATTERSALL	R R			Lieutenant	Rifle Brigade & RAF	
TAYLOR	C G	OBE		Captain	RASC	
TAYLOR	C P			Company Quartermaster Sergeant	RASC	
TAYLOR	D E D	MC, Mentioned in Despatches (2)		Lieutenant	Royal Fusiliers	SR
TAYLOR	E G		02/05/1915	Second Lieutenant	King's Own (Royal Lancaster Regiment)	
TAYLOR	F G	AFC		Second Lieutenant	RAF	
TAYLOR	H A			Captain	Royal Garrison Artillery	
TAYLOR	H D			Second Lieutenant	Royal Garrison Artillery	SR
TAYLOR	H H R			Cadet	King's Liverpool Regiment	
TAYLOR	J	MC		Lieutenant	Royal Field Artillery	
TAYLOR	J T			Lieutenant	Royal Garrison Artillery	T
TAYLOR	P T			Captain	Royal Marine Light Infantry	
TAYLOR	S			Lieutenant	South Staffordshire Regiment	
TAYLOR	S A T		17/04/1917	Second Lieutenant	Worcestershire Regiment	
TAYLOR	W K			Lieutenant	Durham Light Infantry	
TEAPE	A T			Private	Black Watch (Royal Highlanders)	
TENBOSCH	C P		19/07/1916	Second Lieutenant	Australian Engineers	
TENNENT	J H	MC		Lieutenant	Rifle Brigade	
TENNYSON	C A			Captain	Royal Marines	
TERRY	H F			Lieutenant	Royal Field Artillery	
TETLEY	A S	Mentioned in Despatches (2), Croix de Guerre	15/11/1916	Lieutenant Colonel	Royal Marine Light Infantry	
TETLEY	G S	MC		Lieutenant	East Surrey Regiment	
TETLEY	W S			Lieutenant	Oxford and Bucks Light Infantry	

Surname	Initials	Honours and Awards	Died on Service	Rank	Service	T/SR etc.
THICKETT	H			Lieutenant	Royal Lancaster Regiment	
THOMAS	C A G			Lieutenant	Worcestershire Regiment	T
THOMAS	C F			Captain (From Reserve of Officers)	York and Lancaster Regiment	
THOMAS	D C			Captain	RASC	
THOMAS	D C W		12/11/1914	Captain	Argyll and Sutherland Highlanders	
THOMAS	D H R			Not Known	Not Known	
THOMAS	R R		28/06/1915	Petty Officer Motor Mechanic	Royal Naval Air Service	
THOMPSON	A M			Captain	RAMC	
THOMPSON	C J			Private	Motor Transport	
THOMPSON	E D			Cadet	RAF	
THOMPSON	E R	MC		Captain	Manchester Regiment	
THOMPSON	F H			Chief Petty Officer	RAF (formerly RNAS)	
THOMPSON	G K			Captain	RAMC	
THOMPSON	H G	MC		Captain	RASC	
THOMPSON	J C C		25/01/1915	Second Lieutenant	London Regiment (Artists' Rifles)	
THOMPSON	J W	Mentioned in Despatches		Lieutenant	Royal Garrison Artillery	T
THOMPSON	N D			Lieutenant	Lancashire Fusiliers	T
THOMSON	H			Lieutenant	RASC	
THOMSON	K C	Mentioned in Despatches	31/12/1914	Lieutenant	Royal Scots Fusiliers	
THOMSON	S P D		13/05/1915	Lieutenant	Leicestershire Yeomanry	T
THORNE	A H			Captain	Royal Engineers	T
THORNE	W C	OBE		Captain	Royal Engineers	
THORNLEY	F B	MC, Croix de Guerre		Captain	Royal Irish Rifles	
THRUPP	C W			Cadet	Royal Garrison Artillery	
THURBURN	E J P		09/04/1917	Second Lieutenant	Cameronians (Scottish Rifles)	
THURBURN	R W O			Lieutenant	Cameronians (Scottish Rifles)	
THURSBY	F D V			Captain	Suffolk Regiment	
THWAITES	G E			Lieutenant	RASC	
TILLARD	E R			Major	Suffolk Regiment	T
TILLIE	A R		11/05/1916	Captain	Royal Flying Corps	
TILLIE	J A		19/07/1918	Second Lieutenant	Black Watch (Royal Highlanders)	
TINKER	G L	MC		Captain	Duke of Wellington's (West Riding Regiment)	T
TIED	K			Second Lieutenant	Machine Gun Corps (Infantry)	
TOD	T L G			Second Lieutenant	Royal Horse Artillery & Royal Field Artillery	
TOD	W M			The Rev.	CF (4th Class)	

Surname	Initials	Honours and Awards	Died on Service	Rank	Service	T/SR etc.
TOLSON	J M		26/10/1918	Second Lieutenant	Royal Field Artillery	
TOMLIN	C G		09/07/1916	Lieutenant	London Regiment	T
TONGUE-CROXALL	E R			Captain	Royal Field Artillery & RAF	T
TOOTELL	G D L			Lieutenant	Guards Machine Gun Corps	
TOOTHILL	J C P			Second Lieutenant	Royal Engineers	
TOSH	J C P	MC, Mentioned in Despatches		Captain	Royal Engineers	
TOTTIE	R			Lieutenant	Royal Horse Guards	
TOWNSEND	J V		24/09/1918	Lieutenant	Yorkshire Regiment	
TOWNSEND-GREEN	H R		03/03/1915	Captain	London Regiment (Queen's Westminster Rifles)	T
TOWNSEND-GREEN	S L			Captain	London Regiment	T
TOWNSEND	F C			Captain	Rifle Brigade	
TRAVERS	E			Lieutenant	Royal Field Artillery	
TRAVERS	W I	OBE		Lieutenant Colonel	Royal Engineers	
TREACHER	A V			Lieutenant	Royal Garrison Artillery	T
TRENCH	B F			Lieutenant Colonel	Royal Marines	
TRENGROASE	R V			Captain	Gloucestershire Regiment	
TRESIDDER	C T		22/04/1916	Captain	Gloucestershire Regiment	
TROLLOPE	T C S			Second Lieutenant	Yorkshire Light Infantry	
TROLLOPE	W K		03/05/1917	Second Lieutenant	RFC	
TRUBSHAW	A R			Lieutenant	Royal Field Artillery	T
TRUBSHAW	C S			Captain	Royal Welsh Fusiliers	
TRUBSHAW	H E	Mentioned in Despatches		Major	Royal Engineers	T
TRUSTRUM	G R			Lieutenant	Royal Field Artillery	
TRYON	F C H		14/11/1916	Major	Canadian Infantry	
TRYON	G A	MC	07/11/1918	Lieutenant Colonel	King's Royal Rifle Corps	
TUCKER	H B	Mentioned in Despatches		Captain	96th Indian Army	
TUCKER	J A	Mentioned in Despatches	01/11/1914	Second Lieutenant	Royal Field Artillery	
TUFNELL	H C C			Captain	Royal Engineers	T
TURNBULL	D S		15/04/1917	Lieutenant	RFC	
TURNBULL	W A		13/11/1916	Lieutenant	Bedfordshire Regiment	SR
TURNER	A R			Lieutenant	Northants Regiment	
TURNER	C			Major (Staff)	(From Reserve of Officers)	
TURNER	C W	Mentioned in Despatches		Captain	1st Royal Dragoon Guards	

Surname	Initials	Honours and Awards	Died on Service	Rank	Service	T/SR etc.
TURNER	D W		17/02/1919	Second Lieutenant	Essex Regiment	
TURNER	G	Mentioned in Despatches		Major	South West Borderers	
TURNER	G F	Mentioned in Despatches		Lieutenant	5th Dragoon Guards	
TURNER	G R	CB		Surgeon-General	Royal Navy, Chief Consultant, Chatham	T
TURNER	M A		16/07/1916	Captain	Suffolk Regiment	
TURNER	M H			Lieutenant	Dorset Regiment	
TURTON	R D	CMG, Mentioned in Despatches (2)		Lieutenant Colonel	Governor of Military Prison	
TURTON	T C		08/05/1917	Second Lieutenant	The King's (Liverpool Regiment)	
TWEEDALE	A			Lieutenant	Manchester Regiment	
TWEEDY	A C			Major	South African Service Corps	
TYRRELL	G Y	MC		Captain	The Buffs (East Kent Regiment) & RAF	
TYRWHITT-DRAKE	E T			Captain	Berkshire Yeomanry	T
TYRWHITT-DRAKE	H W		01/03/1915	Private	Hussars	
TYSON	C E	MC		Lieutenant	Royal Field Artillery	
TYZACK	E D		15/09/1917	Second Lieutenant	Royal Flying Corps	
UDALL	E H	Mentioned in Despatches		Captain	RAMC	
UDALL	J S	Mentioned in Despatches		Lieutenant	South West Borderers	
UDALL	R G			Lieutenant	Staffordshire Yeomanry	T
UDALL	T C B	Mentioned in Despatches		Lieutenant	Machine Gun Corps (Infantry)	
USHER	J T			Major	9th Lancers	
USHER	R S			Second Lieutenant	6th Inniskillin Dragoons	
VALLANCE	H C			Not Known	London Scottish	
VAN MILLENGEN	C A M	MC and Bar		Major	Rifle Brigade	
VAN MILLENGEN	D F			Second Lieutenant	Black Watch (Royal Highlanders)	
VAN SICKLE	R K			Lieutenant	RAF	
VARDON	H G E			Lieutenant	Royal Wiltshire Yeomanry	
VAUGHAN	L R	CB, DSO, Brevets (2), Mentioned in Despatches (10)		Major-General	G S O (7th Gurkhas)	
VAUGHTON	G E		20/11/1917	Second Lieutenant	Essex Regiment	
VEITCH	D M V		08/07/1916	Captain	1st Duke of York's Lancers (Skinner's Horse)	
VERNET	R	MC, Mentioned in Despatches		Captain	Assistant Provost Marshal	

Appendix I 235

Surname	Initials	Honours and Awards	Died on Service	Rank	Service	T/SR etc.
VERNON	A S	Mentioned in Despatches (2)		Major	Oxford and Bucks Light Infantry & Machine Gun Corps	
VERNON	H W			Lieutenant	London Regiment and RAF	T
VERNON	R J	Mentioned in Despatches		Major	RAMC	
VERRY	R T			Second Lieutenant	RASC	
VICARS	W H			Major (from Reserve of Officers)	Royal Scots	
VICKERS	E B			Captain	RASC	T
VICKERS	J H	Mentioned in Despatches		Major	RAF	
VICKERS	N M		03/08/1916	Lieutenant	Yorkshire Regiment	
VICKERS	V E			Assistant Engineer	Railway Company	
VIGERS	R S G		05/04/1917	Second Lieutenant	King's Royal Rifle Corps	
VINTCENT	C A		13/04/1915	Second Lieutenant	Rifle Brigade	
VINTCENT	L H	MC		Lieutenant	Royal Garrison Artillery	
VIVIAN	H			Captain	RASC	
VON HAAST	J H			Not Known	Not Known	
WADE	H F			Major	Royal Field Artillery	T
WAGHORN	C H			Captain	RNVR & RAF	
WALDOCK	F A			Lieutenant	Royal Field Artillery	
WALDOCK	H F			Second Lieutenant	Royal Marine Light Infantry	
WALE	A		30/05/1918	Captain	Royal Field Artillery	
WALFORD	E			Captain	Royal Engineers	
WALKDEN	G G	Mentioned in Despatches		Major	Royal Field Artillery	T
WALKER	A E J			Second Lieutenant	Labour Corps	
WALKER	A S			Captain	RAMC	
WALKER	A T		30/07/1915	Second Lieutenant	Rifle Brigade	
WALKER	E J P T	OBE, Mentioned in Despatches (3)		Captain	32nd Lancers, Indian Army	
WALKER	Henry		26/07/1917	Colonel	West Yorkshire Regiment (Prince of Wales's Own)	
WALKER	Harold	Mentioned in Despatches		Captain	RAMC	
WALKER	Henry			Captain	Hertfordshire Volunteer Regiment	
WALKER	M			Lieutenant	RAF	
WALKER	M J L		03/05/1917	Second Lieutenant	Queen's Own (Royal West Kent Regiment)	
WALKER	S		09/05/1915	Private	Devonshire Regiment	

Surname	Initials	Honours and Awards	Died on Service	Rank	Service	T/SR etc.
WALLACE	D H			Lieutenant	Cameronians (Scottish Rifles)	
WALLACE	E G			Lieutenant	5th Dragoon Guards	
WALLACE	G R	MC and Bar, Mentioned in Despatches	27/08/1917	Captain	Worcestershire Regiment	T
WALLACE	H A C		22/04/1915	Captain	Canadian Infantry	
WALLICH	C C N			Captain	Devonshire Regiment and Royal Field Artillery	
WALSHAM HOW	F A	Mentioned in Despatches		Major	Worcestershire Regiment	T
WALTER	R J K			Lieutenant	RASC	
WARD	A S			Lieutenant	Hertfordshire Yeomanry	
WARD	D I			Private	New Zealand Rifles	
WARD	F S	Mentioned in Despatches	31/07/1917	Captain	The King's (Liverpool Regiment)	
WARDALE	H			Lieutenant	Royal Field Artillery	T
WARD-JACKSON	R			Captain	Leicestershire Regiment	T
WARDLE	J R		02/01/1916	Major	Glasgow Yeomanry (Queen's Own Royal)	T
WARDLE	R F			Captain	North Staffordshire Regiment & Army Service Corps	T
WARREN	L R	DFC		Captain	RAF	
WARWICK	G N			Lieutenant	RAF	
WARWICK	P			Second Lieutenant	Duke of Cornwall's Light Infantry	
WATERFIELD	A W			Captain	Northants Yeomanry	T
WATERHOUSE	T H			Lieutenant	RASC	
WATNEY	B G			Lieutenant	RNVR	
WATNEY	R W			Captain	East Surrey Regiment	T
WATSON	A C	DSO, Mentioned in Despatches (3)		Lieutenant Colonel	7th Hussars	
WATSON	C D			Lieutenant	Tank Corps	
WATSON	D			Captain	East Yorkshire Regiment and RAF	
WATSON	E C	OBE		Captain (Temporary Major)	7th Dragoon Guards (Princess Royal's)	
WATSON	I N H			Captain	Royal Engineers	SR
WATSON	S McD			Second Lieutenant	Royal Field Artillery	
WATSON	W	Brevet, Mentioned in Despatches (3)	03/05/1917	Lieutenant Colonel	Somerset Light Infantry	
WATTS	M H			Surgeon-Probationer	Royal Navy	
WATTS	E G S			Second Lieutenant	Queen's Royal West Surrey Regiment	
WAUGH	E J			Captain	General List	
WAUTON	A D B			Captain	RASC	
WAUTON	E B			Captain	Nigerian Field Force	

Appendix I

Surname	Initials	Honours and Awards	Died on Service	Rank	Service	T/SR etc.
WAYMAN	H R B	DSO, Mentioned in Despatches		Lieutenant Colonel	Northumberland Fusiliers	
WAYMAN	W L			Captain	116th Mahrattas, Indian Army	
WEATHERELL	R K			Captain	Suffolk Regiment	
WEARNE	K M		20/09/1917	Second Lieutenant	The Queen's (Royal West Surrey Regiment)	
WEAVER	A B			Lieutenant	East Yorkshire Regiment	T
WEBB	D V	MC	16/10/1918	Captain	Leicestershire Regiment	
WEBB	H E			Lieutenant	Royal Engineers	
WEBB	V P			Not Known	Public School Battalion, Royal Fusiliers	
WEBB	W H			Major	Staffordshire Yeomanry	T
WEBSTER	A P			Lieutenant	Grenadier Guards	
WEBSTER	J R		09/09/1916	Captain	London Regiment (Royal Fusiliers)	T
WEEKS	F M	Mentioned in Despatches	11/04/1918	Captain	Northumberland Fusiliers	
WEIR	I E R			Captain	126th Baluchistan, Indian Army	
WELCH	H			Major	Sherwood Foresters (Notts and Derby Regiment)	T
WELCH	T			Captain	RASC	T
WELLS	C B	DSO, Mentioned in Despatches		Lieutenant Colonel	Essex Regiment	T
WELLS	C J			Lieutenant	Sherwood Foresters (Notts and Derby Regiment)	T
WEST	H R A			Not Known	King Edward's Horse	
SACKVILLE-WEST	K F	Twice Mentioned in Despatches	29/06/1921	Captain	2nd Dragoon Guards (Queen's Bays)	
WEST	W R J R			Cadet	Royal Military Academy, Woolwich	
WESTMACOTT	H R	Mentioned in Despatches		Major	Welsh Regiment	
WESTOLL	J			Captain	Durham Light Infantry	T
WHEATLEY	A R	Mentioned in Despatches		Major	East Surrey Regiment	T
WHEATLEY	R		24/11/1916	Second Lieutenant	Sherwood Foresters (Notts and Derby Regiment)	
WHETHERLY	W S	DSO, Mentioned in Despatches (3), Brevet		Major (Brevet Lieutenant-Colonel)	7th Dragoon Guards (Princess Royal's)	
WHILLIS	R W			Second Lieutenant	Northumberland Fusiliers	
WHITBY	E V			Captain	RAMC	
WHITBY	T F			Lieutenant	Royal Welsh Fusiliers	
WHITE	B G	Mentioned in Despatches (2)		Staff Captain	1st Australian Division	
WHITE	C V			Second Lieutenant	Machine Gun Corps (Infantry)	

Surname	Initials	Honours and Awards	Died on Service	Rank	Service	T/SR etc.
WHITE	R H	MC		Lieutenant	King's Own Yorkshire Light Infantry	
WHITE	W L	DSO		Major	Royal Field Artillery	
WHITEHEAD	C			Lieutenant	Royal Field Artillery	
WHITEHEAD	F	Ordre de Couronne, Croix de Guerre		Lieutenant	Duke of Lancaster's Own Yeomanry	T
WHITEHEAD	H			Captain	Loyal North Lancashire Regiment	T
WHITEHURST	H			Lieutenant	Loyal North Lancashire Regiment and Royal Engineers	
WHITLING	H T M			Major	RAMC (Red Cross)	
WHITMORE	P S			Second Lieutenant	RAF	
WHITTAKER	J			Lieutenant	East Lancs. Regiment	
WHITSON	H T		05/09/1918	Captain	The King's (Liverpool Regiment)	
WHITSON	R S	MC		Lieutenant	Royal Scots	
WHITWELL	F A	Croix de Guerre		Lieutenant	RASC	
WHITWELL	H			Lieutenant	RAMC	
WHITWELL	J F			Not Known	British Red Cross Motor Ambulance Corps	
WHITWORTH	C W	MBE		Captain	West Yorkshire Regiment (Prince of Wales's Own)	T
WHITWORTH	R B	MC		Captain	Royal Field Artillery	T
WICKE	T E			Second Lieutenant	King's Royal Rifle Corps	
WIGG	C			Corporal	Royal Engineers	
WIGFULL	C			Second Lieutenant	London Regiment	T
WILCOX	J J	MC, Mentioned in Despatches (2)		Captain	Somerset Light Infantry	SR
WILKIE	H G	Mentioned in Despatches		Captain	Royal Field Artillery	
WILKIE	R S			Lieutenant	Royal Marine Light Infantry	
WILKINSON	C L G			Captain	King's Royal Rifle Corps	SR
WILKINSON	F C E		25/04/1915	Private	Australian Infantry, A.I.F.	
WILKINSON	G G		01/07/1916	Serjeant	Middlesex Regiment	
WILKINSON	G S			Captain	RASC	
WILKINSON	Sir P S	KCMG, CB, CMG, Mentioned in Despatches (4), Commander of the Crown of Italy		Major-General	Colonel, Northumberland Fusiliers	
WILKINSON	W T	DSO and Bar, Mentioned in Despatches (5)		Lieutenant Colonel	King's Own Scottish Borderers	
WILLCOX	B B	MC		Captain	London Regiment	
WILLCOX	C W			Captain	RAF	

Surname	Initials	Honours and Awards	Died on Service	Rank	Service	T/SR etc.
WILLEY	H	Mentioned in Despatches		Major	Royal Garrison Artillery	
WILLIAMS	E			Lieutenant	Yorkshire Regiment	T
WILLIAMS	G G A			Lieutenant	5th Dragoon Guards and RAF	
WILLIAMS	P G		05/06/1916	Fleet Surgeon	Royal Navy	
WILLIAMS	H J	DSO, Mentioned in Despatches (2)		Major	1st Dragoon Guards	
WILLIAMS	P S			Captain	RASC	
WILLIAMS	S S			Major	Suffolk Yeomanry	T
WILLIAMSON	E B			Lieutenant	Royal Fusiliers	
WILLIAMSON	H C			Lieutenant	Royal Field Artillery	
WILLIAMSON	J N			Lieutenant	Life Guards	
WILLIAMSON	J S			Cadet	RAF	
WILLIAMSON	L A			Second Lieutenant	London Regiment	
WILLIS	G A A	MC		Lieutenant	Royal Engineers	
WILLIS	H			Captain	Royal Garrison Artillery	
WILLIS	J C T			Cadet	Royal Military Academy, Woolwich	
WILLOUGHBY	L B			Major	Assistant Inspector, Quartermaster General Services	
WILMOTT	J H			Second Lieutenant	Royal Garrison Artillery	
WILLS	A G	MC		Lieutenant	Cambridgeshire Regiment and Machine Gun Corps	T
WILSHIN	J V	MC		Lieutenant	Royal Field Artillery	
WILSON	C E			Lieutenant	1st Dragoon Guards	
WILSON	Charles E			Lieutenant	Royal Irish Rifles	
WILSON	D			Captain	Royal Field Artillery	T
WILSON	H	OBE, Mentioned in Despatches		Major	Royal Garrison Artillery	T
WILSON	J A (DSO)			Lieutenant Colonel	Gurkha Rifles (Indian Army)	
WILSON	J M			Captain	Life Guards	
WILSON	J R			Captain	Lanarkshire Yeomanry	T
WILSON	L N			Lieutenant	Royal Field Artillery	
WILSON	T J		21/03/1918	Second Lieutenant	Royal Field Artillery	
WILSON	W			Captain	Derbyshire Yeomanry	
WIMBLE	H R		03/05/1915	Corporal	London Regiment (London Rifle Brigade)	
WINDLE	M S			Captain	Royal Field Artillery	
WINGFIELD-DIGBY	F J W			Cadet	RAF	
WINTER	C E			Lieutenant	RAF	
WINTON	A Seton-			Lieutenant	Northumberland Fusiliers	
WINTON	B L Seton-			Lieutenant	RASC	

Surname	Initials	Honours and Awards	Died on Service	Rank	Service	T/SR etc.
WITHINGTON	R L	MC, Mentioned in Despatches		Captain	Royal Engineers	
WITHY	B		02/07/1916	Lieutenant	The King's (Liverpool Regiment)	
WITT	H T			Sergeant-Major	Inns of Court OTC	
WOLTON	R A G			Lieutenant	Royal Garrison Artillery	T
WOOD	C E			Sergeant	Labour Corps	
WOOD	C K	Mentioned in Despatches		Colonel	Royal Engineers	
WOOD	J Hatton			Captain	RASC	
WOOD	J I			Lieutenant	Border Regiment	
WOOD	R B		12/10/1916	Second Lieutenant	Border Regiment	
WOOD	T C L			Lieutenant	Northumberland Hussars and RAF	T
WOOD	W A	MM		Private	RASC	
WOODGATE	H F			Major	Special List	
WOODHEAD	R			Lieutenant	West Yorkshire Regiment (Prince of Wales's Own)	
WOODS	E J		09/10/1917	Lieutenant	West Yorkshire Regiment (Prince of Wales's Own)	
WOODSEND	H D	Silver Medal for Valour (Italy)		Captain	Royal Field Artillery	
WOODSEND	P D			Captain	RASC	
WOOLERTON	E N C			Captain	Oxford and Bucks Light Infantry	T
WOOLLEY	V J			Captain	RAMC	
WOOSTER	F G			Lieutenant	Norfolk Yeomanry	T & POW
WORSLEY	P			Second Lieutenant	Royal Engineers	
WORRALL	B			Lieutenant	Royal Scots Greys	
WORRALL	P			Lieutenant	Army Service Corps	T
WRAGG	N J		18/07/1916	Lieutenant	South Staffordshire Regiment	
WRENFORD	C R B			Lieutenant	Royal Berkshire Regiment	
WRIGHT	C S			Lieutenant	Royal Engineers	T
WRIGHT	D A			Lieutenant	RAF	
WRIGHT	E B Fitzherbert			Captain	Royal Field Artillery	
WRIGHT	H	MC		Captain	Gordon Highlanders	
TATTERSHALL (FORMERLY WRIGHT)	J W W			Gunner	Royal Field Artillery	
WRIGHT	N			Private	RASC	T
WRIGLEY	A E			Captain	Manchester Regiment	
WRIGLEY	W G	Mentioned in Despatches		Captain	Duke of Wellington's (West Riding Regiment)	T
WYNN	R T B			Lieutenant	RAF	

Surname	Initials	Honours and Awards	Died on Service	Rank	Service	T/SR etc.
WYNNE	C H L			Lieutenant	Leicestershire Regiment	
WYNNE	E E		08/06/1917	Captain	Leicestershire Regiment	
WYNNE	H E S	CMG, DSO, Mentioned in Despatches (5)		Lieutenant Colonel	Royal Field Artillery	
YEATMAN	A A B			Private	Honorable Artillery Company	
YEATMAN	M B			Lieutenant	Not Known	
YOUNG	A D B			The Rev.	CF (4th Class)	
YOUNG	C E			Lieutenant	Royal Field Artillery	
YOUNG	E C			Major	Royal Field Artillery	
YOUNG	G C			Sub-Lieutenant	RNVR	
YOUNG	G P			Lieutenant	Loyal North Lancashire Regiment	
YOUNG	H			Lieutenant	Gloucestershire Regiment	T
YOUNG	J D	MC, Mentioned in Despatches		Major	Buckinghamshire Hussars	T
YOUNG	M C B K			Captain	Duke of Wellington's (West Riding Regiment)	POW
YOUNG	R A		22/12/1914	Second Lieutenant	Royal Munster Fusiliers	
YOUNG	R A B	OBE, Mentioned in Despatches		Major	APD	
YOUNG	R P			Not Known	Honorable Artillery Company	
YOUNGER	R D			Lieutenant	3rd Dragoon Guards	
ZINKEISEN	I V			Cadet	London University OTC	

Appendix II

Record of Service for the Assistant Schoolmasters of Uppingham School

Surname	Initials	Honours and Awards	Died on Service	Rank	Service	
Barker	A			Captain	Not Known	T
Bashford	F G			Lieutenant	School OTC Contingent	
Bland	C H	TD		Major	Leicestershire Regiment	
Burnaby	R B			Lieutenant	School OTC Contingent	
Champion	H H			Captain	School OTC Contingent	
Colley	W H	OBE		Lieutenant-Colonel	Yorkshire Regiment & Manchester Regiment	
Griffith	W S H			Captain	School OTC Contingent	SR
Habershon	S H		10/04/1918	Lieutenant	Suffolk Regiment	
Hale	E N	Croix de Guerre		Captain	Royal Engineers, Black Watch and GSO2 GHQ	
Hirst	F E			Second Lieutenant	Labour Corps	
Hughes	T G			Lieutenant	Leicestershire Regiment	T
Johnson	B J			Lieutenant	School OTC Contingent	
Jones	C H	CMG, TD, Legion of Honour		Lieutenant-Colonel	Leicestershire Regiment	
Lloyd-Jones	I G	TD		Major	Not Known	
Lumsden	J A			Cadet	Royal Garrison Artillery	
Mountfort	C C			Captain	School OTC Contingent	
Oberhoffer	G H J		18/02/1916	Private	Royal Fusiliers	
Owen	R H			Lieutenant	School OTC Contingent	
Raynor	K			Captain	Black Watch	
Roberts	A B			Lieutenant	School OTC Contingent	
Shea	R P	Mentioned in Despatches (3)		Major	Leicestershire Regiment	

Surname	Initials	Honours and Awards	Died on Service	Rank	Service
Small	R E	DCM		Regimental Sergeant Major	Leicestershire Regiment
Sterndale Bennett	R	TD		Major	School OTC Contingent
Street	F		07/07/1916	Lieutenant	Royal Fusiliers
Thorne	H S			Lieutenant	Royal Scots
West	Elsa			Music Sister	VAD

Appendix III

Account of the Dedication of the School War Memorial 16 October 1921

December, 1921.

THE SCHOOL MAGAZINE.

No. 466.   Vol. lix.

EDITORIAL.

THE end of term and the publication of the School Magazine are both upon us; and as regards the former, at any rate, it does not seem too soon to speak of its having been successful. A threatened outbreak of scarlet fever fortunately did not spread; the six days' isolation of the School House was not long enough to interfere in any way with the term's programme.

The Fifteen have been giving a good account of themselves; and the football throughout the School has been very keen.

The centenary of the birth of Edward Thring was observed on November 29th; a special service in Chapel was followed by the presentation of the Thring Medal, and speeches in the Schoolroom, after which a wreath was laid on the grave. A full account of this will appear in our next issue.

DEDICATION OF THE SCHOOL WAR MEMORIAL.

[*By kind permission of the "Grantham Journal."*]

"THEIR glory shall not be blotted out, and their name liveth to all generations." With this deep feeling uppermost in the minds of all present, the Memorial Shrine erected to perpetuate the names of 443 Old Uppinghamians

234 DEDICATION OF THE SCHOOL WAR MEMORIAL.

who laid down their lives in the Great War was dedicated, in the Uppingham School Chapel, on Sunday afternoon, October 16th. In addition to the School, very many of the parents and other relatives and friends of the fallen were present, the spacious building being completely filled, and the service was of the most impressive and memorable kind. The dedication ceremony was performed by the Right Rev. Cecil Boutflower, D.D., Bishop of Southampton, and an old Uppinghamian.

The Shrine completes another portion of the three-fold scheme to commemorate the great sacrifice made by those whose names are thus recorded, and is built on the south side of the Chapel, from which entrance to it is given. With regard to the memorial scheme as a whole, another part of it, which has for some time been in existence, is the providing for the education of sons of Old Uppinghamians who fell in the war, and sons of Old Boys who, because of the war, were not able without help, to come to the School; while the third phase is a large Memorial Hall, which it is hoped to put in hand very soon. The subscriptions for the whole work have come from Old Boys, parents of those who fell, and from many friends of the School associated in any way with it.

The Executive Committee consists of the Head Master (the Rev. R. H. Owen, M.A.), Sir Arthur J. Fludyer, Bart. (Chairman of Governors), Mr. Stanley Christopherson, O.U., Mr. Hugh Rotherham, O.U., Mr. T. E. Monckton, Hr. H. Willey, O.U., Colonel W. R. Glover, C.M.G., D.S.O., O.U., with Mr. J. P. Graham as Hon. Secretary. The War Shrine Committee composed originally the Head Master, the late Canon Rawnsley, the late Mr. E. W. Hornung, Sir W. H. Ellis, G.B.E., Mr. Stanley Christopherson, with Mr. Graham as Secretary.

DEDICATION OF THE SCHOOL WAR MEMORIAL. 235

The designing of the Memorial building dedicated on Sunday was entrusted to Mr. Ernest Newton, R.A., O.U., and Lieut.-Col. W. G. Newton, M.C., his son, and the work is characterised by consummate skill and appropriateness, and was greatly admired. The memorial takes the form of an octagonal shrine, entered from the Chapel on the south, and built on the axis of the main entrance to the Chapel. One side of the shrine is taken up with the entrance, and the other seven sides are divided into three panels each, giving 21 panels in all, and 21 names are inscribed on each panel. The floor and the walls up to the cornice are of Portland and Ancaster stone, and the upper part of the interior is of English oak, carved and finished in gold and blue. Round the cornice are the following eight "watchwords," sentences taken from Holy Scripture, and chosen by the late Mr. E. W. Hornung, O.U.:—"With perfect heart they offered willingly to the Lord"; "That jeoparded their lives unto the death"; "They were a wall unto us both by night and day"; "Their sound went out into all the earth"; "Therefore they shall be mine in the day when I make up my jewels"; "Thine, O Lord, is the greatness, and the power, and the glory, and the victory"; "Make them to be numbered with Thy Saints in glory everlasting." At the eight internal angles of the cornice are angels offering the flowers of the Nations. The names upon the panels are shallow cut and gilded in William Morris Kelmscott type. The School seal is let into the floor in black and white. All the light to the Shrine comes from a crown of windows in the roof, and the sun moving round gilds each panel in turn. The outside of the building is in Weldon stone, with lead roof, and surmounted by a gilded ball and cross. The contractors for the work were Messrs. John Thompson and Son, of Peterborough.

DEDICATION OF THE SCHOOL WAR MEMORIAL.

THE SERVICE.

The dedication service took place at four o'clock, and while the congregation was assembling, appropriate selections were played by the organist, Mr. R. Sterndale Bennett. As the School clergy, including the Head Master, and the Bishop of Southampton, proceeded to their places, the hymn, "Hark! the sound of Holy voices," was sung. The special form of service was taken by the Head Master, and the lesson, from Wisdom iii, 1 to 10 v., was read by the Rev. R. F. McNeile. Psalm 23, "The Lord is my Shepherd," was chanted, and during the singing of the hymn, "Holy Father, in Thy Mercy," the Bishop and clergy went to the Shrine, which was then dedicated by his Lordship, "To the glory of God, and in memory of those who gave their lives for England and for Freedom." A period of silence, all kneeling, followed, and after the hymn, "Holy, Holy, Holy! Lord God Almighty," the Bishop of Southampton gave an address, based on the text: "I will not offer burnt offering unto the Lord my God of that which doth cost me nothing," 2nd Samuel xxiv., 24 v. David's spiritual instinct when he had the unexpected chance of a cheap deal, the preacher observed, probably taught him that in God's eyes everything was worth what it cost, and that there was no such thing in his mind as a cheap religion. This was not a funeral service, or anything like it, but a day of proud and humble Thanksgiving. These men for whom they met to give thanks that day certainly did not offer that which cost them nothing. In what sense they offered to the Lord their God he would not then discuss, but they offered and gave up everything that life held dear. And it was no conscript offering. He would not dwell on the pride felt at their voluntary three million men, whether the policy of it were wise or not. He knew that Japanese trained under a

DEDICATION OF THE SCHOOL WAR MEMORIAL.

universal conscript system, and proud of their deep-rooted patriotism, had assured him that were matters left to voluntary enrolment, there would be no "first 100,000" from the Universities, the Colleges, and Higher Schools of Japan. That, they said, was a British speciality, and the spirit they knew was not limited to the public schools and colleges, even if it shone there with special lustre. Besides those whose names—443 of them—were recorded on that memorial, there were others, he did not know their numbers, whom the School gave, who, though it did not happen to them to die, had come out of the struggle, blinded, maimed, or broken for life, and whose sacrifice was sometimes the harder of the two. There were thousands of such around them, and they were daily confronted by their uncomplaining good cheer, the noblest kind of courage. They could not forget these in the high honour and thanksgiving of that day. Then, if words could do it, they would add their tribute of remembering gratitude and sympathy to that great multitude of mourning hearts, parents and wives and dear ones, who did not keep back their best, and had had to pay the bill of cost through it all. One of these, once a youngster in the School with himself, was Ernest Hornung, who gave his only son, and who told in almost his last book the strange story of the finding of his boy's grave, and behind which was an inspiration of Christian faith and unforgetting pride in Uppingham. Among such a great company of sacrifice, they took their stand that day, safe and free, to make their memorial of honour to them and praise to God In such an hour they would be real in all they did. Englishmen believed they did not like sentiment, and were sure they could not endure humbug, but no one who had heard of the pathetic songs contributed to a seamen's "sing-song," or at a football "smoker" of the simpler sort, would believe the

238   DEDICATION OF THE SCHOOL WAR MEMORIAL.

former, and when it came to funerals and the like, there was a certain amount of the latter going about. In connection with war memorials, of which a Bishop naturally got more than his share, it was quite certain that a good deal of humbug was talked, and sung, and sometimes preached. "For all the saints, who from their labours rest," how often that was sung on these occasions. But what about the blackguards who fell in the war as well? He wanted to give thanks for them too; but did they expect him to call them saints for the occasion? We were not Mahommedans. We did not believe that every man was a saint if only he got killed in battle, that to die fighting was to be sure of going straight to heaven. He remembered that saints, in the New Testament use of the word, were very mixed characters, and that the saints at Ephesus to whom St. Paul addressed his letters had still to be advised to give up stealing and not to get drunk. Shaky Christians evidently, but they had gone in for being on God's side, and meant to follow Christ. They knew as a fact that many who fell in the war, some of whom perhaps they were fond, were very far from being saints in any such sense. And yet, if there were one such among their Old Boys, he felt they should put up his name just the same, and give thanks for him with the rest. When he read of the things that these men did, he felt sure that somehow God was behind it, and that He had not done with them. So he would be humble in his prayers, and avoid all Mahommedan humbug, and all un-Christian talk, but commend them to God's fatherly care in confidence that they could never be beyond His love, and give thanks that day for what His spirit made them do. He said they would be real, and please God, practical too; so would they best honour the men who fell. In regard to the Great Law of

Sacrifice, everything was worth what it cost, and not a penny more. In the moral world, it was true, and even, he thought, in the intellectual. There were some few there who could recollect the masterful voice within the walls adjoining those, which proclaimed in language more memorable than ornate: "You may talk what rot you like, but learning is pain, and there are some boys who never will take the pains necessary to learn, except——." The conclusion of that wise saying, remarked the Bishop, he would prefer to tell them out of Chapel. Mr. Thring did not live to encounter the full tide of theories that would remove everything unpleasant from the path of learning; had he done so they would have had cause to remember his words. Think of the degradation in trying to make the high service of Almighty God appear easy and cheap to the eyes of men, watering down our Lord's high standards of life, providing ornate services for the fastidious, and P.S.A.'s for the crowd, eliminating the Cross from religion, when all the time everything was worth what it cost, and not a penny more! The lesson these men on their memorial had left, in his way of thinking of it, did not belong chiefly to school-days or worship hours, but to the whole life of our lads to-day and for many years to come when they had left those walls behind. In a world bleeding and staggering from the greatest war in history, did they suppose there was any easy way, any short cut, to get things righted, but through sweat and sacrifice all round? Were they such fools as to think that, after wasting life-blood and treasure for five long years they could settle down to softer jobs, shorter hours, and bigger money than before the war? Yet that was what a majority of the people appeared to have thought for nigh three years past, and every son of this or other privileged Schools who was trying to live again to pre-war standards of self-aggrandisement or idle devotion to sport and pleasure, was, by his example, helping them to think it. Should their brother go to the war and fall in the fight, and they loaf around in safety, seeking a good time? Was that all they could do for those who died, many of them in the hope to make a new world and a better England? The dreams of a happier world to dawn automatically after the war, with which they cheered themselves during the darkest days, had not come true. The optimists were hard to find; diplomacy seemed to fail. No one, he said, could get the world righted but Jesus Christ, and there was no way but His, the way of sacrifice. He could not do His part to save the world but by the Cross, and did they suppose they could? There was no such thing as cheap blessings for men, or nations, or fellows at School. There were moral skunks who desired cheap religion, who wanted to be Christians on the sly, but our Lord said, if any man would come after Him, let him take up his cross and follow Him. That was the secret of the only way, to follow Him, the Lord of all self-sacrifice and chivalry. The sacrifice of re-making the world, and building the kingdom of God here, must be faced. It was not just honour or duty they had to follow, but their Lord and Leader Himself, made perfect, through suffering, by His Cross.

The service concluded with the hymn, "Ye Holy Angels Bright," and the general thanksgiving and Blessing.

A number of floral tributes were placed in the Shrine, both before and after the service. The late Head Master (the Rev. H. W. McKenzie, M.A.) was amongst those present on Sunday.

241

THE SHRINE.

DEATH called them, and so young they sped
    Where Honour and where Duty led!
What gift can our great debt repay?
The easy tribute of a tear?
Praise and thanksgiving, memory dear?
    Nay, is there yet no better way?

We build a temple of men's hands,
Our Shrine shall ever, while it stands,
    Recall each well-beloved name;
Theirs was no offering men may buy
With money—Faith and Courage high,
    The incense of Love's golden flame.

Could we but call "the meek-eyed Peace"
From Heaven to Earth, and find release
    From envy, hatred, malice, pride,
Thus only might we pay our debt
And be forgiven, and forget
    Our sorrow that so young they died.

Then should we know that Death may be
Forgotten in their Victory,
    And men their baser selves disdain;
Then only shall we cease to mourn
When Envy dieth, and Love is born
    From out the travail of their pain.

                    H.

Appendix IV

Order of Memorial Service 6 July 1919

UPPINGHAM SCHOOL

Mementote cum pietate et desiderio huiusce scholae alumnorum qui pro patriae salute ac fide dimicantes mortem nobilem oppetierunt

July 6, 1919

Commemoration of the Members of the School who have laid down their lives in the War

Abel, John Duncan
Addington, Geoffrey William
Aizlewood, Leslie Peach
Alexander, Harry
Allen, Wellesley Roe
Almack, Edward Poulton
Anderson, Cecil Francis Edward
Archer, Ronald Hedley
Arnold, Alfred Huntriss
Ash, Basil Claudius
Atkins, Herbert de Carteret
Averdieck, George Gerald
Aytoun, Rolls Merlin Graham
Bailey, Clive Maxwell
Bailey, Donald Frank
Baker, Joseph Leffler
Balloch, Humphrey Colquhoun
Bamford, Edwin Scott
Bancroft, Noel
Banks, James
Barber, John Christian
Bardswell, Hamilton Ainsworth
Barnsley, Alan Arthur
Bascombe, Cecil Reginald
Bates, Raymond Plumptre
Beatson, Walter William Gordon
Beck, Bernard
Bedford, Seaton Hall
Beer, Arthur Henry
Bennett, Harold
Benning, Murray Stuart
Bernhard, John Edward
Bewicke, Calverley George
Bishop, Charles Gamble
Blumer, John
Bolland, Theodore Julian
Bolus, Gerald Warren
Borrer, John Maximilian
Boston, Laurence
Bourke, Eustace George Walter
Bowman, William Powell
Brandon, Arthur Chester
Brandreth, Lyall
Brewis, Alfred Percy
Brewis, John Arthur Gardner
Briggs, Claude
Bright, Archibald Viccars
Brittain, Edward Harold
Broad, Alfred Evans
Broadbent, Edgar Richard
Brock, George Selby
Brodie, Philip Wyndham
Brooks, Walter Leslie
Brown, Anthony William Scudamore
Brown, Harold Montagu
Brown, Richard Walter
Browning, Charles Stewart
Bryson, George Landen Unite
Bulkeley, Llewelyn Alfred Henry
Bunce, Hugh Pollock
Burnaby, Hugo Beaumont
Burne, Newdigate Owen
Burrell, William
Caldecott, John Leslie
Callard, Stanley Edwyn
Carr, Stanley Theodore
Carter-Wood, Joseph Alan
Caunter, Richard Lawrence Luscombe

4

Chaloner, Richard Godolphin Hume
Chambers-Hunter, Charles Allardyce Jopp
Chapman, Henry Reynolds
Charlton, John Macfarlan
Charlton, Robert
Checkland, Beaumont Montmorency
Chester, Lewis Charles Bagot
Chipman, Rupert Borrodaile
Christmas, Dudley Vyvyan
Church, Geoffrey William
Clarke, Horace Yelverton Chatfield
Clegg, Robert Leslie
Cliff, Grosvenor Talbot
Clode-Baker, George Edward
Cohan, Edward Molyneux
Cole, Leslie Stuart
Cole, Nigel Edwin Fitzroy
Colley, William Arthur
Collinge, Wharton Rye
Collings-Wells, John Stanhope
Constantine, Herbert Norman
Cook, George Trevor Roper
Cooke, Guy Proudfoot
Cooper, Cecil Fletcher
Corbett, David Bertram
Cousans, Guy Newson
Cowan, John Orr Craig
Cowell, George Edmond Maurice
Cree, James Fleming
Croft, Bernard
Crosby, John Claud Parry
Crosby, Timothy Hugh Stowell
Crosley, Cecil
Cull, Arthur Tulloch
Cumming, Frederick Kenneth
Cunningham, Charles Clemence Francis
Currey, Vere Fortrey
Cutts, Thomas Bernard
Dacres, Leonard Seymour Lambert
Dalziel, Gordon Noel Coleman
D'Arcy-Irvine, Charles William
Darbishire, Lionel Charles
Daukes, Archibald Henry
Davenport, Thomas Lowe
Davies, Henry Llanover
Denman-Jubb, Cyril Oswald
de Pass, Crispin Asahel
de Pierres, Eric Noel
de Pledge, Edward Charles Man
Deuchar, Alexander Guthrie
Dickinson, Digby Cecil Caleb
Dickson, William Tillie
Dow, Walter
Dowson, Humphrey
Dudley, Charles Leonard
Dunn, Gwynne Morgan
Dunn, Philip Morgan
Durlacher, Philip Alfred
Dusgate, Richard Edmund
Dust, Frank William
Edwards, James Harry
Eiloart, Cyril Howard
Eiloart, Frank Oswald
Emsley, John Alfred
Fair, George Patrick Conroy
Farmiloe, George Frederick
Fawcett, Leopold George Frederick Elliott
Fawcett, Robert Heath
Feilden, Oswald Henry
Field, Hassall Dyer
Field, Samuel Hatten
Fletcher, John Holland Ballett
Forrest, Charles Evelyn
Forsell, Alan Richard
Forster, Christopher Jack
Francis, John
Fraser, Henry Hubert

5

Freeman, Edward
Frost, Edmund Lionel
Gaffikin, George Horner
Gamon, Sydney Percival
Garnons-Williams, Percy
Garrod, Roland Perceval
Garvey, Ivan Harold
Gaussen, Aratoon William David
Geary-Smith, Alec
Gemmell, Kenneth Alexander
Gemmell, Stuart Sterling
Geoghegan, William George Richard
Gilpin, Ernest Henry
Glaisby, Kenneth
Gleed, John Victor Ariel
Glover, Richard Bowie Gaskell
Gold, Charles René
Greenhill, Thomas Watson
Greenwell, Thomas William Maddison
Gwynne, Edward Claypole
Hackforth-Jones, Arthur
Hall, Allan Bernard
Hall, Thomas Storey Inglis
Hamilton, George
Harman, John Augustus
Harrison, Cyril Cazalet
Harrison, Charles Gordon
Harrison, Digby Greenwood
Headington, Arthur Hutton
Healey, Richard Elkanah Hownam
Heath, Geoffrey
Heblethwaite, Christopher John
Hedderwick, Guy
Henderson, Duncan Frank
Herron, Walter Fitzroy
Hess, Henry
Hewitt, George Alfred Guest
Heywood, Leonard John
Heywood, Stanley
Hicking, Francis Joseph
Hicking, George Graham
Hickling, John Christopher
Hill, Philip Aubrey
Hillman, Leslie Howis
Hind, Laurence Arthur
Hobson, Owen Ellis
Hodding, Henry Ellis
Holmes, Reginald Eden
Holt, Leslie
Hooley, Basil Terah
Hopkins, Charles Randolph Innes
Horridge, John Leslie
Horsfall, Cedric Fawcett
Hume, George Minchin
Huntriss, Cyril John
Huntriss, Harold Edwards
Huntriss, William
Inglis, Rupert Charles
Jalland, Stephen
Johns, William A.
Johnson, Bernard Angas
Johnstone, Gilbert Lumley
Jones, Eric Arthur Owen
Kellie, Leslie Laurance
Kendall, James Lionel
Kennard, Willoughby Arthur
Kerr, Arthur Douglas Garnett Odel
Keyser, Richard Norman
Knaggs, Victor St. George
Knight, Philip Clifford
Knights-Smith, Bernard Arthur
Knights-Smith, Philip Arnold
Laing, James Gordon
Lascelles, Arthur Moore
Lawes, Thomas Eric
Laws, Philip Umfreville
Lawson, Oswald Head
Leach, Grey de Lèche
Leake, George Arthur
Lee, Cedric

6

Leighton, Roland Aubrey
Leney, Bertram
Lennard, Edward Stuart Russell
Lewis, Donald Swain
Lewis, Harold
Lloyd-Jones, John
Lord, Evelyn Geoffrey
Longmore, Charles Gerald
Lumgair, Robert Robertson Morrison
MacDaniel, Francis George Vernon
MacIntosh, John
Mackenzie, Ulric Knut
Mackie, James Logan
Mackirdy, Charles David Scott
McGeagh, William Morice
MacIver, Ian
McKergow, Robert Dudley Wilson
Malinson, Emil August Hennig
Mann, Humphrey Dalla
Mann, Robert Lamplough
Mansel-Carey, Spencer Lort Mansel
Mansergh, Charles James Carden
Marriage, Andrew Warner
Marriott, Frederick Ernest
Marriott, Norman Clark
Marsh, Francis Bedford
Marsh, John Lockwood
Martin, John Sinclair
Mason, George William
Mather, Noel Edward
Mathews, Hugh Spencer
Mathieson, Kenneth Ronald
Maufe, Statham Broadbent
Maule, Edward Barry
Maxwell, Harley Hyslop
Meakin, Kenneth William Glenny
Meakin, Walter Kendrick
Meares, Cecil Stanley
Merriman, Gordon
Michelmore, Jeffery Edwards Morton
Millar, Robert Curie
Milne, Eric Sutcliffe
Milward, Philip Henry
Monaghan, Denis Laurence
Moore, Roger Ludovic
Moreton, Norman Charles Henry Macdonald
Morgan, George Hamilton
Morgan, George Hungerford
Morgan, Ronald Charles Wybrow
Morton, Elys Arthur
Moyes, Wilfred Blake
Mylne, Euan Louis
Napier, William Lennox
Neame, Eric Gilson
Nevill, Cuthbert St. John
Newbold, Philip
Newton, William Trafford
Nicholson, Alan Gifford
Nicholson, Harold William
Nicholson, Laurence Cail
Nimmo, William Leslie
Norris, Edward Fraser
Norris, Kenneth Arthur Annesley
Northrop, John Eric
Norton, Tom Edgar Grantley
Oldrey, Robert John Blatchford
Osborne, Brian
Palmer, William Lucius
Parr, Wilfrid Wharton
Payn, Reginald Wallace
Peacock, Thomas Gordon
Pearce, Geoffrey Vincent
Penfold, Jeffery Bradley
Phipps, Christopher Leckonby
Pickering, Thomas
Pickup, William Howard
Pilgrim, Stephen Argent Ffennell
Ponsford, Frank Henry Savory

7

Popple, George Marsden
Powell, Maurice
Powell, Townsend George
Pratt, Lionel Henry
Pridmore, Percy Malin
Purser, Frank Dulcken
Pym, Francis Leslie Melville
Rabone, Arthur Brian
Ransome, Herbert Fullarton
Ratcliff, John Edward
Raven, Frederick Gifford
Raven, Henry Reginald Charles Earle
Redfern, Samuel Lees
Redmayne, Giles Blomfield
Reeves-Smith, Denys
Richardson, Victor
Rickards, Hew Wardrop Brooke
Ridgway, Henry Akroyd
Ridley, Clement Archie
Rigg, Samuel
Rigg, Stanley
Riley, Thomas
Roberts, James Thursby
Robertson, John Alexander Tower
Robinson, Frank Bradbury
Rohde, Harold Turner
Roughton, Thomas Hende
Rowley, Gerald
Royle, John Bedward
Ryder, William Harold
Sales, Norman
Salter, Geoffrey Charles Taylor
Sanderson, Archibald James
Satterthwaite, William Herbert
Savill, Frank Ewart
Schiff, Martin Noel
Scholey, Charles Harry Norman
Scrutton, Hugh Urquhart
Sculthorpe, William Vaughan
Searle, Valentine Lang Stuart
Selwyn, Arthur Penrose
Selwyn, Christopher Wakefield
Senior, Herbert Godbert
Shaw, Bernard Hudson
Shaw, Robert Ramsay Stuart
Sinclair, John Norman
Slater, Walter Theodore
Smalley, John Douglas
Smith, Duncan Vaughan
Smith, Edmund Percival
Smith, Herbert Shaw
Smith, Ralph Henry
Smithers, Reginald Cuthbert Welsford
Snowdon, Henry Frederick
Southern, Hugh
Sowerby, Frank Douglas
Speke, Hugh
Springfield, Geoffrey Mandeville Osborn
Springfield, George Patrick Osborn
Springfield, Humphrey Osborn
Stansfeld, John Raymond Evelyn
Stedman, Philip Bertram Kirk
Stephen, James Howie Frederick
Stevenson, Harry Burnett
Stewart, Robert Colin
Storey, Kenneth Cothay Bonnell
Studholme, Lancelot Joseph Moore
Styer, Wilfred Henry
Sutton-Jones, Cecil Gwyn
Swanwick, Russell Kenneth
Sweet, Roy Thornhill
Sykes, Arnold Walker
Sykes, Leslie Gordon
Symondson, Vernon Francis
Symons, Herbert William
Tarr, Francis Nathaniel
Tatham, Geoffrey Bulmer
Taylor, Ernest George

8

Taylor, Sidney Arnold Turner
Tenbosch, Christian
Tetley, Arthur Stanley
Thomas, Duncan Collisson Willey
Thomas, Richard Roy
Thomson, Kenneth Clark
Thomson, Samuel Pestell Donald
Thompson, John Cecil Caster
Thurburn, Erik James Ptolemy
Tillie, Arnold Reed
Tillie, John Archibald
Tolson, James Martin
Tomlin, Charles Geoffrey
Townsend, John Vernon
Townsend-Green, Henry Russell
Tresidder, Charles Tolmie
Trollope, William Kennedy
Tryon, Frederick Charles Hilbers
Tryon, George Arthur
Tucker, John Ayre
Turnbull, David Stevens
Turnbull, William Arthur
Turner, Douglas William
Turner, Maurice Arthur
Turton, Thomas Charles
Tyrwhitt-Drake, Herbert William
Tyzack, Eric Delaney
Vaughton, Guy Eglinton
Veitch, Danyck Moberly
Vickers, Noel Muschamp
Vigers, Robert Stanley Garrard
Vintcent, Charles Aubrey
Wale, Adie
Walker, Anthony Thornton
Walker, Maurice John Lea
Walker, Sam
Wallace, Geoffrey Robert
Wallace, Henry Atholl Charles
Ward, Frank Saxon
Wardle, John Russell
Watson, William
Wearne, Kenneth Martin
Webb, Duncan Vere
Webster, John Richard
Weeks, Francis Mathwin
Wheatley, Roland
Whitson, Henry Thomas
Wilkinson, Frederick Charles Erasmus
Wilkinson, George Jerrard
Wilson, Thomas Johnstone
Wimble, Herbert Reginald
Withy, Basil
Wood, Robert Basil
Woods, Eric Joseph
Wragg, Norman John
Wynne, Edward Ernest
Young, Roger Assheton

Masters of the School.

Habershon, Sidney Heathcote
Oberhoffer, George
Street, Frank

𝕿𝖍𝖊𝖎𝖗 𝖌𝖑𝖔𝖗𝖞 𝖘𝖍𝖆𝖑𝖑 𝖓𝖔𝖙 𝖇𝖊 𝖇𝖑𝖔𝖙𝖙𝖊𝖉 𝖔𝖚𝖙, 𝖆𝖓𝖉 𝖙𝖍𝖊𝖎𝖗
𝖓𝖆𝖒𝖊 𝖑𝖎𝖛𝖊𝖙𝖍 𝖙𝖔 𝖆𝖑𝖑 𝖌𝖊𝖓𝖊𝖗𝖆𝖙𝖎𝖔𝖓𝖘.

HYMN.

Hark! the sound of holy voices, chanting at the crystal sea
Alleluia, Alleluia, Alleluia, Lord, to Thee:
Multitude, which none can number, like the stars in glory stands,
Clothed in white apparel, holding palms of victory in their hands.

They have come from tribulation, and have wash'd their robes in Blood,
Wash'd them in the Blood of Jesus; tried they were, and firm they stood;
Mock'd, imprison'd, stoned, tormented, sawn asunder, slain with sword,
They have conquer'd death and Satan by the might of Christ the Lord.

Marching with Thy Cross their banner, they have triumph'd following
Thee, the Captain of salvation, Thee their Saviour and their King;

10

Gladly, Lord, with Thee they suffer'd; gladly,
  Lord, with Thee they died,
And by death to life immortal they were born,
  and glorified.

Now they reign in heavenly glory, now they
  walk in golden light,
Now they drink, as from a river, holy bliss and
  infinite;
Love and peace they taste for ever, and all truth
  and knowledge see
In the Beatific Vision of the Blessèd Trinity.
                                        Amen.

Then shall be said:

I AM the resurrection and the life, saith the Lord : he that believeth in me, though he were dead, yet shall he live : and whosoever liveth and believeth in me shall never die.

I know that my Redeemer liveth, and that he shall stand at the latter day upon the earth.

Greater love hath no man than this, that a man lay down his life for his friends.

11

PSALM XXIII.

THE Lord is my shepherd : therefore can I lack nothing.

He shall feed me in a green pasture : and lead me forth beside the waters of comfort.

He shall convert my soul : and bring me forth in the paths of righteousness, for his Name's sake.

Yea, though I walk through the valley of the shadow of death, I will fear no evil : for thou art with me; thy rod and thy staff comfort me.

Thou shalt prepare a table before me against them that trouble me : thou hast anointed my head with oil, and my cup shall be full.

But thy loving-kindness and mercy shall follow me all the days of my life : and I will dwell in the house of the Lord for ever.

Glory be to the Father, and to the Son : and to the Holy Ghost;

As it was in the beginning, is now, and ever shall be : world without end. *Amen.*

LESSON, *Wisdom* iii. 1–10.

ANTHEM.

'The souls of the righteous are in the hand of God, and there shall no torment touch them. In the sight of the unwise they seem to die. But they are at peace.'

12

Let us remember before God with thanksgiving and with honour the members of this School who have fallen in the service of their country, who by their life and death have made possible the victory of righteousness and peace.

Then all kneeling, a silence shall be kept for a space.

ALMIGHTY and Everlasting God, unto whom no prayer is ever made without hope of thy compassion; We remember before thee our brothers, the members of this School, who have laid down their lives in the cause wherein their King and country sent them. Grant that they, who have readily obeyed the call of those to whom thou hast given authority on earth, may be accounted worthy of a place among thy faithful servants in the kingdom of heaven; and give both to them and to us forgiveness of all our sins, and an ever increasing understanding of thy will; for his sake who loved us and gave himself for us, thy Son our Saviour Jesus Christ. *Amen.*

O MERCIFUL God, the Father of our Lord Jesus Christ, who is the resurrection and the life; in whom whosoever believeth shall live, though he die; and whosoever liveth, and believeth in him, shall not die eternally; who also hath taught us, by his holy Apostle Saint Paul,

13

not to be sorry, as men without hope, for them that sleep in him; We humbly beseech thee, O Father, to raise us from the death of sin unto the life of righteousness; that, when we shall depart this life, we may rest in him, as our hope is these our brothers do; and that, at the general Resurrection in the last day, we with them may be found acceptable in thy sight; and receive that blessing, which thy well-beloved Son shall then pronounce to all that love and fear thee, saying, Come, ye blessed children of my Father, receive the kingdom prepared for you from the beginning of the world: Grant this, we beseech thee, O merciful Father, through Jesus Christ, our Mediator and Redeemer. *Amen.*

O ALMIGHTY God, who by the incarnation of thy blessed Son hast consecrated for all mankind the life of service, we yield thee heartfelt thanks for the members of this School who in this conflict have proved themselves servants faithful unto death; beseeching thee that each succeeding generation in this place may be so inspired by their example that they also may find their perfect freedom in thy service as faithful soldiers of our Lord and Saviour, Jesus Christ. *Amen.*

14

UNTO God's gracious Mercy and Protection we commit them: the Lord bless them and keep them: the Lord make his face to shine upon them: the Lord lift up the light of his countenance upon them and give them peace. *Amen.*

✠

O GOD, the God of the spirits of all flesh, in whom all creatures live, who by the mouth of thy Son hast taught us that they greatly love who lay down their lives for others; we commit to the arms of thy love the souls of these our brothers who have fallen in this war. Of thy mercy, grant, O Heavenly Father, that we who serve thee still on earth may one day with them be partakers of the inheritance of the Saints in light; through Jesus Christ our Lord. *Amen.*

Lord, have mercy upon us.
Christ, have mercy upon us.
Lord, have mercy upon us.

✠

OUR Father, which art in heaven, Hallowed be thy Name. Thy kingdom come. Thy will be done, in earth as it is in heaven. Give us this day our daily bread. And forgive us our trespasses, As we forgive them that trespass against us. And lead us not into temptation; But deliver us from evil. Amen.

15

V. Turn thee again, O Lord, at the last.
R. And be gracious unto thy servants.
V. O Lord, save the King.
R. And mercifully hear us when we call upon thee.
V. Our help is in the name of the Lord.
R. Who hath made heaven and earth.
V. The souls of the righteous are in the hands of God.
R. And there shall no torment touch them.
V. The Lord is my shepherd.
R. Therefore can I lack nothing.

Then all standing the Priest shall say:

THESE are they which came out of great tribulation, and have washed their robes and made them white in the Blood of the Lamb. Therefore are they before the throne of God, and serve him day and night in his temple. And he that sitteth on the throne shall dwell among them. They shall hunger no more, neither thirst any more; neither shall the sun strike upon them nor any heat. For the Lamb which is in the midst of the throne shall be their shepherd, and shall lead them unto living fountains of waters; and God shall wipe away all tears from their eyes. *Rev.* vii. 14–17.

I heard a voice from heaven saying unto me, Write, From henceforth blessed are the dead which die in the Lord.

16

HYMN.

LET saints on earth in concert sing
    With those whose work is done;
For all the servants of our King
    In Heav'n and earth are one.

One family, we dwell in Him,
    One Church, above, beneath;
Though now divided by the stream,
    The narrow stream of death.

One army of the living God,
    To His command we bow;
Part of the host have cross'd the flood,
    And part are crossing now.

E'en now to their eternal home
    There pass some spirits blest;
While others to the margin come,
    Waiting their call to rest.

Jesu, be Thou our constant Guide;
    Then, when the word is given,
Bid Jordan's narrow stream divide,
    And bring us safe to Heav'n.
                    Amen.

17

Address by the Rev. Canon W. C. E. Newbolt, O.U.

HYMN.

YE holy Angels bright,
 Who wait at God's right hand,
Or through the realms of light
Fly at your Lord's command,
  Assist our song,
  Or else the theme
  Too high doth seem
  For mortal tongue.

Ye blessèd souls at rest,
Who ran this earthly race,
And now, from sin released,
Behold the Saviour's Face,
  His praises sound,
  As in His light
  With sweet delight
  Ye do abound.

Ye saints, who toil below,
Adore your heavenly King,
And onward as ye go
Some joyful anthem sing;
  Take what He gives
  And praise Him still,
  Through good and ill,
  Who ever lives!

18

My soul, bear thou thy part,
Triumph in God above,
And with a well-tuned heart
Sing thou the songs of love!
    Let all thy days
    Till life shall end,
    Whate'er He send,
    Be fill'd with praise. *Amen.*

GENERAL THANKSGIVING.

BLESSING.

LAST POST.

RÉVEILLÉ.

OXFORD: FREDERICK HALL
PRINTER TO THE UNIVERSITY

Bibliography

Archival Sources

Official Sources
The London Gazette
The National Archives
AIR/1/120/15/14/80: Officer Cadets for Officers Cadet Technical Corps
WO 92/9034: Regulations for Officers Training Corp 1908 & Royal Warrant
Officer Files:

Abel	John Duncan	WO 339/70723
Addington	Geoffrey William	WO 339/72970
Akroyd	Henry Cecil	WO 339/13666
Alexander	William Lindsay	ADM 337/56/166
Almack	Edward Poulton	WO 339/6854
Annan	James Gilroy	WO 339/36496
Archer	Ronald Hedley	WO 339/52170
Aytoun	Robert Merlin Graham	WO 339/7602
Badgery	Thomas Samuel Maxwell	WO 339/95495
Baker	Humphrey George Ambrose	WO 339/124614
Barker	Kenneth Edgar Mylne	WO 374/3955
Bascombe	Cecil Reginald	WO 339/115814
Beachcroft	Philip Maurice	WO 339/58550
Beatson	William Gordon	WO 339/58484
Beck	Edwyn Walter Tyrrell	AIR 76/30/177
Becker	Harry Thomas Alfred	WO 339/108894
Bell	Kenneth Pyman	WO 374/5560
Bindloss	Edward Hugh	WO 339/1270
Birley	Maurice	WO 339/1391
Brittain	Edward Harold	WO 339/27827
Browne	Burdett	WO 339/60555
Bunce	Hugh Pollock	WO 339/36949
Burlison	John Clement	WO 339/45176
Caldecott	John Leslie	WO 339/6987
Carey	Wilfred Hardacre	WO 339/33904
Carter-Wood	Joseph Allan	WO 339/19013

Chambers-Hunter	Charles Allardyce Jopp	WO 339/42584
Christopherson	Arnold Bayley	WO 339/17833
Colley	William Arthur	WO 339/21703
Collinge	Arthur	WO 339/5252
Constable	Oswald Clement	WO 339/32422
Cooper	Hugh	WO 339/133494
Ellinger	Maurice Reginald	WO 339/11428
Hett	Alan Stanley	WO 339/60216
Ivatt	Henry George	WO 339/24071
Johnson	William Dalrymple	WO 161/95/38
Parr	Wilfred Wharton	WO 339/27667
Peachey	Hugh Graham	WO 339/10422
Pearson	Algernon George	WO 339/8566
Regnart	Cyrus Hunter	ADM 196/62/386
Thornely	Francis Bodenham	WO 339/16476
Trench	Bernard Frederic	ADM 196/63/58
Webb	Duncan Vere	WO 339/15795
White	William Lambert	WO 339/20320
Whitwell	Francis Albert	WO 339/67763
Willey	Harold	WO 33966398
Williams	George Gilbert Algernon	WO 339/8764
Williamson	James Sprout	AIR 76/551/158
Wilson	John Menzies	WO 76/7/46
Withy	Basil	WO 339/65351
Wood	Leslie Thomas Cyril	AIR 76/559/9
Wood	John Ironside	WO 339/2226
Wragg	Norman John	WO 339/44486
Wright	Desmond Arthur	WO 339/80654
Wynn	Roland Tempest Beresford	WO 339/123636
Young	Hugh	WO 339/55413

Commonwealth War Graves Commission
Casualty Database http://www.cwgc.org/search-for-war-dead.aspx

Liddell Hart Centre for Military Archives
Papers of:
    Burnaby, Lt Col Hugo Beaumont
    Carr, Lt Gen Laurence
    Lethbridge, John
    Liddell Hart, Capt Sir Basil Henry
    Caunter, Brig John Alan Lyde

Lincolnshire Archives
Letters from Christopher Wakefield Selwyn

London Metropolitan Archives
Peachey Family

Somme Museum
Frank Thornley Collection

St Albans School
School Archives

The Imperial War Museum
Papers of:
    Ash, Lieutenant F H
    Briggs, Mrs L K
    Burton, Commander H C
    Cane, Major A S
    Eckenstein, Captain T C
    Ennor, Lieutenant F H
    Gray, Papers of Captain J E B
    Hale, Alfred
    Horridge, Captain G B
    Horridge, Captain J L
    Howitt, Brigadier F D
    Howitt, Captain H G
    Lee, Lieutenant Colonel A N
    Lewis, Major-General H V
    Openshaw, Group Captain E R
Taped Interview:
    Horridge, George B

St Georges School Archives
School Magazines 1914-1918

Uppingham School
Harold Howitt Reminiscences
Charles Herbert Jones
Files of R Sterndale-Bennett (1910-1921)
School Magazines 1884-1930
Uppingham *School Roll* 1824-1905 Third Issue, London 1906
Uppingham *School Roll* 1853-1947 Seventh Issue, (London: 1948)
Uppingham School Archives
Third List of Old Uppinghamians who served in H.M. Forces 1914-1919 (Oxford 1919)
Unknown OU, *Games, Public School and Empire 1840-1900 A Study of Uppingham School to explore the effects of games on the British Empire* unpublished BA dissertation (York)

Official Publications

Edmonds, Sir J, E., *Official History of the Great War: Military Operations France and Belgium 1914-1918, 14 Volumes* (London: HMSO, 1922-1949)

General Works

Tony Ashworth, *Trench Warfare 1914–18: The Live and Let Live System* (London: MacMillan 1980)

Chris Baker, *The Battle for Flanders: German Defeat on the Lys, 1918* (Barnsley: Pen and Sword, 2011)

Stephen Badsey, 'Haig and the Press' in Brian Bond and Nigel Cave (eds), *Haig: A Reappraisal 70 Years On* (Barnsley: Leo Cooper, 1999), pp. 176-195

Corelli Barnett, *The Collapse of British Power* (Paperback edition, Gloucester: Alan Sutton 1984)

Jim Beach, *Haig's Intelligence: GHQ and the German Army, 1916-1918* (Paperback edition, Cambridge: Cambridge University Press, 2015)

Ian Beckett, *Britain's Part-Time Soldiers: The Amateur Military Tradition 1558-1945* (Revised paperback edition Barnsley: Pen and Sword Military, 2011)

Ian Beckett and Keith Simpson (eds), *A Nation in Arms: A Social Study of the British Army in the First World War* (Manchester: Manchester University Press, 1985).

Ian F W Beckett (ed), *The Army and the Curragh Incident*, (Stroud: Army Records Society, 1986)

Shelford Bidwell and Dominick Graham, *Fire-Power: The British Army Weapons and Theories of War 1904-1945* (Paperback edition, Barnsley: Pen and Sword, 2004)

Robert Blake (ed), *The Private Papers of Douglas Haig 1914-1919* (London: Eyre and Spotiswoode, 1952)

Donald F Bittner, 'Royal Marine Spy 1910-1913 Captain Bernard Frederic Trench Royal Marines Light Infantry', in *Royal Marines Spies of World War One Era* (Royal Marines Historical Society, Portsmouth, 1993). pp. 1-60.

Jonathan Boff, *Winning and Losing on the Western Front: The British Third Army and the Defeat of Germany in 1918* (Cambridge: Cambridge University Press, 2012)

Brian Bond, *From Liddell Hart to Joan Littlewood: Studies in British Military History* (Solihull: Helion, 2015)

Bond, B., et al, *'Look to Your Front': Studies in the First World War* (Staplehurst: Spellmount, 1999)

Stephen Brooks (ed), *Montgomery and the Battle of Normandy* (Stroud: Army Records Society, 2008)

Stephen Brooks (ed), *Montgomery and the Eighth Army* (London: Army Records Society, 1991)

John Buckley, *Monty's Men: The British Army and the Liberation of Europe* (Paperback edition, London: Yale University Press, 2014)

David Cannadine, *The Decline and Fall of the British Aristocracy* (Paperback edition, London: Papermac, 1996)

Richard A Chapman, *Leadership in the British Civil Service* (London: Crook Helm, 1984)

Carlo D'Este. *Decision in Normandy The Unwritten Story of Montgomery and the Allied Campaign* (Paperback edition, London: Classic Penguin, 2001)

J R de. S Honey, *Tom Brown's Universe: The Development of the Victorian Public School* (London: Millington, 1977)

Sir Robert Ensor, *The Oxford History of England England 1870-1914* (Oxford: Clarendon, 1936)
Cyril Falls, *The First World War* (London: Longmans, 1960)
Niall Ferguson, *The Pity of War* (Paperback edition, London: Penguin, 1999)
Niall Ferguson, *Empire: How Britain Made the Modern World* (Paperback edition, London: Penguin, 2004)
David French, *British Economic and Strategic Planning 1905-1915* (London: George, Allen and Unwin, 1982)
Jonathan Galthorne-Hardy, *The Public School Phenomenon* (London: Hodder and Stoughton, 1977)
Brian Gardner, *The Public Schools* (London: Hamish Hamilton, 1973)
Adrian Gregory, *The Last Great War: British Society and the First World War* (Cambridge: Cambridge University Press, 2008)
Captain Alan R Haig-Brown, *The OTC and the Great War* (London: Country Life, 1915)
Paul Harris, *The Men Who Planned the War: A Study of the Staff of the British Army on the Western Front, 1914-1918* (Farnham: Ashgate, 2015)
Peter E Hodkinson, *British Infantry Battalion Commanders in the First World War* (Farnham: Ashgate, 2015)
Richard Holmes, *Tommy: The British Soldier on the Western Front 1914-1918* (Paperback edition, London: Harper Perennial, 2005)
Steve Hurst, *The Public Schools Battalion In The Great War* (Barnsley: Pen and Sword, 2007)
Keith Jeffery, *MI6: The History of the Secret Intelligence Service 1909-1949* (Paperback edition, London: Bloomsbury, 2011)
E H Jenkins, *A History of the French Navy* (London: Macdonald and Janes's, 1973)
Alan Judd, *The Quest for Mansfield Cumming and the Founding of the Secret Service* (London: Harper Collins, 1999)
B Cory Kilver Jr, *Echoes of Armageddon, 1914-1918: An American's Search Into the Lives and Deaths of Eight British Soldiers in World War One* (AuthorHouse: Bloomington, 2004)
John Lewis-Stempel, *Six Weeks: The Short and Gallant Life of the British Officer in the First World War* (Paperback edition, London: Orion, 2011)
Edward C Mack, *Public Schools and British Opinion Since 1860: The relationship between contemporary ideas and the evolution of an English institution* (New York: Columbia University Press, 1941)
S P B Mais, *A Public School in War Time* (London: John Murray, 1916)
J A Mangan, *Athleticism in the Victorian and Edwardian Public Schools* (Cambridge: Cambridge University Press, 1981)
Arthur Marwick, *The Deluge: British Society and the First World War* (London: Bodley Head 1965)
Martin Middlebrook, *The First Day on the Somme* (Paperback edition, London: Classic Penguin, 2001)
Martin Middlebrook, *The Kaiser's Battle* (Paperback edition, London: Classic Penguin, 2000)
Christopher Moore-Bick, *Playing the Game* (Solihull: Helion 2011)
Jerry Murland, *Departed Warriors: The Story of One Family in War* (Leicester: Matador, 2008)
V Ogilvie, *The English Public School* (London: B T Batsford, 1957)
Peter Parker, *The Old Lie* (Paperback edition London: Hambledon Continuum, 1987)
Thomas Pakenham, *The Boer War* (Paperback edition London: Abacus, 1992)

William Philpott, *Attrition: Fighting the First World War* (New York: Little & Brown, 2014)
Caroline E Playne, *Society at War, 1914-1916* (London: Allen and Unwin, 1931)
Andrew Rawson, *British Expeditionary Force – The 1914 Campaign* (Barnsley: Pen and Sword, 2014)
W L Reader, *At Duty's Call* (Manchester: Manchester University Press, 1988)
Andrew Renshaw, *Wisden on the Great War: The Lives of Cricket's Fallen 1914-1918* (London: John Wisden and Co 2014)
David Reynolds, *The Long Shadow* (Paperback edition London: Simon and Schuster, 2014)
J D Sainsbury, *Hertfordshire's Army Cadets* (Welwyn: Hart's Books, 2010)
Anthony Seldon and David Walsh, *Public Schools and The Great War The Generation Lost* (Barnsley: Pen and Sword Military, 2013)
Matthew S Seligmann (ed), *Military Intelligence from Germany* (Stroud: Army Records Society, 2014)
Matthew S Seligmann, *The Royal Navy and the German Threat, 1901-1914: Admiralty Plans to Protect British Trade in a War Against Germany* (Oxford: OUP, 2012)
Gary Sheffield and John Bourne, *Douglas Haig: War Diaries and Letters, 1914-1918* (Paperback edition, London: Phoenix, 2006)
Gary Sheffield and Dan Todman (eds.), *Command and Control on the Western Front: The British Army's Experience 1914-18* (Staplehurst: Spellmount, 2004)
Gary Sheffield, *Forgotten Victory: The First World War, Myths and Realities* (Paperback edition, London: Review, 2002).
Alan Shepperd, 'Horrocks', in John Keegan (ed) *Churchill's Generals* (Paperback edition, London: Warner, 1992)
Peter Simkins, 'The Four Armies 1914-1918', in Chandler, D. and Beckett, I. (eds), *The Oxford Illustrated History of the British Army*, (Oxford: OUP, 1994)
Peter Simkins, *From Somme to Victory: The British Army's Experience on the Western Front 1916-1918* (Barnsley: Praetorian,2014)
Peter Simkins, 'Haig and the Army Commanders', in Brian Bond and Nigel Cave (eds) *Haig: A Reappraisal 70 Years On*, (Barnsley: Leo Cooper, 1999), pp. 78-106
Peter Simkins, *Kitchener's Army: The Raising of the New Armies, 1914-1916* (Barnsley: Pen and Sword, 2007).
B Simon & I Bradley, (eds.) *The Victorian Public School* (London: Gill and Macmillan, 1975)
Nick Smart, *Biographical Dictionary of British Generals of the Second World War* (Barnsley: Pen and Sword, 2005)
E M Spiers, *Haldane: An Army Reformer* (Edinburgh: Edinburgh University Press, 1980)
John Springhall, *Youth, Empire and Society: British Youth Movements, 1883-1940* (London: Croom Helm, 1977)
Peter Stanley, *Die in Battle Do Not Despair: The Indians on Gallipoli, 1915* (Solihull: Helion, 2015)
Martin Stephen, *The Price of Pity: Poetry, History and Myth in the Great War* (London: Leo Cooper, 1996)
David Stevenson, *1914-18: The History of the First World War* (Paperback edition London: Penguin, 2005)
Hew Strachan, *The First World War: A New History* (Paperback edition London: Simon and Schuster, 2006)

Andrew Syk (ed), *The Military Papers of Lieutenant-General Frederick Stanley Maude 1914-1917* (Stroud: Army Records Society, 2012)

Dan Todman, *The Great War: Myth and Memory* (London: Hambledon and London, 2005)

Malcolm Tozer, '"To the Glory that was Greece": Classical Images in Public School Athleticism', in Tom Winnifrith and Cyril Barratt (eds) *Leisure in Art and Literature* (London: Macmillan, 1992). pp. 109-129

Malcolm Tozer, *The Ideal of Manliness: The Legacy of Thring's Uppingham* (Truro: Sunnyrest Books, 2015)

Tim Travers, *How the War was Won: Command and Technology in the British Army on the Western Front, 1917-1918* (London: Routledge, 1992)

Alexander Watson, *Enduring the Great War: Combat, Morale and Collapse in the German and British Armies* (Paperback edition, Cambridge: Cambridge University Press, 2009)

Samuel R Williamson, *The Politics of Grand Strategy: Britain and France Prepare for War, 1904-1914* (Cambridge Massachusetts: Harvard University Press, 1969)

Norman T Wills, *Fenland Churches and People between Spalding & Long Sutton* (Long Sutton: Privately published, 1988)

Denis Winter, *Death's Men: Soldiers of the Great War* (Paperback edition, London: Penguin, 1979)

Jay Winter, *Sites of Memory Sites of Mourning* (Paperback edition, Cambridge: Cambridge University Press, 1996)

Robert Wohl, *The Generation of 1914* (London: Weidenfield and Nicholson, 1980)

Christian Wolmar, *Engines of War: How Wars Were Won & Lost on the Railways* (Atlantic Books London 2010).

David, Zabecki, *The German Army 1918 Offensives: A Case Study in the Operational Level of War* (Abingdon: Routledge, 2006)

Autobiographies, Memoirs and Personal Accounts

Philip Bagnal, *Fields & Battle Fields (By No 31540)* (New York: Robert M Macbride & Company, 1918)

Adrian Bell, *My Own Master* (London: Country Book Club, 1962)

Vera Brittain, *Chronicles of Youth 1913-1917* (London: Phoenix Press, 1981)

Vera Brittain, *Chronicle of Friendship 1932-1939* (London: Victor Gollancz, 1986)

Vera Brittain, *Testament of Youth* (Paperback edition London: Virago 2004)

Vera Brittain, *Wartime Chronicle 1939-1945* ((London: Victor Gollancz, 1989)

Alan Bishop, and Mark Bostridge, (eds) *Letters from a Lost Generation – First World War Letters of Vera Brittain and Four Friends: Roland Leighton, Edward Brittain, Victor Richardson, Geoffrey Thurlow* (Paperback edition, London: Abacus, 1998)

Edmund Blunden, *Undertones of War* (Paperback edition, London: Penguin, 2010)

D W Carmalt Jones, *A Physician in Spite of Himself* (London: Royal Society of Medicine Press, 2009)

Captain J A L Caunter, *13 Days: The Chronicle of an Escape from a German Prison* (London: G Bell and Sons, 1918)

Alex Danchev and Daniel Todman (eds), *War Diaries 1939-1945: Field Marshal Lord Alanbrooke* (London: Wiedenfield and Nicolson, 2001)

Paul Fussell (ed), *The Ordeal of Alfred M Hale* (London: Leo Cooper, 1975)
Philip Gibbs, *Now It Can Be Told* (London: Harper, 1920)
John P Graham, *Forty Years of Uppingham Memories and Sketches* (London: Macmillan, 1932)
Robert Graves, *Good-bye to All That* (London: Jonathan Cape, 1929)
Horrocks, Lieut-General Sir B., *Escape To Action* (New York: St Martin's Press 1961)
Cecil Lewis, *Sagitarius Rising* (Paperback edition, London: Penguin, 1977)
C R W Nevinson, *Paint and Prejudice* (New York: Harcourt, Brace and Company, 1938)
Charles E Raven, *A Wanderer's Way* (London: Martin Hopkinson, 1929)
Lieutenant Colonel Charles à Court Repington, *The First World War, 1914-1918: Personal Experiences of Lieut.-Col. C. À Court Repington Vol. 2* (Boston and New York: Houghton Mifflin, 1920)
Field-Marshal Sir William Robertson Bart., *From Private to Field-Marshal* (London: Constable, 1921)
Field Marshal Viscount Slim, *Defeat into Victory* (Paperback edition, London: Pan, 2009)
Sir Charles Walker, *Thirty-Six Years at the Admiralty* (London: Lincoln Williams, 1933)
Wills, J., *World War 1 experiences of my grandfather, Gordon Wills* <http://www.oceanharmony.ca/Alfred%20Gordon%20Wills.html>
Wills, J., *World War II Experiences of Bill Wills* <http://www.oceanharmony.ca/WRWills%20essay.html>

Biographies

Paul Berry and Mark Bostridge, *Vera Brittain: A Life* (Paperback edition, London: Virago, 2008)
Ian Buruma, *Their Promised Land: My Grandparents in Love and War* (Paperback edition, London: Atlantic, 2016)
Simon Davies, *Enemies at Peace* (Privately published, 1993)
Ross Davies., *'A Student in Arms': Donald Hankey and Edwardian Society at War* (Farnham: Ashgate, 2013)
F W Dillistone, *Charles Raven: Naturalist, Historian, Theologian* (London: Hodder and Stoughton, 1975)
Don Farr, *None That Go Return* (Solihull: Helion, 2010)
David Boyd Haycock, *A Crisis of Brilliance* (Paperback edition London: Old Street Publishing, 2010)
Lavinia Greacen, *Chink: A Biography* (London: Macmillan, 1989)
Lawrence James, *Imperial Warrior: The Life and Times of Field-Marshal Viscount Allenby* (London: Weidenfield and Nicolson, 1993)
Penelope Jessel, *Owen of Uppingham* (London: A R Mowbray 1965)
Clare Leighton, *Tempestuous Petticoat: The Story of an Invincible Edwardian* (New York: Rinehart and Company, 1947)
Marie Leighton, *Boy of My Heart* (London: Hodder and Stoughton, 1916)
Russell Miller, *Uncle Bill: The Authorised Biography of Field Marshal Viscount Slim* (Paperback edition London: Phoenix, 2014)
Robin Prior and Trevor Wilson, *Command on the Western Front: The Military Career of Sir Henry Rawlinson 1914–18*, (Barnsley: Leo Cooper, 2004)

Peter Rowland, *Raffles and His Creator: The Life and Works of E.W. Hornung* (London: Nekta, 1999)
Gary Sheffield, *The Chief: Douglas Haig and the British Army* (London: Aurum, 2011)
John Terraine, *Douglas Haig: The Educated Soldier* (Paperback edition, London: Phoenix, 2005)
Philip Warner, *Horrocks: The General Who Led from the Front*, (Paperback edition London: Sphere, 1985)
Jeffery Williams, *Byng of Vimy: General and Governor General* (Paperback edition, London: Leo Cooper, 1992)

Unit Histories

Captain J D Hills, *The Fifth Leicestershire – A Record Of The 1/5th Battalion The Leicestershire Regiment, – T.F., During The War, 1914-1919* (Loughborough: The Echo Press, 1919)
W Shaw Sparrow, *The Fifth Army in March 1918* (London: John Lane, 1921)

School Histories

Anon., *Memorials of Rugbeians who fell in the Great War Volume V* (Rugby: Privately published, 1919)
Anon., *Tonbridge School and the Great War of 1914-1918 A Record of the Services of Tonbridgeans in the Great War of 1914-1918* (Tonbridge: Privately published, 1923)
Mike Garrs, *Valiant Hearts: The Story of Uppingham School VC's* (Nettleham: Privately published, 2010)
Bryan Matthews, *By God's Grace* (London: Whitehall Press, 1984)
Bryan Matthews, *Eminent Uppinghamians* (Cranbrook: Neville & Harding, 1987)
Richard Pearson, *The Boys Of Shakespeare's School In The First World War*, (Stroud: The History Press, 2010)
Asher C J Pirt, *WSS Old Boys and the Great War 1914-1918* (Watchet: Privately published, 2013)
Nigel Richardson, *Thring of Uppingham* (Buckingham: University of Buckingham Press, 2014)
Paddy Storrie, *"Here I am; Send me": The War Dead of St George's School 1914-1918* (Harpenden: St Georges School, 2004)
Derek Winterbottom, *Henry Nevinson and The Spirit of Clifton* (Bristol: Redcliffe, 1986)
Wykehamist War Service Roll 1914-1919 (Winchester: Privately published, 1919)

Fiction and Poetry

Vera Brittain, *Verses of a VAD 1918* (London: Imperial War Museum, 1995)
Vera Brittain, *Because You Died* (London: Hachette Digital 2008)
Erskine Childers, *The Riddle of the Sands* (Paperback edition, London: Penguin, 2007)
E W Hornung, *Fathers of Men* (London: Smith Elder & Co, 1912)
E W Hornung, *The Young Guard* (London: Constable, 1919)

Journal Articles

'Obituary D W Carmalt Jones, D.M., F.R.C.P. F.R.A.C.P.' *British Medical Journal* (16 March 1957), pp. 649-650.

'Obituary D W Carmalt Jones, M.A., D.M. Oxfd, F.R.C.P. F.R.A.C.P.' *The Lancet* (16 March 1957), pp. 59-60.

Bond, B., 'Richard Haldane at the War Office, 1905-1912' *Army Quarterly* 86: 1 (1963), pp. 33-43

Alastair Compston, 'From the Archives', *Brain*, 2013: 136, pp. 1681-1686.

Peter Donaldson, 'The Commemoration of the South African War (1899-1902) in British Public Schools' *History & Memory*, 25: 2. pp. 32-65

R Douglas, 'Voluntary enlistment in the First World War and the work of the Parliamentary Recruiting Committee' *Journal of Modern History*, 42: 4 (1970), pp. 564-585

David French "Official History"? Sir James Edmonds and the Official History of the Great War, *RUSI: Royal United Services Institute for Defence Studies*, 131: 1 (March 1986) pp 58-63

Anthony Fletcher, 'Patriotism, the Great War and the Decline of Victorian Manliness' *History*, 99: 334, pp. 40-72

John Grigg, 'Nobility and War: The Unselfish Commitment?' *Encounter* 74 (1990), pp. 21-27

Timothy Halstead, 'The First World and Public School Ethos: The Case of Uppingham School' *War and Society*, 34: 3 (August 2015), pp. 209-229

Timothy Halstead, 'The Junior OTC: Playing at Soldiers or Nation in Arms?' *British Journal for Military History*, 3: 2 (February 2017), pp. 62-81

Nicholas Hiley, 'Spying for the Kaiser', *History Today*, 38: 6 (1988), pp. 37-43

Nicholas Hiley, 'The Failure of British Espionage against Germany, 1907-1914', *The Historical Journal*, 26: 4 (December 1983), pp. 867-889

Rob Johnson, '"I Shall Die Arms in Hand, Wearing the Warriors' Clothes": Mobilisation and Initial Operations of the Indian Army in France and Flanders' *British Journal for Military History*, 2: 2, (February 2016), pp. 107-109

Alisa Miller, Modern War and Aesthetic Mobilisation: Looking at Europe in 1914, *British Journal for Military History*, 2: 2 (February 2016), pp. 12-41

C B Ottley, 'Militarism and Militarization in the Public Schools 1900-1972', *The British Journal of Sociology*, 29: 3 (September 1978) pp 321-339

Christopher Phillips, Logistics and the BEF: The development of Waterborne Transport on the Western Front, 1914-1916 *British Journal of Military History*, 2: 2 pp. 42-58

F W Shotton, William Bernard Robinson King 1889-1963, *Biographical Memories of Fellows of the Royal Society*, 9 (Nov. 1963) pp. 171-182

Strachan, H., 'Essay and Reflection: On Total War and Modern War', *The International History Review*, 22: 2 (2000) pp 341-370

E M Teagarden, 'Lord Haldane and the origins of the Officer Training Corps' *Journal of the Society for Army Historical Research*, 45: 182 (1967) pp. 91-96

Malcolm Tozer, 'Cricket, school amd empire: E W Hornung and his Young Guard', *The International Journal of the History of Sport*, 6: 2 (March 2007) pp. 156-171

P Wilkinson, 'English Youth Movements, 1908-1930', *Journal of Contemporary History*, 4: 2 (1969) pp. 1-23

Ian Worthington, 'Antecedent education and officer recruitment: The origins and early development of the public school-Army relationship', *Military Affairs*, Vol 41 No. 4 (1977) pp. 183-190

Newspapers

Grantham Journal
Rutland and Stamford Mercury
The Alpine Journal www.alpinejournal.org.uk
The Fifth Gloucester Gazette
The New Zealand Gazette
The Pipeline
The Times 1910-1966
The Morning News Wilmington Delaware
The New Beacon The Magazine Of Blind Welfare
The Western Australian
The Wipers Times

Dissertations and Theses

Phylomena Badsey, 'The Political Thought of Vera Brittain', unpublished PhD thesis (Kingston, 2005)

Stephen Badsey, 'Fire and the Sword The British Army and The Arme Blanche Controversy 1871-1921' unpublished PhD thesis (Cambridge, 1981)

Christopher Hammond, 'The Theory and Practice of Tank Co-operation with Other Arms on the Western Front during the First World War' (Birmingham, 2005)

Christopher Jordan, 'Steering Taste: Ernest Marsh. A study of private collecting in England in the early 20th Century' (University of the Arts London Camberwell College of Arts, 2007)

Changboo Kang, 'The British Infantry Officer on the Western Front in the First World War: With Special Reference to the Royal Warwickshire Regiment' unpublished PhD thesis, (Birmingham, 2007).

Ian Maxwell, 'The importance of being Ernest John: Challenging the misconceptions about the life and works of E.J. Moeran' (Durham, 2014)

Richard John Palmer, 'The Life of F W Sanderson (1857-1922) with special reference to his work and influence at Oundle School' (1892-1922) (Hull, 1981)

Simon Robbins, 'British Generalship in the First World War, 1914-1918' unpublished PhD thesis, (London, 2001)

Gary Sheffield, 'Officer – Man Relations: Morale and Discipline in the British Army, 1902–22' unpublished PhD thesis, (London, 1994)

Malcolm Tozer, 'Manliness: The Evolution of a Victorian Ideal' unpublished PhD thesis (Leicester, 1978)

Malcolm Tozer, 'Physical Education at Thring's Uppingham', unpublished MEd dissertation (Leicester, 1974)

Worthington, 'Antecedent Education and Officer Recruitment An Analysis of the Public School-Army Nexus, 1849-1908' unpublished PhD thesis (Lancaster, 1982)

Miscellaneous

Scott Addington, *For Conspicuous Gallantry… Winners of the Military Cross and Bar during the Great War Volume 1 – Two Bars and Three Bars* (Leicester: Matador, 2006)

Bedford Borough Council http://www.bedfordshire.gov.uk
Blackadder Goes Forth, TX 28 September 1989 to 2 November 1989
Cambridge Regiment Awards 1914-1918 http://www.roll-of-honour.com/Regiments/CambsRegimentAwards1914-18.html
G V Carey, *The War List of the University of Cambridge 1914-1918* (Cambridge: Cambridge University Press, 1921)
Commentary on memorial at St Mary & St Eanswythe Church, Folkestone http://www.kent-fallen.com/PDF%20REPORTS/FOLKESTONE%20ST%20MARY'S.pdf
E S Craig and W M Gibson, *Oxford University Roll of Service*, (Oxford: Clarendon Press, 1920)
Family Records – a short history of the La Fontaine family http://levantineheritage.com/book1.htm
Grace's Guide http://www.gracesguide.co.uk
Kirklees Council https://www.kirklees.gov.uk
Law Society, *Record of Service of Solicitors and Articled Clerks with His Majesty's Forces 1914-1919* (London: Law Society, 1920).
Leicester War Memorials http://www.leics.gov.uk/leicester_war_memorials_v3.pdf
Leicestershire Antills and Connected Families http://antill.org.uk/
S Light, AGM April 14th 2012 Morning Presentation No Task Too Great No Work Too Small *The Western Front Association Bulletin 93 (2012) pp 9-11*
Monty Python's Flying Circus, *Upper Class Twit of the Year*, TX 4 January 1970
Record of War Service 1919-1918 Officers Training Corps (Junior Division) Public School Officers and Other Members of the Staffs, (London: privately published, 1919)
Roll of Honour, Buckinghamshire http://www.roll-of-honour.com/Buckinghamshire/Wendover.html
St George's School, School History <http://www.stgeorges.herts.sch.uk/About-Us/School-History>
P. Simkins, AGM April 14th 2012 – President's Address 'Everyman at War' Revisited, *The Western Front Association Bulletin 93 (2012) pp 3-6*
Statistics of the Military Effort of the British Empire During the Great War, (London: HMSO 1922)
C Stewart, *'War Memoirs of the Dead': Writing and Remembrance in the First World War* http://www.csub.edu/~mbaker2/stewartwwimem.pdf
The Bedfordshire Regiment in the Great War http://www.bedfordregiment.org.uk/index.html
The History of Epsom College a <http://www.epsomcollege.org.uk/a-unique-history>
The Long Long Trail http://www.1914-1918.net/
The V.C. and D.S.O. Distinguished Service Order 1886-1915: Distinguished Service Order. 6Th September 1886 To The 31St December 1915 (London, Naval and Military Press, 2009)
The V.C. and D.S.O. Book Distinguished Service Order 1916 – 1923 (London, Naval and Military Press, 2009)
The Royal Leicestershire Regiment http://www.royalleicestershireregiment.org.uk/
V & A https://www.vam.ac.uk
York and the Great War York http://yorkandthegreatwar.com/

Index

INDEX OF PEOPLE

Addington, Scott 118-119
Aitken, Robert Creighton Seymour 144-145
Albery, Bronson xv
Alexander, Brigadier-General Charles Henry 77-78, 124-125, 127, 131-132, 134
Allenby, General Edmund 126-127, 132
Arnold, Thomas 22-25, 35-37
Ash, Gerald 155
Ashwell, Lena 141

Bagenal, Hope 73
Baker, Humphrey 77
Balfour, Arthur 23
Barber, Colin 156-157
Barnett, Correlli 22
Bascombe, Cyril Reginald 83, 85
Beadle, J P 151
Beale, Lionel xv
Beatson, Walter William Gordon 83
Becker, Harry 77-78
Bell, Adrian 103
Bewicke, George 148
Bindloss, Edward 77-78
Bishop, Major Charles Gamble 85
Bittner, Donald F 55, 58
Blair Oliphant, Major Kington Phillip 72
Bland, Captain Constantine 99
Blunden, Edmund 21
Boff, Jonathan 133
Boucher, Herbert Edward 82
Brandon, Lieutenant Vivian 59-66
Brewis, Alfred Percy 95
Brittain, Edward xix, 38, 52, 70-72, 75, 89, 103-104, 157, 162
Brittain, Vera xi, xvii, 48, 54, 68, 70, 89, 95, 144, 161

Brooke, Field Marshal Alan 156-157, 159
Brooke, Rupert xvii, 89
Bruty, William Glynes 88-89, 92
Buchan, John 115
Bull, Sir William 62
Bunce, Hugh Pollock, 94-95
Burnaby, Hugo Beaumont 43, 53, 75-76, 78, 96, 107
Burrard, Sir Sidney 45-46
Byng, Sir Julian 129, 132

Calvert, Sergeant 96
Campbell, Malcolm 152
Campion, Frederic Eugene 86-87
Carmalt Jones, Dudley W 37-40, 71, 87-88, 97
Carr, Laurence 144, 156-157, 160
Caunter, John Alan Lyde 108
Chaloner, Richard Godolphin Hume 95
Champion, H H 141
Chapman, Guy 22
Cheyne, Lieutenant Joseph Lister 69
Childers, Erskine 26, 42, 56-57
Cohan, Edward Molyneux 95
Cohan, Harry Molyneux 95
Collings-Wells, Lieutenant-Colonel John Stanhope 112, 149
Constable, Reverend W J xv, 103, 155
Couper, Victor 123, 127-129, 134
Cumming, Mansfield 57, 59-60, 62-67
Currey, Vere 151

Daglish, George Grant 106
Daniel, Arthur Egerton Claude 82
David, Paul 38, 44-45
Dorman-Smith, Eric xvi, 53-54, 156-160, 165
Dryland, Gilbert 155

Eccles, Thomas 105
Edmonds, James 127
Evans, Wilfred 125-126

Ferguson, Major-General Sir Charles 69
Finch, Lesley Hales 155
Fothergill, George Algernon 88-89
Frangcon-Davies, Geoffrey 102
French, David 98-99
French, John 125
Fry, Stephen 21

Gaffikin, George 151
Geddes, Sir Eric 86
George V 65, 110
Gibbs, Sir Philip 131
Gibson, Edward 152
Gleed, John 148
Gough, Brigadier-General Hubert 69, 128-129
Gow, Reverend J of Westminster 138
Graham, John P xiii-xv, 103-104
Grant, Reverend Cecil 36, 95, 102
Gray, Captain J E B 71, 118-119
Greaves, Francis 149
Gregory, Adrian xvi-xvii, 107

Habsburg, Archduke Ferdinand 49
Haig, Field-Marshal Douglas 28, 31, 49, 69, 81, 94, 123, 126-129, 134, 144
Haig-Brown, Alan 51
Haldane, Richard xviii, 30-31, 73, 139
Hale, Alfred 72-73, 77-78
Hall, Thomas Storey Inglis 150
Harmer, William Douglas 88
Harris, Paul 132
Hearn, Edmund Risley 82
Helm, Lieutenant 64
Henderson, Archibald 105
Herbert, Sir Ivor 104
Hett, Alan Stanley 82-83, 85
Hill, Philip Aubrey 95
Hind, Jesse 149
Hind, Lieutenant Colonel Laurence 149
Hind, Trooper Oliver 149
Hohenzollern, Kaiser Wilhelm II 47, 55-56, 65, 70
Holden, Henry 35
Holliday, Lionel Brook 105-106
Hooley, Basil Terah 95

Hopkins, Lieutenant Colonel Charles Harrie Innes 150
Hornung, E W xvi-xvii, 147
Horridge, George 50, 80
Horrocks, Brian xvi, 53-54, 108, 131, 156-160, 165
Howe, Philip 71-72, 75, 96
Howitt, Sir Harold xii, 45-46, 88, 114-115, 119, 155
Humbert, Sydney 118-119

Inglis, Harold 115-116, 150
Ivatt, H G 78

Jackson, Thomas 66
Jalland, Stephen 149
James, Captain B T 87
Jameson, Second Lieutenant Frank 119
Jenkins, E H 55-56
Joffre, Marshal Joseph 124-125
Johnson, Robert 35
Johnston, Francis 108, 155
Jones, Carnforth 76, 87-88
Jones, Edgar Montague 136-137
Jones, Lieutenant Colonel Charles Herbert xiii, 29, 49-50, 101, 103, 135, 137, 139, 164

King, Professor William 46, 48, 54, 87
Kitchener, Lord xiv, xviii, 32, 70, 75-78, 81, 94, 99-100, 104-105, 124-125, 132, 150, 163-164

La-Fontaine, James Sydney 152
Lake, Percy 123, 129-131, 134, 156
Langlois, General 30
Lascelles, Captain Arthur Moore 112-113
Le Queux, William 56
Lecky, Major-General Robert 120
Lee, Major Arthur xv, 71, 75, 96-97, 103, 108, 144
Leighton, Marie 103
Leighton, Roland xi, xix, 52, 70-72, 75, 89, 94-95, 103, 157
Lethbridge, John 156-157, 160
Lewis, Bridges 125
Lewis, Donald Swain 86, 117
Liddell, Clive 131
Living, Charles 118
Loch, Lord 126

Lumsden, J A 101
Lux, Captain 64
Lyle, Oliver 106

MacDonald, Norman xiv, 56, 105
Maling, Captain George Allan 112-113
Mann, Rear-Admiral W F S 48
Mansell-Carey, Spencer 103
Marriot, Frederick 148
Marsh, Ernest 150-151
Marsh, Francis Bedford 94-95, 150-151
Martin, John Sinclair 92
Masterman, Charles 108
Matthews, Bryan xvii, 37, 46, 101, 129, 146
Maude, Sir Frederick 130
Maufe, Captain Harold Broadbent 112-113, 115
Maxe, Major-General Ivor 121
McDonough, George 66
McKenzie, Reverend H W 38, 48-49, 90, 100-101
Moeran, Ernest 38
Monk, Second-Lieutenant Bertram 32, 102
Montgomery, Field Marshal 157-160
Moore-Bick, Christopher xvi, 27, 74
Morrish, James Herbert 82
Mott, Charles E 75-76, 88-89
Mott, Eric 103

Nevinson, C R W xvi, 38, 40, 46-47, 52, 73, 108-109
Newbolt, Henry xvii, 43-44
Newton, Ernest 105
Nixon, Sir John 129-130
Northrop, Geoffrey 152

Oberhoffer, George 140-141, 164
Owen, Reginald Herbert 100-101, 103, 141, 145-147

Parkes, Howard Roderick xiv
Parr, Wilfred 76-78
Peachey, Hugh Graham 75-76, 81, 88, 90-92, 121-122, 124

Raven, Canon Charles 46, 54
Regnart, Captain Cyrus ('Roy') Hunter 57-60, 63, 65-67, 156, 162
Repington, Loos 125, 128
Richardson, Victor xi, 70, 75, 89-90, 94-95, 103

Robbins, Simon 27, 33, 74, 126, 144, 156
Roberts, James Thursby 89
Roberts, Lord 161
Robertson, Sir William 130
Robinson, Godfrey 152-153, 155
Rollo, Brigadier-General George 148
Rollo, William Stuart 148
Rose, Major 88
Russell, Lieutenant Colonel 60

Sanday, William 108
Sanderson, F W 100, 102
Sanford, Dudley William 86
Savory, Reginald Arthur 91, 95-96
Scallon, Sir Robert 129
Sculthorpe, W Vaughan 149
Selwyn, Christopher Wakefield 90-91, 96
Selwyn, Edward Carus xii, 38-48, 53, 90, 101, 136-137, 139, 145, 161-162
Shea, R P 99-100, 140
Sheffield, Gary 25, 126
Shuttleworth, Joseph 41
Singh, Ude 96
Slim, General William 157, 160
Southampton, Bishop of xiii, 147
Steinhauer, Gustav 64
Sterndale Bennett, Major Robert 38, 45, 82-83, 85, 100, 141
Street, Frank 100, 140-141, 164
Suddaby, Rod ix, xvi

Thornely, Frank Bodenham 72, 89, 96, 151-153
Thring, Edward xi-xii, 22, 35-41, 45, 50, 97, 161, 163
Tolson, Leigh 150
Tolson, Robert Huntriss 150
Townshend, General 130
Tozer, Malcolm 43, 49
Trench, Captain Bernard Frederic 57-67, 71, 89, 156, 162
Trench, Lieutenant-Colonel 56
Truman, Private J 96
Tryon, George 79

Vass, Air Commodore Gordon 157
Vaughan, Louis 116, 120, 123, 131

Walker, Sir Charles 69, 106-107, 111
Ward, Sir Edward 28

Warre, Dr Edmund 28, 43, 137
Waugh, Alec 46
Wemyss, Sir Rosslyn 107
West, Elsa 141
Westmacott, Colonel Hugh 152

Wilkinson, Major-General Percy 123, 126-127, 132, 134
Wills, Gordon 48, 54, 75
Wilson, Henry 66, 70
Wolfenden, Lord 36

INDEX OF PLACES

Baltic Sea 57, 59
Bedfordshire 41, 112, 149
Belgium 67, 70, 78, 87, 94, 100, 107, 124, 127-128, 145
Berlin 56, 60, 62, 65
Borkum 55, 60-63, 66, 71, 156, 162
Bristol 135
Brussels 66-67

Canada 43, 53, 91, 129
Copenhagen 59-60, 66
The Curragh 69-70

Delfzyl 62-63
Derby 86
Dublin 69, 151

Emden 60, 62
English Channel 39, 128

France xviii, 24, 29, 32, 39, 55-57, 60, 66-67, 70, 76-78, 81, 84, 86, 89, 92, 94, 98, 101, 105-106, 108, 112-113, 116, 118, 123-129, 141, 143-144, 157, 159

Gallipoli 75, 91, 95, 106, 130, 152
Germany xii-xiii, xviii-xix, 24, 26, 29, 42, 47, 54-62, 64-71, 73, 81, 90, 97, 99, 106-108, 112, 131, 133, 140, 154, 156-157, 160-163, 165
Gully Ravine 91, 95

Harpenden 36, 100, 147
Hertfordshire 36, 136
Hull 152-153, 155

India 78, 129-131
Ireland xii, xviii, 67-69, 152

Kiel 59-61, 63

Lancaster 28, 150
Leipzig 45, 62-63
Liverpool 38, 105, 148, 152
Luton 77, 124

Mesopotamia 129-131, 150, 156

Netherlands 62-63, 67
Normandy 157, 160
North Sea 57, 59-60

Plymouth 57, 65
Poland 64, 70, 154
Portsmouth 55, 57, 64

Russia 29, 55-56, 112, 153

South Africa 26-27, 40, 42-43, 75, 125, 136-139, 161, 164
Southampton 98
Sylt 61, 63

Ulster 69, 72, 127, 151-152
USA 77

Verdun 94, 127

Wendover 43, 53
Western Front xvi, 27, 33, 74, 79, 87, 99, 110, 112, 127, 131-135, 158
Wolverhampton 71, 147
Woolwich Arsenal 102

York 77, 128

INDEX OF SCHOOLS & COLLEGES

Bedford 26, 28, 138, 149
Bradfield 28, 135-136

Camberley Staff College, *see* Sandhurst
Cambridge 35, 73, 79, 85-87, 105, 113
Charterhouse 22, 32, 44
Cheltenham 24, 27, 32-34, 114
Clifton 24, 27, 29, 32-34, 43-44, 51, 114, 123, 138, 147

Durham 35, 38, 76, 112, 166

Eton 22, 24, 27-28, 32-33, 43-44, 51, 93-94, 114, 120, 123, 131, 137-138

Haileybury 25, 28, 32-33, 94, 114, 138-139
Harrow 22, 32-33, 44, 114, 120, 123, 147

Lancing 51, 80

Marlborough 27, 32-33, 38

Oakham School 35, 49
Oundle 26, 79, 100, 102-103, 163
Oxbridge 40, 89
Oxford xiv, 24, 35, 47, 58, 95, 131

Rugby 22, 24, 32, 35-37, 39, 103, 113-114, 131, 138, 147-148

Sandhurst (Staff College, Camberley) 27, 41, 51, 53, 81, 131, 158
Shrewsbury 22, 26, 40, 147
St Albans School viii-ix, 136, 147
St Georges, Harpenden 36, 100, 102-103, 147

Tonbridge 44, 120-121, 140

Uppingham xi-xix, 21-22, 26, 29, 33-46, 48-54, 57-58, 67-77, 79-85, 88-89, 93-95, 97-104, 107, 109-114, 119-123, 125-126, 131, 135-136, 138-141, 143-145, 147-148, 150-151, 154, 157-165.
   Fircroft (house), 100-101, 140

Wellington College (Berks) 27, 32-33, 44-45, 51, 114, 138, 145

Wellington College (Somerset) 81
Westminster 22, 33, 138, 141
Winchester xiv, 22, 27, 32, 74, 84-85, 114, 120-121, 140, 147
Woolwich 27, 41, 51, 84, 102

INDEX OF MILITARY UNITS & FORMATIONS

British Expeditionary Force (BEF) 33, 79, 108, 118, 123, 125-128, 131, 144
Indian Army 91, 129, 131, 166
Indian Expeditionary Force (IEF) 129-130
New Armies 77-78, 81, 94, 99, 124-125, 150
Regular Army xviii, 27, 29-32, 50, 52-54, 73-74, 78, 84, 90-91, 93-94, 98, 121-124, 138, 162
Special Reserve (SR) 29-31, 75, 82-83, 97, 138, 140, 163, 166
Territorial Force (TF) 29, 50-51, 71, 75, 77-78, 82, 95, 97, 99, 136, 138-140, 153, 163

Third Army 126-127, 129, 132-134
Fifth Army 128-129

14th Division 127-129

21st Division 76-77
36th (Ulster) Division 72, 127-128, 151
50th (Northumberland) Division 126-127

Army Service Corps 75-78
Home Guard xiii, 107, 155, 165
Imperial Yeomanry 43, 76
Labour Corps 77, 169
Royal Army Medical Corps (RAMC) 53, 73, 88, 112, 155, 158
Royal Engineers 85-86
Royal Field Artillery 73, 77-78, 85, 152, 166

Cambridgeshire Regiment 75, 169
Durham Light Infantry 76, 112
Leicestershire Regiment 84, 99, 139
Sherwood Foresters 149, 155

Suffolk Regiment 77, 151

Royal Air Force (RAF) 73, 80, 84, 157, 166
Royal Flying Corps (RFC) 73, 83-86, 133, 148

Royal Marine Light Infantry (RMLI) 57-58, 67
Royal Naval Volunteer Reserve (RNVR) 106, 166

Royal Navy 57-60, 106

Uppingham School Rifle Corps xiii, 29, 49, 79
Volunteers:
    Artist's Rifles 141
    Leamington Volunteers 136
    Leicester Volunteers 136
    Cambridge University Rifle Volunteers 79
    City Imperial Volunteers 43

INDEX OF GENERAL & MISCELLANEOUS TERMS

Acts of Parliament:
    Endowed Schools Act 22-23
    Military Service Act 104
    Munitions Act 104
    National Registration Act 104
Admiralty 57, 59-60, 65-66, 105-107, 111, 162
Armistice 94, 118, 133, 144-145, 154
athletes, athleticism 24-26, 45-46, 48, 162
auxiliary units 29, 67
Awards:
    Distinguished Service Order (DSO) xii, 76, 108, 110-111, 114-120, 125, 148-149, 157
    Military Cross (MC) 54, 95, 110-111, 118-121, 148, 152
    Victoria Cross (VC) 111-115, 120, 149

Battles:
    Amiens 86-87, 144
    Arras 94-95, 113, 126-127, 132
    Cambrai 112, 126, 132-134
    Loos 77, 106, 112, 124-125, 131-132, 151
    The Somme 71-72, 91, 94-96, 115, 126-127, 140, 147, 149, 151-152
    Spring Offensive (1918) 112, 115, 126-127, 133, 144, 146
    Ypres (First) xviii, (Second) 126-127, (Third, 'Passchendaele') 94, 127-128
Black Week 26, 28, 42, 44, 136, 161
Board of Education 101, 136
Boer War xviii, 26-30, 32, 42, 47-48, 50, 53, 56, 76, 78, 88, 91, 103, 105, 125, 145, 147, 162, 164-165
British Empire xii, xvii-xviii, 24, 26, 31, 42, 44-45, 47-48, 52, 56, 64, 68, 99, 110, 126, 136, 141, 151, 161

cadets 21, 27-28, 29-30, 32, 42, 51, 81-85, 100, 124, 129, 136-139, 154, 162
Christianity, Christian ideals 23, 24, 25, 37, 90, 103, 147-149 24, 148-149
Clarendon Commission 22, 25
Clarendon schools 22, 33
Commonwealth War Graves Commission (CWGC) xiv, 95

Foreign Office 62, 66

games 24-25, 28, 37-41, 45-48, 50-54, 95, 101-103, 113, 135, 156-159, 162

Harvest Camps 102, 163
Head Masters Conference (HMC) 22, 24-25, 28-29, 43, 49, 137-138

Imperial War Museum (IWM) xv-xvi, 50, 71, 96, 103, 109, 148

Latin 25-26, 40, 46, 49, 149, 162
LNWR 78-79
London Metropolitan Archives xvi, 76

memorial halls 44-45, 145, 149, 153
MI6 58-59, 63, 66-67, *see also* Secret Intelligence Service
military volunteer movement 28, 29, 39, 136
Ministry of Munitions 105-106, 130
music xi, 37-38, 40-41, 44-45, 49, 52, 100, 140-141, 162

Newspapers:
    Daily Graphic 91, 105
    Daily Mail 104

London Gazette 79, 82, 117-118, 121
The *Times* 43, 52, 61-65, 70, 73-74, 104-105, 125, 129-131

Officer Cadet Battalion (OCB) system 82-83
Officer Training Corps (OTC) xii-xiii, 21, 29-34, 42, 45, 47, 49-54, 67, 71-73, 77, 79-85, 87-88, 97, 99-101, 103, 107, 124, 135-142, 154, 158, 162-164
Official History 126-127, 152
Old Uppinghamians (OUs) xii-xvii, xix, 33, 43-44, 47, 53-55, 57-58, 67-68, 70-81, 84-90, 92-94, 97-99, 101-112, 114, 116-118, 120-123, 125-126, 129, 131, 134-135, 144-156, 160-165

Parliament 69, 99, 104, 130

Red Cross 73, 105
The Riddle of the Sands 56, 60

The *School Roll* xiv-xv, 40, 42-43, 50, 52-53, 79, 105, 155

Second World War xiii-xiv, 53, 107, 154-157, 159-160, 165
Secret Intelligence Service 58-59, 63, 65-67, *see also* MI6
shooting, proficiency taught 42-43 iv, 42-43, 47-48, 54, 67, 136-139, 151, 161-162
Sikhs 91, 96
South African War 43-44
Sport, *see* Games
St Dunstans 141, 153

Training certificates 29, 30, 51, 52, 53, 54, 72, 139, 158
Trustees (of Uppingham School) 39-41, 44-45, 99-101, 140

Volunteers 30, 136, 138-139

War Office 28-30, 66, 71, 75-76, 78-79, 83, 100-101, 105, 108, 130, 139, 141, 162
Ward Committee 30, 50-51, 137, 139